HACK ATTACK

White Lies: The True Story of Clarence Brandley, Presumed Guilty in the American South

Murder on Ward Four: The Story of Bev Allitt and the Most Terrifying Crime Since the Moors Murders

Dark Heart: The Shocking Truth about Hidden Britain

The School Report: Why Britain's Schools are Failing

Flat Earth News: An Award-Winning Reporter Exposes Falsehood, Distortion and Propaganda in the Global Media

HACK ATTACK

How the truth caught up with
Rupert Murdoch

NICK DAVIES

Chatto & Windus

LONDON

Published by Chatto & Windus 2014

2 4 6 8 10 9 7 5 3 1

First published in Great Britain in 2014 by
Chatto & Windus
Random House, 20 Vauxhall Bridge Road,
London SW1V 2SA
www.randomhouse.co.uk

Addresses for companies within The Random House Group Limited can be found at:
www.randomhouse.co.uk/offices.htm

The Random House Group Limited Reg. No. 954009

A CIP catalogue record for this book
is available from the British Library

ISBN 9780701187309 (hardback)
ISBN 9780701187316 (trade paperback)

The Random House Group Limited supports the Forest Stewardship Council®
(FSC®), the leading international forest-certification organisation. Our books
carrying the FSC label are printed on FSC®-certified paper. FSC is the only
forest-certification scheme supported by the leading environmental organisations,
including Greenpeace. Our paper procurement policy can be found
at www.randomhouse.co.uk/environment

Typeset in Bembo Std by Palimpsest Book Production Limited,
Falkirk, Stirlingshire
Printed and bound in Great Britain by
Clays Ltd, St Ives plc

For Jean Davies, who died in 1986.
She would have loved this story.

Contents

Who's Who

Sue Akers — Deputy assistant commissioner, Metropolitan Police

Tamsin Allen — Lawyer for hacking victims

Matthew Anderson — Right-hand man to James Murdoch

Sky Andrew — Sports agent, hacking victim

Mr Apollo — Code name for original source for story

Joanne Armstrong — Legal adviser to Professional Footballers' Association, hacking victim

Sir Ian Blair — Commisioner, Metropolitan Police, 2005–09, hacking target

David Blunkett — Home Secretary, hacking victim

Charlie Brooks — Racehorse trainer, husband of Rebekah Brooks

Rebekah Brooks — Editor, *News of the World* and the *Sun*, chief executive of News International from September 2009

Chris Bryant — Labour MP, hacking victim

Ian Burton — External lawyer, News International

Lady Buscombe — Chair, Press Complaints Commission, 2009–11

Vince Cable — Liberal Democrat Secretary of State for business

Glenn Campbell — BBC journalist

Richard Caseby — Managing editor, the *Sun*

Jon Chapman — Legal director, News International

Peter Clarke — Deputy assistant commissioner, in command of Op Caryatid

Max Clifford — PR agent, hacking victim

Daniel Cloke — Director of human resources, News International

Dave Cook — Detective chief superintendent, Metropolitan Police

Andy Coulson	Editor *News of the World*, media adviser to the prime minister
Tom Crone	In-house lawyer, *News of the World* and the *Sun*
Ian Edmondson	Assistant editor (news), *News of the World*
Emissary	Code name for government source
Kieren Fallon	Jockey, hacking victim
Paul Farrelly	Labour MP on media select committee
Dick Fedorcio	Director of communications, Metropolitan Police
George Galloway	Respect MP, hacking victim
Clive Goodman	Royal editor, *News of the World*
Andy Gray	TV presenter, hacking victim
Simon Greenberg	Director, corporate affairs, News International
Mark Hanna	Director of security, News International
Charlotte Harris	Lawyer for hacking victims
Dean Haydon	John Yates's staff officer
Andy Hayman	Assistant commissioner, responsible for Op Caryatid
Amelia Hill	*Guardian* reporter
Ross Hindley	*News of the World* reporter
Les Hinton	Chief executive News International until December 2007
Sean Hoare	Show-business reporter, the *Sun* and *News of the World*
Jeremy Hunt	Secretary of State for culture, media and sport
Lawrence 'Lon' Jacobs	In-house counsel, News Corp
Jingle	Code name for police source
Tessa Jowell	Secretary of State for culture, media and sport
Karl	Code name for police source
Ian Katz	Deputy editor, the *Guardian*
Trevor Kavanagh	Political editor, the *Sun*
John Kelly	Lawyer for hacking victims
Joel Klein	Executive vice president, News Corp
Stuart Kuttner	Managing editor, *News of the World*
David Leigh	Investigations editor, the *Guardian*
Mark Lewis	Lawyer for hacking victims

Will Lewis	General manager, News International
Lola	Code name for source in criminal justice system
Mark Maberly	Detective, attached to Op Caryatid
Alice Macandrew	Media adviser to James Murdoch
Ken Macdonald QC	Director of Public Prosecutions, 2003–08
Paul McMullan	Journalist, *News of the World*
Mango	Code name for whistle-blower source
Alex Marunchak	Executive editor, *News of the World*
Sir Christopher Meyer	Chair, Press Complaints Commission, 2003–09
Fred Michel	Lobbyist for James Murdoch
Sienna Miller	Actress, hacking victim
Greg Miskiw	Assistant editor (news), *News of the World*
Dominic Mohan	Editor, the *Sun*
Daniel Morgan	Private investigator, murdered 1987
Piers Morgan	Editor, *Daily Mirror* and *News of the World*
Max Mosley	Victim of *News of the World* story, funded hacking victims
Glenn Mulcaire	Phone-hacking specialist, *News of the World*
James Murdoch	Executive chairman of News International, 2007–11
Rupert Murdoch	Chairman and chief executive of News Corp
Colin Myler	Editor, *News of the World*
Ovid	Code name for Mulcaire's ghostwriter
Alec Owen	Senior investigator, Information Commissioner's Office
Brian Paddick	Deputy assistant commissioner, Metropolitan Police, hacking victim
Lucy Panton	Crime reporter, *News of the World*
David Perry QC	Senior prosecutor
Robert Peston	BBC business editor
Nicola Phillips	PA to Max Clifford, hacking victim
Julian Pike	External lawyer, News International
John Prescott	Deputy prime minister, hacking victim
Adam Price	Plaid Cymru MP on media select committee
Jeremy Reed	Barrister for hacking victims
Ed Richards	Chief executive, Ofcom

Alan Rusbridger   Editor, the *Guardian* from 1995
Gerald Shamash   Lawyer for hacking victims
Michael Silverleaf QC Barrister for News International
Adam Smith   Special adviser to Jeremy Hunt
Keir Starmer QC   Director of Public Prosecutions, 2008–13
Jules Stenson   Features editor, *News of the World*
Sir Paul Stephenson Commissioner, Metropolitan Police, 2009–11
Sir John Stevens   Commissioner, Metropolitan Police, 2000–05
Keith Surtees   Detective, deputy lead investigator on Op Caryatid
Gordon Taylor   Chief executive, Professional Footballers' Association, hacking victim
Mark Thomson   Lawyer for hacking victims
Neville Thurlbeck   Chief reporter, *News of the World*
Hugh Tomlinson QC Barrister for hacking victims
Tim Toulmin   Director, Press Complaints Commission
Mr Justice Vos   Judge in hacking cases
Neil Wallis   Deputy editor, *News of the World*
Tom Watson   Labour MP on media select committee
James Weatherup   News editor, *News of the World*
Derek Webb   Covert surveillance specialist, *News of the World*
John Whittingdale Conservative chair of media select committee
Phil Williams   Detective, lead investigator on Op Caryatid
John Yates   Assistant commissioner, Metropolitan Police

Author's Note

This is the strangest story I've ever written.

In the beginning, it was next to nothing. Two men were arrested – a private investigator and a journalist from the *News of the World*. Both of them ended up in prison, but it was no big deal. The crime they had committed was minor. Their jail sentences were short. The only eye-catching thing about it at the time was that their crime was quite quirky: they had discovered that they could access other people's voicemail messages and had spent months eavesdropping on three staff at Buckingham Palace. Even so, it was a small story, dead and gone from the public eye within a few days.

And yet, I ended up spending more than six years of my working life trying to unravel the bundle of corruption which lay hidden in the background. Soon there was a small group of us working together, discovering that we had stumbled into a fight with the press and the police and the government, all of them linked to an organisation which had been created by one man.

Rupert Murdoch is one of the most powerful people in the world. You could argue that he is, in fact, the most powerful. News Corp is amongst the biggest companies on the planet. Like all his commercial rivals, Murdoch has the financial power to hire or fire multiple thousands of people and the political power to worry governments by threatening to withdraw his capital and transfer it to a more co-operative nation. But, unlike his rivals in business, his power has another dimension. Because he owns newspapers and news channels, he has the ability to worry governments even more, to make them fear that without his favour they will find themselves attacked and destabilised and discredited. Certainly, a man who is both global business baron and multinational kingmaker has a special kind of power.

So the simple crime story turned out to be a story about the secret world of the power elite and their discreet alliances. This is not about conspiracy (not generally) but about the spontaneous recognition of power by power, the everyday occurrence of a natural exchange of assistance between those who occupy positions in society from which they can look down upon and mightily affect the everyday worlds of ordinary men and women. In this case, as often, that mutual favouritism took place amidst the persistent reek of falsehood – not the fevered plotting of Watergate lies, but the casual arrogance of a group of people who take it for granted that they have every right to run the country and, in doing so, to manipulate information, to conceal embarrassing truth, to try to fool all of the people all of the time.

A lot of writers say that they can't do their job – they can't produce the book or the film or the newspaper article – unless they can reach a point of such clarity about their project that they can reduce it to a single sentence. Waiting for a bus one day while I was drafting this book, I finally got there. This is a story about power and truth.

To be more precise, it is about the abuse of power and about the secrets and lies that protect it. In a tyranny, the ruling elite can abuse its power all day long, and anybody who complains about it will get a visit from the secret police. In an established democracy, abuse of power cannot afford to be visible. It needs concealment like a vampire needs the dark. As soon as a corporation or a trade union or a government or any arm of the state is seen to be breaking the rules, it can be attacked, potentially embarrassed, conceivably stopped. The secrets and lies are not an optional extra, they are central to the strategy.

In this case, the concealment had an extra layer, because news organisations which might otherwise have exposed the truth were themselves part of the abuse, and so they kept silent, indulging in a comic parody of misreporting, hiding the emerging scandal from their readers like a Victorian nanny covering the children's eyes from an accident in the street – 'you don't want to see this'. Some did this because they were linked to the crime by common ownership or by their own guilty secrets about the lawbreaking in their own newsrooms; some turned away for fear of upsetting their political allies. Too many journalists had simply ceased to function as independent truth-tellers, separate from and critical of the people they were writing about. The crime reporter made common cause with the police and also with criminals. The political correspondent developed a loyalty to one party or faction. The media reporter became a tool for his or her owner. The news executive turned into a preening power-monger, puffed with wealth and self-importance, happy to join the elite and not to expose it – all rather like the final moment of *Animal Farm*, when the pigs who have led the revolt against the humans have come to adopt the behaviour of the rulers they were supposed to challenge: 'The creatures outside looked from pig to man, and from man to pig, and from pig to man again; but already it was impossible to say which was which.'

The story of the phone-hacking scandal happens to have unfolded in the United Kingdom, but it could have happened anywhere in the world. News Corp itself has spent years playing the power game in Australia and the United States and China, and anywhere else where its commerce has led it. Those other countries have suffered comparable abuse by News Corp and by other similar forces. The structures of power and the weakness of democracy are more or less the same everywhere. A freakish sequence of events allowed us to see the truth in the UK, but it delivers a lesson for anybody anywhere who thinks they have the right to have power over their own lives.

In the end, the struggle by the small group of people who tried to uncover the hacking scandal was taken over by others who exposed even more. In writing this book, I've been able to draw on the mass of evidence which emerged eventually in civil lawsuits, criminal trials, select-committee hearings in the House of Commons and, above all, through the public inquiry which was chaired by Lord Justice Leveson in London from the autumn of 2011.

In the background, however, we relied consistently on the help of tabloid journalists, police officers, private investigators, government officials, former Murdoch allies and others who refused to accept the corruption around them. Some were able to speak openly, but most of them stepped forward on condition of anonymity, which I've maintained. In a few cases, sources who originally were unattributable have decided that they can now be named, and so they are identified here. All of them played their part, and I want to acknowledge the importance of their help and of their willingness to take risks so that the story could be told.

In three particular areas, my own work was backed up by specialist researchers: Jenny Evans, who built bridges to journalists who had worked on the *News of the World*; Adrian Gatton, who went into the netherworld of private investigation; and David Hencke, who made good use of his long-standing links to politicians and their advisers. Tom Mills analysed press cuttings for me. Scarlett MccGwire introduced me to contacts from the political world.

I also drew on several dozen published books and in-depth articles, which are listed in a bibliography on a website which is a companion to this book, www.hack-attack.co.uk. Occasionally, I have identified them as sources in the text. I acknowledge all of them as valuable raw material.

The emergence of this wealth of new information ended up changing the structure of the book, which now has two different kinds of chapters. Some of them form a historical account of the process by which I and others uncovered the scandal, containing only the information that was available to us at the time. Others are attempts to recreate what was happening behind the scenes – the crime and the cover-ups and the political machinations – and these chapters draw on everything that finally emerged, to try to show the truth that was being so busily concealed. The website has further background on events as well as related documents, audio and video.

A couple of notes about names. First, Rupert Murdoch runs a confusing muddle of companies, which have been restructured since the events described here. For the sake of simplicity, the book generally refers to only two of them: the then global parent company, News Corp; and its main UK subsidiary, known at the time as News International. The UK company has its own subsidiaries, but I have used the generic 'News International' to cover all of them. Second, one central character, Rebekah Brooks, was known by her maiden name, Rebekah Wade, until June 2009, when she married. To avoid confusion, I have used her current, married name throughout.

Finally, I should acknowledge the endless support of my colleagues at the *Guardian* – other reporters who worked tirelessly on the story, the in-house lawyers who wrestled with the threats of libel actions, the desk editors who tolerated my tensions, and, above all, the editor, Alan Rusbridger, who backed this story and never flinched in the face of aggression. Those colleagues and all who helped to tell this strange story believe we have the right to know the truth about power.

Part One
Crime and Concealment

All members of the press have a duty to maintain the highest professional standards.

Press Complaints Commission Code of Practice

You don't get to be the editor of the *Mirror* without being a fairly despicable human being.

Piers Morgan

1. February 2008 to July 2009

I was sitting in a BBC radio studio, getting ready to vomit.

They wanted me to talk about a book I had just written, *Flat Earth News*, about the scale and origins of falsehood, distortion and propaganda in the media. In theory, I was happy to talk to them: I'd spent two years breaking my brain to produce the book, which was finally being published now, in February 2008, and this was a chance to persuade people to read the result. But the thought of this interview flooded me with anxiety.

This was live national radio. Worse than that, this was the *Today* programme. The Queen listens to the *Today* programme; the prime minister, foreign ambassadors, the whole damned UK power elite chews its breakfast with one ear on the *Today* programme. And worst of all, a few minutes earlier, while I was pacing up and down outside the studio, just before I sat down for my ordeal, they had revealed that they had brought in Stuart Kuttner to oppose me. Kuttner!

I had never met him, but I'd heard plenty. Kuttner was this figure from the shadows – the managing editor of Rupert Murdoch's *News of the World*, lurking just behind the editor's throne, the guy who kept the secrets, who got rid of the problems, who dealt with the really dirty stuff. You wouldn't spend long trying to describe Stuart Kuttner without using words like 'tough' and 'ruthless' and 'basically very unpleasant'.

The interview started, I mastered my nerves and started to talk. Kuttner stepped in a couple of times, to inform the nation that I must be from a different planet because he certainly didn't recognise the newspaper industry I was describing. Then I got on to the 'dark arts', outlining the few scraps of information I had found about private

investigators who for years had been working for most British newspapers, breaking the law to help them get scoops. Kuttner moved in
quickly. 'If it happens, it shouldn't happen. It happened once at the
News of the World. The reporter was fired; he went to prison. The editor
resigned.'

Certainly it crossed my mind that he was not telling the truth. He
was right on the simple fact that only one reporter from the *News of
the World* had been sent to prison – the royal editor, Clive Goodman
– but the idea of the 'one rogue reporter' had never quite made sense
to me. Goodman had been jailed a year earlier, in January 2007, for
intercepting the voicemail of three people who worked at Buckingham
Palace. The private investigator who had helped him to do that, Glenn
Mulcaire, had been jailed not only for hacking the voicemail of those
three royal targets but also for eavesdropping on the messages of five
other people who had nothing to do with the royal family. Why had
Mulcaire done that? Nobody had suggested for a moment that it had
been the royal editor who had told him to hack non-royal victims. So
who had asked him to? Other reporters? Editors? Mysterious voices
in his head?

Kuttner swept over the top of me, on a rhetorical roll. British
journalism, he declared, was 'a very honourable profession'. A newspaper like the *News of the World* was really a kind of moral watchdog,
keeping an eye out for misbehaviour among the powerful. 'We live
in an age of corrosion of politics and of public life – degradation,' he
warned.

On that high note, the interview finished, and that might have been
the end of it. I didn't believe all this stuff about the *News of the World*
being a defence against the degradation of public life, but I wasn't
interested in the *News of the World.* I didn't read it and I didn't want
to write about it. I was only relieved to be out of the studio and
happy to go off spreading my ideas about *Flat Earth News*, which is
mostly about quality newspapers and the deep flaws in the way they
now operate. But, unknown to me, Stuart Kuttner had just made a
mistake, a very bad mistake. 'It only happened once,' he had said.
Somewhere out across the airwaves, a man I had never met nor heard
of had listened to what Kuttner said and had felt so angry about it

that he decided to contact me. Which is what happened a few days later.

'I would like to have a discussion with you,' he said. 'I think you will like what I have.'

He left me his mobile phone number, but told me never to leave a message on it.

It's fair to say that reporting is a great deal easier than most reporters like to pretend. People tell you things; you do your best to check them out; and then you tell a lot of other people what you've found. There are some hidden subtleties in there and a few simple skills, but generally speaking, there is nothing very clever about it.

I arranged to meet my intriguing caller. I am never going to be able to say who he is. That's a really common problem. Over and again, you find that the people who have the most interesting things to say are the people who are least able to say them, because they are under pressure of some kind – they are worried that they will be arrested or sacked or divorced or beaten up. Anonymity protects them. This man is going to crop up several times, so he needs a memorable name. I'll call him Mr Apollo.

As soon as I met him I liked him, but I didn't necessarily trust him. We sat in his room in a central London hotel, him faffing about with the coffee-making equipment while he started to talk, me wondering how he knew so much and what he wanted in return.

He told me that Kuttner was a liar, that the *News of the World* had been hacking phones all over the place and that this was how they got most of their stories: they picked up their leads by intercepting voicemail, and then they went out to get photographs and quotes to lay a false trail, so that they could pretend that they had found the story by normal, legitimate means. It wasn't just Clive Goodman who had been doing it, he said – that was a complete joke, loads of reporters had been at it. It was such an easy trick, he said. You dial your target's mobile phone number and when you get through to the recorded message, you hit '9', then the recorded message asks you to enter a four-digit PIN code. Most people don't bother to change the code from the factory setting, so you know what it is. Or, if they do change it, they use something really obvious like the year of their birth. You put in the code and that's it, you can listen to their messages. Of course, Mr Apollo explained, you need to work this so that the target doesn't answer their phone when you call in. So maybe you call during the night, or when you know the target is in a meeting.

Most of the time, he said, it was so easy to do this that you didn't need a private investigator like Glenn Mulcaire to make it happen. Mulcaire's main job, he said, had been to 'blag' the mobile phone companies – to call them up and pretend to be one of their staff – so that he could get numbers for people who were ex-directory, or, more important, to get a PIN code changed back to the factory setting if the target had bothered to alter it. Once the *News of the World* were inside one target's voicemail, they would pick up messages with the numbers of their closest associates, then hack their voicemail, get more associates and create a whole network of eavesdropping around the target. The targets would not discover the codes had been changed for weeks. And if they did discover it, they would think it was some kind of techno foul-up.

This was interesting stuff, and it was tempting to get involved. It would be good to put Kuttner back into his box. It would be better still to do something about tabloid journalists behaving badly. It was not just that a small minority of cowboys with notebooks were making up stories and ruining people's lives; they were also making it much more difficult for other journalists to do their jobs, because people generally now expected to be bribed, bullied and cheated by reporters, so they were far more difficult to deal with.

But it wasn't that great a story. Nobody was going to be very surprised to be told that some tabloid reporters behaved badly and, even if I wanted to pursue it, the difficulty was that all this was just the word of Mr Apollo, who might be right or might be wrong but who had made it very clear that he could not be quoted or named to defend anything that I might write.

By now, he had got the better of the coffee-making, and he sat down and started to relax and to talk about the police. He claimed that Scotland Yard had found masses of mobile phone numbers which had been logged by Glenn Mulcaire but they had never followed up on them. They had made no attempt to prosecute Mulcaire for all these other possible victims, nor to find out who else might have been giving instructions to Mulcaire, nor even to tell all these people that they had been targeted. This was getting more interesting. Why would the police behave like that when dealing with a particularly powerful newspaper, which happened to belong to Rupert Murdoch, the biggest media mogul in the country?

We started talking about the trial of Goodman and Mulcaire, about the fact that it never did make sense that Mulcaire admitted hacking five non-royal victims. That was when Mr Apollo finally opened the door so that I could see a way forward. He claimed that one of those five unexplained victims was suing and was trying to get the police to hand over some of the evidence which they had collected and never revealed. Apparently, it was causing some panic at Scotland Yard. Now here was a way to check Mr Apollo's story. If a judge went ahead and ordered Scotland Yard to hand over evidence, the police would have to comply and then, with any luck, I could get access to the court files and see what was in there.

It was only later that evening, after I'd left Mr Apollo with thanks and a guarantee to stay in touch, that my brain finally clicked into gear and I understood the biggest reason for going after this story. It was not just about the most powerful news organisation in the country apparently cheating and breaking the law, and about the most powerful police force in the country failing – maybe deliberately refusing – to go anywhere near exposing the truth about it. I finally realised that what really mattered was that the man who was editing the *News of the World* at the time – Andy Coulson – was now working as media adviser for the leader of the Conservative Party, David Cameron. And although it was the Labour Party who were in government, it looked very likely that the Conservatives would win the next election and Cameron would become prime minister. Andy Coulson was on his way into Downing Street.

I remembered Coulson resigning as editor of the *News of the World* after the trial of Goodman and Mulcaire, explaining that he had known nothing about Goodman's evil ways but saying that he felt he should go because it had happened on his watch. If Kuttner was lying about all this, then maybe Coulson was lying too. And yet he was aiming to take on the job of organising the communication between the government and the people of the country – really a very unsuitable place for a liar. More than that, if he really had presided over a regime of illegal eavesdropping at the *News of the World*, what would he do if he found himself in Downing Street and he wanted to find out who was talking dirty behind the prime minister's back? Would he go back to the dark arts?

What is the difference between a reporter on the *Guardian* and a reporter on a paper like the *News of the World*? Don't believe anybody who tells you that it has anything to do with moral fibre, or intelligence, or sensitivity. There are bastards and moral weaklings, good guys and idealists, in both worlds. All reporters are really very similar. They run on a flammable psychological mixture, like petrol and air, a volatile combination of imagination and anxiety.

You train your imagination, pushing it like you'd push a muscle until it's stronger than other people's, until it becomes almost freakishly powerful. And over and over again, you point it at your problem and you guess, with great energy and vivid mental pictures: what could the truth possibly be; where could I possibly find the evidence; who could know; why would they talk; what's next; what's missing; how do I finish this jigsaw puzzle in the dark? Then, when you go out to check what your imagination has delivered, you complete the mixture by pouring in equal measures of stomach-burning anxiety. What if this goes wrong; if they won't talk to me; if they talk to somebody else with a notebook; if they lie to me; if they tape me; if they grass me to the opposition? What if I'm wrong? What if the stupid news desk won't run the story?

There is one other thing, the equivalent of the spark that ignites the fuel and air. Most of the reporters who survive and thrive are driven by some kind of deep need. I know one who spent years pretending to himself and to the rest of the planet that he was not gay. He diverted his sexual energy and his waking hours, day and night, into fighting all the powers that be, and he did extraordinary work uncovering all kinds of secret scandals until finally he accepted himself and relaxed and never really produced another story worth reading. I know another who says he grew up with a secret in his family – there was this thing that nobody was allowed to say. Eventually, in his late teens, he discovered that his father was Jewish while his mother was not and that, when they married, their two families had protested so bitterly that the couple resolved never to mention This Thing again. So this reporter can't stand secrets, and he has spent years earning a living and winning awards by hunting down concealment wherever he can find it and tearing it apart.

OK, so mine is this: I spent my childhood being hit by people – grown-ups – some of them genuinely vicious, some of them simply believing the noxious idea that if you spare the rod, you spoil the child. I had been working as a reporter for a couple of decades, thinking I was interested in criminal justice and social problems, before I looked back and saw how over and again I had been drawn to stories where I might have saved victims: particularly victims of unfairness (miscarriages of justice, police corruption); and, even more than that, victims who were children (working as prostitutes, losing out at school, being sexually abused, living in poverty, struggling in prison, being attacked by a mentally disordered nurse). Underlying all of this work, I could see, was some deep-seated urge to hit back at anybody at all who takes power and abuses it.

What's the difference between a reporter on the *News of the World* and one on the *Guardian*? The difference is in the office, in the hierarchy – in the Bully Quotient. There is a lot of bullying in Fleet Street – a lot of puffed-up, pissed-up, overpaid, foul-mouthed, self-important editors-in-chief and people who run news desks and features desks, who can't tell the difference between leadership and spite. I've come across it in quality newsrooms but there is no doubt that the worst of the bullying thrives in the downmarket tabloid newsrooms. Why? It begins with train timetables.

There are 50 or 60 million people crammed into England, Scotland and Wales and, ever since the Industrial Revolution, it's been possible to print a paper in London or Glasgow and put it on a train at night, knowing that by dawn it can reach any household in the land. Compare that to the US: until the electronic revolution, a newspaper that set out at night on a journey from New York City, for example, would be halfway to nowhere by the next morning. So while the US developed city papers, usually no more than a couple in each city, the UK developed a national market for newspapers which was bursting with competition as a dozen or so daily titles fought each other for the attention of all these readers. And the competition has always been most intense among the mass-market tabloids. Their very survival depends on circulation, on selling lots of papers – on printing something that the competition has missed. By contrast, the upmarket papers don't expect to sell millions: they aim for the wealthiest people in the market and make most of their money by carrying advertisements which are aimed at their readers' well-padded wallets.

The commercial pressure in UK newsrooms is relentless, particularly for the mass-circulation titles. Tabloid editors will send out their reporters with an unmistakeable message pinned painfully to the back of their heads – 'just get the story'. No excuses are accepted, no failure is allowed, you stand on that doorstep till she talks to you, you keep asking till you get the answer, open that miser's paw, just get the damned story. And a lot of these editors will scream abuse and shout threats and tip verbal acid over the head of any fool reporter who dares to come back with an empty notebook.

If you succeed in a tabloid newsroom, you'll be given big stories and great foreign trips, lots of bylines, a licence to fiddle your expenses, cosy lunches with the editor and private pay rises. If you fail, you'll sit lonely in a corner, being given no stories or just crap stories that will never make it into print; you'll be woken up at dawn and kept going till midnight; you'll be sent away to Sunderland just as you were leaving the office to go to your own birthday party; if you happen to write something that gets into the paper, you'll get no byline, no thanks, no respite; you will wish you were somebody else. (I know some of this at first hand: I spent my first few years as a reporter on tabloid papers and fled to escape one particularly remorseless bully.) So, of course, when those reporters are out there on the road with nothing much more than their imagination and their anxiety for company, some of them may well decide to invent quotes, fabricate facts, cheat sources, steal pictures, ignore rules, break laws – anything to be allowed to feel good.

Compared to that, the life of a reporter on the *Guardian* is as soft as a baby's face. It's not just that – like the other 'quality' papers – there is less pressure to sell copies. Beyond that, unlike the other quality titles, the *Guardian* belongs to a trust. Instead of having shareholders trying to claw profit out of the newsroom, the trust has subsidiary businesses whose profits are used to fund the newsroom. The paper is still run as a business and it has to survive in the marketplace, but the commercial pressure which distorts so much behaviour in so many newsrooms is reduced to the bare minimum.

What's the difference between the *News of the World* and the *Guardian*? From a reporter's angle? The Bully Quotient. Just that really. I'm allowed to fail.

Not everything that Mr Apollo told me was a total shock.

When I was researching *Flat Earth News*, over the previous two years, I had contacted reporters who had worked in Fleet Street newsrooms, looking for the stories behind their stories, to try to understand why it is that so often our work fails to tell the truth. A lot of reporters had helped and a few of them had gone further and started to tell me about their use of private investigators to gather information by illegal means – these 'dark arts'. Coming from the soft world of the *Guardian*, I had known almost nothing of this.

My enlightenment began one evening in a shady bar in Soho, where a very experienced news reporter spent several hours talking me through his own paper's involvement. He started with 'Benji the Binman', a deeply eccentric loner who had spent his nights buzzing around London in a little van, scavenging in the rubbish bins of law firms and record producers and anybody else who might be in touch with celebrities, and then selling the news he found among the filth. Eventually, he was caught and convicted of theft, which hadn't stopped newspapers using private investigators, or sometimes their own staff, to carry on rummaging through garbage in search of scoops. This reporter said his own paper certainly had done so. They had even displayed as a trophy on the newsroom wall a pair of knickers discarded by the daughter of a leading politician and retrieved from her dustbin by somebody who was pleased to call himself a journalist.

Crouched over a candle on a rickety table in the corner of the bar, we talked on, and he told me in some detail how newspapers had started using 'Trojan Horse' emails to steal data from their targets' computers, which was seriously illegal; and how one newspaper – Rupert Murdoch's *Sunday Times* – had ended up doing so much illegal stuff that, in July 2003, they had appointed a specialist reporter, David Connett, to act as a kind of fallback fall guy. They had taken Connett on as a staff reporter but put him on a freelance contract, made sure he didn't have an office phone number or email address, and then given him the job of commissioning the dark arts. That way, if he got caught, the paper could stand back, disown him and pretend that he was just some crazy freelancer who was nothing to do with them. Connett had become the butt of jokes in the office, with colleagues pretending they couldn't hear him 'because you're not here, mate, are you?'

That little scheme had turned bad. The paper had cut back its staff and made Connett redundant. He asked for the pay-off he would have received as a staff member. They told him he was free-lance and so he wasn't entitled to it. Now, he was taking them to an employment tribunal. Weeks later, I sat in on the hearing and listened to the evidence, including the denials of the *Sunday Times*. The tribunal accepted that this master of the dark arts was clearly more than a casual employee and awarded him compensation for unfair dismissal.

Others who had worked for the *Sunday Times* went on to confirm all this. One of their senior journalists later met me in the coffee lounge of a sedate hotel and, in amongst the old ladies with their tea and digestive biscuits, he not only described that paper's long history of illegally 'blagging' confidential data from phone companies and banks and government departments but also gave me the name and contact details of the specialist who had been doing it for them for years – a former actor from Somerset called John Ford. Another described how they had used a con man, Barry Beardall, to try to entrap Labour politicians.

Since the research for *Flat Earth News* was an attempt to investigate truth-telling on quality newspapers, my education about the dark arts tended to come from them. I found scraps of evidence that other quality papers were also hiring blagging specialists to trick organisations into disclosing confidential data – a criminal offence unless it was justified by a clear public interest. The Conservative peer, Lord Ashcroft, named an investigator who had tricked the Royal Bank of Scotland into disclosing details of the party's bank account, on behalf of *The Times*. A reporter from the *Sunday Telegraph* gave me a copy of a fax about Dr David Kelly, the weapons specialist who had committed suicide after being caught up in the furore over false claims about Iraqi weapons of mass destruction. It had been sent to them by a private investigator on 18 July 2003, the day that Dr Kelly's body was found, and it recorded every phone number Kelly had dialled in a previous eight-week period.

Similarly, the reporter who first told me about bribing police officers was not from a red-top tabloid. He had spent years with the *Daily Mail*, probably the most hardline law-and-order newspaper in the country, always ready to call for more police and tougher punishment – unless it is itself the offender. The *Mail* reporter told detailed stories of using a former detective as a go-between, to hand over envelopes of cash for serving officers, to persuade them to disclose material from police computers or from current investigations. I found more journalists, from the *Mail* and other titles, who had also used the same man to bribe police; and yet others who had been paying their bribes through a particularly nasty bunch of private investigators who ran a London agency called Southern Investigations.

It turned out that all this crime had built up slowly among numerous Fleet Street papers, quality and tabloid. It had reached the point in the early 2000s where several news desks had banned their reporters from commissioning investigators, not because so much of their work was illegal but simply because they were costing such a lot. Those papers began to insist that only executives could commission the dark arts.

Of course, little of this had ever reached the public domain. It's not as if papers were about to start reporting it. The one big glimpse for the public was the material which had been published in two reports in 2006 by the Information Commissioner, whose job is to police databases containing confidential information. These two reports described a network which for years had been run by a private investigator called Steve Whittamore, who specialised in blagging confidential information out of key organisations. Whittamore had two men inside the Driver and Vehicle Licensing Agency (DVLA); a civilian worker in the Metropolitan Police; a former Hell's Angel who specialised in tricking British Telecom; and a private investigator who targeted mobile phone companies and banks. Since the mid-1990s, Whittamore had been sitting in his quiet detached house in a small town in Hampshire, taking calls from journalists and using his network to blag the confidential information they wanted. Almost everything he did was illegal.

In March 2003, the Information Commission set up Operation Motorman and raided Whittamore. In April 2005, he and three of his network went on trial for their extraction of confidential information from police computers, but the whole case ended in confusion. Whittamore and his co-defendants were given the minimum possible sentence – a result so weak that a second trial involving Whittamore and five others was scrapped.

In the background, the newspapers who had commissioned all this activity from Whittamore escaped without a graze. A senior figure from the Information Commissioner's Office told me that their lawyers predicted that, if they were charged, the newspapers would hire senior barristers who would fight every inch of the way and run up huge legal bills and simply bust their budget. Fleet Street was just too big and powerful to fight. As a safer alternative, the commissioner had published two reports outlining Whittamore's activity, identifying eight national daily papers and ten national Sundays which, over a three-year period, had made a total of 13,343 requests for confidential data, almost all of which were 'certainly or very probably' obtained through Whittamore by illegal means. Yet with a hypocrisy which turned out to be typical, Fleet Street chose to report almost nothing of this to the outside world.

Working on *Flat Earth News*, I pestered the Information

Commissioner's Office from hell to breakfast, trying to get hold of the material which they had seized from Whittamore during Operation Motorman – his record of the 13,000-plus requests, complete with the names of some 400 journalists, the names of the targets, the nature of the confidential data required, the method used to obtain it and the price paid. Previously, the ICO had released some sample invoices, hoping to generate publicity. The invoices had been edited to conceal the names of Whittamore's targets, but what they clearly showed was that there was no secret about what was happening. Whittamore was explicitly recording illegal searches on his invoices, and Fleet Street newspapers were paying them. In spite of all my wheedling, I could not persuade the ICO to give me more. At one point, one of their senior officials let me into a room and showed me the piles of paperwork which they had seized from Whittamore. All he had to do was walk away and leave me with it. He wouldn't. The whole bundle of evidence remained hidden.

I knew I was a long way from knowing the whole truth. It was enough to irritate Stuart Kuttner on the radio, which was an achievement of a kind, but I also knew that, in spite of the pressure which the Information Commissioner had created by publishing his two reports, nothing had really changed.

In the summer of 2006, I had doorstepped one of the most active members of Whittamore's network. He was a confident, friendly man and, having escaped without effective punishment, he was happy to talk. He explained that they had decided not to steal any more information from police computers, because it was particularly dangerous, but, apart from that, the network was still trading with a smile on its face, as if the law had never tried to stop them. He sat in front of me in his office, illegally trafficking data, and showed me his current list of clients, which included nearly every newspaper in Fleet Street.

Imagination, anxiety – there's also room for some luck. A few weeks after meeting Mr Apollo, early in 2008, I found myself at a media function, where I spoke about *Flat Earth News*. Afterwards, we sat down to eat and I discovered that the man on my right was a very senior figure from Scotland Yard. So I asked him, 'That case with the phone-hacking, where the *News of the World* guy went to prison. How many victims were there? Was it really only eight?'

'No,' he said, casually. 'There were thousands.'

Oh, really?

It also helps if you have somebody like Mr Apollo to guide you. He stayed in touch and started to provide an invaluable stream of information. Crucially, he was able to give me the name of the non-royal victim who was now suing the *News of the World* – Gordon Taylor, the chief executive of the Professional Footballers' Association, a prime target for a Sunday tabloid in search of stories about the private lives of star players, who would turn to Taylor for help if they found themselves in trouble.

And, just as Mr Apollo had suggested during our first meeting, there was indeed some panic about this legal action at Scotland Yard. This was largely because Gordon Taylor was being represented by a lawyer who, for those who oppose him, is like a nightmare in a dark suit – Mark Lewis, very bright, very ambitious and absolutely devoted to the smell of trouble. I found that there were some people who had a crude theory about Lewis and his weirdly unflinching way of walking into enemy fire with a boyish grin on his face. They reckoned it is because he suffers from multiple sclerosis – 'he's dying, so he has no fear'. That missed the point entirely. It is true that he has MS, which gives him a pronounced limp, but that isn't what drives the man. By chance, I came across somebody who had been at primary school with him, who said that he hasn't really changed since the age of nine. Even then, he was the same – clever, cocky and disobedient. Mark Lewis just loves being a nuisance.

Clearly, it was Lewis who was the brains behind Gordon Taylor's legal action, who had spotted the weakness in News International's story and who was now confronting them with one simple allegation – that if it wasn't Clive Goodman who had told Glenn Mulcaire to hack Gordon Taylor's phone, then surely it was somebody else at the *News of the World*. According to Apollo, Lewis had now hired a barrister and gone to court and persuaded a judge to order the police to hand over any evidence which they possessed relating to the hacking of

Taylor's phone. Apollo didn't know what the evidence was, but a few people at the Yard who knew about it were worried.

I soon tracked down Mark Lewis at the office of a Manchester law firm, and did my best to recruit him as an ally. The problem was that he was hemmed in by confidentiality and so he was not allowed to help. Also, as I later discovered, he takes some pride in being maddening and very rarely does anything that he does not want to do.

If ever I was going to be able to write this story, I needed far more detail. In gaps between working on other stories to keep the *Guardian* happy, I went off, following my imagination wherever it led, in search of police officers and Crown prosecutors, lawyers and probation officers, anybody at all who had been involved in the original trial of Goodman and Mulcaire and who might know something about the evidence which had not been disclosed in court. I made some progress. I tried to find anybody who had anything to do with Gordon Taylor – friends, colleagues, enemies. I made less progress.

Over time, I looked for anybody who had ever had any kind of job at the *News of the World*, anybody who had ever had any kind of connection to the top of Scotland Yard. I found a second source who had had some access to the material gathered by police in the original inquiry. He echoed the estimate of the number of victims which I had been given by the senior Yard figure at the media function: 'Two or three thousand,' he suggested.

I went back and looked more closely at the official version of events. In March 2007, two months after Goodman and Mulcaire were sent to prison, the case was examined by the House of Commons select committee on culture, media and sport. The committee called as a witness Les Hinton, the chief executive of the *News of the World*'s UK owner, News International, and asked him if he had conducted 'a full, rigorous internal inquiry' and was 'absolutely convinced' that Goodman had been the only person on the paper who knew about the hacking of phones. 'Yes, we have,' Hinton replied, 'and I believe he was the only person.' Hinton added that the new editor, Colin Myler, who had replaced Andy Coulson, was still investigating. Which was a little odd because twelve days before Hinton gave this evidence, Myler had already told the Press Complaints Commission (PCC) that he had concluded that Goodman's hacking was 'aberrational', 'a rogue exception' and 'an exceptional and unhappy event in the 163-year history of the *News of the World*, involving one journalist'.

The case was also examined by the PCC, which had been established by the newspaper industry in 1991 in an attempt to prove that it was capable of regulating itself. In this case, I found, the PCC's chairman, Sir Christopher Meyer, a former British ambassador to the USA, had promised to investigate 'the entire newspaper and magazine industry of the UK to establish what is their practice'. In May 2007, the PCC had announced the results of its 'wide-ranging inquiry', claiming that it had 'conducted an investigation into the use of subterfuge by the British newspaper and magazine industry'. This 'investigation' turned out to have involved writing to editors to ask about the internal controls which would prevent their journalists abusing their position, without even attempting to find out if they had been breaking the law; opting not to ask any questions of the outgoing editor of the *News of the World*, Andy Coulson, on the grounds that he had left the profession; opting not to ask any questions of any other executive, editor or reporter who had worked there when Glenn Mulcaire was hacking phones; and choosing instead to ask questions only of the incoming editor, Colin Myler, who necessarily had no direct knowledge of what had been going on before his arrival since he had been editing Murdoch's *New York Post* at the time. The PCC report found no evidence of any illegal activity by any media organisation beyond that which had been revealed at the trial of Goodman and Mulcaire. At the time of the report, the chairman of the PCC's powerful Code of Practice Committee was Les Hinton, the chief executive of News International.

'Move along now, there's nothing to see here.'

This was getting more and more interesting. If the information I was collecting was right, then for some reason the police, the House of Commons and the Press Complaints Commission had all failed to get to the truth. It all reeked of power – well, the abuse of power. What did Coulson know? What did Les Hinton or even Murdoch know?

★   ★   ★

The key to the door was Gordon Taylor's legal action. By the summer of 2008, Apollo was telling me that it was not just the police who had been ordered to hand over material. Mark Lewis and his barrister, Jeremy Reed, had also persuaded the judge that the Information Commissioner's Office must part with some treasure. So, while the police had been told to disclose any relevant material they had seized from Glenn Mulcaire, the ICO had been instructed to disclose the entire record of every job which Steve Whittamore and his network had performed for the *News of the World* – a big chunk of the material which I had glimpsed but conspicuously failed to obtain when I was researching *Flat Earth News*. These two caches of evidence would surely nail the story. Apollo reckoned that the court already had them. But how to get hold of them? A British court can be a secretive place.

Apollo discovered that there had already been preliminary hearings at the High Court at which each side had produced formal statements, of claim and defence. Reading them, I began to see the outline of what was happening. When Mark Lewis had first submitted a claim for breach of privacy on behalf of Gordon Taylor, back in 2007, the *News of the World* had hired an expensive law firm, Farrer & Co. – who oddly also sometimes acted for the royal household whose phones had been hacked. In long-winded legal terms, Farrer & Co. had submitted a defence which not only told Gordon Taylor to get lost, it also applied to the court to have his case struck out. But now that the police and the ICO had handed over their evidence, things had changed.

The case had not been struck out. Far from it, the *News of the World* had been forced to change their position completely. The court documents were short on detail but, as far as I could make out, the new evidence which had been disclosed by the police and the ICO showed that some of their reporters had been routinely breaking the law with Steve Whittamore and, furthermore, crucially, that other reporters apart from Clive Goodman had been involved in hacking phones.

Apollo heard that there were some very tense negotiations going on, with News International offering big money – seriously big money – to Gordon Taylor if he would allow the case to be sealed and kept secret. For reasons which became clear later, Taylor was apparently tempted to settle.

Then, that autumn, I heard that the case had expanded. It had emerged (presumably from the evidence which police had handed over) that the *News of the World* had also been listening to the voicemail of two of Gordon Taylor's closest associates – his in-house legal adviser, Jo Armstrong, and an outside solicitor who specialised in sport, John Hewison. Now they, too, were suing through Mark Lewis. With three litigants, the paper was having to offer even more money to keep the whole thing quiet.

In the background, at the end of July 2008, the *News of the World* had lost a High Court case brought by Max Mosley, president of the body which runs Formula One motor racing. Mosley had sued them for breach of privacy. In March of that year, they had secretly videoed him playing sadomasochistic sex games with five prostitutes and then displayed parts of the video on their website, exposing Mosley's naked body for all the world to see. The High Court saw this as an exceptionally brazen breach of privacy and awarded him higher damages than had ever been given by a British court dealing with a privacy action – £60,000.

In the case of Gordon Taylor, I discovered, News International finally agreed to pay more than £400,000 in damages, an enormous sum. The breach of Taylor's privacy was nothing like as severe as that in Max Mosley's case. Surely this was hush money. The paper also agreed to pay up to £300,000 to cover his legal bills. The deal had been struck during the summer of 2008, but News International had then become embroiled in another six months of wrangling to settle the cases brought by Jo Armstrong and John Hewison. That cost them a further £140,000 in damages plus legal bills. The whole package amounted to just over £1 million. And an essential element of every part of the settlement was that all of those involved would keep all of it secret, for ever. One very good informant claimed that the deal had been approved by Rupert Murdoch's son, James, who had recently taken over from Les Hinton as head of News International and who was, in addition, the boss of the whole Murdoch business in Europe and Asia. If that was right, then Murdoch's son could have his fingerprints on a £1 million cover-up.

By the time the settlement was reached, it was the spring of 2009 and I was surfacing from a horribly complicated investigation of offshore tax havens for the *Guardian*. In the meantime, I had found several sources who were willing to help on the hacking story, as long as I did not disclose their role. From one of them, I had managed to get some electrifying material – extracts from the two caches of evidence, from the ICO and the police, which had forced News International to settle the cases brought by Gordon Taylor and his two lawyer colleagues. I had been given this on the strict condition that, although I could summarise it, I could not say I had any of it in my possession. Good enough. It was powerful material, in two different ways.

First, it revealed the huge scale on which the *News of the World* had been routinely and casually invading the privacy of their targets. It turned out that Steve Whittamore had recorded his work in four exercise books, with a different colour for different newspaper groups. A blue book contained everything he had done for News International. Now, at last, I had my hands on the spreadsheet which had been prepared by the Information Commissioner, listing details from the blue book – every request made by News International journalists in the three years before Whittamore was raided in March 2003. There were hundreds and hundreds of them. The reporters had used Whittamore's network of blaggers and insiders routinely to extract information from the confidential records of the police national computer, British Telecom, banks, hotels, the vast database of social security, the DVLA and the mobile phone companies. Some of the targets were famous names – actors like Jude Law and Sadie Frost. Some were linked to the famous – the grandson of Lord Mountbatten, and witnesses to the murder of the TV presenter Jill Dando. Others were simply ordinary people who had caught a reporter's eye – the owners of every car which was parked near a village green where the actor Hugh Grant was playing cricket.

I thought back to the 1970s and 80s, when the secret state routinely invaded the privacy of its targets, and a network of lawyers and politicians and journalists had worked hard to try to make the police and security agencies accountable. Finally, those agencies had been forced to accept strict guidelines for the use of surveillance on citizens. Yet now, tabloid journalists had pulled on the secret policeman's boots and started to engage in wanton surveillance, without any kind of accountability or due process: simply, they spied where they wanted. Unless this kind of blagging was justified by strong public interest, it was illegal. Certainly, it was wrong. And the paperwork from the police, dealing with Glenn Mulcaire, revealed even more of this invasion.

Like the Whittamore paperwork, it showed that Mulcaire had targeted all kinds of public figures as well as ordinary people who had strayed unwittingly into the path of the *News of the World*. I could not be sure exactly what Mulcaire had done to all of them – whether he had blagged their confidential data or hacked their voicemail, whether he had succeeded or failed – but it was clear he was involved in a very big operation. If he had succeeded in hacking their voicemail, that was illegal in all cases – there was no public-interest defence to justify it.

Some of the targets were particularly sensitive. For example, the paperwork I saw included invoices which made it clear that Glenn Mulcaire had been paid by the *News of the World* to target several senior government ministers, including Tessa Jowell, who had been the Secretary of State responsible for the media, and John Prescott, the deputy prime minister throughout Tony Blair's ten years in Downing Street, from May 1997 to June 2007. In Prescott's case, the paperwork suggested that the *News of the World*'s primary interest had been the disclosure in the spring of 2006 that he had been having an affair. The sensitivity, however, was that Prescott at that time had still been in post, handling all kinds of secrets – economic, diplomatic, military. And yet, on the face of it, the police had done nothing about it; they had not even warned the second most senior member of the government that he had been targeted by a man who specialised in intercepting communications.

But there was a second reason why all this paperwork was explosive – because of what it revealed about the perpetrators. The Whittamore material listed the names of twenty-seven different *News of the World* journalists and four others from the Murdoch daily, the *Sun*, who had hired the blagging network. Checking through a database of Fleet Street stories, I found that all of them had been working either for the news desk or for the features department. Neither of those departments was very big. Together, as far as I could tell, they employed no more than thirty or forty reporters and executives. It looked like well over half of them had been commissioning Whittamore. Between them they had made more than 1,000 requests for information over a three-year period, more than one for every working day – requests which, I already knew, had been analysed by the Information Commissioner who had found that almost all of them were 'certainly or very probably' illegal. And some of those who had commissioned Whittamore were very senior journalists: Rebekah Brooks, who had been editor of the *News of the World* at the time of the requests (and who had now become editor of the *Sun*); Greg Miskiw, the assistant editor for news; Doug Wight, the Scottish editor; Neville Thurlbeck, the chief reporter and former news editor; Jules Stenson, the features editor.

More than half the journalists in news and features? And their bosses? Collectively commissioning hundreds of searches which appeared to be potentially illegal. Surely, this was systematic. How could Coulson – the deputy editor at the time – not have known?

The Mulcaire material was even more significant. Quite simply, it kicked a large, gaping hole in the story that News International had told to the police, the public and Parliament; and it raised some very serious questions about the failure of the police and prosecutors to expose the truth. There were two particularly important documents.

One was a printout of an email, from ross.hindley@news-of-the-world.co.uk. A search in the database of Fleet Street stories quickly established that Ross Hindley was a news reporter at the *News of the World*. It had been sent to shadowmen@yahoo.co.uk. That proved to be the email address of Glenn Mulcaire. It was headed 'TRANSCRIPT FOR NEVILLE: WEDNESDAY JUNE 29 2005'. Checking the database of Fleet Street stories, I found that there was only one Neville on the *News of the World* – Neville Thurlbeck, the chief reporter, who had also shown up as a customer of Steve Whittamore. There then followed the transcripts of thirty-five voicemail messages which had been left on the mobile phones of Gordon Taylor and his legal adviser, Jo Armstrong. This was straightforward evidence which suggested that at least two other reporters from the *News of the World* had been involved in handling illegally intercepted voicemail. It gave the lie to the official version – the claim by the *News of the World* and by Rupert Murdoch's executives and by Scotland Yard and by the Press Complaints Commission – that the 'rogue reporter' Clive Goodman had been the only person on the paper who knew about it.

A second document was also highly suspicious – a contract signed by the assistant editor, Greg Miskiw, in February 2005, i.e. four months before Hindley's email was sent, offering Glenn Mulcaire a payment of £7,000 if he brought in a particularly hostile story about Gordon Taylor, which was outlined in the contract. What was most suspicious about the document was that it had been drawn up using one of Mulcaire's false names, Paul Williams. Why would an assistant editor sign a contract with somebody who was using a false name? Because he was commissioning illegal activity, perhaps?

Finally, I also heard that there was a tape-recording of Glenn Mulcaire explaining to a reporter exactly how to get access to Gordon Taylor's voicemail messages, a step-by-step guide in the art of phone-hacking. The reporter's name, I was told, sounded like Ryan or Ryall.

All this was truly damaging for the *News of the World*. Even if they wanted to claim that they knew nothing about hacking when Clive Goodman was arrested, they had known about this paperwork for months, since it was disclosed in the Gordon Taylor legal action earlier in 2008. Yet they had made no attempt to correct the record in any way. And what about Scotland Yard? This material had been seized from Glenn Mulcaire when police arrested him in August 2006. It had been sitting in police hands ever since. Had they done anything at all to pursue it, to interview or arrest other *News of the World* people who were involved? And if not, why not? And why had they not even mentioned this in court at the original trial?

And surely this was only the beginning. As far as I could tell, the court had ordered the police to hand over material which they held specifically in relation to Gordon Taylor. If it was true that there really were thousands of victims, then it looked as if there would be thousands more documents in Scotland Yard's vaults, about other victims and possibly about other perpetrators at the *News of the World*. Just how much were News International concealing? Just how much evidence had the police buried away?

But, of course, as far as News International and the police were concerned, the case had been settled. The money had been handed over to Gordon Taylor and the two others who had joined the action, Jo Armstrong and John Hewison. The paperwork had been sealed with the blessing of the High Court. Nobody was to know anything about any of this.

Well, that was their plan.

Bob Woodward of the *Washington Post* once said that 'the best journalism is often done in defiance of management'. True. At best, news managers are desperate for copy, so they won't give reporters the time they need to work on stories; at worst, they are little people with big titles who think they should prove themselves by interfering all day long.

But I'm freelance. I work from home where I can be almost invisible to the people who employ me. So I hide out in my study down in deepest Sussex with nothing to disturb me but outbreaks of very loud music and a distant view of a thirteenth-century church, happy in the hope that the *Guardian* will forget me and in the knowledge that I don't need a school prefect to stand over me to tell me to work.

By late June 2009, finally armed with enough detail and my collection of explosive paperwork, I was more or less ready to run the hacking story and so I needed to go up to London to get the *Guardian* onside. It had been well over a year since I had encountered Stuart Kuttner on the BBC radio *Today* programme. I had been working on other projects as well, but this one had got bigger and bigger.

I had lunch with the *Guardian* editor, Alan Rusbridger, in the newspaper's swanky new glass office in the area behind King's Cross Station which was once lined with prostitutes and crack dealers but now trades in nothing more dangerous than chai latte and croissants.

Rusbridger is different from other news managers in at least two ways. First, he is a friend. He and I started as junior news reporters on the *Guardian* on the same day in July 1979. Now that he is the editor, we have a very simple deal: I bring him stories; he covers my back. He knows I won't let him down; I know he won't mess me about.

Second, he has a backbone. Fleet Street is well stocked with ambitious cowards, who have risen to the top by grinning obediently at anybody who is higher up the ladder than them. That kind of editor would take one look at a story which was bound to cause trouble with the largest news organisation in the country and the largest police force and the largest political party and, for good measure, the Press Complaints Commission, and they would have killed it or cut it back and tucked it away at the bottom of page five, hoping nobody would notice it. But Rusbridger liked it.

We agreed that we must run it soon, before Parliament rose for its summer recess, so that we could be sure it would have some impact. I had a little bit more work to do on it. I needed to approach some of the key players, including Coulson and News International, to see if they had anything to say. I also had a worry about it.

I was not sure about naming twenty-seven journalists from the *News of the World* and four others from the *Sun* who had been commissioning Steve Whittamore's network; or the news reporter, Ross Hindley, who had sent the email for Neville Thurlbeck, containing the transcripts of voicemail messages. I did not want to create more Clive Goodmans – more reporters who could be dismissed as rogues by senior people who were, in fact, the ones who were really responsible. Blame tends to fall downwards. Also, perhaps wrongly, I had a queasy resistance to naming journalists, just because I am a journalist. We agreed to hold back the names of all but the most senior and the most culpable.

I explained, too, that although I had got hold of a lot of paperwork, I couldn't admit that. Our evidence would have to stay hidden. We frightened each other a little with some speculation about which particular parts of our private life could be dragged out to punish us. And then we agreed to publish in the next week or so.

We'd probably be OK.

2. Inside the *News of the World*

Based on interviews with former journalists from the News of the World *as well as documents and detail which emerged in the Leveson Inquiry and in court hearings.*

Andy Coulson had a good view from his office. Sitting at his desk, he could look out through his glass wall and see the beating heart of the *News of the World*. Right in front of him was the 'back bench' – the row of desks where he would often sit with his lieutenants, filtering all the material that was being pumped into the paper from news agencies and freelancers and from his own staff, making the decisions that shaped the paper.

Beyond the back bench, he could see the picture desk and then the news desk where several executives ran the news reporters who were cramped together in a group on the far side of the room and, next to them, the sub-editors who would check their stories and write their headlines. Around the edges of the newsroom were the feature writers, the sports writers, offices for a few other executives and a special cubicle for the royal editor, Clive Goodman. This was Coulson's world, and he ruled it. But that wasn't the best part of the view.

The best sight was over to his right, just to the side of the back bench, where he could always see it, where everybody could see it – the trophy cabinet. He had just ordered it brand new, in April 2005, because he was proud of what his staff had achieved. This was the biggest-selling paper in the country – 3.5 million copies every Sunday. It was probably the biggest-selling paper in the Western world. It had the biggest budgets, the biggest impact. Nobody beat the *News of the World*. Which was why the new cabinet now displayed the biggest prize in British journalism – the award for Newspaper of the Year for 2004/5.

In the last twelve months, they had brought in one big scoop after another. David Beckham might be a great footballer and he might have thought he was clever enough to have an affair without his wife or anybody else finding out, but they'd caught him and exposed him for sleeping with his personal assistant, Rebecca Loos, and spread the story over seven pages. A few months later, they'd done the same with the England football manager, Sven-Göran Eriksson, when they caught him having an affair with Faria Alam, a secretary at the Football Association. To top that, a month later they had exposed the Home Secretary, David Blunkett, who had been having an affair with a married American publisher, Kimberly Quinn. As a bonus, they discovered that a *Guardian* journalist, Simon Hoggart, was also having an affair with Quinn, so a few weeks later they had tossed him into the mix as well. Week after week, they had pounded the opposition papers.

For Andy Coulson, aged thirty-seven, this was a peak. He had come a long way in a short time. He had left school at the age of eighteen, armed only with some A levels, a very good brain and one burning ambition: to become a showbiz reporter. It took him just two years of working on a local paper in Essex to hit his target. In 1988, aged only twenty, he was hired by the *Sun* to become part of the team that produced the gossip column, Bizarre. The column was brash and loud – just like its editor, Piers Morgan. It was obsessed with the private lives of rock stars, film stars, TV stars, anybody who could sprinkle glitter on the column's gossip. Coulson was pitched into a world of A-list celebrities and Class A drugs.

There were some people working on Bizarre who disappeared headlong into a blur of non-stop partying. One of Coulson's closest friends, Sean Hoare, who worked beside him on the column, used to start the day with what he called 'a rock star's breakfast' – a Jack Daniel's and a line of coke – and then he would carry on partying with whatever PR people or celebs would find him a story to justify his expenses.

'My job,' Hoare used to say, 'is to take drugs with rock stars.'

There was a tradition, known as the Friday Feeling, when Hoare or one of the other journalists would go off to the *Sun* cashier and draw out £300 and buy some charlie (it was an old News International tradition that some of the back-up staff would always have a nice supply) and then they'd get coked out of their heads and start the weekend.

Those who liked Coulson used to say he was calm at the core; he would always stay straight enough to file his copy. In spite of his youth, he seemed to have landed fully formed, with his light blue shirt and his dark blue suit, all neat and grown up. Others said he was cold, that no matter what was going on, Andy would always survive; behind that mask of mild-mannered competence, he was ruthless.

Hoare was furious with him one time when Hoare had brought in a story about a famous actress only to find that Coulson, first, refused to publish it; second, took the famous actress on holiday; third, was clearly being rewarded in her bed; fourth, and worst of all, told the famous actress how Hoare had managed to get the story in the first place, with the result that the source was exposed and lost forever. When Hoare discovered all this, he told Coulson direct and to his face that he was a complete cunt. Coulson replied with a line which became a regular catchphrase as he worked his way upwards: 'I'll make it up to you, mate.' As though it never mattered what you did, because you could always throw a favour in somebody's direction and just move on. Within six years, he had replaced Piers Morgan as editor of the Bizarre column.

Four years later, in January 1998, Coulson climbed further up the tree and became associate editor of the *Sun*, working alongside the new deputy editor – a sharp, sassy, ambitious young woman called Rebekah. They already knew each other a bit. Now, the two of them bonded. People guessed they must be sleeping together, though nobody was sure. They made a team – they were both young and clever, they had both started with nothing and they both shared an intense ambition. And together they made it.

In May 2000, Rupert Murdoch moved Rebekah Brooks to the editor's chair at the *News of the World*. She immediately recruited Coulson as her deputy. He worked hard for her, set up a new investigations department, handled the detail of stories for her and made sure the staff were happy. He had a good reputation in the newsroom. While Brooks was off in the clouds, making contacts among very important people, Coulson would turn up at the staff parties, and say hi to people in the newsroom. He rewarded himself with a Porsche Boxster with a top speed of 165 mph and a price tag of £35,000. But people began to notice that the more powerful he became, the more names he forgot. After a while, he was reduced to calling most of the men 'mate' and most of the women 'sweetheart'.

Three years later, in January 2003, Rupert Murdoch gave Brooks the *Sun* to edit and made Coulson boss at the *News of the World*. His new position gave him power, and he was happy to use it against those who crossed him. For example, he didn't like Roy Greenslade, the former editor of the *Daily Mirror* who had become a professor of journalism at City University, London. So he withdrew the funding for two student places which the *News of the World* had been sponsoring. The head of the City journalism department, Adrian Monck, had lunch with Coulson and sweet-talked him into restoring the funding. But, as he got up to leave, Coulson added: 'One thing, mate. I want you to give me Roy's head on a plate.' Monck refused: City lost its funding.

It was not simply that he was himself capable of being cold. More important, he was required to be ruthless. From his proprietor and the board of News Corp 3,500 miles away in New York, through the chief executive of News International, Les Hinton, who sat in the same building in Wapping, east London, the unstated message to him and to Rebekah Brooks, editing the *Sun* in the same building, and to every other editor in every other part of the empire was constant and simple: 'Get the story – no matter what.'

The previous month, March 2005, Coulson had been to the Hilton Hotel to pick up his big award, for Newspaper of the Year. Afterwards, when he was interviewed by the *Press Gazette*, he had shrugged off the sneering disdain of outsiders who seemed to think his kind of journalism was not really respectable.

'I've got nothing to be ashamed of,' he said. 'And this goes for everyone on the *News of the World*. The readers are the judges. That's the most important thing. And I think we should be proud of what we do.'

It is an odd thing about newspapers, that they live by exposure, yet they keep their own worlds concealed. A little of the truth about Andy Coulson's newspaper begins to emerge in evidence provided by one of his former staff – hundreds of notes and emails and memos which his executives wrote for each other in 2005 as they strove to repeat the triumphs of the previous twelve months.

It begins with the readers. The friends of tabloid newspapers often point out that their journalism exists only because millions of people choose to pay money to read it. The internal messages go one step further, disclosing the fervour with which readers stepped forward to provide a paper like the *News of the World* with the information which it craved.

Take one week early in 2005. The internal messages record that a male prostitute had contacted them to report 'romping' in a sauna with a male TV presenter – 'He wants to do kiss-and-tell and says his mate can corroborate the tale.' And a woman who went out with a Hollywood actor when he was fourteen wants to sell the story of how he cheated on her. And a caller 'claims to have pics of a prominent Crystal Palace player in a gay clinch with pals on holiday'. And another says 'I've got some information regarding [England footballer] and his ex-wife.'

As the weeks go by, the messages disclose an apparently endless line of men and women who have collected some fragment of human interest and are now offering it for sale (almost always for sale). There is a woman who claims that, years ago, she had some kind of relationship with the rock star Pete Doherty: 'I have some interesting details to give for a good price, although I wish to remain anonymous.' There is a man whose English-born daughter was in New Orleans during Hurricane Katrina and who is offering an interview with her, for £1,500. Some simply hope for a sale: 'I was just wondering how much pictures of Premiership footballers with ladyboys in Bangkok are worth. Got a classic if the price is right.' Some are surely hopeless: 'I recently came into possession of a video of [a named male actor] masturbating.

Would your paper be interested in purchasing this from me as I have no need for it?'

But as the messages flow on, the commercial side of this auction takes second place to something else more striking, something more human and more secret – a casual treachery. At the very least, these informants are betraying those they have come across through their work. A hotel porter says he has got his hands on paperwork to prove that two TV presenters have just secretly spent the night together; a prison worker reckons he can prove that an old heroin addict in one of his cells is the secret father of a singer in a girl band; a fashion worker has got hold of colour polaroids of Kate Moss at a shoot. 'She has no make-up on and looks quite washed out. Would you be interested in purchasing these pictures? They have never been published, and I know they were making an effort for them not to be seen by the public.'

At worst, these are people volunteering to sell the secrets of those who most trust them – their friends, lovers, family members. A man is currently having a relationship with a woman whose brother is a notorious criminal. They have been together for seven months, he says. They are still together. No matter: he's selling her. 'Would you be interested? Cos I have a lot to say!' A man was once in drugs rehab with a film director. 'I spent six months in there with him, went to his family home and got to know him quite well.' No problem, he's selling him: 'This would have to be agreed contractually before I met with anybody from the *News of the World* or said another word.' A man has been visiting a prostitute. He has discovered she is the aunt of a TV presenter. He wants to sell her out – as long as they don't identify him: he is married.

Some of them try to make sure of their sale by offering evidence to prove their story. A man has got in touch to say that he has just spent the night with a young actress from a TV soap, and that's a story worth selling and, even better, he says that he managed to sneak a photograph of her giving him oral sex. Another message records a woman's story about an England footballer: 'Paula claims that she had a four-week fling with XX in Dec last year. She says they had sex in the back of his car in XX's pal's pub. Paula also says she has a jumper with XX's semen on it.'

Everything is for sale. Nobody is exempt. What begins to emerge is the internal machinery of a commercial enterprise which has never previously existed, an industry which treats human life itself – the soft tissue of the most private, sensitive moments – as a vast quarry full of raw material to be scooped up and sifted and exploited for entertainment. Back in the 1980s, the *News of the World* had specialised in digging into the privacy of criminals. In the 1990s, enriched by the excavation of Princess Diana's volatile life, they had widened their work to mine the activities of any celebrity, any public figure. Now, they had gone even further. The whole of human life – of anybody, anywhere who had news value – had become one mass of crude bulk for Andy Coulson's newsroom to extract and refine in a ruthless search for the most intimate, embarrassing, often painful details which could then be converted into precious nuggets for sale in a massive marketplace.

Working in Coulson's newsroom was not easy. It was dirty and difficult and, in some ways, it was dangerous. But they had to get the story. To run this place required a special kind of team.

There is a story that Ian Edmondson often liked to tell, about the time when he was still only a junior reporter on the *News of the World* and he had a girlfriend who was a reporter on another newspaper. He liked to call her 'Boobs'. It so happened, he would explain, that Boobs made friends with Tracy Shaw, a particularly eye-catching young actress from the TV soap opera *Coronation Street* who was of great interest to the tabloids. As Edmondson told it, there was one night when the two women had gone out on the town together and afterwards, Boobs had confided in him that Shaw had done some coke. This was obviously a secret, he would say, and one which could cause trouble for Tracy Shaw and potentially for his girlfriend – but also it was obviously a good story for the *News of the World*. So, he recalled with some relish, he had persuaded the trusting Boobs to tell him the whole tale again, secretly recorded her every word and gave it to the paper.

Edmondson liked to play the bastard. It worked for him. From that position at the bottom of the editorial pile at the *News of the World* in the mid-1990s, he rose to become assistant editor, running the newsroom and still playing the bastard. He went through a phase of telling people that his nickname was 'Love Rat'. It wasn't, but Edmondson liked the idea. One reporter says he even taped the name to the front of his pigeonhole, apparently hoping that it would catch on. However, it is clear from those who worked for him that he had no need to go to such lengths to give himself a bad name. A lot of people genuinely didn't like Ian Edmondson. He was relentlessly competitive, with everybody around him. He had to have the biggest car, the biggest salary. He was very fit. He bicycled to work and ran during the lunch hour, but other people ran too, so he made a big show of carrying a rucksack full of bricks when he went out. He used to tell improbable stories about his achievements – that he had rowed for England; that he had a football trial with the Blackburn Rovers youth team and scored the winning goal, in the dying minutes of the game, with an overhead scissors kick; and then told exactly the same story about a trial for Ipswich Town . . .

He had made friends with Dave Courtney, a burly, shaven-headed Londoner who earned a living by playing the part of a media-friendly gangster. Edmondson liked to confide that he spent a lot of time with gangsters and he reckoned that, after spending a particularly intimate day smoking cigars by the pool with a group of them, one of them had taken him for a ride in his Range Rover, stopped in the middle of nowhere, pulled out a gun and told him he had heard too much that day. Edmondson claimed this guy had made it very clear what would happen if ever he talked but that the gangster had then relaxed and handed him an envelope full of cash. Not everybody believed him.

Andy Coulson was apparently quite happy to take advantage of Edmondson's burning urge to compete. In November 2004, when he hired him as associate news editor, he already had somebody doing the same job, Jimmy Weatherup. Coulson left both of them in place to fight for his approval. They loathed each other. The results were often chaotic. Jimmy Weatherup would send out a reporter to cover a story. Ian Edmondson would call the reporter and send him somewhere else. A reporter would come up with a story idea and tell it to Edmondson, who would take him aside and tell him to keep the idea quiet for a week – 'Jimmy's off next week, and I'd like to have something good for myself.'

Weatherup was older and more experienced than Edmondson and he, too, was capable of playing the bastard. He used to like ordering young reporters to go and knock on the door at a particular address, warning them that the man who lived there was notoriously vile-tempered and often physically violent. This was just a trap: the address didn't exist, and if the reporter claimed to have been there and found nobody in, Weatherup would dump ordure on them. But Weatherup was no kind of street fighter. He appeared to be stuck in a 1970s time warp, playing the Travolta part in *Saturday Night Fever*, tall and slim and with a great deal of preening in front of the mirror. His hair was surprisingly dark, and Edmondson regularly accused him of dyeing it. He wore expensive suits and special gloves for driving and he had a well-known tendency, at the first sight of a sunny day, to turn up in the office in tight-fitting white tennis shorts; and an equally well-known tendency to slide up behind the young female reporters and massage their shoulders or even kiss their necks. He was known as Whispering Jimmy partly because of his smooth, oozing style on the phone and partly because he was so obsessively secretive. Some colleagues knew Weatherup as 'Secrets' and Edmondson as 'Lies'.

All this created a regime in which the naturally intense rivalry between a mass-market newspaper and its competitors was made all the more furious by the back-stabbing tension between the two news editors. Coulson managed to raise the friction still higher by aggravating the long-standing competition between the news desk and the features department. The two sections rarely spoke and frequently fought, hiding their plans from each other, constantly attempting to outdo each other.

The features editor, Jules Stenson, was tough, clever, an unrivalled expert on TV soap operas and widely seen as most likely to succeed Coulson in the editor's chair. He was also aggressive, particularly with Clive Goodman, with whom, according to one colleague, he had a relationship of mutual loathing. Stenson's relationship with Ian Edmondson was just as bad. One of the journalists who worked there remembers the news desk in April 2005 trying to buy the story of a woman in Yorkshire who had admitted helping her seriously ill husband to die. She had been cleared in court, and the news desk sent a reporter to offer her £5,000 for the intimate close-up tale of her husband's death, but the reporter found that she had already been offered £6,000 by somebody else. The news desk bid higher; the rival went higher too. At £14,000, the news desk pulled out and then discovered that they had been bidding against Jules Stenson.

Andy Coulson kept his hands close to the steering wheel. He chaired the daily conference when the heads of all the editorial departments – news, features, sport, showbiz, royal, politics – would pitch their ideas. He liked to show that he was on top of stories. During the spring of 2005, for example, he personally oversaw a project to snatch an interview with the Yorkshire Ripper, Peter Sutcliffe, in Broadmoor psychiatric hospital, where he was serving his time for the murder of thirteen women. This was kept very secret. The reporter on the job was instructed not to tell colleagues. For maximum discretion, Edmondson could have managed the job himself, but Coulson liked to think he knew how to run an investigation and he duly authorised the payment of a hefty fee to Sutcliffe's brother, Carl, and also the purchase of a camera and recorder which were specially designed to trick the metal detectors at Broadmoor. Carl Sutcliffe concealed them inside a plaster cast and visited his unsuspecting brother who then found himself splashed across the *News of the World*, primarily on the grounds that he had become fat – 'a balding 17-stone slob', as the paper put it.

Still, there was a limit to how much Coulson could intervene. He would sit in his office, banging out emails with terse instructions to those around him, but he relied on two right-hand men to enforce his will. Each of them had offices which flanked his own at the top end of the newsroom. To Coulson's left, looking out, was Stuart Kuttner, who had been the managing editor at the *News of the World* for nearly fifteen years.

There was something dark about Kuttner with his skeletal face, his slow, calculating manner and his original London accent only slightly disguised as posh. Since 1987, he had served half a dozen editors in a role like that of the Harvey Keitel character in *Pulp Fiction* – he cleaned up mess. If any kind of threat came out of any kind of dark corner – scandals in the newsroom, rebellious reporters, angry victims – Kuttner would deal with it, get rid of the body, clear up the blood. He told one colleague that his favourite book was Machiavelli's *The Prince* with its admiration for manipulation and deceit as the necessary tools of power. Kuttner enjoyed power. Former colleagues say he liked to use the messengers as his private staff, sending them out to buy him fresh fruit in the morning or to take his briefcase down to his car at the end of the day. He was notorious for the violence of his bollockings. But primarily his power was financial. He was responsible for the editorial budget, and all those who worked for him agree that he treated the newspaper's money as though it were his own: he wanted every penny accounted for.

Coulson's second enforcer, in the office to his right, was his deputy editor, Neil Wallis. He was nearly twenty years older than Coulson; he had been in Fleet Street for years, moving from one tabloid to another, earning along the way a reputation for what one colleague described as 'a psychopathic ability to divorce his emotions from his actions'. This colleague recalls Wallis at a leaving party strolling up to an executive whom he had shafted in his earlier career with a cheery smile and an extended hand, only to be told: 'I'm not going to shake your hand until you've washed it.' He collected libel writs like kids used to collect coins – 'the Wallis Collection' as it was known, with a nod to the Wallace Collection of fine art in central London.

Wallis made it his business to go drinking with top cops. In January 2005 he persuaded the retiring Metropolitan Police Commissioner, Sir John Stevens, to write a weekly column for the *News of the World*. It turned out that Wallis had been offering Stevens free PR advice for years and credited himself with helping Stevens into the commissioner's chair. That, plus up to £7,000 a column, plus the promise to call him The Chief, even though Stevens was no longer a chief officer, landed the man.

In some newsrooms, Wallis was known as 'the wolfman', possibly because of a story he had written to the effect that the Yorkshire Ripper was a Jekyll and Hyde character who killed only on full moons. At the *News of the World*, he was known as 'the rasping fuckwit', which was partly a reflection of his breathy voice but also a straightforward sign of disrespect. The truth was a bit more complicated than that. A lot of reporters didn't like him as a person, they didn't trust him and they knew he was the kind of cynic who gives cynics a bad name, but they also knew that he was a highly effective hack. He was quick-witted and tough. He had good contacts, he could spin a story. He understood the business of tabloid journalism.

So News Corp's demand for success at all costs was passed down from Andy Coulson's office through Kuttner and Wallis to the news desk and the features department and then onwards to the journalists beneath them, and with it came a certain style of management, simply and repeatedly described by those who experienced it as 'bullying'. This was a tough place to work.

Hanging on the wall above the news desk, there was a digital clock which counted down the minutes to the next edition of the paper. In the human-resources department, they logged the bylines of all the reporters, who were often reminded that those who slipped down the league table could expect to be hauled in for a bollocking or even to find themselves on the receiving end in the next round of redundancies.

Reporters who worked there speak of a deeply unpleasant 'ideas' meeting on Tuesday mornings when they would all sit in a corner office while Edmondson or Weatherup or one of their deputies told them that their ideas for stories were all useless, a judgement which was often reinforced by an email later in the morning telling them that those were the worst story proposals the news desk had ever heard and demanding three more ideas from each of them. Edmondson, the reporters say, was particularly aggressive. They tell, for example, of him trying to put an electronic tracker on one reporter's phone to check on his movements; of a senior reporter being reduced to tears at his desk because his wife had been diagnosed with cancer and Edmondson refused to let him have any time off work to look after her; of another who was sacked because he became a single parent and would not accept Edmondson's ruling that 'you belong to the *News of the World*'. When they were out on the road, they say, he liked to keep up the pressure by sending them texts – 'tick tock' or simply '??'.

Since Rupert Murdoch broke the print unions and threw out the

National Union of Journalists in 1986, the reporters had had no kind of protection. Some cracked. One is said to have tried to kill herself at a Christmas party. Mostly, however, they passed the bullying along to the people they dealt with. Several of them have described how they were encouraged to rip off the sources who sold them stories.

Some sources were naive. They would tell their story before getting a signed contract and would simply never be paid. One reporter was sent to interview a prostitute who had had sex with a public figure, with instructions not to pay more than £250,000 for her story. The woman opened up by saying she wouldn't talk for a penny under £10,000. Another agreed to talk on the promise that the *News of the World* would pay for her to have a good holiday. When she tried to claim her reward, Ian Edmondson declared that she was from up north, so she could stay in a caravan, for £150. Some got contracts and fell for an easy trick. The contract promised them big money if the story went on the front page. The reporter knew very well it would go inside the paper but kept that quiet. When the story came out and the source begged for something, anything, the reporter would offer them a tiny fee and, as one put it, 'you wear them down and, in the end, they'll take buttons'. A few — including a woman who had been raped by a footballer — fell foul of a clause which said that to the best of the source's knowledge, the story must be true: the *News of the World* printed the story, claimed the source had been knowingly wrong about some part of it and refused to pay up. The subjects of stories also were shown no pity. They were dragged out and exposed in front of millions of readers, for being gay, for liking sex, for having a new partner, for accidentally showing their knickers when they stepped out of a car, for having broken the law when they were an adolescent. If the truth was not good enough to make a story, they could twist it.

Some reporters say they had pangs of conscience, not least because of the eye-watering hypocrisy which was involved. While castigating anybody else who showed any special interest in sex, the *News of the World*'s own newsroom was bubbling with affairs and outbreaks of sexual harassment, including a marked tendency during Andy Coulson's time to recruit pretty young women who were encouraged to come into work wearing as little as possible. The paper had always been keen to expose orgies, but former *News of the World* journalists describe some of their own office parties as a model of drug-fuelled sexual adventure. They recall one mighty booze-up ending with an assistant editor outside the Chocolate Bar in Mayfair, central London, scarcely able to walk and talking to a woman reporter while he held his cock in his hand.

The paper ruined a long list of more or less famous men by exposing the fact that they had visited prostitutes. And yet, in search of more of these stories, one *News of the World* reporter was told to make contacts among high-class sex workers with the specific instruction that he should have sex with them, do cocaine with them and claim it all on expenses. So he did. On another occasion, according to one source, Ian Edmondson wanted to expose a Premiership footballer for using prostitutes – and paid one to have sex with him. In the same way, they were ruthless in exposing any target who used illegal drugs, but there was no shortage of journalists using the same drugs. Former reporters tell stories of a Christmas disco where the dance floor was almost empty while various guests resorted to the toilets to snort cocaine; and of a ripple of panic when the *Sun* let their anti-drug hound, Charlie the Sniffer Dog, loose in the newsroom. Some of the journalists, including executives, were running on alcohol. A few ended up in expensive rehab clinics (noticing the opportunity to find stories about fellow patients).

This was not just about hypocrisy. It was also the key to a crucial editorial distortion: regardless of the reality of the world they lived in, the *News of the World* was pretending in print that the nation lived by an antique moral code which rendered anything other than clean living and straight sex between a married couple improper and, therefore, they wanted to claim, a legitimate subject for exposure. It was fiction. It was also the cornerstone of their justification for their most destructive work.

There was no room for doubt or conscience. Human feelings did not come into it. The *News of the World* was exposing bad people – all in the public interest. Privacy did not come into it. Privacy was for paedophiles, as the former feature writer, Paul McMullan, used to say.

There was no escape. If a public figure admitted to using cocaine or enjoying sex, they had sacrificed their right to privacy. If a public figure refused to admit to using cocaine and enjoying sex, they were misleading the public, so they had no right to privacy in the first place. The *News of the World* might keep its own behaviour private. But that was different. The important thing was to get the story.

Gordon Taylor was a perfect target for the *News of the World*. It was not just that his job as the boss of the Professional Footballers' Association gave him daily access to the private lives of famous players, his own private life also caught their eye.

It started back at the beginning of 2005, when a well-known retired footballer contacted the paper and arranged to meet a reporter from the Manchester office in a pub on Merseyside. There the retired player passed on some scandalous gossip. He claimed – falsely, as it turned out – that Taylor was having an affair with Jo Armstrong, who was not just his in-house legal adviser: she was also his son's former girlfriend. The reporter hurried back to the office and relayed the tale to Greg Miskiw.

Miskiw was a *News of the World* legend, a man who had sacrificed his reputation, his peace of mind and his health to the single glorious goal of living the life of a lad. A lad drinks: Miskiw drank whisky in what he liked to call 'gentleman's measures', so big that he didn't have to ask for a refill while other people were nursing their pints. A lad has madcap adventures: Miskiw's best was in 1982 when he tried to smuggle himself into communist Poland by hiding inside a mailbag and posting himself to Warsaw, only to be arrested and locked up until Mrs Thatcher's government prised him free. A lad shags: Miskiw was deeply committed to the cause.

By 2005, age was catching up with him. He was fifty-six and looked much older. He was getting very fat. Years of smoking had ruined his lungs. A few months earlier, he had left the Manchester office one day and crashed down on the pavement with a heart attack. Worse than that, he had been pushed aside. For years, from the mid-1990s, Miskiw had been cock of the walk in London, where he had been an assistant editor, overseeing the news desk. He had been devious, aggressive, secretive to the point of paranoia – and highly successful, although he spent most of the day every day raving with nervous energy, sometimes physically battering his head against the wall, until he got drunk enough to calm down in the evening. He had also been ruthless, once famously telling a young reporter, Charles Begley, who was depressed about having to dress up as Harry Potter as part of a publicity stunt, that he should toughen up and focus on what the *News of the World* did for a living: 'We go out and destroy other people's lives.'

But Andy Coulson didn't like Miskiw; and Miskiw didn't like Coulson. So, in 2003, as Coulson established himself as editor, Miskiw was moved up to Manchester as northern editor.

When he heard the story about Gordon Taylor, early in 2005, Miskiw did something which would have struck any outsider as very strange. He pretended he had been given the tip by somebody completely different. He even drew up a contract, dated 4 February 2005, which was eventually to fall into the hands of the *Guardian*. It undertook that if the story about Taylor was eventually published, the *News of the World* would pay £7,000 to this supposed source, who was named in the contract as Paul Williams. This was fiction upon fiction. It was not simply that Paul Williams did not exist. Like 'Glenn Williams' and 'John Jenkins', the name was simply a cover for one of Miskiw's few close friends – Glenn Mulcaire, who was in a spot of trouble. After working for years as a prolific source of information for the paper, the investigator was now facing a disastrous suggestion that Stuart Kuttner, on orders from Andy Coulson, might cut his contract in half. It suited Miskiw very well to defy his bosses in London by finding another way to make sure that his mate got his money. Since the former footballer who really was the source of the story about Gordon Taylor would rather have eaten his own leg than admit he had told the tale, Miskiw could safely pretend that the source was his friend and agree a fat payment.

It was Greg Miskiw who had originally discovered Mulcaire and his special skills. Miskiw had first come across him as a blagger, in the late 1990s, working for an investigator called John Boyall, who was one of the three men who later ended up in the dock with Fleet Street's most notorious blagger, Steve Whittamore. Mulcaire was a natural.

Other blaggers may have been better trained, they may have done more research on their targets or come up with better scripts to fool those they dealt with, but for ordinary, natural-born, quick-thinking, silver-tongued, seat-of-the-pants, top-of-the-head spontaneous genius, Mulcaire was the man. He was born to bullshit. And then he taught Miskiw about phone-hacking.

By 1999, according to former *News of the World* reporters, Miskiw was dropping heavy hints to reporters that he was 'a hundred per cent sure' that some tip was accurate. Very soon, others in the newsroom learned his trick and started doing it themselves, swapping good numbers and useful messages like schoolboys swap conkers, openly discussing hacked messages, then writing stories which were sprinkled with imaginary quotes from an imaginary source, often an anonymous 'pal'.

It was no good if the target answered the phone, so they would help each other out – one calling the target and posing as the man from the gas board to keep the line busy, while the other called in and listened to the voicemail. They called this 'double whacking'. Sometimes, reporters did both jobs at once – sitting crouched over their desk with a phone at each ear, one to engage the target, the other to hack. This was known as 'muppeting', because it looked so stupid. Ironically, one of the few who declined to do it in the early days was Clive Goodman: he thought mobile phones would never catch on, so he refused to have anything to do with them.

Early in 2000, Miskiw fell out with John Boyall and poached Mulcaire from Boyall's agency to work for him direct. By 2001, with Miskiw's support, Mulcaire had joined the British Association of Journalists and been given a full-time contract worth £94,000 a year – a big deal, more than the news editor was being paid. Soon, he had an office in Sutton, south London, where he blagged and hacked on such a scale that he had to recruit an assistant to help him.

Now, early in February 2005, Mulcaire went to work on Gordon Taylor. By 22 February, he had recorded eleven messages that had been left on Taylor's phone. Mulcaire passed the tape to Miskiw who gave it to a secretary in the Manchester office, who typed out the messages. This was a well-oiled system.

Miskiw was in contact with Glenn Mulcaire almost every day, sometimes tasking him on his own stories, very often passing on requests from other people on the paper. A few other senior journalists were allowed to deal direct with Mulcaire, but Miskiw made sure he was the main minder. This was partly because it gave him power and prestige within the paper; but also because Miskiw didn't trust other people not to cock it up. Miskiw always ensured that Mulcaire's work was hidden, inventing false sources, omitting key details, always laying false trails. Often, this involved using a former police officer, Derek Webb, who had become an expert in covert surveillance, calling himself Silver Shadow. Mulcaire would locate a target using criminal methods, Webb would follow them for days without breaking the law, then the paper would close in.

If the story was seriously libellous, the *News of the World* would cut a deal with the target. Knowing that they could not defend a libel action without admitting that they had obtained the story by criminal means, they would call the target, pretend that they were ready to publish and then offer to run a less damaging version if the source would give them confirmation. So the actress would confirm she had had a miscarriage if the paper agreed not to say that it was an abortion; the footballer would confirm that he had smoked cannabis, if they agreed not to say he was snorting cocaine. Andy Coulson had often made calls like this and liked to declare with a grin: 'That's tabloid journalism! You turn them over in the morning. And in the afternoon, they thank you for it.'

None of Gordon Taylor's messages revealed any kind of affair between him and Jo Armstrong. On the following Sunday, Liverpool were due to play Chelsea in the Carling Cup final at the new Millennium Stadium in Cardiff. Glenn Mulcaire found out which hotel Taylor was staying in before the game. As a result, Taylor was disturbed early on the Sunday morning by a *News of the World* reporter finding some pretext to call his room to see whether a woman answered. The same reporter lurked outside the hotel, in case a picture would tell the story. It didn't.

But Mulcaire persisted. That was not easy: he was overloaded with work. Coulson's former reporters say he was helping them on just about every story they covered, though not all of them knew he was hacking. Even on a Saturday, when the paper had to cover small news stories, they would ask Miskiw to get Mulcaire to blag phone companies to find close friends of a family who had died in a house fire, or to blag the DVLA for the name and home address of somebody who died in a car crash. They used him to check on kiss-and-tell stories. A train company manager wanted to sell them the tale of his brief affair with the model Kate Moss. He described how he had been staying at a hotel in central London when he had started talking to her at the bar. They had spent the night together, he said, and, when he woke up the next morning, he had found a note from her, asking him to get in touch if he was in town again and leaving her mobile number. Mulcaire blagged the phone company and found that this had indeed been Kate Moss's number, but it was no longer in use. Eventually, the man confessed he had made up the whole tale, and so, to punish him, they got Mulcaire to find his home address and landline number and then called his wife to ask her to comment on her husband's relationship with Kate Moss.

All the stories which had won Coulson the award of Newspaper of the Year were based on Mulcaire hacking voicemail. He had hacked Sven-Göran Eriksson to expose the England manager's affair with a secretary, Faria Alam. He had hacked David Beckham to expose the footballer's affair with his personal assistant, Rebecca Loos. No matter how many times Beckham changed his number, no matter how many extra SIM cards he shuffled through his phone, Mulcaire kept listening to his messages. At one point, Mulcaire claimed, Beckham had hired an expensive security agency to make sure that his phones were safe, and, according to Mulcaire, he had broken through their protection within an hour.

He had hacked messages left by the then Home Secretary David Blunkett, provoking Greg Miskiw, who was usually highly secretive, into boasting to colleagues that if they could listen to the voicemail of the minister who was directly responsible for the Security Service, they could surely listen to anybody's. Having got away with it the previous year when the paper had exposed Blunkett's relationship with Kimberly Quinn, Mulcaire was now hacking him all over again, seeking out the details of the politician's supposed relationship with a former estate agent named Sally Anderson, which, in truth, had nothing sexual about it. He was hacking Sally Anderson. And her father. And her brother, as well as her partner, ex-boyfriend, grandmother, aunt, mother, cousin, a close friend, her osteopath and two of Blunkett's special advisers.

By May 2005 Ian Edmondson was getting impatient for the Gordon Taylor story which Miskiw had been promising to deliver for several months. Internal messages show that during April Edmondson had tried to nail it by sending a reporter, Laura Holland, to spy on Taylor at the PFA's annual awards ceremony in Park Lane, in case he showed up holding hands with Jo Armstrong. She got nothing. (She and a male photographer were told also to swab the toilets in case they could find cocaine traces.) Mulcaire had tried blagging into Taylor's bank account in case that yielded anything. It didn't. So, Edmondson brought in Neville Thurlbeck, chief reporter, winner of awards, tabloid-scoop hero, rather unusual person.

Thurlbeck, then aged forty-three, grew up in down-to-earth, gritty Sunderland in the north-east of England, but he emerged in the fantasy role of a very old-fashioned high Tory. He was obsessed with the 1930s. He liked to wear braces and tweed jackets with a handkerchief neatly placed in the breast pocket. He told colleagues with pride that he had never worn a pair of jeans. He spoke about his wife in equally conservative tones, boasting that he had never ironed a shirt in his life. He was a fan of George Formby and claimed to play the ukulele. He drove a Mercedes and deplored these southerners who thought it was sensible to spend millions to live in Victorian semis, which he regarded as slums, and insisted on finding his own detached house in Surrey, built, of course, in the 1930s. And yet beneath this stuffy, fluffy image, he was a ruthless tabloid man.

He had made his name – and won four different awards for the scoop of the year – in 2000 by exposing the Conservative peer and novelist, Jeffrey Archer. Notoriously, he had once also exposed himself in the course of attempting to prove that a naturist couple in Dorset, Bob and Sue Firth, were offering sexual services to the customers of their bed and breakfast business. Not realising that his attempts to persuade the couple to have sex in front of him had made them so suspicious that they were secretly videoing him, he stripped off to pose as a fellow naturist and then surreptitiously engaged in an act which earned him the nickname Onan the Barbarian. In spite of regularly indulging himself by spending company money on the most expensive restaurants and hotels, Thurlbeck had risen through the ranks, serving as news editor under Greg Miskiw, from 2001 to 2003, and was now chief reporter, the man who did the big stories.

On 9 May 2005, Thurlbeck was sent a transcript of the messages from Gordon Taylor's voicemail which had been typed up by the secretary in Manchester three months earlier. It took a while for him to get moving. He had just revealed that the TV football presenter Andy Gray had broken up with his girlfriend. Gray, too, was being hacked by Mulcaire and by several *News of the World* journalists. He was an easy target: whenever he was commentating on a live football match, they knew he could not answer his phone, so they dialled in and listened to his voicemail. Then, before he could start work on Gordon Taylor, Thurlbeck was sent to Australia to cover the supposedly private medical care of Kylie Minogue, who had been diagnosed with breast cancer. Thurlbeck filed a long piece from Melbourne, quoting her younger brother, Brendan, 'speaking to a family friend'. Brendan Minogue and his sister, Dannii, were being hacked by Mulcaire.

In June, just as Thurlbeck started work in earnest on the Taylor story, something very significant changed at the *News of the World*: Greg Miskiw left the paper. Control of Mulcaire, who had been managed with such cunning by Miskiw, now passed to Ian Edmondson, who was happy to embrace the investigator but who was an altogether less subtle operator. He started using Mulcaire on very sensitive targets, including the specialist PR man Max Clifford, who brokered the tales of people at the centre of tabloid scandals; journalists and editors on rival papers, including even Rebekah Brooks at the *Sun*; George Osborne, the closest political ally of David Cameron who became Conservative leader in October 2005; and the family of the Labour prime minister, Tony Blair. Mulcaire even ended up hacking *News of the World* journalists, including Andy Coulson, and a football reporter, James Fletcher, in case he was picking up titbits about the private lives of famous players.

There was a big leaving party for Miskiw in London. Glenn Mulcaire was a guest, rubbing shoulders with reporters and executives and with Andy Coulson, who was later to deny ever having met the investigator.

Edmondson wanted the Gordon Taylor story badly. On Monday 27 June, he called in Derek Webb, who booked into a hotel in Manchester and started to shadow Taylor, watching him meeting Jo Armstrong, observing no sign of anything sexual and reporting back that it looked as though the story was not true. Edmondson refused to drop it. On Wednesday 29 June, Glenn Mulcaire supplied a new recording of some messages left on the phones of Taylor and Armstrong. These were transcribed and, that afternoon, a London reporter, Ross Hindley, emailed the transcript of thirty-five messages to Mulcaire so that he could pass them on to Neville Thurlbeck. 'Hello,' wrote Hindley in a message which was to become a central exhibit in the exposure of the *News of the World*. 'This is the transcript for Neville.'

Two days later, on Friday 1 July, Edmondson sent a photographer up to Manchester to try to snatch a picture of Taylor with Armstrong. Derek Webb was in a swanky fifth-floor restaurant, watching his two targets having lunch, when the photographer called him to say he had arrived in the city. Webb told him where he was and a few minutes later, to his horror, the photographer walked into the restaurant and sat down beside him. Taylor and Armstrong did not notice. Nor, by sheer luck, did they notice when the photographer walked to the back of the restaurant, turned and openly banged off several shots of them. However, another diner did notice exactly what was happening and, as the photographer headed for the exit and found he had to wait for the lift, the observant diner went to warn Gordon Taylor and pointed out the photographer and also Derek Webb, who was clearly linked to him.

Taylor was furious and went after the photographer, narrowly failing to catch him as a lift arrived to take him downstairs. Taylor followed him. Webb followed the two of them, pausing in the lift to change his coat and put on a hat, before arriving in the street to see Taylor now confronting the photographer – and a passing police officer being drawn into the incident.

That afternoon, Edmondson tasked three photographers and two more reporters to join Thurlbeck in trying to nail the story for that Sunday's paper. Thurlbeck, in his customary style, booked into a very pleasant country hotel outside Manchester. On Saturday morning, the team split up and went off to stage simultaneous confrontations with Jo Armstrong, Gordon Taylor's son and Taylor himself. It was a disaster. Jo Armstrong said the story wasn't true; Taylor's son told the reporter to piss off; and Thurlbeck, having idled over a satisfying breakfast, turned up on Taylor's doorstep too late, found he had gone into town and ended up chasing him through a shopping mall, at the end of which Taylor told him to piss off.

The story was false. It died. At least, that's what the *News of the World* thought at the time. Unknown to them, Gordon Taylor decided to alert his lawyer, Mark Lewis. Lewis wrote to the *News of the World*'s long-serving in-house lawyer, a man with a laid-back and charming style called Tom Crone, who had qualified as a barrister before going to work for News International where he attempted to prevent libels and contempts of court and dealt with the aftermath if he failed. Crone wrote back to Lewis, saying there would be no story and that this was all just legitimate journalistic inquiry.

In the newsroom without boundaries, there was one thing which was not tolerated: failure. This was a problem for Clive Goodman, who had worked for the *News of the World* since 1986. He was portly, pompous, well past his prime, and his career had ploughed into the sand.

After years as a specialist in celebrity gossip and the life of the royal family, he had run out of contacts and started to run out of steam. By 2005, he had the grandiose title of royal editor, a fob watch, his own office and not much hope. Colleagues in the pub once joked that he was like the eternal flame because he never went out.

Goodman did his best to make good. He emailed Coulson from time to time saying he needed cash to pay police officers who worked at the royal palaces, occasionally adding a line to point out that this was a criminal offence. Coulson routinely agreed, the payment was logged in internal paperwork with false names for Goodman's contacts, and the money was served up in cash through the network of offices run by the Thomas Cook travel agency.

And Goodman also resorted to the skills of Glenn Mulcaire. He had been hacking in a small way on his own since January 2005, using a couple of phone numbers and PIN codes for royal staff which Greg Miskiw had given him. But in August, Coulson took him out to lunch and told him he had to find new ways to get stories about Prince William and Prince Harry – and Goodman knew how to do it. Years later, he was to claim it was Mulcaire's idea, that the hacker was worried that his contract was going to be cut so he was looking for an extra deal on the side. Mulcaire says he never wanted to do it, because it was dangerous and that he was pressurised. Whatever the origin, the result was that Goodman agreed to find money to set up a special operation – they called it 'Project Bumblebee' – to trawl systematically through the voicemail of the royal family and their staff. Goodman would revive his career. Mulcaire would earn some extra cash. Over the following couple of months, the investigator started gathering royal phone numbers and PIN codes, dropping heavy hints to Goodman that he was being helped by some secret source in the Security Service.

The only problem with Goodman's plan was Ian Edmondson, who had now pushed Jimmy Weatherup aside to take sole control of the news desk. With Miskiw gone, Edmondson was using the secret weapon to capture masses of stories (and making the rival features department look so weak that one of their writers, Dan Evans, was now routinely hacking phones on the same scale as Mulcaire in an attempt to catch up). Goodman had little chance of getting direct access to Mulcaire for himself. He had the answer. He would simply go over Edmondson's head. On 25 October, Goodman went to see the editor. Coulson was cautious. He had no problem with breaking the law or invading the privacy of the royal household, but he was under relentless pressure from Murdoch's managers to cut back on editorial spending. Nevertheless, if this worked, it could boost the paper's circulation and pay for itself. Coulson agreed that, for a trial period of just four weeks, Mulcaire would be paid an extra £500 a week to target the royal household's voicemail.

They all knew this was legally very risky. They agreed to keep it especially secret. They arranged that the payments to Mulcaire would be sent to him under yet another false name, David Alexander, with a pick-up address which could not be linked to him, in Chelsea, central London.

On 26 October, Mulcaire emailed Goodman – subject 'Bumblebee' – with details of fourteen royal numbers which he could access, adding 'Please file secure folder!!!!' From that afternoon, the two of them were regularly intercepting Palace voicemails; Stuart Kuttner was signing off payments to 'David Alexander'; and, following the established pattern, Goodman was tasking Derek Webb to follow up on hacked intelligence by secretly following royal targets. Webb recognised this was not easy, but he found a solution: he lurked outside palaces and royal houses, noting the descriptions and numbers of police escort vehicles and then, as the escorts followed their royal charges, Webb followed the escorts.

It worked but, for the most part, it produced only small stories, which Goodman chose to run in his diary column, published under the pseudonym Blackadder. On 6 November 2005, he revealed that Prince William had pulled a tendon in his knee playing football and had gone to Prince Charles's personal doctor for treatment. What Goodman did not realise was that the prince's knee had recovered and he had never seen the doctor: all he had done was to leave a voicemail message with one of his staff, saying that he would like to see the doctor. A week later, Blackadder ran another small story about the political editor of ITN, Tom Bradby, lending a portable editing suite to Prince William. Goodman laid a false trail in the story, hinting heavily that he had picked this up from a source in ITN. What he didn't know was that Bradby had told nobody at ITN apart from his secretary, whom he trusted. All he had done was to leave a voicemail message on one of the royal phones.

What Goodman and Mulcaire also did not know was that these signs of their activity had been so loud and so clear that the Palace had complained to the head of the police team at Buckingham Palace, who had passed on the complaint to the Specialist Operations team at the Metropolitan Police, who had decided to start an investigation.

The four-week trial period ended, and Goodman begged a further month's money from Coulson, but by February 2006 the editor's budget worries had become so intense that he instructed Stuart Kuttner to end

Glenn Mulcaire's royal retainer and to start paying him only when he delivered results. Goodman did his best to claim fat fees for any stories that the investigator found, but, in search of success, the two of them became more and more reckless. By now, the police were on to them.

On 9 April 2006, Goodman ran a story with Neville Thurlbeck about a row between Prince Harry and his then girlfriend, Chelsy Davy, after Harry had visited a lap-dancing bar. Under the heading 'Chelsy tears Harry off a strip', it not only reported the argument but quoted a deliberately slighty inaccurate version of a message which had been left on Harry's voicemail by his brother, Prince William, mimicking the voice of Chelsy Davy. A week later, on 18 April, Goodman had the front-page splash with a story about Prince William getting drunk after his brother's passing-out parade at Sandhurst military academy. Goodman was happy. Mulcaire was happy – he got £3,000 for his work. But the story crashed through trip wires in the army and the Palace, by accurately reflecting a complaint which had been made by the head of Sandhurst, General Andrew Ritchie, to Prince Harry's private secretary, Jamie Lowther-Pinkerton. The complaint had been made in a voicemail message.

Very few people knew about Project Bumblebee. But plenty of people knew about Glenn Mulcaire and understood that he was a master of the dark arts. Some knew precisely what he had to offer as a special skill and either practised it themselves or saw other people doing it. They talked about it in conference with the editor. They laughed about it in the pub. Some knew it was illegal. Some didn't. It didn't matter – as long as they could carry on concealing it from the rest of the world. Mulcaire continued with his work, busy as ever.

Early on the morning of 8 August 2006, Goodman and Mulcaire were arrested on suspicion of intercepting voicemail messages from the royal household. A few weeks later, the police contacted Gordon Taylor to tell him his voicemail had been hacked. Taylor told Mark Lewis and it was then, like a boy picking up a stone and starting an avalanche, that Lewis decided to sue.

3. 8 July 2009 to 14 July 2009

At half past four in the afternoon on Wednesday 8 July 2009, we posted my news story on the *Guardian* website, headed 'Murdoch papers paid £1 million to gag phone-hacking victims'. It said:

> Rupert Murdoch's News Group Newspapers has paid out more than £1 million to settle legal cases that threatened to reveal evidence of his journalists' repeated involvement in the use of criminal methods to get stories.
>
> The payments secured secrecy over out-of-court settlements in three cases that threatened to expose evidence of Murdoch journalists using private investigators who illegally hacked into the mobile phone messages of numerous public figures as well as gaining unlawful access to confidential personal data, including tax records, social security files, bank statements and itemised phone bills. Cabinet ministers, MPs, actors and sports stars were all targets of the private investigators.
>
> Today, the *Guardian* reveals details of the suppressed evidence, which may open the door to hundreds more legal actions by victims of News Group, the Murdoch company that publishes the *News of the World* and the *Sun*, as well as provoking police inquiries into reporters who were involved and the senior executives responsible for them. The evidence also poses difficult questions for:
>
> • Conservative leader David Cameron's director of communications, Andy Coulson, who was deputy editor and then editor of the *News of the World* when, the suppressed evidence shows, journalists for whom he was responsible were engaging in hundreds of apparently illegal acts;
> • Murdoch executives who, albeit in good faith, misled a parliamentary select committee, the Press Complaints Commission and the public;

- The Metropolitan Police, which did not alert all those whose phones were targeted, and the Crown Prosecution Service, which did not pursue all possible charges against News Group personnel;
- The Press Complaints Commission, which claimed to have conducted an investigation but failed to uncover any evidence of illegal activity.

The story traced the course of the legal action by Gordon Taylor and his two associates and went on to quote the unnamed police sources who had suggested to me that there were thousands of victims of phone-hacking, adding that these sources 'suggest that MPs from all three parties and Cabinet ministers, including former deputy prime minister John Prescott and former Culture Secretary Tessa Jowell were among the targets'.

As the story was posted on the website, the *Guardian* news desk asked a reporter, Caroline Davies, to call John Prescott, to get a reaction quote. Ten minutes later, she came back, flushed with success after tracking down the famously blunt and plain-speaking politician. She started to reel off a jumble of comments, capturing Prescott's tendency to produce multiple half-formed sentences without finishing any of them. The deputy editor, Paul Johnson, asked her to slow down, go back to the beginning of her notes and just to tell him exactly what Prescott had told her. 'OK,' she said. 'I told him the gist of the story, and he said "FOOKIN HELL!"'

A few hours later, we published a second story on the website, headed 'Trail of hacking and deceit under nose of Tory PR chief', which delivered more detail without referring to the paperwork on which it was based. It explained that in a short period of Mulcaire activity during the spring of 2006, those who had been targeted included not only John Prescott and Tessa Jowell but also the rock star George Michael; the actor Gwyneth Paltrow; the former Conservative MP who had become mayor of London, Boris Johnson; and the radical Scottish politician, Tommy Sheridan. The story went on to publish more of the detail of Steve Whittamore's blagging for the *News of the World*, naming public figures whose information he had stolen and the organisations whose security had been penetrated by his network.

The story had been damped down a little by the *Guardian's* legal department. For fear of UK libel law, which makes it dangerous to criticise people who can afford aggressive lawyers, I had had to steer clear of any direct suggestion that Andy Coulson knew about the illegal activity. A few days before we published, I had submitted a detailed question to him about the Gordon Taylor settlement, and his secretary at Conservative HQ had replied to say that 'it didn't ring any bells with him'. For the same reason, I had had to suggest that Murdoch's executives might have been acting 'in good faith' when they misled a parliamentary select committee, the Press Complaints Commission and the public. Personally, I believed that they had been deliberately lying. If they really had been acting in good faith, surely they would have gone back to the select committee and everybody else a year before, when they were passed the new evidence in the Gordon Taylor case, and they would have announced that, although the details of the legal action were confidential, they now realised that their whole 'rogue reporter' story was untrue. But they hadn't done that.

What was more, News International had put out a lie before we published the story. When I had called them a few days earlier, I had been wary of telling them too much. I was worried that they might try to pre-empt me by putting out some twisted version of the story – a 'spoiler' calculated to make mine look old and unpublishable, without disclosing too much of the truth. So, I had asked – with calculated naivety – if they knew anything about any of their titles paying damages for hacking the mobile phones of possibly three people in the footballing world. That night, a friendly source had called me to say I had caused some kind of collective anxiety attack at News International's headquarters: 'They are all chasing around blaming each other for having given you the story.'

The following morning, the News International press officer called back to say that she had spoken to the managing editors and the lawyers for all four titles: 'No one has any knowledge about this . . . This particular case means nothing to anyone here, and I've talked to all of the people who would be involved.' That certainly was a lie, although the press officer did not know it, calculated on the assumption that we didn't know enough to run a story.

By contrast, Clive Goodman, on whose head News International had shovelled so much blame, chose to be strangely silent. When I called him, he said: 'I'm not even going to say "No comment" as a comment.'

The story went off like dynamite, though there was obviously something wrong with the detonator. Certainly, there was an explosion. John Prescott worked his way through broadcast studios, roaring his indignation like a bull in pain. Several other Labour MPs started chasing Andy Coulson's tail like dogs on a fox, pointing out that it raised questions about David Cameron's judgement in hiring him. And a handful of public figures surfaced to explain how vile it was to have their privacy invaded. But the explosion went off at half strength. It soon became clear that there was a shortage of people who were interested in getting into a fight with Rupert Murdoch.

The rest of Fleet Street did their best to ignore the story. That was no surprise. They had multiple motives for concealing the truth from their readers – because they themselves had a history of playing the same illegal games as the *News of the World* and/or they supported the Conservatives and didn't want to give oxygen to the Andy Coulson angle and/or they were owned by Rupert Murdoch. I heard later from an executive at *The Times* that the editor, James Harding, had been 'puce with rage' at the idea that he had to follow up on this *Guardian* rubbish. The political correspondent of Murdoch's Sky News channel solemnly warned his viewers that 'this is very much being ramped up politically'.

In an attempt to get the story covered elsewhere, the *Guardian* press office had asked me to brief two broadcast journalists from *Channel 4 News* and the BBC. That Wednesday morning, before we posted the story, I had met them in a café at Victoria Station. The Channel 4 man brought a crew and shot an interview, which they used prominently that evening. The BBC man went off to consult his bosses, who then suffered some kind of nervous collapse and refused to run anything until Channel 4 did and, even then, opted to run it low down in the bulletins.

In the political world, the Labour government might have decided to leap on the vulnerability of Andy Coulson and challenge David Cameron to explain what steps he had taken to ensure that Coulson was clean before he hired him; complain that he had hired Coulson with his eyes shut simply so that he could have Murdoch's man in his private office; move to set up some kind of inquiry. The government did no such thing. Instead, the prime minister, Gordon Brown, said merely that it raised serious questions; and a Home Office minister, David Hanson, told the House of Commons that these were serious allegations and he would find out more and report back to them. For his part, the Conservative leader, David Cameron, professed to be indifferent: his office briefed reporters that he was 'very relaxed' about the affair. (The briefings from his office, of course, were given by people who were working for Andy Coulson.)

There was some sign of action from the House of Commons select committee on culture, media and sport, to whom the Murdoch executives had given misleading evidence in 2007. I had called the committee chairman, the Conservative MP John Whittingdale, as we published our first story. He and several Labour members were now saying that the committee would recall the Murdoch witnesses. That night, on BBC's *Newsnight*, Murdoch's former editor at the *Sunday Times*, Andrew Neil, roundly declared that this was 'one of the most significant media stories of modern times'.

Murdoch himself surfaced briefly in New York, where a reporter from Bloomberg asked him for a quote about the Gordon Taylor settlement. Shrugging and shaking his head, he declared that his company couldn't have settled the legal action as the *Guardian* claimed. If they had done, he would have known about it, he said. That raised the interesting possibility that James Murdoch had signed off on a £1 million settlement and decided not to tell his own father in case he went ballistic. There was no word at all from News International.

By the next morning, Thursday 9 July, there was a small storm raging, and the commissioner of the Metropolitan Police, Sir Paul Stephenson, announced that he had asked his assistant commissioner, John Yates, to look into the whole matter.

I was running on adrenalin. I had slept about four hours and was up at dawn, trying to write follow-up stories while simultaneously taking endless calls from foreign news media and BBC radio stations wanting to interview me, and a steady trickle of calls from lawyers and agents acting for public figures who suspected that they had been targeted by Mulcaire. There were also calls from potentially very useful new sources. Several journalists who had worked at the *News of the World* emerged cautiously from the shadows, talking on the strict condition that their identities never be disclosed for fear that their careers would be ended immediately, explaining in detail how Andy Coulson had commissioned crime and the paper had paid for it. Three people, including one just out of jail, got in touch to name other private investigators who had worked for the *News of the World*.

By five o'clock in the afternoon, with my head buzzing, I had written a story for the next day's paper, disclosing that the former England football striker, Alan Shearer, and the manager of Manchester United, Alex Ferguson, were among those whose messages had been intercepted from Gordon Taylor's phone. It was not much of a tale, but it kept the affair alive. Just then, I was surprised to hear that the assistant commissioner, John Yates, was already prepared to make a statement. A small bony hand pinched my heart as it occurred to me that he might rubbish the whole story.

I had never met John Yates nor had anything to do with him, but other journalists said he was intelligent and straight. So, in spite of my anxiety, I was reasonably confident when Yates stepped out in front of Scotland Yard to address a collection of journalists. Dressed in a dark suit, bristling with quiet authority, he explained that that morning the commissioner had asked him to 'establish the facts'. 'I was not involved in the original case,' he said, 'and clearly come at this with an independent mind.' He proceeded to gently demolish our work.

We had suggested there were thousands of victims. Yates said that those targeted by Goodman and Mulcaire 'may have run into hundreds of people, but our inquiries showed that they only used the tactic against a far smaller number of individuals'. We had said a mass of victims had never been contacted by the police. Yates said: 'Where there was clear evidence that people had potentially been the subject of tapping, they were all contacted by the police.' We had said John Prescott was targeted. Yates said police 'had not uncovered any evidence to suggest that John Prescott's phone had been tapped'. This was worrying. I had no way of proving he was wrong. I had good sources – but they were all anonymous and off the record. I had paperwork – but I had promised not to use it. We were wide open to attack.

There was something else that was more worrying. Why was Yates saying this? If he was wrong – if, in fact, what the *Guardian* had published was correct – then this smelled very rotten, as if he thought it was all right to cover up the failures of the original inquiry and/or to do a favour for Murdoch's newspapers. But supposing he was right! Supposing the two sources somehow had misunderstood the number of hacking victims. Supposing Glenn Mulcaire had 'targeted' John Prescott by having him followed, not by hacking his phone or doing anything illegal. Supposing there was something wrong with that paperwork: it really wouldn't be difficult to forge the contents of an email . . . Rusbridger and I had gone in very deep. If Yates was right, if our story was rubbish, we were in a lot of trouble.

Yates went on to say that the whole case had been the object of 'the most careful investigation by very experienced detectives' and that the Crown Prosecution Service had 'carefully examined all the evidence'. Since no additional evidence had come to light, he could see no reason to reopen the inquiry. He finished by acknowledging the real concerns of people who feared their privacy had been breached. 'I therefore need to ensure that we have been diligent, reasonable and sensible and taken all proper steps to ensure that, where we have evidence that people have been the subject of any form of phone-tapping, or that there is any suspicion that they might have been, that they have been informed.'

Yates's statement hurt us. And there was a little more pain, too, from the Director of Public Prosecutions (DPP), Keir Starmer QC, another man with a good reputation for straight dealing, who announced that he was ordering an urgent review of the material which police had given to his prosecutors in 2006 but then appeared to prejudge his own inquiry by adding: 'I have no reason to consider that there was anything inappropriate in the prosecutions that were undertaken in this case.' And something else to worry about: the select committee had decided not only to call back the Murdoch witnesses but also to call me to give a public account of the story on Tuesday of the following week.

The newspapers who had done their best to ignore our story were now happy to report that there would be no new police investigation. Meanwhile, News International still said nothing. It was like we were beggars at their banquet. Who were we to gatecrash their cosy world? We would be ignored, or perhaps we would be punished. You could almost feel them watching, weighing it up: how much did we know, how much could we hurt them, how much could they safely deny? It took a bad mistake from me finally to give them a clear answer to their questions.

That Thursday night, as John Yates's statement made its mark, I went live on BBC *Newsnight* with the celebrity PR agent Max Clifford, who had been identified as a hacking victim at the original trial of Goodman and Mulcaire; the former deputy assistant commissioner of the Metropolitan Police, Brian Paddick; and John Prescott. The anchor, Gavin Esler, immediately asked me how damaging Yates's statement was for the *Guardian*, but the conversation bounced harmlessly around the subject – Clifford suggested he might now sue, Paddick said there should be some kind of independent police inquiry, Prescott worried out loud that Yates had taken so little time to come to his conclusion. Then, in the last minute, Esler turned back to me and asked me what else the *Guardian* might reveal. I babbled a bit about possibly naming executives who were involved but told him: 'You have seen the best of what we've got.' That was my mistake.

For Murdoch's people, calculating their next move, and looking at our stories with the eyes of experienced journalists, it was already obvious that we had quoted no evidence of any kind. We simply stated the facts, but we used no named sources, no quotes from documents. And if that really was the best of what we had, then they could see that we were not going to produce any sources or documents. In other words, we couldn't prove a thing.

By Friday morning, our political correspondents in the House of Commons were reporting that Murdoch journalists were briefing Conservative MPs that the *Guardian* could not back up its story. The House of Commons select committee had already told me and Rusbridger that we must appear before them on the following Tuesday, and now we were warned that several Murdoch-friendly MPs on the committee were 'getting ready to barbecue you'. Then, on Friday evening, the tiger finally showed its claws.

News International released a three-page statement which poured down scorn on the *Guardian*. In the last forty-eight hours, they said, they had conducted a thorough investigation, which augmented the original investigation they had conducted in 2006 when Goodman and Mulcaire were arrested. In addition, the original police investigation, which had included live monitoring of both men, had been 'incredibly thorough'. Based on all this, they concluded that 'there is not and never has been evidence' that *News of the World* journalists had accessed anybody's voicemails, or instructed anybody to access voicemails, or that there was systematic corporate illegality at News International. 'It goes without saying that, had the police uncovered such evidence, charges would have been brought against other *News of the World* personnel. Not only have there been no such charges, but the police have not considered it necessary to arrest or question any other member of *News of the World* staff.' Specifically, the statement continued, it was untrue that police had found evidence that 'thousands' of mobile phones had been hacked; untrue that police had found evidence of the involvement in hacking of other staff; untrue that there was evidence of their hacking the phones of John Prescott or any other victims named by the *Guardian*; untrue that their executives had sanctioned payment for hacking. 'All of these irresponsible and unsubstantiated allegations against the *News of the World* and its journalists are false.'

This was strong stuff. At the same time, they released a letter from Rebekah Brooks to the chairman of the House of Commons media select committee, John Whittingdale. 'The *Guardian* coverage, we believe, has substantially and likely deliberately misled the British public,' she wrote, and the allegation that thousands of people were the objects of illegal phone-hacking had been 'roundly contradicted' by John Yates. Very strong.

All this ran like water down a mountain through the columns of the Murdoch newspapers and the bulletins of his Sky News channel. It was frightening to watch and, since the statement had been released just as Fleet Street was hitting the deadline for its first editions, it was also very difficult to counter.

I was at home, alone in my study, when this torrent of aggression was released. As I saw it break out on to my computer screen, a feeling of dread swamped me. For a moment or two, my brain just stalled and then, like a malignant cell, a horrible thought silently formed itself – I had screwed up. I'd got the story wrong – a big story, that had gone round the world, that had had politicians and public figures standing up on their back legs shouting for action. And it was wrong, or maybe it was wrong, or I couldn't be sure, but if it was wrong – on that kind of scale – Rusbridger and I really were in a deep pit of foul-smelling trouble.

And then it got worse. I took a call from the *Independent on Sunday*, who lobbed a highly destructive verbal bombshell in my direction. They told me they wanted to run a story accusing me of paying bribes to police officers, specifically of paying bribes in order to obtain the phone-hacking stories which we had just published. I started gabbling down the phone – I'd never paid a bribe in my life, why were they saying this, who had said this to them, which officer was I supposed to have paid, when, where, why, didn't they understand they were accusing me of crime, didn't they understand they couldn't just publish crap like that? The reporter said they had a good source. It was as if he could not hear me telling him that this just wasn't true.

I called Rusbridger in his office in London, who told me that he had just taken a call from David Leppard at Murdoch's *Sunday Times*. Leppard! Of all the reporters in all the newsrooms in all the world, Leppard was the person you least wanted to have on the end of your phone. He was no friend of the *Guardian* and nor was his editor, John Witherow, who had once flared up at a story about his paper in the *Guardian* and told Rusbridger that 'I will always retaliate and I have many more readers than you do, so I can cause you much more pain.'

I had written harsh things about Leppard in *Flat Earth News*, and he had publicly declared he was suing me, although he never did. Now, he told Rusbridger he planned to run a story that Sunday, accusing him of hiring a private investigator who had illegally hacked into voicemail.

Leppard claimed this had happened some ten years earlier in the late 1990s, that Rusbridger had hired a high-powered security consultant to check out allegations that a senior civil servant was being paid backhanders by the multinational biotech company Monsanto. Leppard was saying that the consultant had subcontracted work to an investigator who had hacked the target's voicemail. Rusbridger's deputy, Paul Johnson, was in the room when Leppard made this call. He said he had never seen Rusbridger look so shocked, that he had put down the phone, sat in his chair looking pale and dazed, and said: 'I don't know what he's talking about.'

Trying to work out a reply to News International's statement, trying to find a way to stop the *Independent on Sunday* and the *Sunday Times* smearing us as criminals and hypocrites, we then heard that the first edition of the next day's *Times* – also owned by Rupert Murdoch – was carrying a column written by Scotland Yard's former assistant commissioner, Andy Hayman, who had supervised the original hacking inquiry in 2006. 'We put our best detectives on the case and left no stone unturned,' he wrote. And when he turned to the scale of the hacking which they had uncovered, this assistant commissioner who had personally supervised the whole inquiry directly contradicted my off-the-record sources: 'There was a small number – perhaps a handful – where there was evidence that the phones had actually been tampered with.'

This was not good.

We couldn't stop, so we had to fight back.

As far as most of the world was concerned, the *Guardian* had been wrong about every significant statement in our stories – John Yates and Andy Hayman had implied as much, News International had shouted it loud, the rest of Fleet Street had reported it. Furthermore, two other newspapers were now out to expose Rusbridger and me as criminals. And the two of us were waiting to be barbecued by the select committee on Tuesday.

I hardly slept. Even so, by Saturday morning, I had cleared my head and felt sure once more that our story was right. News International were surely blowing up a blizzard of lies to conceal the truth and, for some reason, the police and the DPP seemed to be going along with them. I spoke again to the *Independent on Sunday*, who finally accepted that I had not bribed any police officers. They withdrew the story.

The smear against Alan Rusbridger, however, came direct from News International. But it turned out that it was partly my fault. On the Friday morning, I had written a feature for the *Guardian's* media section, which was due to be published on Monday. It pulled together everything I knew about Fleet Street and the dark arts, including the *Sunday Times's* long history of involvement. Unknown to me, the media section had called the *Sunday Times* for a comment, and John Witherow had lived up to his promise that he would always retaliate and cause Rusbridger pain, by releasing David Leppard like a dirty bomb in Rusbridger's office.

Also on that Saturday morning, Rusbridger had the *Guardian* archives searched and found that the beginning of Leppard's story was true. In 2000, the *Guardian* had been investigating Monsanto and hired a high-calibre security consultancy, Ciex, to produce a 'due diligence' report on the company. Leppard was claiming that Ciex had subcontracted some of the work to a man who had gathered information by illegally hacking voicemail, a former actor called John Ford. Rusbridger knew nothing about it. But I knew something. In *Flat Earth News*, I had identified Ford as a specialist blagger – who worked for years for the *Sunday Times* and David Leppard!

The difficulty for Rusbridger was that it was not going to matter very much that the story was not true or that it was an exercise in hypocrisy. There were hostile newspapers and Conservative MPs lining up to feast on his flesh, and they would use this as a carving knife. He spoke to Witherow who insisted he would run the story.

Rusbridger and I talked tactics. Ford was not the only skeleton in the *Sunday Times's* cupboard. Researching *Flat Earth News*, I had got hold of tapes of a con man, Barry Beardall, who worked regularly for David Leppard, attempting to entrap various politicians. They included a phone call in which Beardall had conned the posh London law firm Allen & Overy into handing over confidential material about Gordon Brown. That was sleazy and, in the case of Allen & Overy, potentially illegal. How would Witherow like it if the *Guardian* posted those tapes on its website?

By late morning, the two editors had agreed to pull their tanks off each other's lawns. Witherow withdrew the story which Leppard had been working on. Rusbridger withdrew the story about Fleet Street's use of the dark arts which I had written for Monday's *Media Guardian* and agreed not to use the Barry Beardall tape. Rusbridger and I were both happy enough to be fighting on only one front.

Then my phone rang and, for the second time in this saga, I benefited from News International's dishonesty. Just as Mr Apollo had first contacted me because he wanted to answer Stuart Kuttner's outburst on BBC radio, so now a well-meaning supporter reacted to the long and aggressive statement which News International had put out the previous evening. It was designed to deceive, according to this source. Probably, I said, but we had no way of proving it since I was not allowed to reveal the evidence I had collected from various sources. However, my caller persuaded me that to defend the *Guardian* at Tuesday's select-committee meeting I could safely use two of the documents which I had got my hands on – the email for Neville Thurlbeck containing transcripts of thirty-five of Gordon Taylor's voicemail messages, and the contract signed by the assistant editor, Greg Miskiw, offering a £7,000 bonus to 'Paul Williams' if he delivered a story about Gordon Taylor's private life. Both had been passed through enough people's hands that nobody could be sure where I had obtained them. They also happened to be the two most powerful documents in my possession.

Now maybe we had a chance, but I didn't tell anybody, not even Rusbridger. I didn't want any risk of some hostile MP on the select committee hearing about this and changing direction in search of their barbecue.

That Sunday, I went up to the office to be interviewed by foreign

TV crews and to meet Gordon Taylor's lawyer, Mark Lewis, who was a far more relaxed man now that the story had been published. He was still bound by some confidentiality but he was willing to work with me, to find new clients and new ways of breaking down News International's door. He brought with him his former assistant, Charlotte Harris. The two of them wanted to set up a new legal partnership and they had just acquired their first potential client, the celebrity publicist Max Clifford.

Like Gordon Taylor, Clifford had been approached by police back in 2006 and been told that they had evidence that his phone had been hacked. Like Taylor, he had been named in court as a victim of Glenn Mulcaire with the same mysterious idea that Mulcaire had hacked him without anybody ever having asked him to do so. Now Clifford, too, was going to sue the *News of the World*. Unlike Taylor, however, Clifford was saying that he would not settle. He was suing so that the truth would come out and he was not going to sell his silence for any of Murdoch's millions.

The pressure on the *Guardian* was beginning to show. One executive sent Rusbridger a long email that Sunday morning, arguing that some parts of our original story must have been wrong. He quoted the statements made by Yates and Hayman, said that in his experience Yates was crafty but not a liar, and added: 'They have made it clear that the Goodman inquiry didn't find evidence of other reporters being directly involved . . . I think we are vulnerable, and the Tories on the committee will hammer us.' The paper, he suggested, needed to acknowledge that some parts of the story were inaccurate. I felt a strong desire to strangle the author of the email. Rusbridger was unmoved.

News International were busy in the background. Friendly journalists from other papers called to tell me that, speaking off the record, News International were pushing hard against the *Guardian*. Nobody was interested in this story, they said, and the *Guardian* were being 'obsessive' in pursuing it. The whole story was untrue and the subject was old. It was just being reheated by people who had a liberal agenda, who wanted to attack Rupert Murdoch: the BBC and the *Guardian* had concocted the whole thing.

Oddly, however, in spite of insisting that the whole story was fiction, News International were using a second line of defence with journalists who contacted them – it was all Andy Coulson's fault. He had lost control of the paper. One of the journalists who had been fed this line explained: 'They're happy to throw Coulson to the wolves. All they care about is protecting James Murdoch and Rebekah.'

News International were busy, too, in print. On Sunday, the *News of the World* ran a leader comment denouncing our story as 'inaccurate, selective and purposely misleading' and republished Andy Hayman's column from *The Times*. That same day, the *Sunday Times* performed an interesting manoeuvre. They ran a long feature about the phone-hacking. In the top half of the story, they included a series of sceptical lines, describing the claims in the *Guardian* story as 'extravagant' and recycling the denials of News International, John Yates and Andy Hayman. However, buried towards the end of the story, the paper disclosed that, according to 'a senior source with good knowledge of the case', the potential victims of hacking identified by the original inquiry included the then commissioner of the Metropolitan Police, Sir Ian Blair.

This was very strange journalism. If they believed that the police commissioner may have had his messages intercepted, that was a big story – straight to the front page – not just because of the security implications when the commissioner was responsible for secret inquiries but also because it raised more loudly than ever the underlying question about whether Scotland Yard had concealed far more than they had revealed. Why would the police not have said openly that their own boss had been a target? The *Sunday Times*, however, had buried the claim. It looked very much as though somebody was trying to run a 'spoiler'.

Sadly, it looked as though other journalists were picking up on News International's briefings. On Monday, the *Independent* published a column by its right-wing media commentator, Stephen Glover, which simply recycled the gospel according to News International as though it were true: 'The BBC has conspired with the *Guardian* to heat up an old story and attack Murdoch.' It didn't seem to matter that the BBC had had nothing to do with the story and had been reluctant even to follow it up. The whole affair was hysteria, wrote Glover. Nick Davies was 'the sort of journalist who can find a scandal in a jar of tadpoles'. The story was old, he said, the *Guardian* didn't claim the hacking was still going on. 'If there is new evidence, let it be brought forward.'

And that was exactly what News International wanted him to say. On the following day, Tuesday 14 July, I had to give evidence to the select committee. Rusbridger had postponed a holiday to come with me. And, as far as News International knew, we would walk naked into that committee room, completely unable to produce any evidence to back up our story. If they had their way, there was a good chance that Rusbridger and I would be humiliated and, if they kept pushing, we could lose our jobs.

But I had some protection. Although I believed that it was safe to use my documents, I was worried that if I simply handed them over to the select committee, I would lay myself open to the charge that I was breaching Gordon Taylor's privacy just as badly as the *News of the World* had. Since then, newspapers have published the fact that this was about the false story about his supposed affair with Jo Armstrong, but at the time, this was clearly private. So, I decided to organise some home-made redaction.

That Monday morning, I sat my teenaged children round our dining-room table with a pot of glue, a pair of scissors, some black paper and a photocopy of the documents and asked them to stick slices of black paper over all the passages that could breach Gordon Taylor's privacy. While they redacted the paperwork, I sat in my study to think.

It was Scotland Yard who were the real threat. They were giving News International credibility. But the more I looked at Yates's state-ment, the more I worried about what he was up to. I reckoned I could see clear signs that he knew much more than he was saying.

For example, how many people had been warned? Yates said that the original inquiry in 2006 had warned all the potential victims. Really? A sharp-witted editor on the *Guardian* news desk had noticed that, after News International circulated their damning statement on Friday evening, Scotland Yard's press bureau also had put out a short press release, which had been overlooked in the turmoil (and which always was likely to be overlooked, being put out at 7.37 on a Friday evening when most reporters have gone home). It repeated the closing words from Yates's statement from the previous evening, about how he wanted to make sure that police had been diligent and sensible and taken all proper steps to make sure victims had been informed – and then it revealed that they had begun contacting people to tell them their phones may have been hacked 'and we expect this to take some time to complete'.

Why on earth had John Yates not said that plainly on the Thursday – 'We're terribly sorry, we've discovered we didn't do the job properly in 2006, the *Guardian* are quite right that we failed to inform all the potential victims, so we're going to have to do that now'? Why on earth had he chosen instead to say 'Where there was clear evidence that people had potentially been the subject of tapping, they were all contacted by the police'?

And just how many victims were there? The official version was that there were eight, who had been named at the original trial. But Yates had kept it very vague, saying only that it was 'a far smaller number' than hundreds. If it was eight, why not say so? And if it was not eight, then why not say that the official version failed to disclose the whole story?

And why had he said nothing about the involvement of other journalists? He said he had been asked to 'establish the facts'. So why not mention the fact that since August 2006 when they seized material from Mulcaire, the police had been in possession of an email which clearly suggested that Clive Goodman was not the only *News of the World* journalist involved in all this? What other evidence might they be failing to disclose?

I also noticed a few odd points in the statement which News International had put out on Friday evening. The original police investigation, they said, had included 'live monitoring' of Goodman and Mulcaire. How could they know that? The statement went on to cite the evidence which the police found. Again, how could they know what the police did or did not find? Maybe they were lying. If they were telling the truth, the police must have given them this information. How many organisations which are the object of police inquiries are given a briefing about the result of those inquiries?

I made several calls to Scotland Yard's press bureau, trying to find out whether the original inquiry had interviewed anybody from the *News of the World* apart from Clive Goodman; and why they had slipped out this weird statement so late on a Friday evening; and how many other victims they were now approaching. They were unhelpful to the point of being obstructive.

Select committees are famous for being boring. They have no real power to get anything done, they hold meetings which nobody watches and nobody cares about, and most of their members are particularly well known for being useless at the interrogation of their witnesses. This one was a little bit different.

The committee room was stuffed with people. The public seats were filled; there were spectators sitting on windowsills and standing round the doors, all watching the dozen MPs who sat behind a horseshoe-shaped desk. Rusbridger and I were suffering from some stage fright. At a nervy early morning meeting in a greasy café in Whitehall, I had told him about the documents which I was going to give to the committee, but we had no idea quite how things would play out, whether hostile MPs would nevertheless be able to make skewered pork of us. There was a real tension in the air: somebody was going to have a very bad day.

First, there was a warm-up act, a solo performance by the director of the Press Complaints Commission, Tim Toulmin, a tall, thin dark-haired man in his mid-thirties. He lounged backwards in his seat, with one arm tossed over the back of the empty chair beside him, a model of confidence. I could only watch him and wonder whether he had any idea of how wrong he was.

Toulmin explained that there was no problem with the phone-hacking report which the PCC had produced in 2007: 'Of course, there is absolutely nothing in it for the PCC to cover anything up at all.' None of the MPs asked him if there might be something in the fact that a large chunk of the PCC's funding came from News International, or that their ethics committee had been chaired by a Fleet Street executive – Les Hinton – at the same time as he was chief executive of News International.

Toulmin was asked how he could be sure that phone-hacking was not continuing. 'We cannot be one hundred per cent sure without having some sort of God-given powers of seeing into journalists' minds and private activity. The point is, if you have any suspicion, you can go to the police, you can complain to a lawyer, you can come to the PCC, you can go to a newspaper, you can tell Nick Davies about it and he will probably write a lengthy story about how frightful journalists are.'

Was this man speaking as the supposedly independent arbiter of press complaints, or was he just a spokesman for Fleet Street? Two or three of the MPs showed signs of standing up to him. A Labour MP, Paul Farrelly, challenged him to follow up on an old report in *Private Eye* magazine that News International had paid Glenn Mulcaire £200,000 in exchange for his silence. Toulmin questioned how that could be relevant, and Farrelly spelled it out to him, that this looked like hush money, the purchase of silence about the very facts in which Toulmin claimed to be interested. Toulmin was not interested: 'We are not going to chase up every rumour and bit of tittle-tattle that we read in *Private Eye*.'

Farrelly fired back: 'People will gain a very poor impression of the PCC if that is the line you continue to maintain.'

Farrelly, I knew, had been a Fleet Street journalist before he became a Labour MP, and there were clear signs that he knew what he was talking about and, like a lot of other journalists, might well feel angry at the way that News Corp had dragged newspapers downhill in search of bigger profits. He was also naturally pugnacious: he ran the House of Commons rugby team, playing at scrum half.

There was one other potential ally. Over the weekend, two of the *Guardian's* political correspondents had emailed me to say that there was a new Labour MP on the committee, Tom Watson, who had told them he wanted to get to the bottom of the hacking scandal. They had explained that he was a former defence minister who had no love at all for the Murdoch papers, which had hounded him because he had been part of the 'curry-house plot' in 2006, which had tried to force Tony Blair to resign to make way for Gordon Brown at a time when Blair was the darling of the Murdoch titles.

Toulmin slipped away, evidently content in the knowledge that Rusbridger and I were heading for disaster. Indeed, Rusbridger also had his doubts about me. He knows my mouth sometimes works much faster than my brain and, as we took our seats, he explained that if I started to get wild, he would squeeze my knee under the table. Rusbridger made an opening statement about the regulation of the media and then, with the vague distraction of my editor's fingers drifting towards my inner thigh, I started talking.

I explained about the gap that often develops between what a reporter knows and what the reporter can say publicly, because so many sources insist on keeping themselves and their evidence hidden. 'On Friday evening, News International put out a statement which was deemed by one particularly important source to be "designed to deceive" and, as a result, I have now been authorised to show you things that previously were stuck in that gap, and I am talking about paperwork. So what I want to do is to show you, first of all, copies of an email.'

I handed them copies of the email for Neville (as redacted by my children). 'Now, perhaps I could just leave that with you and move on to a second document which I want to be able to show you—'

John Whittingdale, the chairman, interrupted. 'With respect, we have quite a lot of questions for you, rather than just—'

I shrugged at him. 'Do you want the evidence or not? It is up to you.'

Several of the MPs said certainly they wanted it. I could see Paul Farrelly and Tom Watson nodding with particular energy.

Whittingdale gave in. 'Go on.'

We were winning. Happy that somebody else's plans were coming unstuck, I handed out the redacted copies of the contract signed by Greg Miskiw, offering £7,000 to Mulcaire if he would bring in the story about Gordon Taylor. I talked about the police, who had been sitting on these two documents since they had raided Mulcaire three years earlier and the curious fact that, if News International were to be believed, detectives had never arrested or interviewed Neville Thurlbeck who had been sent all these voicemail transcripts, or the junior reporter who had sent them to him (I held back Ross Hindley's name), or Greg

Miskiw, who had signed a contract with a private investigator using a false name.

'If News International are correct in saying that these people have not been arrested or questioned,' I told them, 'the implications, I am sure you can see, are very, very worrying. I spent yesterday on the phone, asking Scotland Yard for an answer to this question. At the end of the day, they eventually confirmed that they had not arrested any other *News of the World* staff other than Clive Goodman, but they would not tell me whether they had questioned any. Clearly, that is terribly important.'

And what about John Yates? 'For reasons which I cannot explain, he made no reference to the fact that Scotland Yard has had in its possession for well over two years paperwork which implicates other *News of the World* journalists. I do not know why he did not tell us, but again it worries me.'

Just what was the truth about whether the police had warned all the victims of the hacking? 'Why were we told on Thursday that everybody had been approached and then quietly, in this almost invisible fashion – because I do not think any newspaper picked this up for Saturday morning – on Friday evening were we told "We are now contacting people"?' Why had Yates said blandly that there was no evidence that John Prescott's phone had been hacked? 'So far as we know, there was no attempt by Scotland Yard to investigate what it was that Mulcaire had done in relation to Prescott – and, therefore, of course there is no evidence.'

By now, the atmosphere in the room had changed. The MPs on the committee were flicking through the paperwork I had given them, frowning, shaking their heads, exchanging whispers. Rusbridger had relaxed and taken his hand off my knee.

I handed the committee a third clutch of paperwork, a collection of rather elderly invoices which had been released years earlier, in redacted form, by the Information Commissioner as samples of the material which his officers had seized from Steve Whittamore in March 2003. 'The reason I am showing this to you is not because it tracks down some specific criminal offence but because it shows the systematic and open character of what is going on. These payments have not been made with bags of cash under the counter, they are being made by the News International accounts department.' The invoices explicitly recorded Whittamore being paid for extracting confidential data from phone companies and the DVLA, all potentially illegal.

I explained that I had seen records of Whittamore's dealings with the *News of the World*, identifying twenty-seven journalists who had commissioned him. I named the former assistant editor, Greg Miskiw, who was recorded making ninety requests, thirty-five of which would be illegal if they could not be justified in the public interest. 'I want to say, because it is important to make it clear, that Andy Coulson's name does not show up in that list.' I decided not to name any others: 'I would just feel uneasy if I started running around with a blue light on my head . . . The organisation will blame the lowly individuals rather than accepting whatever responsibility is due to themselves.'

There was a brief puff of barbecue smoke from one of the Tory MPs who quoted Stephen Glover, the right-wing columnist from the *Independent*, with his odd theory that the story was 'to do with the BBC and the *Guardian* ganging up on the Murdoch press'. It was all that was left of News International's attack, and it was too little and too late. We were safe.

I tried to end on a clear note: 'I think it is very hard to resist the conclusion that News International have been involved in covering up their journalists' involvement with private investigators who are breaking the law, and it is very worrying that Scotland Yard do not appear to have always said or done as much as they could have done to stop that cover-up.'

Later that day, I phoned a friendly source at News International. 'We're depressed,' she said.

Of course, we hadn't really won much of a victory. All we had done was to avoid the barbecue.

The fact was that we had started a fight and we couldn't stop it. There was a small sign of that when Rebekah Brooks backed out of a *Guardian* project which the *Sun* had been planning to support, the 10/10 campaign to cut carbon emissions by 10% during the year 2010, which was due to be launched in September 2009. It was made clear that she was backing out because of our coverage of the hacking affair. James Murdoch evidently agreed with her, even though he makes much of his concern about the environment. 'He's passionately green,' according to one source who knows him well, 'but that's second. First, he's tribal.'

There was an even clearer sign of News International's mood a few days later when an MP contacted me to report a conversation with Rebekah Brooks. On the day after the select-committee hearing, she had been asked how she thought the hacking affair might end. 'With Alan Rusbridger on his knees, begging for mercy,' she had replied.

Murdoch's *Times* disposed of the *Guardian*'s evidence to the select committee in 115 words tucked away on page 20. The *Sun* did not mention it at all.

It was as if now there were two versions of reality. There was the official version, aggressively promoted by News International and endorsed by the police and the PCC and the Conservative Party and most of the rest of Fleet Street. Then there was the version which was being shown to me by a small collection of nervous off-the-record sources – journalists, private investigators, the managers and lawyers of various celebrities – who told a very different story. They weren't talking about a rogue reporter. What they were describing was a rogue newspaper.

4. Crime in Fleet Street

Based on interviews with private investigators who worked for newspapers; journalists who hired them; evidence collected by police officers and others who investigated the investigators; 'Stick it Up Your Punter! by Peter Chippindale and Chris Horrie; as well as material obtained by the Leveson Inquiry.

Rupert Murdoch has consistently denied ever having any knowledge of illegal activity in his newsrooms. Not everyone sees it that way.

Some claim that, whatever he knew, he was responsible because he imposed on his editors such a ruthless drive for sales; and that, although he might not have known of specific offences, he always understood in general terms that his journalists might break the law to deliver results. This idea was given some traction in March 2013, when one of his own reporters secretly recorded him declaring that the bribing of police by journalists had been 'going on a hundred years'. Furthermore, there is an interesting pattern which became clear as the truth finally emerged about the epidemic of crime in British newspapers. Whether the offence was blagging, or hacking phones or computers, or tapping live phone calls, or paying bribes to police, the new evidence suggests that, with every kind of crime, the trouble began in the Murdoch papers.

Ian Withers is possibly the best-known and longest-surviving private investigator in the UK. He is old style: been around since 1960, used to be a police officer, has had a few run-ins with the law. By sheer fluke, the dusty archives of the *Guardian* hold a memo, written on 26 April 1971, in which an experienced reporter summarised an interview with him.

According to the memo, all those years ago Withers was saying that it was 'easy and very common' to make a phone call to extract sensitive personal information from the Inland Revenue, the Department of Social Services, police and other government agencies: 'No trouble at all in the majority of cases,' he said. 'One can usually adopt a fairly effective cover story, pretending to be someone in another branch of the same department.'

The memo described Withers' work for foreign embassies, US and UK corporations and the Liberal Party, who allegedly asked him to check out the anti-apartheid campaigner Peter Hain (who years later became a Labour Cabinet minister). It presented Withers as a man who was not too worried about breaking the law, recording his bland admission that he was awaiting trial under the Wireless Telegraphy Act, which then banned bugging and phone-tapping: 'The case has not yet come to court, but it will end in a fine when it does.' In the same year, 1971, he and three others were prosecuted for blagging, using the antique common-law charge that they had conspired to effect public mischief. They were convicted although they won an appeal to the House of Lords, which said effectively that it was not a crime to tell a lie.

From the mid-1980s, Ian Withers sold his services to the *Sunday Times*, which had been the property of Rupert Murdoch's company since 1981. He worked in particular for the paper's investigative specialist, Barrie Penrose. By this time, the 1984 Data Protection Act had passed into law, making it a crime to take information from a confidential database unless it was necessary in the public interest.

Withers was the beginning. In the end, there were several dozen specialists following in his footsteps, digging out confidential information for newspapers by fair means or foul. Forty-two of them are named, many for the first time, in the appendix to this book. The link between them and Withers' early work was forged by one man who became involved in the strangest development in Fleet Street crime.

In the early 1980s, this man was a young stage manager, bored with his work in small London theatres. One day he was reading his local paper, the *Richmond and Twickenham Times*, when he saw an advertisement offering jobs in a private-investigation agency. It so happened that, for no clear reason, the respectable suburbs of Richmond and

Twickenham had attracted a cluster of private investigators who had become involved in the fast-growing industry of 'tracing'.

Some private investigators – commonly known as 'PIs' – blame Margaret Thatcher. They say that there had always been a small number of specialists who traced people who had disappeared without paying their debts. These tracers were expert at mining public records for information, but they also blagged, calling up people and organisations to trick them into disclosing information about the target's current whereabouts. The 1980s saw Mrs Thatcher engineer a credit boom with millions borrowing for mortgages, bank loans, hire purchase. This, in turn, generated a debt boom as a mass of these new borrowers took the money and ran. The demand for tracers went through the roof. Dozens of new staff were hired by the existing specialists, including Ian Withers' company, Nationwide. Other PIs joined in, creating new tracing agencies. It was one of these new agencies – based over a sandwich shop in Twickenham – whose advertisement caught the young stage manager's eye.

He was hired and, for professional purposes, he adopted the pseudonym 'Al Green'. He was quite unlike most PIs, who tended to be ex-cops like Ian Withers. Al Green had never been in the police and generally despised them as thugs. He was highly strung, highly intelligent, instinctively left wing. And there was one other thing about Green which was most unusual in his new profession, and which was to have a decisive impact: he was addicted to heroin.

Green quickly discovered that he was oddly adept at tracing. He used to tell friends that the job suited him because he had always felt inadequate and this was a rare chance for him to take on a challenge and win. He also recognised that when it came to blagging, a heroin addict develops a horribly effective skill at deceiving all those around him, including himself, and he would tell the joke about the difference between an alcoholic and a drug addict: 'The alcoholic will steal your wallet. The heroin addict will steal your wallet and then help you to look for it.'

Soon, he learned how to trick police into disclosing information from their confidential records (known as making a 'club call'); and how to trick British Telecom into handing over the itemised bills which they started to produce in 1987 (known as rocs, 'records of calls'). Other tracers were calling banks and blagging the new home address of an account holder; Green started to blag their bank statements as well. When Barclays Bank proved difficult to penetrate, he posed as a postgraduate student researching a thesis about computer systems and spent a day as a guest of one of the companies who supplied the bank's software.

Green quickly rose through the ranks and became a trainer for one of the older tracing outfits, run by an Italian called Dick Rinaldi in Ealing, west London. There he passed on his skills to dozens, possibly hundreds of others; and then, in 1987, he moved to the Streatham branch of Nationwide. It was here for the first time that he connected with Fleet Street, picking up on Withers' connection with the *Sunday Times*, for example blagging military sources for the personal details of the special-forces soldiers who had controversially shot dead three IRA terrorists in Gibraltar in March 1988. Then the heroin played its part.

By 1988, Green had reached a point where, according to one source who worked with him, he was 'off his face' all day and having to stop his car to vomit on the way to see clients. Realising the trouble he was in, he started going to meetings of Narcotics Anonymous. And, during those meetings – by the kind of chance that often lies behind game-changing events – he heard of another tracer with a heroin history who also was going to NA meetings. He is entitled to keep his past addiction private, so I will call him 'Blue'.

Like Al Green, Blue was one of the few PIs then who was not an ex-cop, and he too had been working as a tracer, for an agency in Fulham. He had a natural charm and he had found ways to blag the three government agencies for sickness, unemployment and supplementary benefits. People might leave their partners without paying their alimony or abandon their businesses without paying their suppliers, but very few of them cut themselves off from the benefits of the welfare state. Blue discovered the numeric codes by which local offices identified themselves when they called in to the centre, he learned their internal jargon and then he would call up and, with a few minutes' work, he would uncover the whereabouts of his target. 'The trick,' he used to say, 'is to pick the lock nice and carefully, not leave any mark, lock it up and leave it so that nobody knows you've had the information.'

In 1986, Blue had struck out on his own, running a specialist tracing business in south London, with an offshore sideline which specialised in blagging international banks. Although he had been clean for some years, he still went to London meetings of Narcotics Anonymous – where Al Green found him. In 1988, they started working together. They formed a perfect partnership. Both knew the trade. Both had had enough of earning money for other people. Al Green could train new recruits. Blue could find those recruits and a steady cluster of good clients at NA meetings (Chelsea meetings delivered some particularly wealthy ones). So it was that his south London base became a kind of blagging factory, populated by a steady flow of recovering addicts.

Their finest recruit was Michael Boddy, known as 'Micky the Mouse', a public schoolboy who had become addicted to heroin and spent years sleeping rough and living off the streets. He had developed septicaemia, probably through using dirty needles, and surgeons had amputated one of his arms. As he recovered his health, with the help of Narcotics Anonymous, he returned to a more stable life, gardening, joining the Orchid Society of Great Britain and collecting antique prints of plants. Under Al Green's expert tuition, he also became a specialist in blagging British Telecom and mobile phone companies, from whom he extracted ex-directory numbers, lists of Friends and Family numbers, and rocs. He claimed that his thousands of victims included the Queen, Princess Diana and David Beckham. He became widely regarded in his profession as the UK's premier blagger of phone companies – or, as he himself put it, he was 'the ace trace from outer space'. He was also known to be emotionally highly volatile and was dispatched from Blue's base to work from his own flat.

Members of the network claim they really didn't know that some of what they were doing was against the law. One says he knew it was 'naughty' but since they were often tracing fraudsters and debtors, he believed it was acceptable. Operating quite separately from mainstream PI agencies, this highly skilled group rose on the tide of debtor-tracing, working regularly for the mortgage outfits of Lloyds Bank and National Westminster Bank. And also for Rupert Murdoch's papers.

Al Green kept up his link to the *Sunday Times* and did jobs for the paper's investigative team, Insight. Now, Blue started working for them too. By one means or another, he was able to help them find a way through the banking labyrinth of Polly Peck, the giant textile company which collapsed in debt and scandal in 1990, and to trace cash that had been laundered by some of London's leading gangsters.

It was through this network that the former actor John Ford learned his skills before going on to become a full-time blagger for the *Sunday Times*. Ford had been struggling, his career reaching a low peak in a TV advertisement for McDonald's. He became a brilliant generalist, blagging any target he chose. Numerous reporters on the *Sunday Times* had his number. He worked on serious stories – exposing corruption and alleged sexual abuse in sport – and on pure gossip, succeeding, for example, in extracting personal data about the then Labour minister Peter Mandelson in an attempt to prove that he was in a gay relationship.

Along the way, other newspapers started to use the group. One member of the NA network says that in 2000, Andy Coulson, as deputy editor of the *News of the World*, was dealing direct with them. Blue developed a relationship with the *Mail on Sunday*. One *Mail on Sunday* journalist recalls his network blagging records of calls made by the former prime minister's son, Mark Thatcher, and by the Indian steel billionaire, Lakshmi Mittal, who was accused of buying influence in Tony Blair's government.

But the main link from the Narcotics Anonymous group to the rest of Fleet Street was forged by a middleman, a stocky former soldier from south London called Gary Lowe, occasionally known as The Corporal. Lowe ran his own investigation company, Chimera, from his home in Croydon and was also a partner in Blue's offshore venture. When clients needed tracing, Lowe subcontracted the work to Al Green and Blue and their network. At first, Lowe was involved with commercial clients but, according to some of those who worked in this field, Lowe became the most prolific of all the private investigators who worked for Fleet Street – and, as ever, it appears he began with a

Murdoch paper, the mid-market daily *Today*, which News International bought in 1987 and closed in 1995.

One of the NA network recalls that this started as a hostile move. A journalist from *Today* contacted Lowe and asked him to do some tracing. Lowe relayed the job to Al Green who was told to do the work at top speed. Green did so, and twenty-four hours later, the result was splashed across *Today* – as part of an exposé of the hidden world of private investigators. A disaster for the secretive bloggers. But then, in a dazzling display of double standards, the Murdoch paper appreciated the value of a man like Lowe and started to hire him. Lowe picked up more work from the Murdoch titles, particularly the *News of the World* and the *Sunday Times*.

And in the classic shape of Fleet Street crime, the infection then spread from the Murdoch papers outwards to their competitors. By his own account to friends, Lowe went on to work for fifty different national newspaper journalists including those at the Mirror Group, frequently subcontracting work back to the NA group. For example, when the *Daily Mirror* in 1990 investigated the financial affairs of the miners' leader, Arthur Scargill, according to one source, it was that alliance which blagged Scargill's bank accounts.

Lowe had his problems with the law. He has told friends that, at one point, he was charged with corruption for allegedly buying confidential information which came from an employee of the DVLA in Swansea, but, he has said, the charge against him was dropped before trial. He continued working for newspapers until 2010.

Numerous other bloggers followed the path to Fleet Street (see appendix), including Steve Whittamore, who was a commercial tracer until 1991 when he was approached by the *News of the World* who offered to pay far more than other clients. All of this activity was potentially illegal if it was not necessary for the public interest. Some of it doubtless was lawful. But the reality is that in Fleet Street at this time, nobody was really very worried. There were no rules.

For anybody who wants to understand why things went so wrong in British newspapers, there is a very simple answer which consists of only two words – 'Kelvin' and 'MacKenzie'.

When Rupert Murdoch made him editor of the *Sun* in 1981, MacKenzie effectively took the book of journalistic rules and flushed it down one of the office's famously horrible toilets. From then, until finally he was removed from his post in 1994, MacKenzie's world ran on very simple lines: anything goes, nobody cares, nothing can stop us now. Appointed by a man who prided himself on being an outsider and on pushing boundaries, Kelvin MacKenzie was an editor who precisely matched his employer's approach to life – a journalist uninterested even in the most fundamental rule of all, to try to tell the truth. As he later told a seminar organised by Lord Justice Leveson, MacKenzie had a simple approach to fact-checking: 'Basically my view was that if it sounded right, it was probably right and therefore we should lob it in.'

This was the editor who referred to the office computers as 'scamulators' and who scamulated a long list of phoney stories, including most notoriously the 'world exclusive interview' with Marica McKay, widow of a British soldier killed in the Falklands, who, in truth, had given the *Sun* no interview at all; the vicious libel on Liverpool football fans, accused by the *Sun* of pissing on police and picking the pockets of the dead at the Hillsborough stadium disaster; the fictional front page claiming that the comedian Freddie Starr had eaten a live hamster in a sandwich; the completely false story about Elton John paying to have sex with a rent boy. For Lord Justice Leveson, MacKenzie recalled how the *Sun* had paid Elton John £1 million in damages for that particular piece of scamulation and how he had then reflected on the *Sun*'s attempts to check their facts and succeeded in drawing the most perverse of conclusions. 'So much for checking a story,' he grumbled. 'I never did it again.'

The PCC Code of Practice said journalists should not invade people's privacy. MacKenzie simply and baldly said that he 'had no regard for it'. As one particularly sensitive example of protected privacy, the law said that newspapers should not publicly identify the victims of rape – MacKenzie went right ahead and published a front-page photograph of a woman who had been raped with special violence.

The rule-breaking was taken to a peak after the coincidence that in the same year that MacKenzie became editor of the *Sun*, the United

Kingdom saw the opening chapter of what was to become the biggest human-interest story in the world. In 1981, the royal family acquired a new princess. For better and worse, the Diana story busted straight through the wall of deference which previously had concealed most of the private lives of those who lived in the Palace. MacKenzie's *Sun* led the way. If that meant publishing photographs of Diana six months pregnant in a bikini, taken on a telephoto lens without her knowledge, then that was fine because he was merely showing 'a legitimate interest in the royal family as living, breathing people'. If it meant making up stories, that too was no problem. In their brilliant account of life at the *Sun*, *Stick it Up Your Punter!*, Peter Chippindale and Chris Horrie describe MacKenzie telling his royal correspondent, Harry Arnold, that he needed a front-page story about the royal family every Monday morning, adding: 'Don't worry if it's not true – so long as there's not too much of a fuss about it afterwards.'

Once Diana's life had been dragged into the newsroom and converted into raw material to be exploited without limit, the private lives of other public figures were hauled in behind her. And then the private lives of private figures. There were no boundaries. MacKenzie adopted a crude populist view of the world, designed simply to please an imaginary *Sun* reader, defined in his own words as 'the bloke you see in the pub, a right old fascist, wants to send the wogs back, buy his poxy council house. He's afraid of the unions, afraid of the Russians, hates the queers and the weirdos and drug dealers.'

MacKenzie not only produced a paper to please this imaginary bigot, he himself was the bigot. Chippindale and Horrie record his habit of referring to gay men as 'botty burglars' and 'pooftahs'. He published a story falsely quoting a psychologist who was supposed to have said 'All homosexuals should be exterminated to stop the spread of AIDS.' He was no better with race, for example dismissing Richard Attenborough's film about Gandhi as 'a lot of fucking bollocks about an emaciated coon'.

From this position it followed logically that he abandoned any pretence of fair reporting about the governing of the country. A couple of hundred years ago, British journalists had disgraced their trade by selling their collaboration to politicians – for a fee, these 'hacks' would write whatever their paymasters required. In spite of all the twists and turns through which journalism had tried to redeem itself, MacKenzie acted as an unpaid political hack, turning the *Sun* into a weapon to attack all those who might upset his 'right old fascist' reader, scamulating as he went.

MacKenzie inflicted his ways on those who worked for him. There probably never was a rule against bullying, but if there was, MacKenzie would have shattered it. He was an Olympic-gold-medal-winning office tyrant. Colin Dunne, a feature writer who had worked on the *Sun* before MacKenzie took over, described the regime of relentless labour which he introduced: 'Whenever Kelvin saw an empty office, or even an empty chair, he was overcome with the fear that someone some-where was having a good time. And it was his personal mission to put a stop to it.' Chippindale and Horrie record the advice which MacKenzie offered to an elderly graphic artist whose presence upset him: 'Do us all a favour, you useless cunt: cut your throat.'

The infection spread through the *Sun* and was then compounded as those who had served under him moved to rival titles, taking his reckless ways with them. And in newsrooms without rules, why would anybody obey the law?

Rupert Murdoch was right: the business of bribes had been bubbling in the dark gutters of Fleet Street for years. In the 1970s, the commis-sioner of the Metropolitan Police, Robert Mark, discovered that crime reporters were buying information from serving officers and denounced it as 'one of the most long-lasting and successful hypoc-risies ever to influence public opinion'. The bribery stopped. What Murdoch did not say was that it was one of his own most senior editorial executives in the UK who revived it – Alex Marunchak, a crime reporter who rose to become executive editor of the *News of the World*.

Ukrainian by birth, devious and hard by nature, Marunchak ran a famous double act with Greg Miskiw, who is also Ukrainian. The two of them worked together, spoke Ukrainian together and broke the law together. Marunchak was always the leader. In order to get stories and praise; in order to beat the opposition and pay for his massive alcohol and gambling habits; and finally in order to have himself promoted to the highest ranks of the paper, he bathed in a sea of corruption. He made little secret of it. He didn't need to.

His former colleagues say that from the mid-1980s, Marunchak was a prime user of the former detective who I had come across when researching *Flat Earth News*, who had been pushed out of the Metropolitan Police after a corruption scandal and reinvented himself as a conduit for bribes from Fleet Street to serving officers. His name – published here for the first time – is John Ross, known to *News of the World* journalists as 'Rossy'.

Marunchak and the ruddy-faced former cop formed a powerful alliance, drinking together at the Old Rose on The Highway in Wapping; going to police Christmas parties which are said to have been awash with drugs and prostitutes; setting up stories with serving officers; even paying some officers to moonlight for the paper by doing surveillance on targets or appearing as backup when a reporter got into trouble in a crack house. The former colleagues claim that, with Rossy's help, police officers were being paid 'left, right and centre'. It was all against the law. But nobody cared. At one point, they say, Marunchak even hired a couple of Flying Squad officers to drive out to Eastern Europe to bring back a load of vodka he wanted to import.

Rossy's way soon spread into a network of bent police contacts. Word travels in an organisation like the Metropolitan Police, where people move from one station to another, from one squad to another, and so it became well known that if you came across a celebrity breaking the law or as a victim of crime, or if you came across a bit of scandal or a juicy sex crime, you could dip into confidential police files and earn yourself some extra cash by contacting John Ross. This hit a high in February 1994, when police found the dead body of a Conservative MP, Stephen Milligan, who had accidentally suffocated, apparently during a bout of autoerotic asphyxiation. An officer tipped off Ross, who sold the story and pocketed thousands of pounds. One source who knows both Rossy and Marunchak claims that at one point, some serious money was being paid to a very senior officer at

Scotland Yard. One of the Yard's press officers, now dead, was disciplined for selling information to John Ross.

Rossy wasn't Marunchak's only way of dealing with dodgy police. In March 1987 – as Marunchak was being promoted to work on the news desk – there was a murder in south London. A private investigator called Daniel Morgan, aged thirty-seven, was found with an axe in his face in the car park of a pub in Sydenham. For some journalists, this was an important story because it soon became clear that the police investigation into the murder had run into a rat's nest of crime and bent policing and so they set out to expose it. For Marunchak, the evident corruption was an irresistible opportunity, and he set out to take part in it.

Two men sat in the middle of that nest. One was Daniel Morgan's business partner, a heavy-set, heavy-drinking Yorkshireman named Jonathan Rees, then aged thirty-two. Within days of Morgan's murder, investigating officers came to see Rees as their prime suspect. As a private investigator, Rees was a man without any special skill: he had been in the merchant navy and then he had worked as a store detective and, in the late 1970s, as a bailiff for an outfit where Morgan also had worked. In 1981, he and Morgan set up their own investigation agency, working for local law firms, serving writs, collecting information. Since all their business, their contacts and their drinking life were embedded in the dreary, red-brick maze of south London, they called themselves Southern Investigations.

The second key figure was a big, burly, bent detective sergeant, who ran the local crime squad in Catford, south London, Sid Fillery, then aged forty. Fillery, according to his former colleagues, often cut corners, bashed prisoners, 'fitted up' suspects with false evidence, drank copiously while on duty and kept in an office drawer a stash of photographs of young boys being used for sex. Within days of Morgan's murder, investigating officers came to the conclusion that their inquiries were being obstructed by Fillery. They discovered that for the last five years, he had been a close friend of Jonathan Rees: both of them were Freemasons, and the two of them had routinely shown up in local pubs buying rounds, slapping backs and talking business, often with other police officers. Rees had been hiring Fillery and police colleagues to do jobs for Southern and paying them for information from the police computer. In fact, Rees had been spending so much time with Fillery and his colleagues that some officers thought he must be a detective and allowed him the run of local stations.

When Jonathan Rees emerged as the prime suspect for the murder of Daniel Morgan, it was Fillery who went to interview him, and Fillery who went to his office to seize crucial paperwork which then disappeared. A year after Morgan's body was found slashed and bleeding in that car park, it was Fillery who left the police and replaced the dead man as Rees's business partner in Southern Investigations.

Their activities had caught my eye when I was working on *Flat Earth News*. Far more detail has emerged since then, largely because it turned out that Scotland Yard's Directorate of Professional Standards, the DPS, finally became so concerned about the unsolved murder of Daniel Morgan and the network of corruption around Southern Investigations that they ran a covert operation against Rees and Fillery, uncovering a mass of information, including their links to Fleet Street. In 1997, the DPS approached a retired detective, Derek Haslam, and persuaded him to work as an undercover informant. As a serving officer, Haslam had known Jonathan Rees and seen the corruption of some of the officers who mixed with him. Now, he agreed to renew his connection with Southern and to report back each week to a handler whom he would meet in crowded public places, often airports. To protect him from leaks within Scotland Yard, all his information was recorded under a false name. They called him Joe Poulton. Early in 1999, alarmed by the scale of crime which Haslam was reporting, the DPS planted an electronic listening device in Southern's office. For months, it sat there undetected, recording hundreds of hours of casual criminality.

Some of the intelligence was connected to pure crime, nothing to do with newspapers – associates of Rees and Fillery importing drugs from Ireland and stashing kilos of cocaine in a London cemetery, laundering cash for a south London drug baron, stealing drugs from a rival dealer, trying to pass information to the police to cause trouble for two other south London drugs families, plotting to plant drugs in the car of a detective who was investigating Morgan's murder. And always, there were the signs of serious police corruption, as ordinary as oxygen in the world of Southern Investigations. The hidden bug one day caught Rees discussing a bent officer. 'He's fucking bent as fuck,' he said. 'I love a bent Old Bill.'

There were plenty of them and eventually some were caught: Detective Constable 'Skinny' Tom Kingston, jailed for his part in stealing two kilos of amphetamine from a dealer; former Detective Constable Martin King, imprisoned for corruption and perverting the course of justice; former detective 'Drunken' Duncan Hanrahan, jailed for conspiracy to supply drugs, rob, steal and pervert the course of justice; and a very powerful police commander who, according to Haslam, was up to his elbows in armed robbery, fencing stolen goods and the protection of one of London's most powerful gangsters. He was not caught. All of them had their own contacts among other bent officers. The network of corruption, according to Rees and Fillery's recorded words, spread beyond the police to a bent VAT inspector (who had access to confidential information on anybody running any business) and also to bent customs officers. And if all other contacts failed, according to one source who was close to Southern, Rees said he could always borrow a police warrant card and just pose as a serving officer himself.

Among other benefits, the network granted Rees and Fillery promiscuous access to the confidential records held on Scotland Yard's computers. The hidden bug caught them laughing about friends in the force who were stealing other officers' swipe cards so that they could log on in their names. One of their contacts had left the force and taken with him the book of codes which allows officers on the road to call in for information from the computer. Rees's immediate reaction was to wonder whether they could steal the code book.

These contacts allowed Rees and Fillery to pursue their criminal ends – selling inside information or a little discreet assistance to a client who had been charged with a crime, extracting confidential police data on who was wanted for what offence, providing help to associates who were involved in major drug deals. In one call which was caught by the bug, Rees discussed using a customs contact to plant false evidence on a client's enemy. In another, he boasted that he was paying £100 a month to a police contact to check the Met's internal computer system for any intelligence on himself or Fillery: in this way, Rees claimed, they had discovered that a hostile officer had filed an intelligence report linking them to a conspiracy to sell £500,000 of amphetamine.

The DPS tried to summarise their knowledge of Southern's activities in an internal report, which concluded: 'Scanning intelligence around police corruption in London, it can be stated that Rees and Fillery are a crucial link between the criminal fraternity and serving police officers. There is nothing that they do that in any way benefits the criminal justice system.'

Alex Marunchak waded into the cesspit at Southern Investigations, scooping up whatever he could find for the *News of the World*. Journalists who worked with him have described how 'Sid's men' were a familiar sight – in the newsroom; in the bar of the Old Rose; sitting outside targets' homes, watching and snatching covert pictures which would then be served up in dossiers; going out on stories as bodyguards; and, above all, selling information which they had obtained by criminal means. Rees liked to boast that there was nothing he could not get his hands on – 'even the Queen's medical records', he told Derek Haslam. In a single year, 1996/7, the *News of the World* paid Southern a total of more than £166,000.

They targeted rock stars. They went after criminals. They hit the royal family, senior politicians and anybody else who caught Marunchak's eye. When Marunchak wanted a Special Branch intelligence bulletin for a story, Detective Constable 'Skinny' Tom Kingston supplied it. When Southern asked about the movements of the royal family or government ministers or prisoners liable to escape, a motorcycle escort officer from the police Special Escort Group told them all they needed to know. When the *News of the World* wanted to expose the then Foreign Secretary, Robin Cook, for having an extramarital affair, it was Southern who provided a former police officer, Steven 'Sid' Creasey, to follow him around.

They even managed to find bent police contacts abroad. Marunchak needed information from the US about Darius Guppy, an Old Etonian who was wanted for staging a phoney jewellery robbery in New York and defrauding an insurance company. Rees had the answer, as the hidden bug recorded: 'We got some fantastic contact in America. Their ex-police officers' association is just like a serving police force, still get hold of things that are going on, they get access.' Rees went on to describe how he had got in touch with a former FBI agent: 'He said "Yeah, yeah, leave it with me," and, before Guppy got picked up, we had copies of his arrest notes, the photographs, the information, confidential top-secret file that had come from the Met Police . . . So before they even got him, the *News of the World* had it on their desks.'

Independently of Rees, Marunchak had his own dark sources. He heard that another *News of the World* journalist knew a civilian worker in the police and Marunchak paid him £800 to leak confidential information. He also procured a contact in the Passport Office, who could supply the personal details of anybody who had applied for a passport, including a photograph, if Marunchak was willing to wait twenty-four hours.

Marunchak did well out of all this. He rose through the ranks to become senior executive editor and then editor of the Irish edition, based in Dublin. He remained hard, unrelenting towards the targets of *News of the World* stories. During his rise, in May 1996, a Catholic priest, Father Benjamin O'Sullivan, killed himself after being accused of being a paedophile by one of Marunchak's reporters. Marunchak reacted by sending a jokey message on the newsroom's internal system, about 'the death of that homo monk'.

He also remained mysterious. Several colleagues believe Marunchak had links with intelligence agencies, a clear possibility for a Ukrainian based in the West during the Cold War. Certainly, he did work as a translator for the Metropolitan Police. One reporter recalls being invited by him for a drink in the Ritz hotel where they were joined by the former detective John Ross and a man from the US Embassy, who then tried to recruit the reporter as an asset for the CIA. Marunchak himself encouraged the rumours. According to one source who dealt with him in 2010, Marunchak pulled out his mobile phone and flashed several numbers which he claimed were his MI5 contacts.

And, as ever, the collusion with Rees and Fillery spread from the

Murdoch newsroom to others. Once Marunchak had established the link to Southern, several *News of the World* reporters found out what he was doing and took the link with them when they moved papers. Doug Kempster, who had worked in London and Birmingham for the *News of the World*, went to the *Sunday Mirror* in 1996 and became a regular customer of Rees and Fillery's network. Gary Jones, who had worked with Marunchak in London, moved to the *Daily Mirror* as crime correspondent, and was soon in touch with Southern. A similar route was followed by Mark Thomas, chief reporter at the *News of the World*, then deputy editor at the *Daily Mirror* and finally editor of the *Sunday People*.

The police bug recorded Kempster, at the *Sunday Mirror*, arranging for Southern to get inside the bank account of Prince Edward and the Countess of Wessex; sharing his opinion that 'Asians look better dead'; and cracking a joke with Rees about 'a one-legged nigger'. It also recorded Rees arguing with Gary Jones about payment of the large bill which Jones and Mark Thomas had run up for the *Daily Mirror*, and telling him bluntly that he could not submit invoices which listed the phone numbers which had been blagged 'because what we're doing is illegal, innit? I don't want people coming in and nicking us for criminal offences, you know.'

But that is exactly what happened. Through Derek Haslam and the listening device, in late 1999 the DPS became aware that Rees had been hired by a client called Simon James, who wanted to stop his wife, Kim, getting custody of their child in divorce proceedings. Rees agreed to use his police contacts to plant some cocaine in her car and to record a false intelligence alert about her supposed possession of drugs so that she would be arrested and prosecuted. The DPS moved in. Simon James and Rees were jailed for six years for conspiring to pervert the course of justice, extended in Rees's case to seven years by the court of appeal.

In 2002, with Rees still behind bars, police raided Southern again, seized Sid Fillery's computer, and found his collection of pornographic pictures of young boys. In October 2003 at Bow Street Magistrates' Court, Fillery pleaded guilty to making and possessing indecent images of children and was placed on the sex offenders' register. Police also sent files to the Crown Prosecution Service summarising alleged involvement in illegal information-gathering by Rees and Fillery, naming members of his network and including evidence about Alex Marunchak, Doug Kempster from the *Sunday Mirror* and Gary Jones from the *Daily Mirror*.

In all cases, the CPS concluded that there was insufficient evidence to justify a prosecution.

After four police inquiries, the murder of Daniel Morgan remains unsolved. Neither Rees nor Fillery nor any of their associates has been found guilty of any offence in relation to his death.

It was in the fertile soil of the *Sun* that the crime of phone-hacking first took root in Fleet Street, in 1998. According to some who worked there, it was a young reporter from the provinces who introduced the trick. For legal reasons, he cannot be named, so I will call him Sand.

MacKenzie had left four years earlier, but the culture of his destructive genius remained, and that included the bullying. Sand appears to have suffered badly from one particularly demanding editor. 'He had no contacts,' according to one former colleague, 'and anyway if he had had any, his boss would have stolen them.'

Quite how Sand learned to hack is not clear, but certainly by 1998, the hole in the security of mobile phone messages was becoming common knowledge. Struggling to survive, Sand started eavesdropping on voicemail. Apparently keen to advertise his cleverness, he made no secret of what he was doing. A former colleague, whom I will call Diamond, says that Sand's phone-hacking was well known to be the source for the *Sun*'s long-running coverage in 1999 of Mick Jagger's divorce from Jerry Hall and identifies Jagger's PR man, Bernard Doherty, as a particular target.

'He was an industry,' according to Diamond, who was also new to the *Sun* and was shocked to see other reporters soon copying Sand. 'I thought that journalists had just stopped having contacts, a whole generation coming up without being able to talk to people, wandering around electronically through these people's lives.'

One of those who saw the crime circulate through the *Sun* was Sean Hoare, who worked alongside Sand and later confessed openly to what was happening: 'I hacked messages. Everyone was at it. All of a sudden, you have this power. You can access anything. You can tell their movements, where they've been. Everybody got a bit carried away with this power that they had. No one came close to catching us.' Hoare cited the splits and tensions within the Spice Girls, and a high-volume dispute between David Beckham and Posh Spice as examples of stories which he landed through hacking. 'It was so competitive,' he said. 'You are going to go beyond the call of duty. You are going to do things that no sane man would do. You're in a machine. Everyone was drinking everyone's blood.' And so it spread like bindweed – outwards to other newspapers, who could not afford to be beaten by the *Sun's* antics; and, according to some sources, allegedly upwards into the most senior ranks of Fleet Street.

The *Sun's* associate editor at this time was Andy Coulson. Diamond has no doubt that Coulson soon heard what Sand was doing, and claims to have seen Coulson playing some of the hacked messages about Mick Jagger's divorce. Diamond also claims that Coulson said of Sand: 'He's a one-trick pony. But what a trick!'

By the time that Coulson moved to be deputy editor of the *News of the World* in 2000, Glenn Mulcaire, with the help of Greg Miskiw, had already planted the hacking seed there. However, under the leadership of Coulson and his editor, Rebekah Brooks, who had also come from the *Sun*, hacking became embedded as a core activity in the newsroom. One of Brooks's first moves as the new editor was to contact Miskiw, who had been master of the dark arts when she was features editor there from 1996 to 1998. Miskiw had just been sent to New York as US editor. Brooks recalled him to London, although she has always insisted that she had no idea that he was involved in crime.

Back at the *Sun*, Diamond, Hoare and one other reporter, 'Sapphire', all claim that the editor of Bizarre, Dominic Mohan, became an enthusiastic hacker. Mohan has made it clear that he denies this. Diamond and Hoare independently claim that Mohan hacked Andy Coulson's own messages and then told him so – 'I know what you did last night' – thinking that Coulson would find it funny. As it was, they recalled, Mohan found himself on the receiving end of a furious verbal kicking. Hoare claimed that he had his own messages hacked by Mohan. At the Leveson Inquiry, Mohan was asked a series of questions about his possible knowledge of phone-hacking and denied being aware of any such activity.

Counsel for Leveson, Robert Jay QC, asked him whether there was a pattern in the sources of seven different stories, published by him in the Bizarre column, which reported that Liam Gallagher from Oasis and his partner, Patsy Kensit, had had 'a stream of fierce rows over the phone'; that the TV soap actress Martine McCutcheon and her partner 'had phoned each other every day since they met'; that TV soap actor Sid Owen had 'made a series of phone calls' begging his girlfriend to come back to him; that Anthony Kiedis from Red Hot Chili Peppers had been dating one of the Spice Girls and 'has been bombarding her with phone calls'; that the rock singer Robbie Williams had been 'making late-night calls'; that the fashion model Caprice had been 'bombarding 5ive singer J with phone calls'; and that a Manchester United footballer 'has been bombarding' a model with phone calls.

Mohan said it was difficult to remember the source of stories many years after they had been written, that they had probably been obtained from contacts and that he was not aware that anyone on Bizarre had hacked messages to obtain any of them although he could not be 100% certain of that. In his report, Leveson specifically refrained from criticising Mohan. By this time, Mohan had been promoted by Rupert Murdoch to be editor of the *Sun*. Later, he became an assistant to News Corp's chief executive.

Sand in turn left the *Sun* and moved to the Mirror Group. Former colleagues claim he continued to hack voicemail, that he did so openly and that he showed his trick to reporters on the group's national titles – the *Daily Mirror, Sunday Mirror* and the *People*. There are unconfirmed allegations that some editors at all three titles were either aware of criminal hacking in their newsrooms or actively took part in it.

At the Leveson Inquiry, Piers Morgan – by then the renowned presenter of CNN's *Tonight with Piers Morgan* – found himself accused of supervising hacking during his time as editor of the *Daily Mirror*. One of Morgan's finance reporters, James Hipwell, told Leveson of the 'unfettered activities' of the paper's show-business team, whose desk was close to his own: 'The openness and frequency of their hacking activities gave me the impression that hacking was considered a bog-standard journalistic tool . . . I would go so far as to say it happened every day, and that it became apparent that a great many of the *Mirror's* show-business stories would come from that source.' Hipwell said he had no proof that Morgan knew about the hacking but he added: 'I would say that it is very unlikely that he didn't know that it was going on . . . The newspaper was built around the cult of Piers. He was the newspaper. Nothing happened at the newspaper without him knowing.'

Morgan replied by saying that 'I have no reason or knowledge to believe it was going on.' He drew attention to the fact that Hipwell had later been jailed for insider trading, buying the same shares which he was tipping in his column. Hipwell was 'a convicted criminal', Morgan said, who had changed his story on a number of occasions when his share-dealing was investigated. 'I believe any testimony he gives to be inherently unbelievable.'

Morgan specifically denied an allegation that he had listened to voicemail messages exchanged by Britain's two most famous Swedish residents at the time – the TV presenter Ulrika Jonsson and the England football manager Sven-Göran Eriksson – who were having an affair. He said he did not remember a lunch at which, according to the BBC anchorman Jeremy Paxman, Morgan had been seated opposite Ulrika Jonsson and had teased her about the messages which she had left for Eriksson, mimicking her Swedish accent. Paxman told the Leveson Inquiry that Morgan had then turned to him and explained how messages could be hacked.

Piers Morgan was also taxed over a column that he had written in October 2006, describing the tense relationship between Paul McCartney and his then wife Heather Mills. He had written: 'At one stage, I was played a tape of a message Paul had left for her on her mobile phone.' Heather Mills told Leveson that in January 2001 she had had an argument with McCartney, after which he had left a sequence of apologetic messages, including one in which he sang 'Please forgive me', and that later that day, a reporter who had worked for the *Mirror* had called her to say that he knew the couple had argued and that 'I've just heard a message of him singing on the phone to ask you for forgiveness.'

Morgan agreed that he had heard a voicemail message, but he said: 'I have no reason to believe that the tape was obtained in an unlawful manner.' He said he would not identify the source of the tape but implied that it could have been leaked by Heather Mills. She denied sharing any voicemail with him.

Three men who had edited the *People* also found themselves facing unconfirmed allegations that they had hacked phones during their careers. Neil Wallis, who edited the paper before becoming Andy Coulson's deputy at the *News of the World*, was eventually arrested on suspicion of conspiring to intercept communications. He was not charged. When Wallis later said that the police had no evidence of his involvement in hacking, the Crown Prosecution Service corrected him, saying that they did have evidence but that it was insufficient to take to court. Two of Wallis's successors at the *People*, Mark Thomas and James Scott, were also arrested by police on suspicion of the same offence. At the same time, the former editor of the *Sunday Mirror*, Tina Weaver, and her head of news, Nick Buckley, were also arrested. At the time of this book's publication, prosecutors had not decided whether or not they should be charged.

Kelvin MacKenzie himself was never implicated in the hacking. On the contrary, as his culture of recklessness spread across Fleet Street, his own voicemail was targeted – by Glenn Mulcaire from the *News of the World*.

One of the most striking features of all this crime is that the police failed to tackle it. This was true not only in relation to the hacking of voicemail but also with the more serious offence of tapping live phone calls – even when it was used against the most sensitive of victims, the royal family.

In August 1992, MacKenzie's *Sun* published extracts from a phone call between Princess Diana and her childhood friend James Gilbey, during which he famously and repeatedly called her 'Squidgy'. The princess described the sadness of her marriage to Prince Charles and the tension in her relationship with the royal family. That call had been intercepted. Oddly, the call had taken place in December 1989, nearly three years before it was published. Even odder, it had first surfaced in the United States, in *National Enquirer* magazine, which frequently employed former British tabloid journalists. The possibility was raised but never confirmed that this had been done to cast the *Sun* in the lawful role of merely reproducing material that had already been published abroad. Whatever the detail of the way it was done, there was no doubt that this was a serious offence, punishable with up to two years in prison under the 1985 Interception of Communications Act. Police took no action against the *Sun*.

Then the *Sun* did it again. In December 1993, they published highly embarrassing extracts from a long call made by Prince Charles to his then lover, Camilla Parker Bowles, explaining that he envied the role of her tampon. Alex Mitchell, an Australian journalist who was based in London at the time, later reported that the Queen's private secretary, Lord Fellowes, had found that there was evidence of interference with the landline at Eaton Hall, Cheshire, the country seat of the Duke of Westminster, where Prince Charles is believed to have been staying when he made the call. Strangely, the call had been made in December 1989, the same month as the 'Squidgy' call and four years before it was published. Equally strange, it appeared first in an obscure women's magazine in Australia, *New Idea*, which happened to belong to Rupert Murdoch. When it was suggested that the story had been effectively laundered through *New Idea* to avoid punishment by the British authorities, Murdoch issued a formal statement that 'any suggestion of collusion or conspiracy between companies is totally without foundation'. The police took no action.

The royal family were not the only ones to find their phone calls being tapped and then published in the *Sun*. In 2002, the paper was pursuing the story of a convicted fraudster, Peter Foster, who had helped the then prime minister's wife, Cherie Blair, to buy two flats in Bristol. On 13 December, the paper published 'sensational details . . . gleaned from a series of taped phone calls to which the *Sun* has listened'. They reported that Foster was thinking of capitalising on the scandal around him by selling his story for up to £100,000. The *Sun* did not deny that, within hours of the calls being made, it had obtained tapes of 'money-grabbing Foster', his mother and his brother, without Foster's consent. The Press Complaints Commission merely 'censured' the *Sun* for the tapping. The police took no action.

Who was tapping calls for Fleet Street? While the police failed to expose the truth, some journalists and private investigators were well aware of the answer, published here for the first time. It involved a former police officer, two serving officers and one deeply eccentric character with an obsession with cats. And News International titles.

On 24 September 1995, the *News of the World* ran a picture of the former England rugby captain, Will Carling, poking his head out of the door of a health club in west London. The point of the story was that Carling had just had a secret meeting in the club with Princess Diana, who was alleged to be having an affair with him. One of those who was directly involved with taking this picture says that it was obtained by intercepting the princess's phone calls. The job was commissioned, he says, by Alex Marunchak of the *News of the World*, and it was carried out by a former Metropolitan Police officer, Steve Clarke, who had set up an investigation agency called Metshield.

This source has described how he saw Steve Clarke use a device 'about the size of a car radio' to access Princess Diana's number and to tune into the calls which she was making. This sounds like a radio scanner of the kind which could be used to intercept calls in 1995 when phone systems were still using analogue, not digital systems.

The source says that, having discovered the princess was due to meet Carling at the health club, Clarke tasked a former Met detective, Sid Creasey, who also worked for Southern Investigations, to go to the club with a photographer. The source says that Creasey saw Diana leave the club and then waited until, some minutes later, Carling started poking his head out of the door to check that the coast was clear, failed to spot the threat and was caught on camera.

Alex Marunchak went on to find two serving detective constables from the Metropolitan Police, Jimmy Young and Scott Gelsthorpe, who offered the same service. With funding from a senior London criminal, David Carroll, they set up Active Investigation Services (AIS) with an office in Cloth Fair in the East End of London. They used a network of former and serving officers to gather intelligence, and they also intercepted telephone calls, with devices made by hand in the shed of a suburban garden.

The bugs originally were designed and constructed in the mid-1990s by an elderly man, Arthur Strong. He suffered from cerebral palsy which made his hands shake and so, in the late 1990s, he recruited a near neighbour, Stuart Dowling, as his assistant and apprentice. Dowling learned quickly and then devised a more sophisticated version of the bug, using a microchip. He called it the Digital Analogue Crossover, or DAX for short. Placed on a landline, the DAX would relay conversations in real time to a mobile phone. He started making the bugs in his bedroom, but the resin which he used to make them waterproof smelled bad, and his wife, Jodie, complained. So he started using the shed at the bottom of his garden in Langley Road, Sittingbourne, as a workshop for bugging.

Unknown to his wife, Dowling used the bugs to monitor her movements. He was also hired by AIS. Mickey Hall, a former telecoms engineer from Battersea, south London, installed them up telephone poles or inside the green British Telecom junction boxes which stand on pavements around the country, using a fluorescent jacket as well as official barriers and signs to pass himself off as a BT worker.

AIS and the bugging team worked primarily for commercial clients and were eventually caught and convicted. What was not revealed in court is that this network was also working for Marunchak and allegedly for other news organisations. Old AIS invoices specifically record Marunchak hiring them. This seems to have started in 2004 – after the raid on Steve Whittamore – and continued even after the police raided AIS. The key players were released on bail, and AIS simply resurfaced with a new name, Alpha. Sources who worked for the company describe meetings with other unidentified journalists, including a conference organised by an upmarket security company run by a former MI5 officer. They say that Stuart Dowling demonstrated his DAX bug by hooking it up to a nearby shop to listen to its calls, and that journalists were present, not to report the event but as potential customers.

They claim that among the jobs which they took on for Fleet Street was the tapping of the Sussex home of the model and tabloid obsession Katie Price, in January 2011; and the phone calls of the journalist Andrew Morton, who has written biographies of Princess Diana,

Monica Lewinsky and Tom Cruise. One source says that the team were asked to bug Morton's phone 'near Regent's Park'. Andrew Morton has confirmed that he had an office in Drummond Street, two minutes' walk from the park.

And then there is Phil Winton, for years the proud owner of the No Hiding Place investigation agency, a short, tubby character, like Danny DeVito with a full head of dyed black hair and a thoroughly strange life. Winton is obsessed with cats. In 1996, he changed his surname to Catt; he drove a battered old Jaguar car with CAT 343X as the number plate; he kept up to a dozen rare cats in his office, above a café in Finchley, north London; he persuaded his local council to change the name of the alley behind the office to Siamese Mews; and enraged neighbours of his home by building a vast cattery in the back garden. Visitors to his office report that he also appeared to be a stranger to hygiene.

Winton bugged phones. On 20 January 1995, aged thirty-three, he was jailed for twelve months after being convicted of intercepting communications. A jury at Chelmsford Crown Court found that he had arranged for a shortwave transmitter to be placed on a target's phone line in a BT manhole in the village of Witham, Essex. Two other men were jailed with him: David Coghlan, aged fifty-three, a former army intelligence officer; and David Edwards, aged thirty-five, a former BT engineer.

David Coghlan bugged for Ian Withers, who worked for the *Sunday Times*. He is also believed to have bugged commercial enemies of the former owner of the *Observer*, Tiny Rowland. David Edwards has told friends he worked for Gary Lowe and for the network of recovering addicts. Winton, too, was a regular contact of Lowe and the NA network. He had been at school with two of the NA recruits and was often seen visiting Blue. Gary Lowe, as ever, linked them to Fleet Street, although he disliked Winton and humiliated him when he was released from prison by hiring two actors to dress up as policemen and arrest him as he came through the gate.

Winton once boasted in an interview about his media clients, claiming to be getting regular and lucrative work from two contacts on the news desk of 'a popular tabloid': 'One of them will say "Here's the deadline, this is what I want, how much will it cost?" The other just calls up and says "Get the info, I don't care how much it costs."'

Breaking into stolen mobile phones . . . Hiding tracking devices on targets' cars . . . 'Bin spinning' to find stories in rubbish . . . Using police officers and/or employees of phone companies to monitor the precise location of their targets' mobile phones (known as 'pinging'). The criminal ingenuity was almost endless. Ian Edmondson from the *News of the World* devised a scheme to send public figures free mobile phones containing spyware which would relay back to him the call data, contact numbers and pictures in the phone's memory.

There was email hacking. In the summer of 2006, Derek Haslam, who was still spying on Jonathan Rees for Scotland Yard, was alarmed to discover that Rees had found a specialist who had succeeded in hacking into his computer and retrieving the secret reports which he had filed. Through Rees, the same specialist worked for the *News of the World*. Sienna Miller the actress, and Chris Shipman – the son of the murderous Dr Harold Shipman – had their emails hacked at a time when the paper was researching them.

There were burglaries – PIs and journalists working together to break into the homes of public figures. Whether or not they were connected to this, the actor Hugh Grant, the Labour MP Chris Bryant, and the chief executive of the Football Association, David Davies, all reported being burgled at a time when they were the objects of tabloid attention and in circumstances which suggested the burglar was looking for information, not valuables. Two separate sources who were close to Southern Investigations say that Rees and Fillery were breaking into houses, to remove material or plant listening devices. Other evidence shows them attempting to hire a former police officer to commit a burglary, apparently at the home of an unidentified MP. When police searched Fillery's computer, they found a record of Southern reporting to Alex Marunchak the results of a burglary which they appeared to have carried out at the home of an unidentified woman.

Crimes which had been nurtured by three Murdoch papers had spread through almost all of the other national titles. What was being concealed after the arrest of Goodman and Mulcaire was not simply one rogue reporter, nor even one rogue newspaper. This was an industry which had gone rogue, driven by profit, regardless of rules, privileged by its power. Crime paid. Concealment was easy.

5. 14 July 2009 to November 2009

We could have let it drop. The truth is that, if we'd been left to decide for ourselves, we might well have let the whole phone-hacking saga go after Rusbridger and I had stopped the barbecue at the media select committee. We'd published a big story and kicked some powerful people in the shins; we'd proved we weren't lying; there was a long queue of other stories waiting to be covered: why hang around in the cage with the tiger? The answer is that the tiger wouldn't let us go.

It was a Tuesday morning, 14 July 2009, when we appeared before the select committee. That evening, we picked up reports that News International were sending their political correspondents into the House of Commons to spread the word among MPs about David Leppard's story, that Rusbridger had hired the specialist blagger John Ford to hack voicemail. It didn't seem to matter whether this was true or not (or that they had agreed not to publish it). By Wednesday morning, it was travelling fast around Parliament. We were going to have to go and find Ford.

I drove up to the M4 west of London, met the *Guardian*'s investigations editor, David Leigh, in a service station, dumped my car and together we headed off to Ford's last known address, in Somerset. Leigh had been doing this kind of work for even longer than me: when I started out as a messenger boy at the *Guardian*, in 1976, he was already working for the pre-Murdoch *Times*. For both of us, the Leppard smear story was personal. Rusbridger was not just our editor, he was also our friend, and his wife is the sister of Leigh's wife.

By Thursday morning, with the help of one or two journalists who had worked for the *Sunday Times*, we had tracked Ford down to his new home, a terraced house in Bradford on Avon. There was no sign of him, and so there we sat, in the front seat of Leigh's car

like two cops in a B-movie, drinking disgusting coffee from polysty-
rene cups, bitching about office politics and waiting for Ford to turn
up. It rained steadily. In mid-afternoon, our phones suddenly started
buzzing to tell us that the Director of Public Prosecutions had released
a statement. In a nearby shop, we got hold of it by fax and learned
that the DPP had reviewed all the evidence which the police had
handed over in 2006 and concluded that it would not be appropriate
to reopen the case or to revisit the decisions taken. A door slammed.

However, Leigh immediately saw something important buried in
the second page of the statement. The DPP described how, in August
2006, police had searched Glenn Mulcaire's office and seized material
which indicated that some non-royal targets had been hacked.
Prosecutors had agreed that they should select only a sample of these
cases to take to court: 'Any other approach would have made the case
unmanageable.' That suggested a scale of activity by Mulcaire which
went well beyond what had been described by Assistant Commissioner
John Yates with his 'small number' of cases where hacking had been
successful, or by the former assistant commissioner, Andy Hayman, in
his article in *The Times* with his 'handful' of victims.

In the front seat of the car, with the rain pouring down the windows,
we started drafting a story, but then my eye was caught by something
else in the DPP's statement. Towards the end, he said: 'Having examined
the material that was supplied to the CPS by the police in this case,
I can confirm that no victims or suspects other than those referred to
above were identified to the CPS at the time. I am not in a position
to say whether the police had any information on any other victims
or suspects that was not passed to the CPS.' No other suspects? But
what about the email for Neville? Surely that was evidence of other
suspects – a named junior reporter sending thirty-five hacked messages
to the chief reporter, Neville Thurlbeck.

I stepped out of the car so that Leigh could concentrate on drafting
the story and, under the dripping branches of a rain-sodden tree, I
called the DPP's office and asked whether the email for Neville had
been amongst the evidence which the police had passed to prosecutors
in 2006. Clearly, they should have handed it over. It dealt with one of
the very few cases which had been brought to court, that of Gordon

Taylor. It was direct and damning evidence of the offence that had been committed. But the DPP's statement seemed to be hinting that the police had not passed it to prosecutors, in which case Scotland Yard had yet more serious questions to answer. The only alternative was that the police had handed it over, and the DPP was simply lying when he said he had seen no information on other suspects. The DPP's office said they would come back to me.

We filed our story and carried on lurking suspiciously, waiting for John Ford to show up. He never did and we concluded that he was probably clasped safely in Leppard's arms somewhere, precisely to make sure that we didn't get a chance to talk to him. We stayed overnight in a small hotel and, when there was still no sign of Ford the next day, we headed back to London.

Without Ford to explain what had happened, Leigh returned to the office and contacted Ciex, the company which had been hired by Rusbridger. It turned out that Leppard had been in touch with one of their security consultants, a former head of MI6's counter-terrorism division called Hamilton Macmillan, trying to persuade him to confirm the story. Macmillan now talked to Leigh and gave him a valuable on-the-record quote: 'The *Sunday Times* allegations are false. The information they supplied to me to support this allegation was also patently invented.'

Back home in Sussex, I decided to turn the fire back on the *Sunday Times* and phoned their managing editor's office to ask them to tell me on the record a) how many times they had made payments to John Ford to blag into confidential databases, and b) the period of time over which these payments had been made. Within minutes, I had an email from David Leigh in the *Guardian* office: '*Sunday Times* going ballistic. Give me a ring.' Clearly, they didn't want the truth about John Ford being told. The result was that, for a second time, Witherow agreed to drop the smear against Rusbridger.

But the dirty play continued. Rebekah Brooks met a friend of Rusbridger and explained that she was very disappointed that he would publish these terrible stories about the *News of the World*, particularly as 'we were so good to him over his love child'. Since Rusbridger had never fathered an illegitimate child, this was interesting. Since Brooks was editing the *Sun*, which specialised in publishing damaging stories

– true or false – about the private lives of public figures, this was also slightly worrying. Rusbridger and I had a paranoid conversation about whether we were going to find some twisted tabloid version of our sex lives in the *Sun* and we decided that the best way to stop it happening was to carry on publishing stories about the hacking. That way, it would be disgustingly obvious that any story like that was nothing more than vengeance.

In the meantime, as if to confirm our anxiety, the smear about Rusbridger using John Ford found its way into the column of the *Independent*'s right-wing media commentator, Stephen Glover, who produced a lip-smacking account in which he announced once more that our Gordon Taylor story had been 'aided and abetted by the BBC' and that Rusbridger had a 'holier-than-thou aura' while in truth he was 'like the grubbiest reporter on the *News of the World*'.

We couldn't let it drop.

The truth really wasn't hard to find. It was sitting there winking and waving and defying us to come and get it.

Paul Farrelly, the Labour MP who was leading the way on the media select committee, got hold of a transcript of the hearing at which Goodman and Mulcaire had pleaded guilty and been sentenced in January 2007. It turned out to be littered with clues that Mulcaire was not just working for Goodman on some dodgy, rogue project but was clearly breaking the law for the *News of the World* as a whole.

For example, here was the prosecution counsel talking about Mulcaire's hacking of the five non-royal victims who were named in court: 'His purpose in doing this was to obtain information concerning the private lives of the individuals concerned, as well as other celebrities, and pass it on to the *News of the World*.' Couldn't be clearer! Clive Goodman's counsel had repeated the point and explained that the non-royal hacking was the responsibility of 'whoever else may be involved at the *News of the World*' – and the judge had agreed. These comments were really significant, because the barristers and the judge had had access to the evidence which the police had supplied for the trial – and yet not one newspaper had reported them.

There was more in the trial transcript. It listed the exact dates when the five non-royal victims had been hacked – which happened to coincide precisely with times when the *News of the World* was working on stories about them. Mulcaire had targeted Gordon Taylor in 2005 when they were pursuing the story about his private life, and again between February and March 2006, when they were chasing allegations about Premiership footballers taking part in gay sex orgies; Max Clifford when he was representing two different women who were alleged to have had affairs with government ministers (John Prescott and David Blunkett); a football agent, Sky Andrew, when one of his clients, the Premiership player Sol Campbell, had mysteriously walked out of an Arsenal game; the Liberal Democrat MP Simon Hughes when Fleet Street was hounding him for being gay; and the fashion model Elle Macpherson when they were pursuing her relationship with a new partner.

In theory, Mulcaire might have been doing this for another newspaper but the transcript disclosed that his contract with the *News of the World* explicitly forbade him from working for any other paper. And since the court was told he had been working at least seventy hours a week for them, it was not clear how he could have been hacking for anybody else even if he had been allowed to.

And this was obviously not some big secret. The court heard a claim from Mulcaire that hacking was so widespread that he had not even realised it was illegal. Phone records quoted in court showed that Goodman was not hiding in a dark hole in a distant field to listen to royal messages: he was often doing it from his desk in the *News of the World* newsroom. The records showed that over a period of 143 working days, he had done this on at least 348 occasions – an average rate of two or three times a day. Goodman apologised in court for deceiving the royal household but he made no such apology to the *News of the World*.

The transcript also had interesting clues about the police. The prosecution version of events was that Goodman had persuaded Mulcaire to hack phones for him by smuggling cash to him. He had done this, they said, by inventing a non-existent super-secret source at Buckingham Palace, code-named 'Alexander', and claiming £500 a week in tip fees for him and then passing this on to Mulcaire. But the dates didn't fit. The prosecution's own case was that Mulcaire had been hacking royal phones since February 2005, possibly even earlier, but the first payment to Alexander was not until November 2005. So why would the police accept such a daft version of events?

Meanwhile, the DPP's office called back with an answer to the question which I had put to them while I was standing under the rain-sodden tree outside John Ford's house. Had the police in 2006 given prosecutors the email for Neville? And the answer was no. They had not shown the prosecutors clear documentary evidence which was directly relevant to one of the very few non-royal victims who had been named in court – documentary evidence which clearly implicated two other named journalists in handling illegally intercepted voicemail. So why would the police do that?

I banged out a story about the police failing to show prosecutors the email for Neville and carried on poking around in my imagination, looking for the rest of the picture.

I tracked down Brian Paddick, who had been a very senior officer in the Metropolitan Police back in 2006, an interesting man who had been reviled by the tabloid newspapers, partly because he took a liberal line on the policing of cannabis and partly because he committed the unforgiveable sin of being openly gay. He explained how things worked at the top of Scotland Yard. The key man, he said, was Dick Fedorcio – the director of communications, responsible for the Met's links with Fleet Street. Fedorcio, he explained, had become a very powerful voice in the internal politics of Scotland Yard.

Every Monday, Wednesday and Friday, he said, the Met's senior management team, the SMT, would meet to discuss policy. This was a small group which included Dick Fedorcio, who was allowed to have a direct impact on operational decisions: 'The Met is desperate to get newspapers to run good news and not to run bad news. Dick Fedorcio is extremely close to editors. One big point of the commissioner's SMT meetings is to discuss cases which are going well and to talk about how to get those out into the press, and to talk about the bad news and how to keep it out of the press. The meetings are dominated by that kind of conversation. Dick will persuade a paper to drop a bad story by giving them exclusive access to a big raid, that kind of thing.'

Paddick had had no direct involvement in the original phone-hacking inquiry in 2006, but he knew a fair bit about it. Simply because the original complaint had come from the royal household, the job had been passed to Specialist Operations, whose main focus is counter-terrorism and whose boss at the time was Assistant Commissioner Andy Hayman. Based on his previous experience, Paddick reckoned the job would have been discussed from time to time at the SMT meetings. 'Andy Hayman would give an update, and there would be a discussion around the table, including Dick: Hayman reports that they have concluded inquiries on the royal family but there is all this other material, and that's when Dick would speak up, and they would decide not to pursue it, not to get into a fight with one of the biggest media organisations in the world.' It was understandable, according to Paddick, that Specialist Ops had not wanted to get bogged down in a long inquiry that would divert them from their proper role. 'It should have been passed to the Serious Crime Directorate. But it wasn't.'

Why? Fear of News International? Favouritism for a powerful news organisation? Simply crap judgement?

It was Paddick who pointed out something which I should already have recognised, that the column in *The Times* in which Andy Hayman claimed there had been only a handful of victims was not a one-off. Hayman had left Scotland Yard in December 2007 and had then got himself a job as a regular columnist with *The Times* – he had gone to work for the organisation he had been investigating!

When I checked a database of media stories, I found Hayman had not only been writing regular columns for *The Times*, he had also sold them the serial rights for his memoirs. Since leaving the police, I reckoned he must have earned at least £100,000 from News International.

The same database disclosed that Hayman was not alone. The man who had been Director of Public Prosecutions at the time of the original inquiry, Ken Macdonald, had stepped down in October 2008 – and in February 2009, he too had started working as a columnist for *The Times*! The point here was not that Hayman or Macdonald was corrupt.

This was about cosiness, the easy assumption that News International was a friendly and respectable organisation to be cultivated, rather than an organisation which might be routinely engaged in illegal activity and which needed to be brought to book.

Just as I was coming to terms with that, *Private Eye* magazine reported that on 16 July, seven days after he announced that no further investigation was required into News International's involvement in phone-hacking, Assistant Commissioner John Yates had sat next to Rebekah Brooks at a police bravery awards ceremony at the Dorchester hotel, sponsored by the *Sun*. Also sitting there was the current commissioner, Sir Paul Stephenson, and one of his predecessors, Sir John Stevens, who had left Scotland Yard and became a columnist for the *News of the World*. Cosy indeed. And that was not all.

Hayman had left the Met under a cloud. In December 2007, eleven months after the trial of Goodman and Mulcaire, he had had to resign after an anti-corruption inquiry accused him of using his corporate credit card to spend thousands of pounds on his own personal pleasure, including restaurants and hotel bills for a female officer with whom he was having an affair. I spoke to a couple of crime reporters who said that it had been well known among them that Hayman was having affairs, not only with the officer who had benefited from his corporate credit card but also with a civilian worker at the Independent Police Complaints Commission.

Simply by checking back through press cuttings, I then found an extraordinary picture. It was not just that the officer in charge of the original inquiry (Hayman) had been having a secret affair. In addition, the DPP at that time (Ken Macdonald), who was ultimately responsible for the prosecution, had been having a secret affair; and the Attorney General at that time, Lord Goldsmith, who was ultimately responsible for the DPP, had been having a secret affair. All three affairs had subsequently been exposed by tabloid journalists. And shortly after this, it was disclosed that the officer who was now responsible for the subject and who was refusing to reopen the inquiry, John Yates, was also having a secret affair.

Apart from the fact that it appeared that nobody in the senior ranks of the criminal justice system was capable of keeping his trousers on, this bizarre coincidence was worrying. To be clear: I had absolutely no evidence that the *News of the World* had tried to use this information to put pressure on any of these senior figures. Nor did I have any evidence that any of these senior figures had compromised their work for fear of what the *News of the World* might do to them. But what was alarmingly obvious was the sheer potential power of a newspaper which specialises in gathering painful and embarrassing secrets about the private lives of influential people. Whether or not that potential power had made any difference in this case was frustratingly invisible.

The more I poked around, the more I saw the truth. Two whistle-blowers helped.

One contacted the *Guardian* office and had a series of conversations with a bright young reporter called Paul Lewis. This source needs to remain unidentified, and I'll call him 'Mango'.

Mango claimed to know a lot about the activities of Greg Miskiw. He said Miskiw had targeted the call centres of the main mobile phone companies by paying cash bribes to some staff there and possibly also by inserting a journalist into one of them as an employee and spy. Mango reckoned that some call-centre workers were earning between £500 and £1,000 a week from the *News of the World*, doubling their legitimate salary by selling confidential information. If true, this would help to explain a mystery.

The trial transcript revealed that when Glenn Mulcaire called the mobile phone companies to blag them, he was able to pose as a member of staff because he could quote an internal password, even though it changed every twenty-four hours. If Miskiw was bribing people in the phone companies, that would explain how Mulcaire was able to do that.

Mango also claimed that Miskiw was involved in paying cash bribes to police officers to extract information from the police national computer and that it was possible that he had a 'high-up contact' in the Metropolitan Police. Miskiw was supposedly being helped by a former police officer named Boyle, who had become a private investigator. All of this evidently had been the subject of a police inquiry at some stage. Mango reckoned that the police had got close to Miskiw and that at one point they had arrested and interviewed him at Colindale police station in north London, but that Miskiw had refused to comment and there had been a lack of will at the top of the Met Police to pursue him.

The other whistle-blower had fallen out of the sky with the rain when I was sitting in the car with David Leigh outside John Ford's house. A complete stranger who had seen our Gordon Taylor story had called me and offered me access to the treasure which had eluded me when I was researching *Flat Earth News* – the material which had been seized by the Information Commissioner's Office when they raided the home of Steve Whittamore back in March 2003, dealing with all the newspapers who had hired him, not just the News International titles.

The source was most anxious to remain anonymous and over the next few weeks we worked together very cautiously. I lent him a pay-as-you-go mobile phone so that I could call him without leaving any trace of his identity on my billing records. When we met, I used cash to pay for drinks or food so that my credit card left no footprints. Much later, this source stepped forward publicly and identified himself, so it is OK now to say that this was Alec Owen, a grey-haired, gravel-voiced former police officer who had worked on counter-subversion in Merseyside Special Branch and had then moved to become an investigator with the ICO. He was now retired.

After some tentative negotiations, I went to his home in Cheshire where the two of us perched on the side of the bed in his spare room and stared at the screen of an ageing computer on the bedside table. Here at last was the database which the ICO had assembled from the Whittamore material – thousands and thousands of requests from more than 400 named journalists, targeting thousands of people, rifling through confidential data about them on the police national computer, the DVLA, phone records, bank records. And, according to the ICO's analysis, the vast bulk of this activity was illegal.

I had already seen the contents of the blue book, in which Whittamore recorded requests from the News International titles, and I had summarised it in the Gordon Taylor story. Now, with an apparently eternal cigarette burning between his fingers, Owen showed me the contents of the red, green and yellow books in which Whittamore had recorded the requests from the *Daily Mail*, the *Daily Mirror*, the *Daily Express* and all of their respective Sunday titles as well as numerous magazines and (embarrassingly) the *Guardian's* sister paper, the *Observer*. Owen wouldn't let me copy the material or even read it at my own pace. He scrolled slowly through it, and, with my eyeballs leaping around the screen, I stopped him and took detailed notes whenever I spotted an interesting line.

On 31 August 2009, we published the result, naming scores of victims and describing 'the casual regularity with which newsrooms have treated confidential databases as a library of convenience and the alarming ease with which the security around supposedly well-guarded databases has been repeatedly penetrated'. Some of the victims had real reason to be frightened: the former Metropolitan Police Commissioner, Lord Imbert, who had a long history of investigating terrorist groups and whose private address had been handed out by British Telecom; the then head of MI6, Sir Richard Dearlove; well-known footballers whose homes had been burgled while they were at matches; and two leading journalists who had exposed the activities of gangsters. The summaries of stories on Whittamore's invoices made it clear how little of this had anything to do with public interest: 'Bonking headmaster . . . Dirty vicar . . . Miss World bonks sailor . . . Witchdoctor . . . TV love child . . . Junkie flunkie', and so on and on.

The significance of this was not just the snapshot of promiscuous criminality in Fleet Street but the fact that they had got away with it. Just as the Metropolitan Police had failed to dig deep into the *News of the World* or warn Mulcaire's victims, so the Information Commissioner had failed to prosecute the newspapers or alert Whittamore's victims. Alec Owen had no doubt about the explanation: the ICO didn't want to get into a fight with Fleet Street.

Seeing the truth was not enough. On the best of days, British libel law is so ferocious that newspapers frequently end up concealing the truth about rich or powerful people who can go to court and win hundreds of thousands of pounds in damages and legal costs if the journalists cannot produce hard evidence to defend themselves. In a case like this, where a powerful organisation had already proved itself willing to lie on a grand scale, my knowing the truth meant nothing unless I had documents or on-the-record human sources to prove it. This is where the lawyers came in.

As soon as the *Guardian* published that first story about Gordon Taylor, I'd started to get approaches from lawyers who represented public figures, all of whom seemed to have suspected for years that tabloid journalists had been tapping their phones. They were natural allies: I could help them with information; they could help me with a little bit of power. They could follow the path beaten by Mark Lewis on behalf of Gordon Taylor, by suing the *News of the World* and asking the courts to order Scotland Yard to hand over extracts from Glenn Mulcaire's paperwork and any other relevant evidence which they had gathered during the original 2006 inquiry. That evidence would be confidential until it came to court, at which point I would be allowed to sit there and take notes and write stories – and possibly to get hard evidence that other journalists, including maybe even Andy Coulson, had been involved.

Mark Lewis and Charlotte Harris were both working with Max Clifford, hoping he would be the first client of the law firm they wanted to set up. They were an extraordinary combination. When Lewis first turned up with Harris in the *Guardian* office a few days after we published the Gordon Taylor story, he introduced her: 'This is Charlotte Harris, who's ruining my life at the moment.' What he meant was that the two of them had dived into one of the world's most volatile romantic relationships.

Charlotte Harris plays a brilliant game. She is small and vivacious, in her early thirties. She wears high heels, low tops and short skirts. She totters through life batting her big bright eyes at men, who make the simplest and most self-serving of mistakes, which is to assume that she is a dim-witted sex object whose primary function is to sleep with them. The truth is that she has a brain like a Rolls-Royce. She is very sharp, absolutely determined to win her point and perfectly willing to allow men to behave like idiots around her if that's what their egos demand.

She had sailed through university, won a national award as a student drama critic, written a play which reached the finals of the National Student Drama Festival and marked her graduation with a major confrontation with her mother, who demanded that she drop two things from her life – her boyfriend, whom her mother thought undesirable, and her decision to become a journalist, which her mother thought was even worse. Harris cut a deal, kept the boyfriend, dropped the journalism and trained as a lawyer instead. Seven years later, in December 2006, she had started work at the Manchester law firm George Davies, where Lewis was a senior solicitor.

They had collaborated on the early stages of the Gordon Taylor case. Since then, several things had changed. She had left to work for another Manchester law firm; Lewis was on the verge of a terminal fallout with George Davies; Lewis had left his wife; and the two of them had started their double act. That first day, at the *Guardian* office, they staged the opening performance of what was to become a familiar show, a strange and compelling combination of flirtatious sparring and brilliant legal strategy. I liked both of them a lot.

For the Murdoch organisation, they were a perfect nightmare. Lewis simply wasn't scared of them: the more they snarled at him, the more he liked it. Harris wasn't scared either: she had a very strong, just about unstoppable tendency to deal with people who tried to mess her about by smiling like a cherub and telling them to fuck off.

Max Clifford's case was obviously a strong one. Like Gordon Taylor, he had been named in court as a victim, so there was no doubt that the police were holding evidence that he had been hacked. For most of his long career, Clifford had used the *News of the World* as one of his best clients for the sensational stories he brokered, but in 2005, while Andy Coulson was editor, he had fallen out with them and refused to deal with them any more. So the paper had evidently found their own sweet way of monitoring what he was up to.

Lewis and Harris were also in touch with another of the five original non-royal victims, Sky Andrew, whose work as an agent for Premiership footballers and other sporting figures gave his private life an addictive attraction for the *News of the World*. I undertook to tell Lewis and Harris whatever I could find to help with the two cases in the hope that they would prise information out of the police.

One of the other lawyers who had contacted me also started to play a central role. Mark Thomson shares one particular feature with all of those who were eventually to lead the way against Murdoch – he has a rebel streak. As a student at Cambridge, he had toyed with being an anarchist and he had then worked as a courier, racing a van around London and joining street demonstrations against apartheid in his spare time. He had had no interest in spending his life on a treadmill and had gone off on a poor man's tour of the world before accidentally drifting into law, simply because a friend in London offered him some work as a legal clerk. He liked it, he stayed, he qualified and, twenty-five years later, he had become highly successful, pioneering the development of the new law of privacy in order to protect clients from the aggressive intrusion of tabloid newspapers.

Most of his clients were seriously famous people. For years he had watched them suffering agonies of doubt, trying to explain how a tabloid newspaper could possibly have discovered some detail of their private lives, sometimes accusing close friends or employees of selling them out, occasionally even imagining that the papers must be intercepting their communications in some way. Thomson had no doubt that the papers were playing dirty. On one occasion, he had directly accused a newspaper of listening to a client's voicemail messages. The paper had immediately killed the story and Thomson later had heard that his accusation had sent the paper's editors into meltdown. On 1 June 2009, he had opened his own law firm, with cramped offices in Covent Garden. He and his partner, Graham Atkins, had an impressive list of well-known clients including high-profile actors – Sienna Miller, Jude Law, Ewan McGregor, Hugh Grant and others – and the former prime minister, Tony Blair, and his family.

Clearly, the immediate target for these three lawyers was Scotland Yard, who were sitting on the stash of paperwork and other records which they had seized from Glenn Mulcaire when they arrested him in August 2006. Their first objective was to identify clients who had been victims and, since the police were refusing to do so, the lawyers had to take the initiative, to use the civil courts to force them to disclose their evidence. Then finally we might see the scale of all this.

Thomson now wrote to Scotland Yard on behalf of a dozen clients, asking if they had any kind of evidence that any of them had been the victims of illegal activity by Glenn Mulcaire. If they got a yes, they would go to the High Court for an order requiring the police to disclose that evidence. Lewis and Harris were already at that next stage, seeking orders on behalf of Max Clifford and Sky Andrew.

Other lawyers who had got in touch with me also wrote to the police on behalf of George Michael, whose private life had been exposed relentlessly by the tabloid press, largely because he was gay; the former champion jockey Kieren Fallon, who had been accused of taking bribes in a *News of the World* story which had fallen apart when police took it to court; and Gwyneth Paltrow, whose sole offence was to have given birth to a baby boy.

Maybe we were getting somewhere.

But doors were already slamming.

On 21 July, Andy Coulson and three current executives from the *News of the World* gave evidence to the media select committee. I had been feeding information to the two most active Labour MPs, Paul Farrelly and Tom Watson; and also to Adam Price, a clever young Plaid Cymru MP who had shown signs of wanting to get to the truth. There were lots of leads to follow. But, according to Coulson and the three other witnesses, none of them led anywhere.

Coulson cut a confident figure, his haircut as neat as his suit, his manner as clipped as his speech. And he knew nothing – nothing about hacking phones, nothing about blagging confidential data, nothing about any form of illegal activity on any of the newspapers he had worked on. 'I never had any involvement in it at all,' he said.

He said he didn't know about Steve Whittamore. He had never even heard his name. He said he didn't know about Glenn Mulcaire. He had never even heard his name. He didn't know about anybody paying money to police officers. He didn't know anything that the world did not already know. 'I am absolutely sure that Clive's case was a very unfortunate rogue case,' he told the committee.

The three other witnesses also said they knew nothing about anything illegal. The committee asked numerous questions about Glenn Mulcaire.

The new editor of the *News of the World*, Colin Myler, said he could not help. 'I don't know the man,' he said. The long-serving managing editor, Stuart Kuttner, said he knew no more. The long-serving in-house lawyer, Tom Crone, said he knew equally little. He had never even heard his name until he was arrested, he said.

The MPs confronted them with the email for Neville. Here were leads to follow. The witnesses produced more dead ends than a cemetery.

Tom Crone explained that, when the email had been disclosed some twelve months earlier, during Gordon Taylor's legal action, he had tried to find out more. He had spoken to the reporter who wrote the email, Ross Hindley, but it had turned out that he was very junior at the time, only twenty, and had only just been promoted from being a messenger boy, so he had spent a lot of time typing up stuff, so he just could not remember anything at all about this particular email. And unfortunately, there was no way to ask him any more. He was in Peru.

Crone said he had also spoken to Neville Thurlbeck but unfortunately it turned out that Thurlbeck had never received the email. Thurlbeck thought it was the London news desk who had told him to work on the Gordon Taylor story but unfortunately the relevant person on the news desk said he had never seen the email. Crone had asked the IT department to check whether Ross Hindley might have sent the email to anybody else, but unfortunately the IT department had found nothing.

What about the contract in which Greg Miskiw had offered £7,000 for the Gordon Taylor story to Glenn Mulcaire, using a false name? Kuttner said he knew nothing about it, because the money promised in the contract had never actually been paid. Coulson said he knew nothing about it, because Miskiw had been up in Manchester. And, as it happened, he said, he couldn't remember anything at all about any Gordon Taylor story.

What about an interesting story which the *News of the World* had published during Coulson's time as editor, headlined 'Chelsy tears Harry off a strip', written by Clive Goodman and Neville Thurlbeck, quoting from a voicemail message left by Prince William on Prince Harry's mobile phone? Unfortunately, Andy Coulson said he could not remember it. Nor could Tom Crone, apparently.

Still, in their campaign to prove their innocence, they fired off a co-ordinated volley which flew over the *Guardian's* head and wounded their friends at Scotland Yard. Answering a question which had troubled me, they disclosed that the police had not interviewed a single one of the journalists on the paper – not Ross Hindley and Neville Thurlbeck, who were named in the email for Neville; not Andy Coulson, who was responsible for the journalists; nor Stuart Kuttner, who was responsible for the money they spent; nor Tom Crone, who was responsible for checking the stories they produced. The Yard press office had refused to answer my questions about this. Naively, I had assumed that detectives must have interviewed somebody from the *News of the World* apart from Clive Goodman. And they hadn't. Nobody else at all. What kind of police inquiry was that?

Coulson offered one other bit of news, which he brought up as the hearing ended, almost as though – as a professional media adviser – he was feeding a sound bite to the press. He disclosed that the day after John Yates had made his statement declaring that there was no need to reopen the inquiry, a detective had called him to tell him that he had been a victim of Mulcaire's hacking. Coulson underlined his point: 'I clearly did not know what Glenn Mulcaire was up to.' The tabloids duly reported this as the main point of the hearing.

A blind man in a dark room could see that these people were lying and, sure enough, very quickly we caught them out on one point. The whole idea of Ross Hindley being a junior reporter, newly promoted from messenger boy, turned out to be high-grade garbage. I passed a tip to the investigative magazine *Private Eye* whose reporter, Tim Minogue, discovered that Hindley had not been twenty at the time, but twenty-eight; had not been newly promoted from being a messenger boy but had been reporting for the *News of the World* for five years; and happened to be the nephew of a former editor of the paper, Phil Hall. News International eventually admitted that Crone's evidence had been wrong and claimed that Hindley had 'seemed to be a messenger' and that Crone had been misled by 'provocative questioning and interrupting'. Several members of the select committee thought that that reply was genuinely comic.

But for the most part, they got away with their lies. With the police backing them, there was not much to stop them doing so. None of them knew anything about payments that might have been made to Goodman and Mulcaire to keep them quiet when they came out of prison. Nobody offered any convincing explanation as to how they could come to pay more than £1 million to settle the Gordon Taylor case without understanding that this meant they had crime and criminals in their newsroom; nor why they had never mentioned this to press, Parliament or public.

Separately, Les Hinton, the chief executive of News International, came to the same committee to tell a very similar story. 'There was never any evidence delivered to me that suggested that the conduct of Clive Goodman spread beyond him.'

In amongst all this, I was intrigued by two particular lines which seemed to reek of falsehood. Both of them involved law firms who had supposedly run investigations for News International and found no sign of crime.

Coulson claimed that as soon as Goodman and Mulcaire were arrested, he had called in a firm called Burton Copeland to carry out an investigation. 'There was nothing that they asked for, that they were not given.' Crone made the same claim. Either they were telling the truth, in which case Burton Copeland had the investigative skills of a goldfish; or they were lying. I called Burton Copeland and put it to a senior partner, Ian Burton, that their name was being used in vain. He refused to comment.

In a memo to the committee, News International also claimed to have called in a second law firm, Harbottle & Lewis, to check the contents of 2,500 emails and that the lawyers had found no new evidence of hacking. This was tantalising. News International produced a letter from a senior partner at Harbottle & Lewis, dated 29 May 2007. It was headed 'Re Clive Goodman', and it said: 'We have on your instructions reviewed the emails to which you have provided access from the accounts of: Andy Coulson, Stuart Kuttner, Ian Edmondson, Clive Goodman, Neil Wallis, Jules Stenson. I can confirm that we did not find anything in those emails which appeared to us to be reasonable evidence that Clive Goodman's illegal actions were known about and supported by both or either of Andy Coulson, the editor; Neil Wallis, the deputy editor; and/or that Ian Edmondson, the news editor, and others were carrying out similar illegal procedures.'

I let my imagination loose and emailed Paul Farrelly: 'Why do that in May 2007? It's four months after the trial, three months after Colin Myler's arrival, eleven months before they find out that Gordon Taylor has the paperwork from Scotland Yard. Surely, somebody must have done something in or around May 2007 that made them decide suddenly to take that defensive action. Surely, somebody specifically threatened to accuse those six named execs of being involved in the illegal activity. Is it just a coincidence that it was at this time that Goodman and Mulcaire were threatening to take them to an employment tribunal? . . . Bear in mind that Goodman's former colleagues tell me that he pleaded guilty because he understood that News Int would stand by him. Having agreed to take the rap, he was then told he was being sacked, which was not the deal he was expecting.'

I strongly suspected that Goodman and/or Mulcaire had come out of jail and threatened to implicate those executives unless they were compensated; and that they had been paid to stay quiet; and that, whatever Harbottle & Lewis had said about these emails which they had studied, the *News of the World* had been breaking the law whenever it suited them.

You don't lie if the truth won't hurt you. News International had emerged from the select committee without having to admit any wrongdoing, so they had won the day, but in the longer term, they were very vulnerable. I sent an email to Rusbridger: 'Where we are: select committee will call more witnesses and will produce report which is likely to be v hostile to News Int. Scotland Yard may find it difficult to hold on to their policy of not reopening inquiry. Information

Commission under pressure to disclose all the material they seized from Steve Whittamore. PCC floundering around looking for an excuse to do nothing. News Int appear to have dropped all attacks on the *Guardian* – not a word since we disclosed documents to the select committee. Nightmare for News Int is either that Yard reopen inquiry and/or that Max Clifford et al. win court orders for disclosure of more material held by Yard. They are sitting on a powder keg with carpet on fire with nothing but spit for protection. Nick.'

Then it was the turn of the police. On 2 September 2009, Assistant Commissioner John Yates gave evidence to the media select committee.

A few days before that, searching the select committee's website, I discovered that the office of the DPP, which was showing alarming signs that it was failing to act independently from the police, had given Scotland Yard a new gift. He had sent a memo to the committee with a strange interpretation of the Regulation of Investigatory Powers Act 2000, known as RIPA – the law which made voicemail-hacking a crime.

According to this memo, it was a crime to hack into voicemail only if the intended recipient had not already heard the message that was hacked. Once the message had been heard by the intended recipient, according to the DPP's memo, anybody at all could dial in and listen to it, and that would not be a crime. If that was right, it would dramatically cut the number of victims and the number of perpetrators – and give big support to the Yard's version of events. I didn't believe it for a moment.

I checked the transcript of the trial and found that this interpretation of RIPA had never been mentioned, by the prosecutors or the defence or the judge. I checked back on parliamentary debates when RIPA was being passed into law and found no mention of anybody intending it to be read in this way. And I recalled that when he made his statement after our Gordon Taylor story, John Yates also had not mentioned this. Indeed, his language had been clear and wide: those targeted by Goodman and Mulcaire might have run into the hundreds, he had said, 'but our inquiries showed that they only used the tactic against a far smaller number of individuals'. Still, for a police force coming under pressure, it was indeed a valuable gift. Recognising that this interpretation was almost certainly rubbish, I came to know this as 'RIPA bollocks'.

When Yates gave his evidence to the committee, Paul Farrelly, Tom Watson and Adam Price worked hard to unsettle him, but he stuck resolutely to his script. The *Guardian* story about Gordon Taylor had been nothing more than 'a conflation of old stories', he said, unconsciously echoing the line which News International had been using in their briefings for politicians and other journalists. More important, there was simply no evidence to justify reopening the inquiry. In all the material they had gathered in 2006, he added, 'there was nothing to take us any further forward from an investigation point of view'.

They had tried to obtain more evidence from the *News of the World*, Yates explained, by writing them a letter, asking them for information on a list of points. The newspaper, however, had refused to give them what they wanted. Had they gone to court, to get a production order from a judge which would have forced the *News of the World* to hand over its evidence? No, they had not.

Sitting beside him, Detective Chief Superintendent Phil Williams, who had run the original inquiry under Andy Hayman, casually disclosed that among those identified as victims in 2006 had been Prince William and Prince Harry. Yet for three years, their names had been kept hidden, apparently out of nothing more than old-fashioned British deference to the royal family, whose names could not possibly be spoken somewhere so vulgar as a court of law.

But Yates held firm to his claim that the affair had had few victims. Apart from the small number who had been identified and approached in 2006, there were only 'a couple, a handful of people potentially' who had not been warned and who were now being informed by police. And he recycled the 'RIPA bollocks' from the DPP.

Behind this veil of smug denial, you could see the outline of their failure. Even though Scotland Yard wanted to claim that they were intent on identifying any other lawbreaker at the *News of the World*, they had not tried to interview anybody apart from the hapless

Clive Goodman. And they had been just as weak in dealing with the victims. A statement from the DPP had revealed that back in 2006, when prosecutors agreed to go to court with only eight named victims, the police had agreed to approach and warn 'any potential victim not reflected in the charges actually brought'. Clearly, they had broken that agreement. They had not even approached and warned Jo Armstrong, whose messages were clearly transcribed alongside Gordon Taylor's in the email for Neville. They had not approached Andy Coulson, even though the evidence that he was a victim was clear enough that they could finally warn him within a day of Yates announcing that there was no need to reopen the inquiry.

'There's nothing to see here. Move along now.'

Meanwhile, the lawyers had engaged the enemy and were fighting hand to hand on two fronts.

News International had tried to eliminate Mark Lewis from the game. Their solicitors, Farrer & Co., wrote to complain about the possibility of his acting for Max Clifford. 'Your involvement in this case is plainly wrong,' they had urged in a letter dated 6 August 2009, claiming that his role in the secret settlement of Gordon Taylor's case meant that he had confidential information which he was not allowed to disclose. Indeed, they claimed, he could not do any more work on any phone-hacking case. 'Were you to act for any other would-be claimant in respect of the voicemail accessing allegations, at the very least there is an undoubted risk that the confidential information would be put to use . . . You have an opportunity to correct matters by confirming that you will now accept that you cannot act for any individual wishing to bring a claim against News Group in respect of the voicemail accessing allegations.' They threatened to go to court to take out an injunction to stop him. Lewis saw it as bluff and simply grinned and binned it. Farrer & Co. took no action.

More serious, Scotland Yard persistently failed to hand over the information to lawyers who were trying to find out if their clients had been victims. First, they stalled, sending back a standard letter: 'We are in the process of checking our records to see if your client was subjected to unlawful monitoring. As I hope you can appreciate, this process will take time but we will revert to you as soon as we are able.' Weeks passed and then months during which the lawyers wrote again; and again they received no answer.

Eventually, Scotland Yard began to reply, with letters which soon had the various lawyers complaining bitterly. Like a shy bride on her honeymoon, the police disclosed just a little of what they had. The letters would acknowledge that in the material seized from Glenn Mulcaire, they had found a client's name and/or mobile phone number and/or the PIN code used for accessing their voicemail and that this meant that the client was a 'person of interest' to Mulcaire, but they would then add a standard line which was the equivalent of the shy bride announcing that she had a headache, to the effect that 'there is no documentation in our possession to suggest that your client has been the victim of unlawful interception'.

This enraged several of the lawyers because it seemed to them to be gratuitous and misleading: gratuitous because it was up to the courts, not the police, to decide what the documentation suggested; and misleading because the police could just as easily have said that 'this information clearly suggests that your client was targeted by Mulcaire and may well have been a victim of hacking'.

Several public figures took them at face value and assumed that that must mean they had not been hacked. George Michael and Kieren Fallon, for example, had both believed that they must have been victims (as indeed they were), but both accepted that they must have been wrong and instructed their lawyers not to pursue the case.

Some of the Yard letters showed signs of genuine bad faith. Lawyers for a senior media figure wrote asking whether his mobile phone number showed up anywhere in Mulcaire's records. The police wrote back and said it was not there. Since this man was suspicious for a living, he found this hard to believe and so asked a different lawyer to write again, using different wording, this time asking if his name showed up. The police then admitted that he was named in Mulcaire's hacking notes on three separate occasions.

Similarly, the lawyer for a globally famous actress wrote asking whether police had documentation to suggest that a) her mobile phone had been unlawfully intercepted, or b) she was the intended target of unlawful interception, or c) her private information had been obtained by News International, or d) that she may have been the subject of any unlawful surveillance. After a delay of months, Scotland Yard wrote back saying no to all four questions – but failed to add that they did have documentation which clearly identified the actress as one of Mulcaire's targets, and that they had made no attempt to find out whether that meant that the answer to any of the four questions might be yes. She, too, was misled by the answer and instructed her lawyer not to pursue the case.

Mark Thomson waited a full three months for a reply to the letter he had sent police on behalf of a dozen famous clients in mid-July. Finally, on 14 October 2009, the police responded, claiming that they held no evidence on ten of the twelve public figures on whose behalf he had written to them. This later proved to be false. The Yard's letter ended with a suggestion that his clients should contact their phone companies 'who may be able to assist further'. This was as helpful as a swimsuit on a snowy day: the phone companies are required by law to destroy all their billing data when it is twelve months old and it was now more than three years since they had seized this material from Mulcaire.

It was then that an extraordinary possibility dawned. Why were the police taking so long to answer these letters about potential victims? Why had they broken their original agreement with the DPP to inform all potential victims? Could it possibly be that they had no idea who all the potential victims were?

Mark Thomson succeeded in getting a tip from Scotland Yard. And there was the answer. Back in 2006, detectives had seized a massive quantity of paperwork and computer records from Glenn Mulcaire – and they had never bothered to search it. They might have raced through it and produced a quick summary, but they had never done the job properly. They had taken a great heap of evidence of criminal activity – with whatever it disclosed about victims and offenders – and they had stuffed it into storage. So, now, thanks to these nuisance lawyers and their clients, finally they were producing a database of all the people who had been targeted by Mulcaire. Three years too late.

And, of course, nobody – not the assistant commissioner, John Yates, nor anybody else from Scotland Yard – had said a single word about this to press, public or Parliament. Indeed, Yates had insisted that there was no need to reopen the investigation without ever explaining that neither he nor anybody else at Scotland Yard knew what evidence was lying unexplored in their possession. Even now, in the late autumn of 2009, as a group of officers finished scanning it all on to their database and indexing the contents, Scotland Yard still chose to say nothing. There was no press release; no letter to potential victims to inform them. There was only silence and a self-serving decision that if any potential victim wanted to know about the crimes committed against them, they would have to work it out for themselves and then hire a lawyer to force the evidence out of them.

You win some ground. You lose some ground.

On the evening of Friday 6 November 2009, I flew into Copenhagen, to speak at a journalism conference. An hour or so later, my phone rang, and Alan Rusbridger told me that the Press Complaints Commission had produced a report about our Gordon Taylor story and seemed to have leaked it to *The Times* (prop: R. Murdoch). He had not yet seen the whole thing but he had heard enough, he said, to fear that the report was hostile to us. I met up with friends for a meal and tried to eat while my stomach went tight and refused to co-operate. A little later, Rusbridger got hold of a copy of the report and forwarded it to me. In the subject heading of the email, he wrote 'Snow job'.

The PCC had asked themselves only two questions. First, had the *News of the World* misled them during their original phone-hacking inquiry in 2007 by claiming that Clive Goodman was the only one of their journalists who had been involved? In answering, they managed to ignore the comments of the prosecution, the defence and the judge at the original trial and even to dismiss the email for Neville as 'speculation'. They were happy to declare: 'The PCC has seen no new evidence to suggest that the practice of phone-message tapping was undertaken by others beyond Goodman and Mulcaire.'

Second, they asked whether their earlier actions had failed to prevent renewed hacking. They concluded happily that they had done a good job but, in doing so, they cut the *Guardian*'s legs off. They reported that our story about Gordon Taylor had claimed to have evidence that the hacking had continued after the jailing of Goodman and Mulcaire in January 2007. This happened to be untrue: there was nothing in the *Guardian* story about anything that had occurred after January 2007. The PCC then explained that they had asked me and Alan Rusbridger whether we had any evidence of hacking after January 2007. Since this was not something we had looked at, we had said we had none. The PCC now announced that we had confessed that we had no evidence to support our story. 'The *Guardian*'s stories did not quite live up to the dramatic billing they were initially given,' they concluded.

Four months earlier, when I read News International's attack on our first story, I had felt swamped by dread, that we had just got it wrong. Now, I knew better. This time, I just felt angry. I thought of the PCC's director, Tim Toulmin, in July, lounging back in his seat in front of the select committee smugly declaring that the PCC had no reason to cover up anything at all. How dare they claim to be a regulator? They regulated the journalism industry the way a poodle regulates its master.

Now, I was stuck in Copenhagen without a computer, and Rusbridger was in Nairobi, about to board an eight-hour flight back to London. Somehow, we had to catch up and get the truth across.

Rusbridger took charge and, by email, orchestrated the paper's response – reporters in London 'to make sure we have a point-by-point destruction of their feebleness, their straw men and diversions'; the *Guardian* press office to put out a snappy response; me to write 800 words for Monday morning's paper; the website to run something sooner; somebody to contact Paul Farrelly and other MPs; somebody to draft a letter to John Whittingdale, chair of the media select committee. I persuaded a kindly Danish editor to let me use his office and started writing.

By Monday morning, we were fighting back. 'MPs express anger at PCC phone-hacking "whitewash"', said the headline on the front-page story, which quoted Farrelly and Adam Price laying into the report and Charlotte Harris saying its findings were 'contradictory and self-serving'. Inside the paper, I tried to describe what was wrong with the report and to list a few of the things which they did not say.

I compared the PCC to a boxer who threw punches at shadows on the wall and then, having failed to land a blow on any real target, assumed the role of referee and declared himself the winner. I listed some of the things which they had failed to say and explained how lawyers for public figures were pressing to see the evidence which Scotland Yard was holding on them. 'The PCC may yet discover that the only real victim of their attack is their own credibility.'

Other newspapers did not see it that way, recycling the PCC report as though it were telling the truth. '"Phone hacking" journos cleared', said Murdoch's *Sun*. 'Watchdog rejects paper's phone-tapping allegations', said Murdoch's *Times*. Both repeated prominently the PCC's line that the *Guardian* stories did not 'live up to their dramatic billing'.

The *Independent* again were particularly hostile. Their media columnist, Stephen Glover, went to work once more, firmly clasping Murdoch's hand to his lips. In July, he had suggested that the Gordon Taylor story was not only old but also now irrelevant since these illegal practices had surely stopped. 'The *Guardian* does not suggest they still go on,' he had written. Now, four months later, obediently following the PCC's fictional line, he casually rearranged the facts. 'The *Guardian*'s reporter Nick Davies suggested such practices were still widespread,' he wrote.

This was not simply a spat between the *Guardian* and the PCC. Beneath the surface, this was a test of the idea that newspapers could regulate their own business. When Alan Rusbridger told a BBC radio interviewer that the report was 'worse than useless', he meant it. He and one other Fleet Street editor privately discussed the possibility that both of them would simply withdraw entirely from the PCC in order to register their protest. As it was, Rusbridger settled for resigning from the Editors' Code of Practice Committee and making his views very clear. Whether self-regulation could survive remained to be seen.

A few days later, in central London, I hailed a taxi. The driver wanted to talk, asked me what I did for a living, what kind of stories I wrote, so I told him I'd been doing this stuff about the phone-hacking.

'Oh, yes,' he said. 'I know the thing you mean. That all turned out to be wrong, didn't it?'

6. Secrets and lies

Based on interviews with current and former police officers; sources who worked for companies owned by Rupert Murdoch; and evidence disclosed to select committees, court hearings and to the Leveson Inquiry.

Behind layers of official secrecy and public denial, the reality was that the police knew a very great deal about the crimes which were being committed by powerful newspapers. It was years later that the scale of their knowledge finally emerged. Looking back, it is clear that the *Guardian* and others were uncovering only tiny fragments of the truth. This is the story of what the police had hidden in their files, as finally revealed.

It begins in June 2002, when a senior officer in the Metropolitan Police, Detective Chief Superintendent Dave Cook, a clever Scot, then aged forty-three, was asked to appear on the BBC *Crimewatch* programme. His job was to appeal to the public for help in the long-running effort to catch the people responsible for slamming an axe into the head of the private investigator Daniel Morgan in a south London pub car park fifteen years earlier.

The broadcast had a hidden agenda. Secretly, the Met's anti-corruption squad were starting a new investigation into the murder and into the links between bent police officers and their two prime suspects – Jonathan Rees and Sid Fillery, who now ran the murdered man's agency, Southern Investigations. They wanted to use *Crimewatch* to announce a £50,000 reward in the hope of provoking one or more of the suspects to discuss it – and to record them with covert listening devices. Cook had been chosen as a frontman, to conceal the role of the anti-corruption officers. He was a natural choice, a specialist homicide detective who also happened to have been married for several years to one of the presenters of *Crimewatch*, a serving detective sergeant named Jacqui Hames. On 25 June, the day before the broadcast, an odd thing happened.

Scotland Yard received sensitive intelligence (probably from a phone-tap, although that has not been proved) which indicated that Sid Fillery had discussed Cook's forthcoming appearance with Alex Marunchak, the executive editor of the *News of the World*, and that Marunchak had agreed to 'sort him out'. That sounded very much like a conspiracy to pervert the course of justice and possibly a threat of violence. A few days later, Cook was warned by the Yard to watch his back. Several more odd things then happened.

A week later, on 3 July, as court documents later disclosed, somebody who was almost certainly Glenn Mulcaire called the finance department of Surrey police, where Cook had worked previously as head of CID, and, posing as an official from the Inland Revenue, tried to blag the detective's home address. He failed but evidently succeeded elsewhere. The following week, Cook noticed two vans hanging around his home, following him and his wife when they went out. He checked their numbers and found that both were leased to News International. Scotland Yard tasked a covert surveillance unit to follow the vans and then, using the pretext that one of them had a broken tail light, arranged for uniformed officers to stop it and question the driver, who turned out to be a photographer working for the *News of the World*.

Cook complained. Scotland Yard's director of communications, Dick Fedorcio, contacted the *News of the World* who claimed that they had been pursuing a straightforward story, that Cook was having an affair with Jacqui Hames – a claim much weakened by the fact that Cook and Hames were married with two children.

Later that year, Cook was appointed to formally take over the investigation of Daniel Morgan's murder. He raised his concerns about the *News of the World*'s surveillance with his commander, André Baker. Baker arranged a meeting, on 9 January 2003, between himself and Cook, Dick Fedorcio and the paper's then editor, Rebekah Brooks. Cook told her the story of the two vans, with the clear implication that her executive editor, directly or via others at the *News of the World*, had obtained his home address at the behest of a murder suspect and then organised the surveillance in order to discredit or harass him.

Cook went on to tell the meeting that there was further evidence that Marunchak was a rogue journalist. He said that a former secretary at Southern Investigations had made a sworn statement that the agency had paid thousands of pounds to Marunchak, who had used the money to pay off his credit card and, she believed, his son's school fees. Clearly it was possible that Marunchak had been defrauding the *News of the World* by authorising unearned payments for Southern who had then passed him the surplus; or that he was taking bribes to send business in Southern's direction. And then, to Cook's alarm . . . nothing was done.

In sworn evidence to the Leveson Inquiry, Fedorcio described how he had led Rebekah Brooks from the meeting to a drinks party then taking place at Scotland Yard and left her talking to the then commissioner, Sir John Stevens. Scotland Yard conducted no investigation into what could have been interpreted as a conspiracy to pervert the course of justice in a murder inquiry and an allegation of fraud. Marunchak remained in post as one of the most senior journalists at the *News of the World*.

Much later, Dave Cook's team discovered that the Yard's anti-corruption command were sitting on the hundreds of hours of conversation which had been secretly recorded in Southern's office in 1999, revealing Marunchak's deep involvement in buying information from Southern's network of corrupt police contacts. The tapes included another suggestion that Southern were recycling *News of the World* money to him: Rees described how he had fallen out with Marunchak and warned him that 'your fucking paper will get fucking tipped off about who gets fucking backhanders'. Cook's team also received unconfirmed intelligence reports claiming that Marunchak had bribed an officer in Cambridge to get information on the murder of two young girls, Jessica Chapman and Holly Wells, in Soham in August 2002; and that he was close to the former Met detective John Ross, who was a conduit for press stories provided by corrupt officers in London.

Most serious, Cook's officers found a statement which had been sworn by a close associate of Daniel Morgan who said that in the weeks before he was murdered, Morgan had contacted a Sunday newspaper to try to sell information about very powerful corrupt officers. There was no evidence that this involved Marunchak, let alone that he had tipped off Rees; but Cook's team sent a detailed report to the Directorate of Professional Standards, suggesting that Marunchak be investigated. Nothing was done.

Later it emerged that back in 2000, the team which had placed the listening device in Southern's office had been equally disturbed by what they heard. Their operational head, Detective Superintendent Bob Quick, had sent his own report to the Directorate of Professional Standards, urging them to investigate the payment of police bribes by newspapers. Nothing was done.

March 2003 was a bad month for News International.

In London, Rebekah Brooks, now editing the *Sun*, gave evidence to the media select committee in the House of Commons and admitted that 'we have paid the police for information in the past'. She appeared to have no idea that this was an admission of crime. Sitting beside her, Andy Coulson, who had just replaced her as editor of the *News of the World*, dived in to rescue her, explaining that they would do this only if it were in the public interest. He appeared to have no idea that this made no difference – bribing police was still a crime.

It was in that same month that investigators from the Information Commissioner's Office raided Steve Whittamore and seized his cache of paperwork detailing his dealings with Fleet Street. This proved to be a turning point in the development of three separate police investigations. All three exposed potentially illegal information-gathering on behalf of the Murdoch papers and other news organisations.

The first was *Operation Reproof*, which had been opened in January 2002, when a businessman in Devon complained that he was being blackmailed by people who had obtained details of his criminal record from a private investigator. Within months, police had identified seventeen police personnel who were suspected of leaking confidential data to a network of half a dozen PIs. At least one of the PIs – Glen Lawson of Abbey Investigations in Newcastle upon Tyne – was working for newspapers. He had commissioned searches of police records for information on three Labour MPs: the then chancellor, Gordon Brown; his close ally, Nick Brown; and the MP for Reading, Martin Salter. Lawson would not identify his client, but police noted that he had made the searches at a time when the *News of the World* were attacking Salter for daring to oppose Rebekah Brooks's controversial campaign to introduce 'Sarah's Law', requiring police to disclose the home addresses of convicted paedophiles.

Total number of journalists interviewed: zero.

Operation Motorman was a spin-off from this inquiry. Reproof raided a PI called Chris Dewse based in Horley, Surrey, and found a host of evidence that he had been obtaining data from two men who worked for the DVLA and that he was then selling some of it to Steve Whittamore. They passed this to the ICO, who organised the raid on Whittamore in March 2003 – and who then failed to interview any of the journalists who had commissioned his criminal activity. Internal ICO paperwork confirms that they simply chose not to confront the power of the newspapers, recording that a senior barrister told them that although there was evidence to support a prosecution of the press, the prospect of Fleet Street fighting them in a series of expensive pre-trial hearings persuaded them to accept the barrister's advice that 'the cost would be excessive both to investigate and prosecute'.

Total number of journalists interviewed: zero.

Operation Glade was a spin-off from Motorman. Searching through Whittamore's paperwork, the ICO soon found evidence that the network had a source with access to Scotland Yard's sensitive computer records. They handed their evidence to the Metropolitan Police, whose anti-corruption command in August 2003 set up Glade and raided Whittamore for a second time. Glade decided to dig deeper, which soon took them back to Rebekah Brooks's bold admission to the select committee about making payments to serving officers. Police sources claim that they tapped her phone. Brooks has told friends that she believes this happened. Glade also dug into the web of 'dark arts' contacts set up by her assistant editor, Greg Miskiw (later to surface in calls to the *Guardian* from the source known as Mango). By 10 November 2003, an internal Glade log recorded: 'Evidence exists which implicates a number of journalists in the offence of conspiracy to corrupt.' Anticipating a hostile reaction from Fleet Street, they called in Dick Fedorcio and one of his press officers for advice about how to handle any media storm. In January 2004, they interviewed as suspects seven journalists from the Mirror Group, the *Daily Mail* and News International, including Greg Miskiw (just as Mango later alleged). All admitted hiring Whittamore, but denied knowing that he used illegal methods to obtain his information. In March 2004, Glade sent a file to the CPS, who decided there was insufficient evidence to justify a charge against any of them.

Total number of journalists interviewed: seven. Total journalists prosecuted: zero.

In December 2004, twenty-one months after publicly admitting that her journalists had paid police officers in the past, Rebekah Brooks dined at the exclusive Ivy restaurant in London with the commissioner of the Metropolitan Police, Sir John Stevens.

In November 2005, there was a strange and notorious incident when Rebekah Brooks was arrested after her husband, the TV actor Ross Kemp, reported that she had assaulted him. She was held overnight in a cell. According to unconfirmed police sources, she was released in the morning without being interviewed, an apparent breach of normal procedure.

And then in early 2006 there was *Operation Caryatid*, Scotland Yard's inquiry into the hacking at the *News of the World* – an inquiry, we now know, that uncovered very much more than was ever admitted when Goodman and Mulcaire were jailed.

While the court and the world were told of only eight victims, the reality was that, in a brief and superficial search of the 11,000 pages of paperwork seized from Mulcaire's office, detectives had found the names of 418 people. A senior Caryatid officer, DCI Keith Surtees, had no doubt what this meant, recording in his daily log on 10 August 2006: 'I take the view that the research work is and has been undertaken with the intention of eventually obtaining access to voicemail messages.' If they had completed a thorough search of the seized material, they would have found that it contained references to 6,349 people who had been targeted by Mulcaire over the previous five years. They also said nothing public about the audio recordings of 745 hacked messages which they found in Mulcaire's possession including some which had been left by David Blunkett when he was Home Secretary and ultimately responsible for Scotland Yard.

And while Goodman alone from the *News of the World* faced prosecution, Caryatid found clear clues that other journalists were involved. Having noticed that Mulcaire wrote 'Clive' in the top left-hand corner of his notes whenever he was working for Goodman, Caryatid went on to find twenty-eight other names written in the same position on his notes about non-royal targets, including the first names of Greg Miskiw, Ian Edmondson, Neville Thurlbeck and James Weatherup. Studying Mulcaire's phone records, they observed a regular pattern, that the investigator would call the paper, hack a target's voicemail and then call the paper again. The implication was clear.

It was not just that detectives had reason to believe that others at the paper were receiving hacked material from their investigator; Caryatid had also discovered that journalists themselves were probably listening to voicemail. They had uncovered phone company records which showed that on hundreds of occasions, target phones had been accessed from two particular numbers which belonged to News International. They established that these were 'hub' numbers, a billing arrangement which allowed the company to collate numerous handsets and landline extensions into one bill with one collective number. A Caryatid detective sergeant, Mark Maberly, later told Leveson that he had identified three *News of the World* journalists he would like to have questioned.

Scotland Yard opted not only to stay silent about these findings, they also chose not to mention two significant facts about their inquiry. The first was that they had been obstructed repeatedly by News International. This started in brazen form on the day Clive Goodman was arrested in August 2006, when they sent a team of specialist officers to the *News of the World* to use their standard power to search the premises of anybody who has been arrested for an indictable offence. As four officers started to collect paperwork from Goodman's desk, they were confronted by executives who argued that they had no right to search a journalist's property, which has some special protections in law. The officers hesitated. Somebody called in a couple of photographers who started taking pictures. The inspector in charge reported that he feared they would be attacked. Outside the building, more officers were barred from getting through the front door.

Three News International lawyers turned up, took the four officers into a conference room and persuaded them to stop searching Goodman's desk and, in particular, not to seize his computer or the contents of his locked personal safe. The police argued that nevertheless they must be allowed to search the accounts department, which contained material that was not journalistic. They went to do so but, according to evidence at the Leveson Inquiry, the managing editor, Stuart Kuttner, joined the lawyers and physically blocked them. The raid was abandoned.

Later in the inquiry, Caryatid wrote to News International to ask them to hand over a list of material, including records of Mulcaire's work; information from Clive Goodman's computer and safe; and the detail of which extensions and handsets had made calls via the 'hub' numbers, as well as the owners of numbers which had been called by Mulcaire before and after he accessed a target's voicemail. Through their lawyers, News International agreed to co-operate but then failed to hand over every item, with one exception. They disclosed details of the total of £12,300 which Clive Goodman had paid in cash to Mulcaire, which had been recorded internally as payments to the non-existent source called David Alexander. This proved to be the cornerstone of News International's cover-up.

UK law allows police to go to court for a production order to compel journalists to hand over evidence if they fail to co-operate with an inquiry, and Caryatid had enclosed a draft order in their letter. The officer who dealt with this, Detective Sergeant Mark Maberly, later told Leveson that he suspected he was being 'fobbed off' by News International. Leveson himself concluded that the company were offering only the 'veneer of co-operation'. But senior officers chose to take no further action. The draft production order was never used.

The second point on which Scotland Yard chose to stay silent was the key fact that in the early autumn of 2006, a month or two after arresting Goodman and Mulcaire, they had closed down Operation Caryatid without completing the investigation. The precise date when they did this is not known: they made no record of the decision nor of their justification for doing so.

It was as part of this decision, it eventually emerged, that they agreed with prosecutors to contact all potential victims. The police themselves would warn all those in four 'national security' categories – royal, military, police, political – while the phone companies would be told to warn others who they would identify from their own call data.

If they had mentioned this plan in public, they might well have been told, as Lord Justice Leveson eventually concluded, that this was 'poorly thought out' and 'lacked coherence' since it left out any potential victims whose names had not been found in the initial search of Mulcaire's paperwork; and, in relying on the phone companies to find the evidence, it also excluded the bulk of Mulcaire's targets over his years of hacking since the companies are allowed to keep call data for only twelve months.

In the event, they simply failed to execute the plan. They succeeded in warning all of the royal targets – nineteen of them (as distinct from the three who were mentioned in court). They then failed to warn the two military targets they had identified; failed even to warn all senior police including their own commissioner, Sir Ian Blair; and failed to warn most of the seventeen politicians. That included leaving in the dark three Home Secretaries – David Blunkett, Charles Clarke and the incumbent at the time, John Reid – in spite of the fact that they were responsible for police and the Security Service, and John Prescott and two of his staff, who were handling even more sensitive material. Of the 418 people they had identified as targets, they actually only warned twenty-eight, including Rebekah Brooks.

Beyond that, they also failed to tell the phone companies to contact the apparent victims among their customers. O2 took the initiative and informed some forty customers, but the other companies stuck to the standard police requirement that all information connected to their inquiries must be kept secret.

Having decided in the early autumn to close down Caryatid, they stood by that decision on 23 November when they received a delayed report from their forensic specialists about the contents of Mulcaire's computers. This revealed that he had selected 320 victims as 'special projects', hacking not only their own voicemail but also those of their friends and family. These included their former deputy assistant commissioner, Brian Paddick, but they did not tell him that. Even more significant, the report contained one line which was bristling with threat to Scotland Yard: 'It is also believed attempts may have been made to corrupt serving officers and misuse the Police National Computer.'

The allegation of corruption of their own officers was clearly very serious. Worse, the signs of corruption included evidence that in some way Mulcaire and/or the *News of the World* had penetrated the ring of security around the Witness Protection Programme, to uncover the new identities of witnesses and, in some cases, offenders who were deemed to be at serious physical risk. This is believed to have included Robert Thomson and Jon Venables, tabloid hate figures who had been convicted in 1993, as ten-year-old boys, of the abduction and murder in Liverpool of the two-year-old James Bulger. Caryatid sent a warning to the Witness Protection Programme and conducted no further inquiries themselves.

This was not the only material in Caryatid's hands which hinted that the *News of the World* had been paying bribes. In Glenn Mulcaire's home, they found whiteboards on his walls which included the daily security passwords for mobile phone companies, supposedly known only to trusted employees. Caryatid made no attempt to find out how Mulcaire had obtained them. In Clive Goodman's home, they found fifteen internal phone directories from the royal household, all of them confidential, some of them containing sensitive details of the private phone lines of the royal family as well as security plans for the protection of Kensington Palace. Caryatid made no attempt to find out how Goodman had obtained them and did not even inform the Palace that he had done so.

Set aside for a moment the question of why the police acted as they did. The immediate point is that by opting to say nothing, the effect was to enable the success of a dishonest conspiracy that was taking place outside Scotland Yard, at the headquarters of Rupert Murdoch's UK company.

To begin with, it all focused on Clive Goodman. On Thursday 10 August 2006, two days after his arrest, Goodman was visited at his home in Putney, west London, by the *News of the World*'s clean-up specialist, the managing editor, Stuart Kuttner. Goodman confronted him with a series of alarming claims. According to notes which Kuttner made at the time, the royal editor told him that Mulcaire had claimed to be getting help in hacking the Palace phones from a contact in the Security Service and that he had 'told Andy this at the start'; the police thought that there were other targets of Mulcaire's hacking, including the paedophile former rock star Gary Glitter and the former Serbian president, Slobodan Milosevic; they had spotted how Mulcaire would speak to the *News of the World* before and after some hacks; and they were looking at the paper's payment records as a way of possibly widening their inquiry. The only good news was that Goodman had refused to answer police questions. So far. That afternoon Kuttner reported back to Coulson.

Giving evidence years later, Goodman described how over the following few weeks, he felt an increasing pressure from News International to take all the blame for the paper's hacking on his own shoulders. He said he was surprised that his own solicitor, Henri Brandman, who was being paid by News International, suggested he might say that he was acting 'under stress – some kind of lone wolf'. He also claimed that Coulson phoned him, agreed to suspend him on full pay and then suggested that he had had some kind of contact with the police or the Home Office and that they did not want to send him to prison as long as he admitted his guilt and got the case out of the way.

Goodman and Coulson were friends: Coulson had been one of the few people from work who had been invited to his wedding two months earlier. But now the royal editor was so worried that he was being set up to take the blame for all of the *News of the World*'s hacking that he found himself an insurance policy: he accessed his office email account and downloaded messages which recorded him discussing hacked stories with his editors, including Coulson, and which reflected Coulson's approval of the 'David Alexander' payments for the royal hacking. Apparently aware that a news organisation might be willing to hack into a computer, he took the precaution of doing this in an Internet café.

Coulson was evidently just as suspicious. He asked to meet Goodman

Rebekah Brooks makes her connection with the then prime minister, Tony Blair, in 2004

Rupert Murdoch with his UK chief executive, Les Hinton, at the Fleet Street church, St Brides, in June 2005. Coulson and Brooks in the background

Party power: Wendi Murdoch and Rupert Murdoch at News Corp's 2007 summer gathering with the then prime minister, Gordon Brown, and Sarah Brown

Above: Three former editors of the *News of the World*: Piers Morgan, Rebekah Brooks and Andy Coulson

Right: Right-hand man: David Cameron in London with Andy Coulson in April 2009, a year before Cameron became prime minister

Before it all went wrong: David Cameron and Rupert Murdoch at the wedding of Rebekah and Charlie Brooks, June 2009

Left: The royal editor meets his fate: Clive Goodman on the way to being sentenced to prison, 26 January 2007

Above: Formula One racing president Max Mosley after winning his privacy action against the *News of the World*, July 2008

FREE Spanish phrasebook

Spanish phrasebook 4

£0.90
Thursday 09.07.09
Published
in London and
Manchester
guardian.co.uk

Today family & relationships
Tomorrow
business & politics

theguardian

Revealed: Murdoch's £1m bill for hiding dirty tricks

● Tory PR chief under fire over tabloid hacking

● Politicians and celebrities among victims

Nick Davies

Rupert Murdoch's News Group Newspapers has paid out more than £1m to settle legal cases that threatened to reveal evidence of his journalists' repeated involvement in the use of criminal methods to get stories.

The payments secured secrecy over out-of-court settlements in three cases that threatened to expose evidence of Murdoch journalists using private investigators who illegally hacked into the mobile phone messages of numerous public figures to gain unlawful access to confidential personal data, including tax records, social security files, bank statements and itemised phone bills. Cabinet ministers, MPs, actors and sports stars were all targets of the private investigators.

Today, the Guardian reveals details of the suppressed evidence, which may open the door to hundreds more legal actions by victims of News Group, the Murdoch company that publishes the News of the World and the Sun, as well as provoking police inquiries into reporters who were involved and the senior executives responsible for them. The evidence also poses difficult questions for:

● Conservative leader David Cameron's director of communications, Andy Coulson, who was deputy editor and then editor of the News of the World when, the suppressed evidence shows, journalists for whom he was responsible were engaging in hundreds of apparently illegal acts.

● Murdoch executives who, albeit in good faith, misled a parliamentary select committee, the Press Complaints Commission and the public.

● The Metropolitan police, which did not alert all those whose phones were targeted, and the Crown Prosecution Service, which did not pursue all possible charges against News Group personnel.

Andy Coulson, David Cameron's director of communications and the former editor of the News of the World

● The Press Complaints Commission, which claimed to have conducted an investigation, but failed to uncover any evidence of illegal activity.

The suppressed legal cases are linked to the jailing in January 2007 of a News of the World reporter, Clive Goodman, for hacking into the mobile phones of three royal staff, an offence under the Regulation of Investigatory Powers Act. At the time, News International said it knew of no other journalist who was involved in hacking phones and that Goodman had acted without their knowledge.

But one senior source at the Met told

the Guardian that during the Goodman inquiry, officers found evidence of News Group staff using private investigators who hacked into "thousands" of mobile phones. Another source with direct knowledge of the police findings put the figure at "two or three thousand" mobiles. They suggest that MPs from all three parties and cabinet ministers, including former deputy prime minister John Prescott and former culture secretary Tessa Jowell, were among the targets.

Last night, Prescott said: "I think Mr Cameron should be thinking of getting rid of Coulson."

News International has always maintained it had no knowledge of phone hacking by anybody acting on its behalf.

Murdoch told Bloomberg news last night that he knew nothing about the payments. "If that had happened I would know about it," he said.

A private investigator who had worked for News Group, Glenn Mulcaire, was also jailed in January 2007. He admitted hacking into the phones of five other targets, including the chief

6-7»

Continued on page 2 »

Reaction

"I think it is one of the most significant media stories of modern times. It was systemic throughout the News of the World. This newsroom was out of control."
Andrew Neil

"The whole thing is deplorable. Mr Cameron should be thinking of getting rid of Coulson."
John Prescott

"There is a question as to whether this news group ... is liable to other actions. The lesson is they shouldn't presume this will only be dealt with in criminal courts, but it will also be dealt with in civil courts."
Simon Hughes

Amid G8's rubble and aftershocks, Brown is in his element

Patrick Wintour

It was a late start by Gordon Brown's standards. He burst onto his British Airways chartered plane bound for the G8 summit in L'Aquila, Italy, a little before 6.30am.

Sarah Brown, recently appointed as the prime minister's special envoy to Planet Normal, cheerfully wrote on her blog that she and her husband had been "up at the crack of dawn", though by the time she climbed out of bed her husband had almost certainly fired off several waves of emails across Whitehall.

Brown has never got up at the crack of dawn. He is always up before it,

especially if a world summit on the economy is in prospect. Brown is in his element at the G8.

He knows the detail of IMF structures backwards, the future trajectory of oil prices, the debt-GDP ratio of Papua New Guinea and the intricacies of climate change technology transfer funds. He has also been at this game for so long he hardly needs civil servants to come

'Italy's leader has eased the pain by providing luxurious, silk bed linen – a Berlusconi speciality'

with him, and with admirable seriousness of purpose, he drives his G8 colleagues through with his commitment and knowledge.

But at this summit, he has come up against another irresistible force in the shape of the mercurial Italian prime minister, Silvio Berlusconi, a man who has organised a playboy summit of high comedy, chaos and emotion.

The summit, including a 25-nation guest list and 5,000 or so hangers-on, was shifted in April from a luxurious island off Sardinia to the dusty, earthquake-hit town of L'Aquila. Fifty thousand lost their homes in the capital city of Abruzzo.

The logo for the summit still depicts swimming Sardinian turtles, even

though the event is taking place in some functional financial police barracks in the heart of the mountains - the kind of spartan quarters to which voters would like to see Britain's errant MPs consigned in future.

Italy's leader has eased the pain by providing some luxurious, silk bed linen - a Berlusconi speciality.

In the conference area, poignant pictures of the many Renaissance gems destroyed by the earthquake are displayed. Blue tents still pockmark the area, housing many residents who believe Berlusconi has not kept his promises to help them. One poster on a hilltop reads "Yes we camp".

Continued on page 2 »

'There is a distinct St Augustine feel about financial reform plans: O Lord help me be tough on the City - but not yet'

Will Hutton
Comment
page 29 »

The story that started it all – the Guardian splash Nick Davies' first hacking article on 9 July 2009

Assistant Commissioner John Yates 'establishes the facts' after Nick Davies' first hacking story, 9 July 2009

Deputy Assistant Commissioner Sue Akers explains Operation Weeting to the home affairs select committee, July 2011

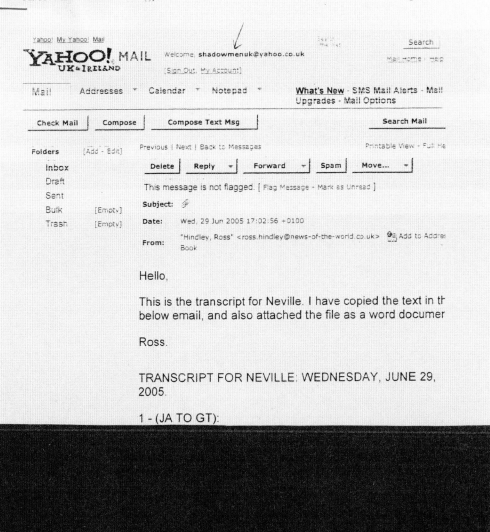

Yahoo! My Yahoo! Mail

YAHOO! MAIL
UK & IRELAND

Welcome, **shadowmenuk@yahoo.co.uk**
[Sign Out, My Account]

Search

Mail Home - Help

| Mail | Addresses ▾ | Calendar ▾ | Notepad ▾ | **What's New** - SMS Mail Alerts - Mail Upgrades - Mail Options |

| Check Mail | Compose | Compose Text Msg | Search Mail |

Folders [Add - Edit]

Previous | Next | Back to Messages   Printable View - Full He

Inbox
Draft
Sent
Bulk   [Empty]
Trash   [Empty]

| Delete | Reply ▾ | Forward ▾ | Spam | Move... ▾ |

This message is not flagged. [Flag Message - Mark as Unread]

Subject: ✐
Date: Wed, 29 Jun 2005 17:02:56 +0100
From: "Hindley, Ross" <ross.hindley@news-of-the-world.co.uk> 📇 Add to Addres Book

Hello,

This is the transcript for Neville. I have copied the text in th below email, and also attached the file as a word documer

Ross.

TRANSCRIPT FOR NEVILLE: WEDNESDAY, JUNE 29, 2005.

1 - (JA TO GT):

2 - (MT TO GT):

The notorious 'email for Neville', as redacted by Nick Davies' children

NEWS OF THE WORLD

NORTHERN OFFICE, NEWS INTERNATIONAL NEWSPAPERS LIMITED
FIRST FLOOR, 111 PICCADILLY, MANCHESTER, M1 2HY
TEL: 0161-228 0210 FAX: 0161-228 2927

THE NEWS OF THE WORLD undertakes not to publish any information/ pictures supplied by PAUL WILLIAMS in connection with ████████████████ PFA Chief Executive Gordon Taylor.

The News of the World agrees to pay a minimum sum of £7,000.00 on publication of the story based on information provided by Mr. Williams. This figure will be re-negotiable on the basis of prominence given to the story.

Signed......

Dated: 4th February 2005

The contract which Greg Miskiw gave Glenn Mulcaire in his false name, Paul Williams

Above: Nick Davies hands over paperwork to the House of Commons select committee for culture, media and sport, July 2009

Left: Alan Rusbridger, editor of the *Guardian*

but, according to one source close to him, he feared that his royal editor would secretly tape record him and so he refused to go to Goodman's house and rehearsed his lines to make sure they were safe before finally meeting him in the Café Rouge restaurant in Wimbledon. He was right to be suspicious: Goodman secretly taped the conversation (although he made a mess of it). Recalling this meeting years later, Goodman claimed that Coulson once more had implied that he or somebody else at News International was in touch with the police attempting to use their influence to ensure that he would not go to prison. Goodman said his editor urged him again to plead guilty, assuring him that he would still have a job: 'You can be one of the people who come back.' He added that Coulson had encouraged him to say that he had 'gone off the reservation' adding: 'All you've got to say is that you're a lone wolf.' Goodman said that he noted the echo of his own solicitor's words and that this 'put the fear of God into him' that he was being set up, although a judge later ruled that this fear was unfounded.

There is no evidence to confirm Coulson's claim that he or somebody close to him had a contact in the police. But internal paperwork from the Crown Prosecution Service does reveal that on 22 August – eight days after the meeting in the Café Rouge – a senior prosecutor sent an email indicating that it was unlikely that anyone other than Goodman and Mulcaire would be charged.

Certainly, News International did their best to find out what the police were doing. On 15 September, a Caryatid officer, DCI Keith Surtees, met Rebekah Brooks to tell her that her own phone had been hacked and to ask if she would act as a witness for the prosecution. She declined to do so but attempted to discover as much as she could and reported back to News International's in-house lawyer, Tom Crone. Crone in turn sent a worrying email to Coulson: police had a list of more than a hundred victims; evidence that Mulcaire could have been paid as much as £1 million by the *News of the World*; and no evidence of his being paid by anybody else. Searching Mulcaire's office and home, Crone reported, police had seized 'numerous recordings' as well as verbatim notes of voicemail messages. They had spotted a story in the *News of the World* which reproduced precisely a phrase from a voicemail between the actor Hugh Grant and his then partner, Jemima Khan.

But Crone also reported better news, that 'the cops' were thinking along the same reassuring lines as the prosecutors: 'They suggested they are not widening the case to include other *NoW* people but would do so if they got direct evidence, say *NoW* journalists directly accessing the voicemails. (This is what did for Clive). . . There are no recordings of *NoW* people speaking to GM [Mulcaire] or accessing voicemails. They do have GM's phone records which show sequences of contacts before and after accesses. Obviously, they don't have the content of the calls, so this is, at best, circumstantial.'

All looked well – as long as Clive Goodman kept his silence. Over the next two months, Crone made it his business to attend Goodman's meetings with his lawyers, often in the teeth of Goodman's objections, reporting back to Coulson. When the CPS in late October served Goodman with five lever-arch files of evidence, Crone succeeded in persuading Henri Brandman to give him a copy. Goodman later insisted that this was directly contrary to his instructions. The file, which was also seen by Coulson, revealed just how close the police had come to implicating others at the *News of the World*. It included contracts with Mulcaire which had been signed by Greg Miskiw and Neville Thurlbeck. In early November, Coulson spoke on the phone with Goodman, who made a better job this time of using his tape recorder, capturing their nervous references to the material in the prosecution file and their worry that Mulcaire was 'hostile' and might not 'keep schtum' as well as the editor's seductive reassurance: 'You need looking after, and that's what we'll do . . . We're on the same side here . . . You have it from me that, you know, I absolutely see a future for you here.'

Goodman claims that, with a key court hearing due at the end of November, he felt a persistent pressure to admit his own guilt while concealing the guilt of others. He wrote a 'proof of evidence' which named senior executives, including Coulson, as conspirators in the hacking. By the time he submitted it to the court, that material had been deleted. He says Crone made it clear that he could keep his job only if he agreed not to implicate others at the paper. After Crone attended one of his legal meetings, Goodman emailed Henri Brandman to complain that Crone had delivered 'a fairly crude carrot and stick from the *NoW*'. He added: 'I felt more threatened by the message he was asked to deliver today than I had been by much of the prosecution case.'

With Goodman apparently accepting that he should hold his tongue, Tom Crone then warned the editor that Mulcaire, who understood that his work for the paper was finished, had hired an employment lawyer who was making 'a thinly disguised blackmail threat', and advised that they should offer the investigator at least a year's money as a severance deal 'despite the concerns and lack of enforceability re a confidentiality clause'.

It was clear that in Mulcaire's mind, the most acute anxiety was financial. The police and prosecutors had to decide how much of his past income had been derived from crime, so that it could be confiscated by the courts. They had evidence to suggest that, as DCI Surtees told the Leveson Inquiry, 'a substantial amount of his time was spent in illegal activity'. A confiscation on that scale would bring ruin on Mulcaire and his family.

As it was, police and prosecutors agreed to confiscate only the £12,300 cash which had been paid to him as 'David Alexander'. This had the advantage of being uncontentious: there was no dispute from any quarter that this money had been earned through crime. It also had the effect of giving Mulcaire a motive to forget all thoughts of speaking out on the true scale of his crime for the paper.

On 29 November, Goodman and Mulcaire went to court and pleaded guilty. It was a nervous time for the *News of the World*. On the eve of the hearing, Coulson exchanged emails with Crone and others, debating whether to make a public apology to the victims who were to be named in court, anxiously reflecting that this might provoke Goodman and Mulcaire into 'reacting badly'. They decided to say nothing. As Goodman and Mulcaire pleaded guilty, Coulson used email to discuss with Rebekah Brooks the merits of leaking the fact that Brooks herself had been a victim of the hacking, with Coulson arguing that it was a mistake. 'It's all going so well,' he said – an odd remark from an editor seeing a senior employee pleading guilty to crime. Later, as Goodman prepared to be interviewed by the probation service in advance of his sentencing, Crone emailed Coulson, worrying that Goodman might not stick to 'the preferred line'. Goodman and Mulcaire stuck to the script, both of them rewarded with continuing pay from the *News of the World* in spite of having now admitted criminal conduct.

In truth, Goodman did discreetly wander a little from the script. When his probation officer wrote his report for the court, he included one killer line which Goodman had given him about the hacking of the royal phones: 'He contends that his senior editor knows about and gave tacit agreement to the conduct in question, willingly opening a revenue source with the paper's financial department to pay for Mulcaire's activity.' At the sentencing hearing, in January 2007, the judge said he was particularly interested in that line, but he did not read it out, and nor did anybody else. Nothing more was said in public.

By the time the two men were jailed in January 2007, Stuart Kuttner, Rebekah Brooks, Andy Coulson and Tom Crone all had good reason to conclude that Goodman was not the only one of their journalists who was involved and that Mulcaire's hacking was widespread. Coulson resigned, accepting responsibility but denying all knowledge of the crime. The obvious conclusion was that he and some of the others had chosen to conceal what they knew – to cover up. And the objective fact – regardless of motive – is that Scotland Yard's behaviour allowed them to succeed.

For an outsider, all this provided reasonable grounds to cry 'foul' – to speculate that Scotland Yard must have compromised its work because it feared falling out with the country's most powerful news organisation; or even because someone somewhere was receiving bribes or wanted to conceal the history of bribes. That speculation found more fuel as detail emerged of the close and friendly relationship between the Metropolitan Police and Murdoch's journalists. They were particularly close to Assistant Commissioner Andy Hayman, who was ultimately responsible for Operation Caryatid.

Andy Hayman is a controversial figure. Some of his former colleagues dismiss him as a 'yob' and a 'wide boy', who spent too much time and police money in bars and restaurants. On one occasion, he took eight fellow officers for lunch in a West End restaurant and spent £556 from the public purse, including £181 on alcohol. His decision, on resigning from Scotland Yard, to become a columnist for Murdoch's *Times* proved to be only one part of an unusually friendly relationship with journalists. He told Leveson that, as part of an authorised effort to build bridges with the press, he had shared breakfasts, lunches, dinners and drinks with them. His commissioner, Sir Ian Blair, wrote in his memoirs that some of this had worried him: 'I began to pick up that Andy seemed to be spending a great deal of time with the press. Quite early on, there were rumours that he was briefing in a careless and sometimes disloyal manner, although I never had any proof.'

Among these journalists was the *News of the World*'s crime correspondent, Lucy Panton, the wife of a Scotland Yard detective. Hayman had phone calls, private meetings and occasional dinners with her. He also knew Rebekah Brooks and other senior people from News International. He continued this contact even while his own officers were investigating the hacking.

On 26 April 2006, four months into Caryatid's inquiry, Hayman went to the trendy Soho House club in central London. He was accompanied by Dick Fedorcio. The two of them had a private dinner with Andy Coulson and his deputy editor, Neil Wallis – the two men who ran the paper which was suspected of crime by one of Hayman's own teams. Six months later, after Caryatid had decided to stop their investigation but before Goodman and Mulcaire had said whether they would plead guilty or not, Hayman spent two hours drinking with Neil Wallis.

Hayman insists that he did not discuss the hacking inquiry in any way on either occasion. There is no direct evidence to contradict him. But even on its best interpretation, these meetings seem to suggest a degree of friendship between a senior officer and the target of his detectives' work, an easy assumption that there was no reason to treat News International as a suspect organisation in spite of its track record of obstructing his officers. At the Leveson Inquiry, Hayman acknowledged that his decision to go and work for *The Times* after resigning under a cloud of scandal could be seen as 'ethically difficult'.

It may or may not be important that crime reporters suggest that while Hayman was still an assistant commissioner, they were aware of rumours that he was having affairs, one of which was with a woman who worked for the Independent Police Complaints Commission. Since the IPCC at the time were investigating the role of Hayman's officers in the shooting of the Brazilian student Jean Charles de Menezes, who had been mistaken for an al-Qaeda terrorist, this appeared to create a genuine public interest in publishing a story. They published nothing, leaving Hayman with an implicit debt to them.

Hayman's personal closeness to the press was part of a wider set of links between the top of Scotland Yard and Fleet Street. Ian Blair's predecessor as commissioner, John Stevens, had decided that the Met was taking an unfair battering in the press and set out to build closer links with them. He had frequent meetings with editors, columnists and reporters. When his term ended in January 2005, Stevens was hired as a columnist, for up to £7,000 a column, by the *News of the World*. His work was ghostwritten for him by the deputy editor, Neil Wallis.

To build these bridges to Fleet Street, Stevens had relied on the contacts of Dick Fedorcio, who was in constant contact with journalists, including those at News International. This was a natural and inevitable part of his job, but the Leveson Inquiry heard evidence which indicated that Fedorcio may have been particularly close to Rupert Murdoch's titles. He had hired ten former News International journalists to work for him; in July 2005, when Ian Blair was looking for somewhere for his fifteen-year-old son to get a week's work experience, Fedorcio set it up with the *Sun*; when Lucy Panton from the *News of the World* was at Scotland Yard one day, under pressure to file a story, he allowed her to use his personal computer and email; when Rebekah Brooks was looking for a horse, it was Fedorcio, with Ian Blair's knowledge, who arranged for her to be loaned a retired police animal; during the Caryatid inquiry, in June 2006, Fedorcio and Ian Blair had a meeting with Rebekah Brooks; three months later, after Goodman and Mulcaire had been arrested, Fedorcio took the then deputy commissioner, Sir Paul Stephenson, to dinner with Neil Wallis. On 29 November 2006, the day that Goodman and Mulcaire entered their guilty pleas at the Old Bailey, Rebekah Brooks was at Scotland Yard with Fedorcio.

Sir Ian told the Leveson Inquiry: 'I have nothing to suggest that any individual took a decision based on an overestimate of the importance of the influence of any organisation. The problem is that the levels of contact with people from that organisation were so frequent that the defence of "It didn't matter" is very difficult to maintain.'

This close contact with News International fuelled speculation that Operation Caryatid must have been influenced in the company's favour. But the evidence points in a different direction.

Nearly five years after Caryatid ended, when the hacking scandal finally exploded in July 2011, the man directly in charge of the inquiry, Deputy Assistant Commissioner Peter Clarke, was called to explain himself to the House of Commons home affairs select committee. Later, he was called to the Leveson Inquiry. On both occasions, Clarke – a gruff, solid bear of a man with a reputation for total straightness – was a compelling witness who gave a clear and powerful account of his decision to stop the investigation. There were three key points.

First, and most important, Clarke said that his counter-terrorism branch had been overwhelmed with work aimed at preventing mass murder. This had been bad enough at the beginning of their inquiry into the hacking but, on the day after the arrests of Goodman and Mulcaire in August 2006, it had got significantly worse when they launched the biggest counter-terrorism operation in British history, Operation Overt, to deal with a plot to blow up nine passenger planes over the Atlantic. Desperate for resources, Clarke said he had had to stall some of his other terrorist inquiries and borrow 300 detectives from forces around the UK. By comparison, the inquiry into voicemail-hacking was no threat to anybody's life, and they had done enough to prosecute two offenders, to alert the public and government and to ensure that phone companies improved their security.

Second, he had considered and rejected the possibility of passing on the unfinished investigation to some other branch of Scotland Yard. It emerged that DCI Keith Surtees had been suggesting this since May but Clarke had decided that it would be unreasonable to pass so much work to another team which would be struggling with its own prior-ities, particularly as the arrests of Goodman and Mulcaire meant that others involved would have had a chance to destroy evidence.

Third, they had misunderstood the law (what later became known to the *Guardian* as the RIPA bollocks). Caryatid officers told Leveson that their whole approach to the investigation had been defined by advice from the CPS that the hacking of voicemail was an offence only if the message was hacked before it had been heard by the intended recipient. It turned out that at one early point, the CPS had given this advice, albeit in very tentative form; but that later, after they had checked with the lead prosecutor, David Perry QC, they told police that they had changed their view.

However, internal Caryatid logs showed that the lead investigator, Detective Chief Superintendent Phil Williams, and his team simply failed to take this new view on board. They continued to refer to the narrow view of the RIPA law as though it were correct and even arranged for one of the royal household, Jamie Lowther-Pinkerton, not to access his voicemail while they monitored Goodman and Mulcaire calling into his phone, precisely so that they could prove that the investigator was listening to the messages before his target. This misunderstanding significantly restricted their work.

Having heard the evidence of Caryatid officers and examined their logs, Lord Justice Leveson criticised some of their decisions but he concluded that they had always acted in good faith: 'I am entirely satisfied that each of the decisions taken was justified and based on reasoning that was clear, rational and entirely in keeping with the imperatives of the police at that time.'

He found that they had failed to pursue and interview suspects because they could not have done so without searching through all of the seized material and making hundreds of separate legal applications for call data, all of which was beyond their resources. They had failed to warn John Prescott and others because 'they took their eye off the ball'. They had agreed that Mulcaire should lose only £12,300 of his income but they had originally pressed for more to be confiscated.

It was not all simple. There were some thorny questions about whether the police had failed to alert the prosecutors as well as the public that there was evidence which appeared to implicate other journalists at the *News of the World*. The senior prosecutor, David Perry, told Leveson that when he met Caryatid officers a fortnight after the arrest of Goodman and Mulcaire, he had asked them whether there was any evidence to suggest that the editor, Andy Coulson, had been involved, and he had been told there was none. 'We also inquired whether there was any evidence connecting Mulcaire to other *NoW* journalists. Again, we were told there was not, and we never saw any such evidence.' Police witnesses replied that they had misunderstood Perry's question: they said they had thought he was asking whether there was evidence strong enough to justify a prosecution, not simply whether there was any evidence at all, and they had told Perry in general terms that others might be involved.

They were taxed too on their failure to hand prosecutors the email for Neville, which was to become central to the *Guardian's* inquiries and which appeared to be important evidence of Mulcaire's guilt in the hacking of Gordon Taylor's phone. They explained that the email was dated June 2005 while the conspiracy charge covered a period from November 2005. Yet the police had handed prosecutors the contract which Greg Miskiw had signed with Mulcaire for the Gordon Taylor story, which was dated even earlier, February 2005.

There was a similar question in the handling of evidence for another of the non-royal victims, the Liberal Democrat MP Simon Hughes. It emerged that Caryatid had handed prosecutors Mulcaire's notes about the royal victims with the telltale corner name, Clive; and yet in Simon Hughes's case, they had not handed over the notes, which carried corner names of three other *News of the World* journalists. Nor, contrary to common practice, had they shown this paperwork to Simon Hughes.

The police pointed out that they had given access to all of the unused material to the junior prosecution counsel, Louis Mably, but CPS witnesses told the Leveson Inquiry that Mably's sole task had been to check for any evidence which tended to undermine the prosecution, as the law required. He had not looked for anything which might have assisted a wider prosecution. Leveson accepted that these police decisions were part of the wider legitimate decision to limit and close down Caryatid. 'No evidence was concealed,' he concluded.

Finally, Leveson considered the cosy links between News International and some senior officers. The links were real. In the case of Andy Hayman, they were positively controversial, but Leveson found that there was no evidence that this had made any difference to Caryatid's activity.

However, there were signs that that was not for want of the Murdoch company trying. A solicitor who worked briefly for News International, Lawrence Abramson, told Leveson he had read internal emails which suggested 'quite an active involvement in Clive Goodman's prosecution, trying to influence the way the prosecution was being conducted or the defence being conducted'. Quite what this involved was never disclosed.

Leveson uncovered one incident which appeared at first to be linked. He published the email dated 15 September 2006 in which Tom Crone reported to his editor the information which 'the cops' had given to Rebekah Brooks about the progress of their inquiry.

Leveson confronted the potential implication: 'On the face of the email, it appeared that the police had given Mrs Brooks details of the prosecution strategy over and above that which any other victim of crime could expect to be given and it is suggested that, in doing so, the police were improperly alerting her to the state of the investigation by the Metropolitan Police, inviting her to take action internally.' Caryatid officers, however, explained to Leveson that they had spoken to Brooks simply because their evidence of Mulcaire hacking her voicemail was so clear that they thought they might name her in court as one of the non-royal victims. As Phil Williams put it: 'This is purely: "You are a potential victim. Would you like to join our prosecution?"' Brooks had declined the offer. Leveson accepted this. A subsequent investigation by the Independent Police Complaints Commission found that DCI Surtees had committed no crime nor any disciplinary offence.

One other sign that News International's power was having some impact on police thinking was reported much later by the *New York Times*, who said that within days of the arrest of Goodman and Mulcaire, several detectives had started to feel internal pressure. One described being approached by Dick Fedorcio's then deputy, Chris Webb, 'waving his arms up in the air, saying, "Wait a minute – let's talk about this."' The detective had rejected the request. Webb said he did not recall the alleged incident.

The bottom line here is that there is no evidence to support the idea of a deliberate conspiracy by Caryatid to help Murdoch's company. As Leveson said: 'I have no doubt that neither Peter Clarke nor any of the other officers were or would have been affected by any relationships between some senior officers and News International personnel. There is no evidence that the relevant officers approached their task from the standing point of seeking to deal with wrongdoers other than properly and so as to bring the force of the law to bear.'

Bribes had indeed been paid by News International journalists to Scotland Yard officers, but there was no evidence, nor even any hint of an allegation, that any had been paid to any Caryatid officer. The decisions which had limited the investigation all had reasonable explanations. The Caryatid team, Leveson said, had been 'robust, tenacious, well motivated and skilful'. He added: 'I have no doubt that they approached their task with complete integrity.'

There is no reason to doubt Leveson's conclusions. Questions remain whether the *News of the World* was able to use any of its contacts to find out what Caryatid was doing or even to influence its decisions. Beyond that, what the evidence revealed about Scotland Yard was something more basic and more widespread than conspiracy: the casual, routine assumption among those responsible for the Yard's public face that even though this was a police force acting on behalf of the public, spending public money and enforcing laws agreed by those elected by the public, there was nothing controversial about keeping the public in the dark.

Power and secrecy walk hand in hand. Power enjoys secrecy, because it increases its scope. Power generates secrecy, simply because it can. The police – particularly the counter-terrorism branch – have good reasons for keeping some of their work highly secret; but the secrecy of Caryatid went well beyond operational necessity. And there is nothing unusual about that. Scotland Yard is no different to other powerful organisations. They find secrecy easy, natural and extremely helpful, regardless of whether or not it may cheat the public of the information to which they have a profound right. On this occasion, it also helped the conspiracy in News International, not only while Caryatid was working but over the following years as the truth threatened nevertheless to emerge.

On 2 March 2007, Clive Goodman dropped a bomb on News International.

He had been sorely provoked a month earlier when, having held his tongue and gone to prison on the promise from Andy Coulson that he would still be employed at the *News of the World*, he received a letter, informing him that the promise had been broken. Les Hinton wrote that there was 'no choice but to terminate your employment'. Hinton offered him an apology and a year's salary. It was not enough to placate him.

Goodman's bomb took the form of a letter to the director of human resources at News International, Daniel Cloke, written a few days after his release complaining that the decision to sack him was perverse because he was acting with 'the full knowledge and approval' of senior executives, and also inconsistent because 'other members of staff were carrying out similar illegal procedures'. Specifically, he said that Andy Coulson had supported his hacking of the royal household; the extra payments to Mulcaire had been approved by Stuart Kuttner; and similar hacking had been commissioned by the assistant editor (news), Ian Edmondson. 'This practice was widely discussed in the daily editorial conference until explicit reference to it was banned by the editor . . . Tom Crone and the editor promised on many occasions that I could come back to a job at the newspaper if I did not implicate the paper or any of its staff in my mitigation plea. I did not, and I expect the paper to honour its promise to me.'

On 20 March, Goodman was given an appeal hearing with the paper. It was held well away from the *News of the World*'s office, in the company's magazine HQ, off the King's Road in Chelsea. The company refused to hand over documents which Goodman had requested to prove his case, or to allow him further time to prepare his defence, or to bring his lawyer with him, or to record the hearing. Unusually, the appeals panel had no employee representative nor anybody from the company's management. This would have been 'inappropriate' when dealing with such serious allegations, according to News International. Goodman put his case to the human-resources director, Daniel Cloke; the company's legal director, Jon Chapman; and to the *News of the World*'s new editor, Colin Myler.

Goodman hit them hard. He repeated his allegations against those he had already named, adding specific detail about the involvement of Greg Miskiw, and he claimed that in the past two years there had not been a single story controlled by the news desk which had not involved hacking voicemail or accessing some other form of confidential information, and threw in the claim that, with Mulcaire's help, Ian Edmondson had been hacking the voicemail of Andy Coulson on a daily basis.

It got worse. Goodman claimed that in addition to hacking, the paper routinely had been getting hold of targets' call records and tracking their location by 'triangulating' their mobile phones. This was a particularly serious allegation. A mobile phone can be located in this way only by obtaining precise detail of the three phone towers nearest to the handset, mapping the standard radius of all three and then spotting any point where they intersect. Necessarily, that would involve having inside sources in the phone companies or one source in some special section of a law-enforcement agency. This was not simply illegal access to confidential information; it raised the clear possibility that a law-enforcement source had been paid a bribe, for which the courts would impose a heavy prison sentence. All this, Goodman said, was well known.

And he produced his insurance policy – the emails which he had downloaded when he was released from police custody in August 2006, implicating Coulson in the hacking. He told them too that he had taped conversations with Coulson, including their secret meeting at the Café Rouge. He produced the transcript of a voicemail which, he claimed, had been shown to Coulson; Mulcaire's phone records which showed multiple conversations with Ian Edmondson; notes of his meetings with Tom Crone when they discussed his decision to stay silent and the promise that he would keep his job. He argued that the fact that the paper had continued to pay him even after he had pleaded guilty confirmed this promise.

And it got worse still. A lawyer acting for Glenn Mulcaire emailed Tom Crone to inform him that Mulcaire, too, was making similar allegations. Specifically, Mulcaire claimed that Ian Edmondson had instructed him to hack voicemails including those of Rebekah Brooks, Andy Coulson and a member of the House of Lords; that he had email to prove it; and that, while he was driving Ian Edmondson in his car one day, the assistant editor had told him to hack the celebrity PR Max Clifford. Mulcaire also announced that he was planning to write a book about his work for the *News of the World* and, with help from his friend Greg Miskiw, to make a TV documentary.

Over the following ten days, Daniel Cloke and Colin Myler interviewed Stuart Kuttner, who agreed that Coulson and Goodman had been in touch after Goodman's arrest; Ian Edmondson, who declined to say which executives knew Mulcaire was hacking for the paper; and Neil Wallis, who said Goodman was a paranoid troublemaker and that he had never heard of Glenn Mulcaire until he was arrested. The following week, on 29 March, Wallis and the crime reporter Lucy Panton had lunch with Assistant Commissioner Andy Hayman.

Rebekah Brooks intervened, taking Goodman out for lunch at the RAC Club on 12 April. The official policy of News International was that any journalist who broke the law would be instantly dismissed. She had just repeated the point in a letter to the Press Complaints Commission, who were conducting their 'investigation' into the hacking at the *News of the World*. However, at lunch with Goodman, she offered the convicted journalist a job at the *Sun*. Goodman declined.

It was at this point that, with Les Hinton's backing, Cloke and Myler decided to collect emails which Goodman had exchanged with Glenn Mulcaire and the five executives who, he claimed, were co-conspirators – Coulson, Wallis, Kuttner, Edmondson and the features editor, Jules Stenson – and to hand them to the upmarket law firm Harbottle & Lewis. This was later found to be riddled with controversy of two different kinds.

First, the evidence strongly suggests that the law firm were not shown all of the emails. They were collected into seven files, but only five of them were shown to Harbottle & Lewis; and among the messages they did see, several were missing key passages. It may be significant that, according to one source, when Andy Coulson was asked if he would consent to having his emails searched, he said he was not sure and would have to check with his lawyers.

Second, the emails contained evidence which appeared to suggest that Goodman was right, at least in some respects. When the former Director of Public Prosecutions, Ken Macdonald, later read a sample of them, he suggested it was 'blindingly obvious' that they included 'evidence of serious criminal offences'. The messages included strong hints that Coulson and others were aware of Goodman's hacking, both while he was working with Mulcaire and later when he had been arrested and was awaiting trial; and apparently overt references to payments to royal police officers, complete with several warnings from Goodman that these had to be handled carefully because they amounted to criminal offences – for example, in an email to Coulson: 'These people will not be paid in anything other than cash because if they're discovered selling stuff to us, they end up on criminal charges, as could we.' They also reflected some of the contacts between Coulson and Tom Crone as they tried to limit the damage from Goodman's arrest.

But News International's brief for the law firm was very narrow – not to look generally for evidence of wrongdoing but simply to check for evidence to support Goodman's specific claims. On 9 May 2007, Harbottle & Lewis were given remote access to the emails on News International's system. Without waiting for a reply, News International went ahead with a second hearing with Goodman on 10 May, at an even more discreet location, the Antoinette hotel, ten miles from central London, in Kingston upon Thames. There, Cloke and Myler argued that Goodman's allegations were irrelevant to his claim for wrongful dismissal, and that all they should consider was whether Goodman's sacking had been reasonable and conducted by a proper process. They refused to give him copies of the Harbottle & Lewis emails. A furious Goodman told them that their minute of their earlier hearing was inaccurate, repeated his allegations and added that, in spite of Andy Coulson's involvement in the hacking, Coulson had been rewarded with a pay-off of £400,000, a car and a nod that he would be allowed to return to News International in the future.

A fortnight later, on 24 May, a senior partner from Harbottle & Lewis, Lawrence Abramson, spoke by phone with News International's legal director, Jon Chapman. According to evidence which Abramson later gave to the Leveson Inquiry, he drew some of the emails to Chapman's attention because they 'contained potentially confidential or sensitive matters that News International may not want to give disclosure of'. But none of this apparent wrongdoing was covered by the brief which News International had given to Harbottle & Lewis: Abramson said that he was told that these were not matters on which he was required to comment. After a brief negotiation with Chapman about precise wording, Abramson formally wrote the letter which News International were to disclose to the media select committee two years later as evidence of their innocence of crime, confirming that 'we did not find anything in those emails which appeared to us to be reasonable evidence that Clive Goodman's illegal actions were known about and supported by' those whom Goodman had named. Abramson later told Leveson that some of the emails which News International claimed to have sent him 'must have escaped my attention'.

News International then struck a peculiarly generous deal with their criminal former employee: in addition to the one year's salary of £90,000 which Goodman had been offered by Les Hinton in February, he would be paid a further £140,000 plus £13,000 for his legal bill. This payment was on condition that he sign an agreement not to disclose the existence of the agreement or the circumstances surrounding it, and that he must make no public statement which might damage the good name of the *News of the World*. Separately, they agreed to pay Glenn Mulcaire a total of £80,050 with the same agreement of secrecy. Mulcaire abandoned his plans to produce a book and a TV documentary about the *News of the World*.

Both men stayed silent. Murdoch's company – armed now with even more detailed allegations about the crime in one of their newsrooms – chose to say nothing and do nothing.

While News International were pacifying Goodman and Mulcaire in the spring of 2007, Mark Lewis was moving forward with his plan to sue the company on behalf of Gordon Taylor, opening the fight with a formal 'letter before action'. Rapidly, Tom Crone took a train to Manchester where, according to public evidence later given by Mark Lewis, an outwardly calm Crone said that he had thought this had all gone away, to which Lewis had replied that Gordon Taylor was entitled to damages of £250,000. Crone later recalled that he thought 'Wow. That's a lot of money.'

Legal wheels turn slowly. Lewis submitted a claim. News International resisted stoutly. When Lewis then obtained devastating new evidence, including the email for Neville, the Murdoch company switched track, pointing out with little subtlety that, if Gordon Taylor pursued this case, the false story about his supposed affair would become public. That may have worried Taylor; it also made him angry. Lewis continued. At the beginning of May 2008, News International offered to pay £50,000 in damages – five times the amount which had just been paid in a privacy case brought by the actress Catherine Zeta Jones. Lewis rejected it. At the end of May, News International upped their offer to £150,000. Lewis rejected it.

News International went to a senior specialist in media law, Michael Silverleaf QC, showed him the bundle of evidence and asked him what he thought. In a powerful opinion – later released to a select committee – Silverleaf concluded on 3 June 2008 that 'there is a powerful case that there is or was a culture of illegal information access used at News Group Newspapers, to produce stories for publication'. Silverleaf suggested that they might have to go as high as £250,000 to settle the case. News International upped their offer to £350,000, and Mark Lewis rejected it.

On Friday 6 June, one of News International's external solicitors, Julian Pike of Farrer & Co., spoke to Lewis by phone, an uncomfortable conversation during which Lewis evidently told Pike that it was obvious that hacking was 'rife' at the *News of the World*, that either they went to court, which would expose the scandal, or they would have to settle out of court, in which case his client would agree to sign a confidentiality agreement but he would want £1 million in damages: 'One way or another, this is going to hurt.'

Pike emailed Tom Crone his note of the conversation, repeating Mark Lewis's claim that hacking was 'rife' at the paper and adding that, before submitting a formal defence, he would speak to Glenn Mulcaire 'to avoid (as much as possible) hostages to fortune'. Crone sent it on to Colin Myler, explaining his thinking and warning that there was 'a further nightmare scenario' if Gordon Taylor's in-house legal adviser, Jo Armstrong, also sued for messages which had been taken from her voicemail and transcribed in the email for Neville Thurlbeck.

Crone and Pike consulted James Murdoch – a move which was later to jeopardise the young Murdoch's career – and duly settled the case, agreeing to pay £425,000 plus £210,000 legal costs to Gordon Taylor. The 'nightmare scenario' then unfolded as not only Jo Armstrong but also Taylor's external solicitor, John Hewison, sued. Nevertheless, News International had the answer. It may have cost them £1 million, but they ensured that all three litigants signed confidentiality agreements and that the case papers were sealed for ever by the court.

Some of Murdoch's UK executives had been pushed to the very edge of the precipice, to the brink of a fall that would destroy their careers and ruin the reputation of News International, but they had stood their ground, obstructing the police, suppressing the voices of Goodman and Mulcaire, paying off the threat from Gordon Taylor and his two fellow claimants. They had survived. They had kept it all hidden. Now, all would be well for them – for as long as they could continue with their secrets and lies.

Part Two
The Power Game

There is only one thing in this world, and this is to keep acquiring money and more money, power and more power. All the rest is meaningless.

Napoleon Bonaparte

I work for a man who wants it all and doesn't understand anybody telling him he can't have it all.

Paul Carlucci, senior executive in News Corp

7. A wedding in the country

Based on interviews with wedding guests and with journalists and others who have worked with News Corp; biographies of Rupert Murdoch and of UK prime ministers; and evidence disclosed to the Leveson Inquiry.

On a bright shining Saturday afternoon in the middle of June 2009, in the rolling green downland of west Oxfordshire, there is a wedding party. Several hundred men and women are gathered by the side of a great lake, 350 metres long, crowned at the far end with an eighteenth-century boathouse disguised as a Doric temple. The sun pours down. The guests sparkle like the champagne in their gleaming flute glasses. The bride arrives to the sound of Handel's 'Rejoice!', written for the arrival of the Queen of Sheba. Amongst the onlookers, two men lean their heads towards each other.

'So what do you make of all this?' one asks quietly.

'It is a statement,' says the other, in an equally discreet whisper, 'of power.'

At first sight, the power appears to rest with the guests. The man who wants to know what he should make of all this is a senior member of Gordon Brown's Labour government, one of a small group of ministers who are scattered through the gathering. Alongside them is a group of other senior politicians from the Conservative opposition, including its leader, David Cameron. The other man in the whispered conversation is a famously aggressive national newspaper editor, a creator of storms, a destroyer of reputations – and just one of a substantial collection of editors, former editors, political editors, political consultants, newspaper executives, TV presenters, political lobbyists, political PR specialists, political correspondents, all now pressed together by the lakeside. This is a gathering of the country's power elite, and yet the power which is being stated here is not that of the guests.

As the Christian wedding blessing begins, there is an extraordinary interruption. A large car with dark windows arrives at the top of the slope which leads down through the trees to the lake and, instead of halting there with all of the Bentleys and Mercedes (and the chauffeurs slowly baking in the sun), it ploughs on down the hill, its engine horribly loud, its presence horribly wrong, and when several hundred heads turn to understand the commotion, they see the doors of the intruding vehicle open to reveal the familiar form of the prime minister, Gordon Brown, arriving late.

Brown starts to move among the guests, but his body language screams his discomfort. He shakes hands, offers a rictus smile and moves on, obviously ill at ease and out of place. Other guests watch and conclude that he simply does not want to be here. He has just attended the Trooping of the Colour ceremony. He is due back in London to meet President Bush. But the fact is that he had to be here, to show respect.

An alien intruder would assume naturally that this respect is being shown to the bride and groom. The groom is Charlie Brooks – easy-going, clubbable, a trainer of racehorses and a liver of the good life, a man who only a few weeks earlier had explained to the posh socialites' magazine, *Tatler*, that he liked nothing better than to wake up in the morning in his two-bedroomed, taupe-painted converted barn, with his bride-to-be by his side, and for the two of them to fly off to Venice, for lunch at Harry's Bar, followed by some sightseeing and shopping by the canals, and then to fly back to London, for dinner in the famously elegant surroundings of Wilton's oyster bar in Jermyn Street. A perfect day. Charlie is from old English money – nothing flash, nothing vulgar, just solid, comfortable, horse-loving, Home Counties country folk.

But, for the most part, it is not the amiable Charlie who catches the eye in this gathering. His bride captures far more attention. Rebekah is beautiful, with her red hair falling in crazy corkscrews around her elfin face. She is also charming – really quite famous (among this power elite) for her ability to make anybody feel that she is their special friend, that she is part of their team, always ready with a favour, always willing to confide. She is particularly good with men, her fingers resting gently on their forearm and her gaze resting direct on their eyes. Not quite sexual, not quite romantic but so intimate that a well-married, conservative kind of man, several decades older than her, reflects that sometimes he finds himself sighing and wondering whether 'maybe, if things had been a little different, maybe we would have been together'.

This is Rebekah who was so close to Tony Blair when he was prime minister that Downing Street aides recall Blair's wife, Cherie, finding her in their flat and hissing privately 'Is she still here? When is she going?'; Rebekah who then effortlessly transferred her affection to the next prime minister, Blair's great political rival Gordon Brown, who showed his own affection for her by allowing his official country residence, Chequers, to be used one night last summer for an all-girls pyjama party and sleepover to mark her fortieth birthday; Rebekah who now spends her weekends swapping canapés and gossip with Brown's newest political rival, David Cameron, who could possibly be prime minister within a year and who is said to sign off his notes to her with the words 'Love, Dave'. Everybody (who is anybody) is Rebekah's friend.

There are those who say that this is not entirely natural, that they have seen her, for example, on the eve of an important dinner, studying the table plan like a schoolgirl actress with her script, spending several hours revising until she knows all the names and the partners' names and the children's names and the personal interests and the important topics; and then she goes out and performs. And everybody feels so special. Some say that, in truth, Rebekah has no friends at all, only contacts; that all these charming conversations she holds with all these guests are really nothing more than transactions; that all of her relationships are simply a means calculated to attain an end for 'the World's Number One Networker'. Her obvious and immediate end would be journalistic. She is the editor of the *Sun*, the biggest-selling daily newspaper in the country, and, of course, she wants contacts, to give her the stories which she needs to succeed. So, in these transactions which pass as conversations, clearly she has more than her charm to offer. She also has power – the power to make and break a reputation; quite an incentive for those who are offered her friendship.

And she will break as well as make: she is famous not only for her charm but also for her temper like a tornado. Some at the *Sun* remember the morning when she woke up to discover the rival *Daily Mirror* had beaten them to a particular story and how she expressed her feelings by walking into the office and targeting the news desk with a well-aimed missile, hastily identified as a heavy glass ashtray. One of the guests at this wedding, who has been close to her for years, says that here in Oxfordshire, Rebekah is a country wife, riding horses and organising shooting parties, but that, in London, where the real transactions take place, she is 'the beating heart of the Devil'.

The word that follows Rebekah around is 'ambitious'. Most of the journalists who have worked for her love her. In the language of Fleet Street, she has earned the highest accolade – she is 'an operator'. When she wants a story, nothing will stand in her way. Years ago at the *News of the World*, she once dressed up as a cleaning lady to infiltrate the office of the *Sunday Times* and steal their story. But some of those who know her say that it is not really journalism that moves her – that she knows exactly how it works and exactly how to pull in a story and turn out a headline, but that she has no real love of it, no pulse of excitement at the very idea of it. They say that, for Rebekah, journalism is simply a ladder reaching from her not-particularly-well-off middle-class origins in a village in Cheshire, up through her first humble jobs in various newsrooms, then rapidly over the next few rungs to the editor's office at the *News of the World*, and then to the editor's office at the *Sun* – and then higher and higher, as far as the eye of her ambition can see. This summer day in 2009, she is still only forty-one, still climbing. For her, they say, the power of an editor is simply a mechanism for acquiring still more power. 'Where there is power,' says one of those who acts as her friend, 'there is Rebekah.'

Yet, any intruder who imagines that it is the power of Rebekah Brooks which is being stated here today has entirely missed the point. She is merely an avatar. It may not be immediately obvious but the man with the real power is the elderly gentleman, aged seventy-eight, with the avuncular smile and the clumsily dyed orange hair, chatting quietly in the crowd. He is entirely undistinguished in this gathering, but it is he who has raised Rebekah up the ladder of her ambition, and it is his presence which makes the simple, central statement to the members of this power elite: 'You need to be here.' He is one of the small global group who have reached that special position where they are commonly identified simply by a first name. It may be Rebekah's wedding, but this is Rupert's day.

Since 1979, no British government has been elected without the support of Rupert Murdoch. Between then and this wedding, all those who have been prime minister – Thatcher, Major, Blair and Brown – have consistently cleared their diaries and welcomed him to the inner sanctum of their governments (and then disclosed as little as possible of what passed between them). It is certain that other national leaders have done the same, in Beijing and Washington and Canberra and in numerous capitals across the planet. This is the current state of the democratic deal: each man has one vote; this man has power.

The fact of the power is clear. Even here, at the wedding, it colours every move around him. At one point, for example, Tony Blair's former media adviser, Alastair Campbell, strolls up to David Cameron and tells him that, although naturally he hopes Cameron will lose the general election which is due next year, he would support the Conservative leader if, on winning office, he tried to do something about the press. Campbell starts to unwind a well-rehearsed speech about the mendacity and negativity of so much political coverage, and Cameron focuses and is in the process of saying that he does think that newspaper behaviour has got even worse, when suddenly he catches his breath and freezes, like a schoolboy spotted by the teacher, as Rupert materialises at his shoulder, smiling. When Murdoch smiles, respectable politicians burst with appreciation.

Why? That is less clear.

Outsiders often misunderstand the power of a man like Rupert Murdoch. They look at him and they see the very model of a media megalomaniac. Certainly, by fair means and foul, with cleverness and cunning, he has built a vast media organisation – News Corp – which has more than 800 subsidiaries and total assets worth some $60 billion. He and his family trust directly own 12% of the shares (although a subtle legal manoeuvre means that they control 39.7% of the votes). This day in June 2009, News Corp owns one of the world's Big Six film studios, Twentieth Century Fox; one of the world's twenty biggest book publishers, HarperCollins; what was once the world's most visited social networking site, MySpace; but, most important of all, News Corp owns TV channels and newspapers.

Murdoch creates media triangles. Country by country, he has bought a downmarket tabloid (the *Sun* in the UK, the *New York Post* in the US, the *Herald Sun* and the *Telegraph* in Australia); then he has found himself a quality title (the London *Times*, the *Wall Street Journal*, the *Australian*); and alongside them, he has locked in a TV network (BSkyB, Fox in the US, Foxtel in Australia). Each triangle in its own way is the foundation of great wealth and political power.

News Corp's reach is enormous. Through News International, it owns the four titles which together capture 37% of Britain's newspaper readers; plus 39.1% of the BSkyB satellite TV business, beaming movies and sports and the Sky News channel into 10 million homes in the United Kingdom and Ireland. It supplies 60% of Australia's daily papers and 70% on Sundays. Its TV holdings have spread across Europe (west and east), across southern Africa and into Latin America. Its Asian TV network, Star, reaches all of India and all of China, most of the rest of Asia and now, through Star Select, the Middle East too. News Corp's TV channels broadcast movies which are made by its own studios and then reviewed by its own journalists in any of its hundreds of magazines. News Corp broadcasts sports whose rights it owns, played by sportsmen whose teams it owns, in games whose results are published by newspapers it owns.

Seeing how Murdoch has hoarded media outlets like a miser gathers gold, outsiders often imagine that he behaves like a caricature media boss, who jabs a finger in the face of the dependent politician and dictates how things are gonna be if they wanna stay healthy. On this version of events, the mogul forces the government to cut a deal: he agrees not to attack the government's policies (and not to expose the grubby personal secrets of its members); in return, the government agrees to reshape its policies to suit the mogul's ideology; the mogul then whips his compliant reporters into line, and they produce the political propaganda he requires; the government rewards the mogul with lucrative favours for his business.

And yet government ministers and special advisers and civil servants who have dealt with Murdoch, and executives and editors and journalists who have worked for him, tell a different story. The difference between the two stories is itself a clue to one part of the mogul's method. Those who know him say that this is a man who loves information: he uses his journalists as a network of listeners; he taps up every contact for the inside story; he collects political gossip; he is given secret briefings by intelligence agencies; and he has made a fortune out of selling news. Yet, with his own life and particularly with his business life, he is well-walled and secretive: the outsiders are there to be misled.

The insiders say that his use of power is far more subtle than the outsiders imagine. They say first of all that there is something very deep which drives him very hard – maybe, some suggest, that he grew up believing that he could never be good enough for his father, Sir Keith Murdoch, a towering patriarch who built businesses and broke opponents, and so, all his life, his son has been compelled to make his own business bigger and bigger, as though one day his dead father might finally signal that it was enough. With that in mind, they say that his primary interest in politicians is not political; it's commercial. He may be a highly political animal, they say – obsessed with the detail of life in the corridors of power and personally possessed of some extremely right-wing opinions – but what he most wants from politicians is favours for his business. He'll betray his own principles, he'll embrace politicians for whom he has very little respect, just as long as they have the power to help the company get bigger.

In practical terms, this comes down to a repeated demand to be freed from regulation. He and his senior journalists all sing from the same song sheet on the virtues of deregulated free markets, in the UK and the US and Australia, wherever Murdoch owns outlets: theirs is the world's loudest voice calling for the state to be cut back to make way for private enterprise. They do this as though it were simply a point of political philosophy. Clearly, however, it is a matter of overwhelming commercial interest for a businessman who wants to expand, to beat competitors, to dominate the very markets whose freedom he so often proclaims. Democratic governments across the world create regulators to speak up for the public interest – to protect their markets against the power of dominant corporations, to stop them crushing the competition or setting unfair prices or otherwise abusing their position. Repeatedly Murdoch has had to find ways to beat them, to sideline the public interest in order to advance his own. Legal fences obstruct him – so he looks to friendly politicians to quietly open gates and wave him through.

The outsiders may assume that this involves striking a deal. The insiders again say it is more subtle than that – not so much a deal (finite, static, a conscious agreement) as a somewhat cynical relationship (each side pretending friendship but seeking advantage, both offering a little more than they hope finally to give, neither side ever quite sure of the outcome). And that special relationship, they say, is born and brought up and free to flourish in places like this wedding.

Here, by the side of this lake, Murdoch and his executives and his senior journalists enjoy the first privilege of power: that they are given for free the kind of access for which unscrupulous lobbyists will pay fat packets of cash. The prime minister, his likely successor and their respective followers queue up to hear his views, to pick up the signals, to understand what he wants, to send him their own signals, to bond. Some 46 million voters in the United Kingdom might like that kind of access to their leaders, but it is this foreign billionaire – who does not even have the right to vote in the UK – who enjoys it and the special relationship with governments which it brings.

So he moves among the wedding guests, casual and relaxed, chatting quietly. He does not display his power in any overt way – no bodyguards, no sitting apart and holding court like some silver-screen godfather. There is no hint of threat or enforcement. Effortlessly, and with some charm, he harvests the respect of those around him. But . . .

Ultimately, of course, there is something else at work here. It is not respect. It is fear. It is a curious fact that Murdoch holds no fear for ordinary people: most could not care less about him; the few who do care, tend to hold him in contempt as a model of avarice with his seven homes around the globe and his annual income touching $22 million. Yet among those who play the power game, certainly, beneath the courtesy and the conversation, there is a quiet fear.

That, in turn, is a little to do with his character. He can show his charm, he can tell a blue joke to the lads, but the truth is that many of those who shake his hand can see the snarl behind his smile. An Australian associate recalls what happened one day when he suggested to Murdoch that he might like to rebuild bridges with a businessman with whom he had argued and who had since seen his business empire collapse. As he remembers it, the snarl pounced out as Murdoch explained: 'I didn't like talking to that cunt when he had money, and now he's broke, he can get fucked.' One member of this powerful gathering recalls a much gentler but equally revealing comment from the Queen, who asked about Rupert's son, James, and then added sotto voce: 'The father is awful.'

The man's character in turn is at the heart of his approach to business. Rupert Murdoch is a man who will crush an opponent like a beetle beneath his boot, and he will do it for one simple reason – for News Corp. One of the guests who is closest to him says: 'Rupert does not discriminate – he does not care about anybody more than he cares about the business. That includes himself, his kids, his political allies. The business comes first. His plan is "kill or be killed". Every single corporate battle that he's fought over the last fifty years, he's gone head to head to win. You have to win. You don't acknowledge that politics is a higher power. You don't yield to the law of the land. You don't submit to any higher code than your own.'

Notoriously, in 1975, Murdoch abused his position as a newspaper owner to support a plot which ousted the democratically elected prime minister of Australia, Gough Whitlam, who had dared to wander away from the mogul's path. Murdoch is the man who threw 6,000 men out of work when he broke away from the printing unions in London; who dumped his own citizenship as an Australian in order to become an American so that he could own more than 25% of a TV network; who pushed the *Daily Telegraph* and the *Independent* to the edge of destruction in a UK price-cutting war which doubled the circulation of *The Times*; who adopted Christianity like a new suit and then dumped it when he tired of it.

But above all, the fear is generated by the people he hires to work for him. 'He loves thugs,' as one of his senior executives puts it. Roger Ailes at Fox TV; Kelvin MacKenzie at the *Sun*; Col Allan at the *New York Post*; Sam Chisholm at Sky TV: they all came out of the same box, marked 'bully'. And when Murdoch's men bully, their victims really feel it. All these members of the power elite have seen what Murdoch's news outlets can do, using their stories in the same way that muggers in back alleys use their boots, to kick a victim to pulp. 'Monstering', they call it – a savage and prolonged public attack on a target's life, often aimed at the most private and sensitive part of their existence, their sexual behaviour, inflicting maximum pain, maximum humiliation.

Very often, this will have nothing to do with Murdoch's own manoeuvres; it will simply be a matter of filling news space at the expense of some hapless individual who has caught the tabloid eye. Most journalists will refuse to do it, just as most men would refuse to be torturers. But some of those who carry press cards are like the droogs in Anthony Burgess's *A Clockwork Orange*: they kick their victims because they love it. It sells newspapers, it pays well, it's fun.

A monstering from Murdoch's droogs is a terrible experience. If the damage they did were physical – visible – courts could jail them for years. As it is, they inflict grievous emotional harm, the kind of injury from which some victims simply never recover. Indeed, there are some who have been left suicidal by the experience. It can come out of nowhere, picking on some off-the-cuff statement or some tiny detail which has caught nobody else's eye, least of all the victim's, and suddenly the violence begins. It can be completely arbitrary in its choice of target. If Miss Muffet abandons her tuffet because of the approaching spider, the droogs can choose to attack her for cowardice; or to attack the spider for indecency and threatening behaviour.

Once it starts, the monstering cannot be stopped by the victim. If the spider says he meant no harm, he was simply looking for somewhere to sit, then 'an unrepentant spider last night threatened to spread his regime of fear'. Apologising will not work – 'a humiliating climbdown'. Nor will refusing to apologise – 'an increasingly isolated spider'. There is no end to the potential angles. The droogs will call everybody who ever sat next to the spider until they find somebody else who didn't like him. They will comb through arachnophobes everywhere, in search of alarmist quotes and calls for action. They can keep it going for days. A little distortion here, some fabrication there. The fact of the focus is itself a distortion: the relentless return to the same victim, the desire to destroy that corrupts normal editorial judgement. Often, other newspapers and broadcast bulletins will join in, so that simple commercial competition encourages the hunt for a new angle. The spider is helpless – if he speaks out, he fuels the story; if he stays quiet, the story tramples him.

Eventually, the monstering stops, usually because some new target has arrived; or because the target has been destroyed. Sometimes, even destruction is not enough. In his diary, Alastair Campbell recalls the ferocious monstering which was given to the then Transport Secretary Stephen Byers, in the spring of 2002, which continued even after he had resigned: 'It's like they get a corpse but then are disappointed there is nothing left to try and kill, so they kill the dead body too.'

And the fear of this monstering generates power far beyond the relatively small number of victims who are attacked. All those in the power elite are prone to fear Murdoch because none can be sure that they will not be next to be kicked by the tabloid boot. They all saw what happened to the former Labour minister Clare Short. Several times she criticised the *Sun*'s use of topless women to sell the paper and found herself denounced to millions as 'killjoy Clare . . . fat . . . jealous . . . ugly . . . Short on looks . . . Short on brains'. At various points, the paper offered readers free car stickers ('Stop Crazy Clare'); sent half-naked women to her home; and ran a beauty contest to ask their readers whether they would prefer to see her face or the back of a bus. Separately, the *News of the World* ran two bogus stories suggesting she was involved with pornography; tried to buy old photographs of her as a twenty-year-old in a nightdress; and published a smear story which attempted to link her to a West Indian gangster.

Her fellow Labour MP, the former Anglican priest Chris Bryant, provoked the full wrath of the Murdoch papers when he trapped Rebekah Brooks into admitting that her journalists had paid police officers for information at the media select-committee hearing in March 2003. Immediately afterwards, Bryant was warned by a reporter from the *Sun* that 'they will get you for that'. They got him a little bit a few months later when he told the House of Commons that he opposed the idea of a referendum on the new EU constitution and found the *Sun* telling its readers that he was a 'Euro fanatic' who thought they were too stupid to vote. They got him more severely that December when the *Mail on Sunday* exposed his sex life, complete with an embarrassing photograph of him wearing only a tight-fitting pair of briefs, and Brooks at the *Sun* and Andy Coulson at the *News of the World* joined in a vicious monstering. Brooks made it very clear that this was personal, sashaying up to Bryant at a subsequent Labour Party conference to deliver a sharp dig at his sexuality, calculated to remind him of the embarrassment of one of his former colleagues who had been accused of cruising a London park for gay sex: 'Oh, Mr Bryant, it's after dark. I'm surprised you're not out on Clapham Common.'

The punishment was equally harsh for the American writer Michael Wolff. In March 2009 he found himself on the receiving end of a thorough monstering from the *New York Post* when he was working on a biography of Murdoch. By some unexplained means, the mogul's people had laid hands on an unpublished typescript and started to send clear warnings that the boss was not happy with some its contents. Wolff recalls a senior executive calling to ask him to make changes before the book was published.

'What will you do if I don't?' Wolff asked.

'Then we will not support the book.'

'How bad is that?'

'It could be bad.'

And it was bad. The *New York Post* discovered that Wolff had been having an affair and ran stories on 2, 3, 6, 25 and 30 March and 3 and 9 April, publishing along the way a secondary story which accused Wolff of evicting his mother-in-law from her apartment as well as a cartoon of Wolff in bed with his lover, portraying the Jewish writer in a style which might reasonably be described as anti-Semitic.

At its worst, everybody in the power elite has heard that the punishment can amount to crude blackmail. They have all heard the stories about how Murdoch editors have safes containing dossiers of evidence about the private lives of politicians and competing businessmen; and that Murdoch and his people agree to suppress these gross embarrassments in exchange for yet more favours. There are specific rumours – about a senior figure in British sport who is said to have complied with Murdoch's plans for TV rights when he was informed that the *Sun* was ready to tell its readers that he had had sexual relationships with young men; and about a middle-ranking Labour politician who is said to have spoken up on behalf of Murdoch's UK newspapers after journalists obtained a video of him having sex with a prostitute while the prostitute's husband watched. It is true that the sports administrator and the Labour politician offered their support to Murdoch. Whether they did so out of fear of the dossiers – or whether the dossiers even exist – is not so clear. The power is in the belief and in the fear which it engenders. Which is widespread.

Certainly, many have come across a gentler version of this, something more like whitemail – a favour done rather than a threat made. There are senior politicians, police officers and others who know that senior Murdoch journalists have privately put in a word for them, to help with a promotion, to defuse some threat. Most of the wedding guests know that Rebekah worked a clever piece of whitemail with the deputy prime minister John Prescott when, as editor of the *News of the World*, she got hold of the story that many years earlier Prescott's wife, Pauline, had given up a baby for adoption. This had happened before the Prescotts had met, but now the long-lost son had made contact. Prescott pleaded with Rebekah not to publish the story until his wife and her adult son had had a chance to get to know each other. She agreed, a decent act and one which earned her a sense of indebtedness from Prescott who later, when his family were ready, opted to take the story to her at the *Sun*, where she had become editor. Favours are valuable currency in the corridors of power.

The power to conceal or reveal sensitive personal information turns out to be just like the power of the bully in the school playground. The bully need only batter one or two other children for the fact of his power to be established: fear will then ensure that the others do all they can to placate him. In the same way, the really big power which Murdoch is said to wield – that he can swing the result of elections – does not have to be entirely real. What matters is the fear that it could be real. Far safer to be an ally, even to join the shuffling queue of current and former members of the power elite who take his money, writing columns for his newspapers or selling their memoirs to HarperCollins: the then Speaker of the US House of Representatives Newt Gingrich; the daughter of the then leader of the Chinese Communist Party, Deng Xiaoping; the former Conservative leader William Hague; the former Metropolitan Police Commissioner Sir John Stevens; the former Labour minister David Blunkett; the former Downing Street press adviser Alastair Campbell; the former Metropolitan Police Assistant Commissioner Andy Hayman; and so on and on.

Nobody is sure whether an aggressive newspaper really can decide the outcome of a national ballot. The newspapers like to claim that they can; politicians claim not to believe it; psephologists argue about the impact of news on voters and the distribution of any newspaper's readers among the swing voters in marginal seats which dictate results. In the best-known UK case, Kelvin MacKenzie's *Sun* in 1992 bloodied its toecaps all over the political career of the former Labour leader Neil Kinnock and then loudly claimed to have won the election for the Conservative leader, John Major. MacKenzie's claim was widely seen as unfounded, if only because of his notorious estrangement from the truth.

There is no doubt that the droogs can cause grievous political harm. A cynical newspaper which targets a political party – in or out of government – can inject it with chaos. All debates become splits, all problems become crises, all changes become climbdowns, all setbacks are humiliating, all successes are ignored. It can change the news agenda so that on any day, the party or government is diverted into managing some crisis which the newspaper has manufactured. It can ruin reputations, with falsehood as easily as with truth. It can wreck the public debate of whole subjects by pumping it full of distortion. (Britain's relationship with the European Union, for example, has been fundamentally shaped by a relentless sequence of notoriously false stories about the EU supposedly banning the British Army, Scottish kilts, pints of beer, bent bananas, charity shops and Christian teachers, as well as supposedly suffocating daily life with an imaginary set of petty regulations.) The impact is like the effect which a screaming brat has on a family: the family may not break up, but ordinary life becomes impossible.

Murdoch controls his company's money with obsessive care, checking daily 'flash reports' from every subsidiary to ensure that they are sticking to the budget he has laid down for each of them. But very little of the editorial distortion in his empire comes direct from him. He intervenes in the round by requiring his outlets to work within the boundaries of policies which will favour businesses like News Corp – cut taxes, cut welfare, cut government, cut regulation, all of the essentials of neoliberalism. From time to time, he directly intervenes in particular stories – to help an ally, to promote his business, to reflect some random personal bias. His senior journalists admit privately that this is unacceptable, a clear form of editorial corruption, but they insist that he intervenes far less often than outsiders imagine. The vast bulk of Murdoch's news output, including the huge majority of any falsehood and distortion, is simply the spontaneous product of his highly commercialised newsrooms. It sells.

In the same way, very little of the aggression needs to be directed by Murdoch himself. The fear is all. In the balance of power, a government wins easily over a newspaper group with its vast budget, its military and police, its bureaucracy and all the limbs of the state. But in the balance of fear, the outcome is the opposite. The government lives in fear of what the mogul might do to its collective standing (and perhaps to some individual reputations) by causing chaos in its coverage. The mogul has little to fear from the government. For the most part, politicians will step round him and, in the unlikely event that they do attack, he has the ultimate sanction: he can sell up and leave, avoiding everything they throw at him, taking his investment and his jobs with him.

The point about real power is that it does its own work, particularly among those who deal in power. Nobody in the power elite needs to be told. They all recognise the mogul's power and, with few exceptions, they do everything they can to pacify him, to ingratiate themselves. The mogul, for the most part, does not have to make threats or issue instructions. He just has to show up. Not even that – he just has to exist, somewhere in the background. Everybody understands; the fact of power is enough. If there's a bull in the field, everybody steps carefully. The fear gives him access; the access, gives him influence. Real power is passive.

The wedding blessing ends. The sound of 'Windmills of your Mind' drifts across the lake, and the TV presenter Jeremy Clarkson steps up to read 'Riders in the Stand' by Banjo Paterson. 'The rule holds good in everything in life's uncertain fight; You'll find the winner can't go wrong, the loser can't go right.'

There are prayers and a hymn and then the guests are ushered away, some with the help of their chauffeurs and some on foot across the fields, to Jubilee Barn, where Rebekah and Charlie live, close by the homes of Charlie's mother and sister. Gordon Brown discreetly takes his leave, but the others wander into a vision of the good life – two donkeys grazing peacefully in a paddock like a picture from a children's book; a marquee dressed in the style of a Victorian carnival with tables laid out for a banquet; and a private fairground for their entertainment, complete with a big wheel.

When the power elite meet to play, they work. On this particular day in June 2009, there are all kinds of plots swimming beneath the surface of the idle chatter at the banquet, but one plot in particular is big enough to be clearly visible. Everybody in the power elite knows that at some point in the next twelve months, Gordon Brown must call an election and so Rupert Murdoch will bestow his blessing on his chosen party with all the presumption of entitlement of a Renaissance pope. They know, too, that there is a new player in the game.

In spite of all the fuss that follows him in the UK, like a flock of seagulls behind a trawler, the old man is no longer very interested in what happens in London. He is still interested in the *Sun* and he likes the money it makes; there are rumours that he has his eye on one particularly big deal, involving BSkyB; but, for the most part, the UK has become a sideshow for him. He is happy now, they say, to use it as a kind of playpit, somewhere for his son James to develop his talents before he moves on to join his father in New York, where the big game is being played.

Ultimately, for sure, it will be Rupert who decides where his political blessing will fall, but it is James Murdoch, now aged thirty-six, who will deliver the intelligence on which his father will act, and who now sits surrounded by the smiles of those who feel a profound desire to please him. David Cameron, for example, who sits near him, has worked hard to build a bond. Six times in the last three years, Cameron has shared breakfast, lunch or dinner with the mogul's heir. It hasn't been easy to manufacture a friendship.

A year before, in July 2008, the right-wing journalist Martin Ivens, who writes for Murdoch's *Sunday Times*, hosted a dinner at which Cameron was seated opposite James Murdoch. There were other guests – a couple of newspaper columnists, a PR consultant, a novelist and a conservative historian – but, according to one of those who was there, this was clearly an occasion which had been staged as a summit meeting for the two men. Cameron and James Murdoch appeared to get on well, exchanging enthusiastic agreement about the value of green politics; James frequently disappearing to stoke up on nicotine and equally frequently spicing his views with expletives ('This country is fucked,' he confided at one point). All might have ended well if one of the other guests had not mischievously raised the subject of wealthy residents of the UK who exploit a loophole in UK tax law and claim that they are domiciled elsewhere for tax purposes, thus depriving the government of significant income. Cameron's wife, Samantha, evidently agreed that this was a disgrace, which immediately alarmed the Conservative leader who guessed that James Murdoch himself might well be exploiting this very loophole. According to this guest: 'Cameron jumped to his feet and said they really ought to go "before you say anything else indiscreet, darling" and because he had Prime Minister's Questions the next day.'

The truth is that James is not universally loved. It does not help him that he has been pushed so quickly up the family fast stream. It is only thirteen years since his father persuaded him to abandon his chosen path of producing indie music and join the family business by giving him a generous gift: he made him News Corp's vice president in charge of music and new media. Four years later, in 2000, when he was only twenty-seven, father gave son the Star TV network and an office in Hong Kong. Three more years later, in November 2003, he handed him a prime post in London as chief executive of BSkyB. He was then the youngest chief executive of any FTSE 100 company. Four years later, as James turned thirty-five in December 2007, when Murdoch moved his old ally Les Hinton to New York to take charge of Dow Jones and the *Wall Street Journal*, he moved James even closer to the top of the tree, promoting him to chairman of BSkyB but also appointing him executive chairman of News International and chief executive for all of News Corp's activity in Europe and Asia.

His critics, who cry nepotism, concede that James is clever and hard-working, but many of them say that they find him, well, difficult. In part, this is because James has a slightly robotic quality. He is a walking, talking model of a corporate man: the steel-rimmed glasses and the bristling crew cut, the power suit, the power swearing, the twenty-four-hour drive to succeed, the right-wing politics, and the strained language. James is famous for his addiction to the uniquely twisted talk of the corporate world: he doesn't agree with people but he'll be 'on the same page'; some make plans, he has 'projections going forward'; others are too busy to deal with some problem, he 'doesn't have the bandwidth to firefight that contingency right now'.

But beyond that, the cruel truth is that a lot of people just don't like him. In his father, they can see some charm and even a little humility; this is a man who has built the empire he runs. In James, they see a man with a sense of entitlement and little skill with people. 'He's bloodless,' they say. 'No sense of humour at all . . . Geeky – he wants to talk about wind turbines and iPads, he won't talk about people . . . No warmth . . . An all-round knob.' The work rate which serves him so well in business makes him seem neurotic and even paranoid in a social setting. He chain-smokes and speaks in staccato bursts. One person who has studied him up close claims that James is so paranoid that he keeps a gun under his bed in London, in case the proletariat try to break in and do him an injury.

He can be as abrasive as acid. Whereas his father can hide his snarl if it serves his interests to do so, James has a reputation for indulging in sudden outbursts of ruddy-faced shouting. Years ago, in January 2002, his father took him to a private dinner with Tony Blair in Downing Street, a useful encounter for a man who was due to take over as chief executive of BSkyB and who would need political connections. Alastair Campbell's diary records that James, briefly reverting to the left-wing views of his rebellious youth, made his mark on the prime minister by loudly contradicting his father's claim that the Palestinians had nothing to complain about, explaining that they 'were kicked out of their fucking homes and had nowhere to fucking live'.

Those close to Gordon Brown say that at the time of this wedding, he is still on good terms with the old mogul, but he finds it hard to talk to James. Rupert Murdoch adopted the language of neoliberalism as respectable clothing for the otherwise naked ambition of his plans for global corporate expansion; the son really believes it. He is on a moral crusade for free enterprise and free markets and everything that makes the neoliberal heart beat strong. And anything and anybody that gets in his way must be swept aside. Brown struggles to have any kind of bond with him or with most of the others in Murdoch's UK network. Brown's wife Sarah, however, has worked tirelessly to shore up his standing with the Murdochs by befriending their women: Rupert's third wife, Wendi Deng; Rupert's daughter, Elisabeth; James's wife, Kathryn; and spending so much time with Rebekah Brooks that one of those who works with her says that she is dangerously close to believing that Rebekah genuinely is a friend.

But Cameron has luck on his side. It just so happens that his country home and his political constituency are in this part of Oxfordshire, which has become a kind of Camelot, the new stamping ground of the consciously casual Conservative elite: a land of cocaine and shepherd's pie, where the very rich and famous live a baggy-jeans-and-T-shirt kind of life; where everybody who is anybody shops down the road at Daylesford Organic Foods, known as 'the mother ship' and famed for its £100 hampers with damson vodka and four different kinds of handmade cheese; where the prime minister will crack a can of beer with a rock star like Alex James from Blur, who makes cheese at his farm nearby; and where Bono will partner Rupert Murdoch for a hand of bridge, as he did a few months ago.

Elisabeth Murdoch and her husband, the brilliant and bumptious PR millionaire Matthew Freud, live just down the road. Freud likes Cameron – they high-five when they meet at the lakeside blessing. It was Freud last summer who provided the Gulfstream IV private jet in which Cameron flew out to the Greek islands for a meeting with Rupert Murdoch on board Murdoch's yacht, the *Rosehearty*. (This meeting went better than Cameron's first encounter with Murdoch, in 2005, when Cameron is said to have trilled enthusiastically about the gay Western movie *Brokeback Mountain* without noticing the old man retching at the idea of anybody wanting to watch two cowboys coupling.) Freud is in the midst of creating his own personal Xanadu in a vast old priory which is set to become a hub of partying and power-broking with twenty-two bedrooms, fifteen acres of garden, a seventeenth-century rectory as a guest house, a rectory cottage as a spare guest house, a private chapel and plans for a cinema, an outdoor pool, an indoor pool, a gym, a tennis court, a riding school for Elisabeth's horses, a shed for Matthew's quad bikes and maybe a helipad. Cameron goes to parties there.

Rebekah and Charlie Brooks live in the same patch. Cameron's older brother, Alexander, was at Eton with Charlie and they ride out together on Charlie's horses. And Rebekah, of course, is close to everybody. She goes on business trips with James Murdoch; has girly chats and cigarette breaks with Elisabeth Murdoch and produced a special 32-page edition of the *Sun* for her fortieth birthday; plays the part of daughter, nursemaid and plotter-in-chief to Rupert Murdoch; and, certainly, she has done her best to get close to Cameron.

One of the wedding guests recalls that on the day in October 2007 when her supposed friend, the new prime minister Gordon Brown, shot a near-fatal hole in his credibility by cancelling the general election which he had been planning, Rebekah was straight on the phone to Cameron. 'Shall I bring the champagne?' she was heard to ask him. Another suggests that, although the Camerons respond to her endless invitations to come over for a drink, they know her game and that Mrs Cameron has said that 'I have my old friends, I have my new friends . . . and I have Rebekah.'

At this moment at the wedding banquet, Rebekah causes a stir by insisting not only on making a speech but on using it to further some plot of hers, to broker a peace between the editor of the *Daily Mail*, Paul Dacre, and Matthew Freud, citing the amount which Freud gives to charity as some kind of counter-balance to Dacre's view of the young PR wizard as a yob with a gob. 'I just wish that Paul could see the right side of Matthew,' she explains to guests, some of whom wonder at the inner workings of a woman using her own wedding day as a platform for politics.

In his struggle to win Murdoch's favour, Cameron has one other asset on his side – Andy Coulson. For the first eighteen months after Cameron became leader, he tried to avoid playing the newspaper game, attempting to make his pitch to the public through television news bulletins. It didn't work, and so, in July 2007, he hired Coulson as his director of communications. It changed Cameron's fortunes. Coulson has several strengths: he comes from a working-class background in Essex and knows what messages to send to help the Conservatives break out of their middle-class electoral ghetto; he spent twenty years working for tabloid newspapers and so he knows how to convert that message into stories which newspapers will use; and, above all, he is connected to Rebekah and Rupert and to all that they represent.

It is dark now at the wedding. The banquet is long over. Most of the guests have taken their Range Rovers into the night; some are sprawled around the mansion gardens; and a few are still playing in the fairground.

There, a small group of them, inspired by much alcohol, clamber into the swinging buckets of the big wheel and, gripping the handrails and grinning as though none of this frightened them in the slightest, they rise slowly into the heights, from where they can gaze down on the world that lies at their feet and on the little people below them until, suddenly and alarmingly, the machine that has raised them up simply breaks down, the big wheel thuds to a halt and they are stuck – stranded in the darkness, exposed for all to see, wagging their legs and waving their arms, like so many beetles flipped over on their backs, totally and obviously powerless.

The moment passes, the big wheel moves on and surely it occurs to nobody that this could be even slightly symbolic of anybody's future. They are cocooned in security. Indeed, some of them know that they are not just safe; they are moving on up.

James has his eye on the big prize. He wants his father's job. Since taking over News Corp in Europe and Asia in December 2007, he has made no secret of his ambition to run the whole global corporation. 'He thinks he's the smartest person in the world, reckons his father really doesn't get the modern world,' according to one of those at the wedding. The grab for power has not been subtle. He alarmed his father's closest advisers in New York by inserting one of his own people, Beryl Cook, into the key position of head of human resources there, with the potential to give James the final say over all future appointments; and by pushing plans which clearly shifted News Corp's centre of gravity towards Europe and Asia. He appointed his own chief finance officer, general counsel and director of communications, slicing into the power of those who have the same titles in New York. In 2008, he persuaded the main board to increase its stake in the German pay-TV company Premier, which is about to be rebranded as Sky Deutschland. Now, he is pushing for more money to take over Turkey's biggest pay-TV company, Digiturk. 'He is taking on his father. He's like a young stag locking antlers with an old stag.' But Murdoch will not confront James's challenge.

Those close to the old man say he hires bullies because he personally cannot handle any kind of direct confrontation. One recalls how, soon after he separated from his second wife, Anna, she tried to call him in his New York office but, fearing a difficult conversation, he refused to speak to her. Eventually, she called his chief operating officer, Chase Carey, and persuaded him to ask her husband to pick up the phone, but Murdoch swatted him aside, muttering: 'That's water under the bridge.'

Murdoch's refusal to put James in his place is worrying his advisers, because the truth about News Corp is that it is a family business and they have seen before how his failure to deal with family problems can boil over to threaten the company's welfare. A few years earlier, there was a crisis when Wendi Deng insisted that her two young children, Grace and Chloe, be given votes in the family trust which owns the key shares in News Corp. Murdoch's four oldest children resisted, not wanting their own voting power to be diluted. Murdoch failed to confront the problem until it reached a point where he had to agree to pay $150 million to each of the six children – to Wendi's as compensation for not finally being given votes in the trust, and to the four others so that they did not lose out. He failed, too, to deal with the conflict between his oldest son, Lachlan, who had moved to New York as deputy chief operating officer, and several of his most senior executives. That finally blew up with Lachlan quitting and going back to Australia.

As James aims high, so too does Rebekah. For months it has been clear that, with Les Hinton gone and James busy in Europe and Asia, Murdoch needed to find a new chief executive for his UK company. With her eye on the prize, Rebekah has been doing a part-time course in business management at the London School of Economics. She knows Murdoch adores her, because she solves his problems for him and because she's a 'larrikin' – a mischievous free spirit, who, unlike him, is not afraid to confront anybody. Now Murdoch has given Rebekah a lucrative wedding gift. She gets the job. In three months' time, in September 2009 – twenty years after she started work as a newsroom secretary – she will take over as chief executive of News International, overseeing all four of Murdoch's UK newspapers.

And, if all goes to plan, Andy Coulson also will move up. He was one of those who was caught in the broken big wheel, in a bucket with the former Labour Secretary of State for the media, Tessa Jowell. Only two and a half years after he was forced to resign as editor of the *News of the World*, he stands poised to move into Downing Street. There is an election to win, and politics is never predictable, but all the indications are that sometime next year, Cameron will become prime minister, and Coulson will become one of his closest advisers, managing the government's communication with the nation and the world and serving too as a crucial link between the government and the Murdoch network.

They are wealthy, they are powerful and they have nothing to fear.

8. November 2009 to March 2010

An outsider might have looked at our efforts to crack the walls around Rupert Murdoch's castle and concluded that we were puny no-hopers.

By November 2009, I had spent four months since the *Guardian's* original story about crime at the *News of the World* trying to break through Murdoch's defences – looking for more evidence, writing more stories – but News International, Scotland Yard, the Director of Public Prosecutions and the Press Complaints Commission had all stepped forward like well-drilled guardsmen and told the world that we were wrong. I kept trying, but the truth is that a lot of the shots I fired missed their targets or simply bounced harmlessly off the barricades.

I tried to get Glenn Mulcaire to talk. He is very sharp, but also paranoid. I had to wait in my car near his house until I saw him pull up and walk in. He never so much as glanced my way, but when I knocked on the door, he said immediately: 'Yeah, I saw you sitting there, eight cars down on the right.' Which was correct. He was very likeable and showed a real affection for his wife and four daughters, but he was also very highly strung, his thoughts leaping all over the place, constantly on the alert in case I was taping him or tricking him. I visited him several times. We talked, but he told me nothing. I chased down rumours that when he came out of prison, he had written a book proposal, but it turned out to be an extremely dull piece of work, advising people how to improve their personal security and revealing nothing at all about the phone-hacking.

I traced some of the officers who had worked on Operation Glade, the Scotland Yard inquiry into Steve Whittamore, and was politely told to get lost. I called Greg Miskiw several times, urging him to get out of the rotten house before the masonry collapsed on his head: he just breathed heavily and uttered not a word. I tried to identify the mysterious 'Ryan' or 'Ryall' who was said to figure in a taped recording of Mulcaire explaining how to hack Gordon Taylor's phone – and failed with that too.

Through an old friend who has worked in the darker end of Fleet Street, I made contact with a very interesting private investigator. He had bent the law for newspapers but he seemed to have a conscience, to have worked only on stories where real wrongdoing was being exposed. He took a dim view of cowboy investigators who would do anything for a dollar bill. He named a few of them and started to explain their history. He also came up with one stunning piece of information – that there was a second phone-hacker on the *News of the World*, not a private investigator, but a features writer called Dan Evans who specialised in eavesdropping on phone messages. I checked and found he was still working for the paper – and so possibly still hacking, while News International and the police and the PCC said that all this had stopped with the jailing of Clive Goodman. But I couldn't publish that without hard evidence.

And while I was failing, the enemy were reinforcing their position. The media select committee were being stalled by News International's new chief executive, Rebekah Brooks: the committee wanted her to testify; she was politely refusing; some of the committee wanted to compel her to appear before them; one or two committee members were showing signs of nerves and were not so sure that they wanted to start a fight with Murdoch's new UK chief executive; the dispute dragged on, delaying the committee's report.

The PCC's whitewash had been reinforced by a bizarre move by its new chair, Lady Buscombe, a Conservative peer, who made a speech to the Society of Editors in which she suggested that Mark Lewis had misled Parliament. Lewis had given evidence to the media select committee and had said that, during the Gordon Taylor case, he had spoken to one of the Caryatid officers, Mark Maberly, who had told him that there could be as many as 6,000 people who had either had their own phones hacked or had their messages intercepted on the phones of others. Scotland Yard, however, had told the PCC that Maberly never said this. Instead of treating that as a claim which might or might not be true, Lady Buscombe had made no attempt to check and had announced Scotland Yard's denial in her speech as 'new evidence', thus suggesting that she was not operating as an entirely independent judge of the facts. She had also recycled the police claim that there had been only a handful of victims and undertaken to report her new evidence to the media select committee: 'Any suggestion that a parliamentary inquiry has been misled is, of course, an extremely serious matter.' Faithful editors reported this as though it were true. Mark Lewis sued her for defamation.

In the same week, an employment tribunal in London awarded nearly £800,000 to Matt Driscoll, who had been forced out of his job as a *News of the World* sports reporter after what the tribunal called 'a consistent pattern of bullying behaviour', led by the then editor Andy Coulson. It was believed to be the highest award ever made against a media company. The tribunal found witnesses from the *News of the World* to have been variously unsatisfactory, evasive and dishonest. The *Guardian* carried a report. The story had a special significance because Coulson was now clearly likely to be working in Downing Street within six months. Not one other national newspaper published a single word about it.

In spite of all these signs of our weakness, the reality was that there was never much serious doubt that we were going to break through. In part, this was because of the sheer scale of the buried truth. If newspapers had routinely been exposing the crime in their own newsrooms; if the Press Complaints Commission had been any kind of regulator; if the police and the ICO had had a history of enforcing the law against powerful media companies; if News Corp had ever acquired the habit of honesty: the truth would have been exposed in stories and scandals over the years. As it was, of course, inside the walls of Murdoch's castle, there was something like a mass grave full of several decades of buried secrets, so big and so stinking that once you started to dig, there really was no doubt at all about what was down there.

There was another reason why we were always going to break through – the amazing vigour of the alliance of oddballs who had decided to start digging. This was a collection of strangers. Most of them had never come across each other before. Yet, in spite of the fact that each of them had a natural tendency to be confrontational and generally difficult, they locked together with extraordinary ease. That's because rebels don't like bullies. And in Rupert Murdoch, they had found their perfect target. You can't become a master of the universe unless you are willing to hurt people along the way − a man like Murdoch accumulates far more than his share of money and power but also of victims and enemies. Resentment of his history bound together the alliance. It also continually attracted more support, some of it covert, some of it open, from journalists, private investigators, police officers and others.

Another lawyer joined the fight − Tamsin Allen from Bindmans, a law firm with strong historical links to the Labour Party and an interest in human rights. On the phone, Allen sounds like the Queen's own lawyer, possibly even like the Queen herself, sharp as a diamond, intimidating and posh. In real life, she is deeply relaxed and inclined to turn up at rock festivals in muddy boots. She became involved because two of her clients strongly suspected that they had been hacked: Brian Paddick, the former deputy assistant commissioner at Scotland Yard, who had talked to me about Dick Fedorcio's influence on policy; and Chris Bryant, the minister for Europe in Gordon Brown's government. Both men had been tormented by the tabloids because they are gay.

Tamsin Allen wrote to Scotland Yard on behalf of Paddick and Bryant to see whether John Yates's officers would admit to holding any evidence on them, so that they could sue the *News of the World* for breach of privacy. She also came up with a second line of legal attack. She would apply to the courts for a judicial review of Scotland Yard's handling of the original inquiry in 2006. As with the privacy actions, this would force the police to disclose evidence. Unlike the privacy actions, however, this could not be closed down by the *News of the World* handing out big money to those bringing the case. If the courts agreed that Scotland Yard had failed in its public duty, the only way to settle the case would be for the police to offer a remedy, probably a new investigation.

For sure, this was how we would win − through the courts. The lawyers would enlist the power of the judges. Mark Lewis and Mark Thomson were preparing cases. Charlotte Harris was heading for the front line with Max Clifford. But it was slow! It was like waiting for heavy artillery to be dragged laboriously through the mud while we sat around outside Murdoch's castle, watching him and his court feasting inside.

It was winter. I worked alone in my study, although sometimes cabin fever would get the better of me and I would take a friend's horse out on the hills near my home town, riding alone, thinking about Murdoch's castle, occasionally whipping out my mobile to call the answer machine back in my study to record some devious idea about how to break in.

I got into the habit of visiting the website of the media select committee, where occasionally they posted new written evidence. One day, I found an interesting memo which had been submitted by the police. Down in its detail, it disclosed for the first time a claim that Caryatid had warned victims in four 'national security' categories and then asked the phone companies to warn others. That was news to me; but it was frustratingly limited. It was not just that this was yet another hint that they knew of far more victims than they had admitted. It also raised more questions. Had Mulcaire actually jeopardised national security? Who were these people? Why on earth had the police not even hinted at this before? And anyway, were they telling the truth?

In pursuit of more detail, I decided to recruit a new ally – Scotland Yard. This looked like a good tactic. Surely they could see that if the truth came out, the Metropolitan Police were going to look bad if they carried on acting as though they were colluding with News International. Surely they had no need to defend the errors and weaknesses of the original inquiry – that had been Andy Hayman's work, and Hayman had left in some disgrace, accused of fiddling with his female colleagues as well as with his expenses. Surely I could persuade the Yard to talk to me off the record, to give me some of the truth that they were sitting on, which would help me with my story and also help them to stop the whole affair dragging on and dragging them down.

On the horse on the hills one afternoon that November, I called Dick Fedorcio, who agreed that this was a good idea. After weeks of delay, it was arranged that I would talk to a senior officer without identifying him, referring simply to an anonymous police source. (Much later, that officer disclosed publicly that he had held this meeting with me, so I can say now that this was Assistant Commissioner John Yates.) My bright idea turned out to be a dud. As soon as I sat down in his office, Yates told me that he doubted whether he could help. I started by offering him the chance to give me a story that would surely make Scotland Yard look good, by confirming that in order to be able to inform all potential victims, they had set up a new database containing all of the evidence which they had gathered in 2006.

He shrugged hard, his eyebrows popping upwards in mock disbelief. 'Have we?'

I told him I knew very well that they had, that I had a lot of detail from lawyers who had been in touch with the Yard. Reluctantly, he conceded the point. But it was a bad sign.

He went on to declare that the *Guardian* stories were 'all old stuff'; that there was a perception that this was the *Guardian* running a vendetta against the *News of the World* while everybody else just wanted to move on; that we had claimed to have new evidence when in fact we had none; and that, when he had given evidence to the media select committee, he had decoded the eye movements of the MPs and concluded that I had briefed all but one of them. Weird.

We went round in several circles about the number of victims who had been warned. I wanted to know how many people had been approached as possible witnesses in 2006; how many had then been approached in the four 'national security' categories; how many more they had warned in the last few months. He said the *Guardian* could not be trusted to write a straight story, so he would not give me the numbers. I considered using foul language but opted to carry on negotiating. He shifted a little and said he would think about it but assured me that there were not thousands of victims. The total number of names in Mulcaire's material was more like 600 – and those were just names. The total number of victims was much smaller.

The meeting ended badly. He said he was not allowed to tell me the things I was asking for. I told him I had been in and out of Scotland Yard for off-the-record briefings since before he joined the police and had often been given information that was far more sensitive than this. He told me he had never fallen out with a journalist. I told him that he had finally done so, and that I was sorry we had wasted each other's time.

End of that meeting. End of that tactic. And if there was any doubt about Scotland Yard's attitude, it cleared a couple of weeks later when the commissioner himself, Sir Paul Stephenson, went to see Alan Rusbridger with Dick Fedorcio by his side. Sir Paul explained that my coverage of the hacking story was exaggerated and incorrect. Evidently he expected the editor to tell me to stop digging. To his great credit, Rusbridger ignored him.

With nothing but obstruction from Scotland Yard, I decided to use the Freedom of Information Act to try to force them to disclose something of the evidence they were sitting on. I thought I would start with something simple and unthreatening, so I asked them to look at the database which they had now created from the material which they had seized in August 2006 and to give me five numbers. How many names, mobile numbers, PIN codes, voicemail recordings and voicemail transcripts were recorded in that database?

Their response was as unhelpful as ever. They received my request on 1 December 2009. The law allowed them twenty working days to reply. So, allowing for weekends and Christmas, I would receive an answer by 31 December. No chance. I received nothing by that date, not even a note to say that there was a delay. I made calls, sent emails, made more calls, pointed out that they were breaking the law, lodged a formal complaint and finally, four weeks later than the limit prescribed by law, on 28 January 2010, they sent me just two of the five numbers I had asked for.

There were ninety-one PIN codes in the seized material, they admitted. That was very significant. Since Mulcaire was a man who specialised in hacking voicemail, it suggested that he had had at least ninety-one victims. Why else would he have obtained their PIN codes? But, since we knew that the vast majority of people did not bother to change the factory settings on their phone, it implied that he had probably had a great many more victims. Certainly not 'a handful'.

The police gave me one other answer – that the only example of transcribed voicemail messages in the seized material was already in the public domain, i.e. the email for Neville Thurlbeck. I wasn't sure whether to believe that. But if it was true, it made it even more difficult to understand why they had failed to show this unique document to the Crown Prosecution Service in 2006.

I lodged an appeal in search of the remaining three numbers I had asked for. In the meantime, I had been trying to follow up on the police claim in their memo to the select committee, that they had asked the phone companies to trace other victims of Mulcaire and Goodman and to take appropriate action. I approached the four big mobile phone companies.

One of them – T-mobile – said the police had never been in touch with them at all. Which suggested that the police memo was not entirely reliable. The other three phone companies declined to help. So I sent the three of them a deliberately provocative email, suggesting that I would write a news story about their refusal to disclose how many of their customers had been victims and how many of them had been warned: 'The fact that you have now chosen to suppress these numbers clearly raises the possibility that the company failed to contact and warn a significant proportion of those whose voicemail was targeted or accessed.'

That jogged one of them into action: O2 replied that they had identified 'about forty' victims and had warned them all. Armed with that, I went back to the other two companies and told them that O2 were co-operating, so if they carried on concealing, it would look more and more like they had something to hide. Vodafone then replied that they had found a 'broadly similar' number of victims to O2 and that they had warned them 'as appropriate' – whatever that meant. Orange finally replied that they had found forty-five victims but had warned none of them – because the police had never asked them to. A total of some 120 victims, most of whom evidently had never been warned in spite of what Scotland Yard had told the select committee.

The numbers were very significant, because the true scale was likely to be much greater: these were victims who had been hacked from phone numbers used by Mulcaire and Goodman, but they didn't include those who had been hacked by other journalists. And the phone companies keep call data for only twelve months, but journalists who had worked at the *News of the World* were saying that Mulcaire and various reporters had been hacking phones for at least five years.

On 2 February 2010, the *Guardian* published a front-page story revealing the 120 extra victims found by the phone companies and the ninety-one PIN codes which had been obtained by Glenn Mulcaire and which had never previously been disclosed by Scotland Yard. I wrote that this directly contradicted the 'handful of victims' in the official version of events which was being promoted by the *News of the World* and the police. The story also pointed out that this was further evidence that Scotland Yard had breached their agreement with the Director of Public Prosecutions that they would warn 'all potential victims'. They also appeared to have misled the select committee by submitting a memo which claimed that 'for anybody else that may have been affected', they had made an agreement with the phone companies to research their customers and to take appropriate action.

Scotland Yard did not like this. The story got Yates into trouble with the media select committee, whose chairman, John Whittingdale, wanted to know why on earth Yates had not told them about the ninety-one PIN codes when he had appeared before them in September. Yates explained that in September, they had not known about the PIN codes – thus accidentally confirming that it had taken Scotland Yard more than three years to get round to searching the material they had seized in August 2006.

The Yard's head of communications, Dick Fedorcio, wrote to Alan Rusbridger to complain that my story 'once again presents an inaccurate position from our perspective and continues to imply that this case has not been handled properly and that we are party to a conspiracy'. He followed up by visiting Rusbridger once more, on 19 February 2010, this time with John Yates at his side. I was able to get a very accurate account of what went on.

Yates told Rusbridger that he was 'mystified' that he could not get his message across. He then proceeded to recite the RIPA bollocks which I felt sure was a false version of the law. 'I managed to fall out with Nick slightly,' he said. 'First time I've ever fallen out with a journalist. Nick thinks I'm being pedantic.' That wasn't the word I would have used. 'It's just the law,' he chorused. 'That's RIPA.' Later he added that on this basis, it was correct to say that there had been 'only a handful' of victims. But when Rusbridger pushed him to explain exactly what he was saying, Yates agreed that if you set aside the question of how RIPA should be interpreted, the simple reality was that there had been 'a mass attempt at penetrating people's voicemail systematically' by Goodman and Mulcaire and 'gross systematic breaches of privacy' and 'a systematic process of interception'. Yates added: 'It was dirty business, it is unpleasant.' At last! He was confirming the scale of the hacking – and yet he had never once attempted to say anything like this to the press, public or Parliament.

He went on to claim that most of the ninety-one people whose PIN codes had been found in the Mulcaire material had been contacted by the phone companies, i.e. they were among the 120 victims identified by those companies. This was very surprising since that same week, Scotland Yard's legal department had been writing to Mark Lewis saying that the police did not even know how many people had been contacted by the phone companies, let alone their identities.

He conceded that it was not ideal that Andy Hayman had gone to work for News International. 'Unfortunately, we have no control over what he does and doesn't do. Is it distasteful? Some people say it probably is.' But he tried to claim that the original inquiry had treated the investigation very seriously and had used 'significant resources' and 'very experienced investigators'. Yet they had failed to analyse the evidence which they seized, failed to persuade the *News of the World* to hand over internal paperwork, failed to interview a single other suspect, and failed to inform the potential victims in spite of agreeing with prosecutors that they would do so.

If I had any doubt about whether John Yates was a reliable source of information for my editor, that vanished when he came to the subject of the former deputy prime minister, John Prescott. Our original story about Gordon Taylor had said that Prescott was a target for Mulcaire. I now knew, from John Prescott's son, David, that in December 2009, after five months of pestering, Prescott had finally wrung out of Scotland Yard confirmation that he was indeed named as a target in the Mulcaire paperwork, on two different invoices, dated – exactly as we had said in our story – spring 2006. David Prescott had asked me not to publish this while his father's lawyers decided how to handle it. Now, two months later, John Yates calmly told Alan Rusbridger that there was no evidence at all to suggest Prescott had been a target. His exact words were: 'He doesn't appear anywhere in Goodman's material or in Mulcaire's material. There is no reference to John Prescott at all.'

Rusbridger ignored everything that Yates told him.

There was one other important meeting that week in February 2010. Late one evening, Rusbridger phoned me and started by saying that he sometimes felt as though he were living in a Stieg Larsson novel, full of endless plots and dark machinations. At short notice, he had been summoned to see a senior member of the Labour government and had found himself confronted by a minister brandishing a copy of the *Guardian*, pointing feverishly to my story about the ninety-one PIN codes and the 120 victims identified by the phone companies, insisting (as if Rusbridger did not know it) that this was very important, that Murdoch was out to destroy the governments of Barack Obama in the USA and of Kevin Rudd in Australia and just possibly this story could stop him doing the same to Gordon Brown's. This source had suggested to Rusbridger that the prime minister himself may have had his bank and phone records penetrated by Murdoch's journalists. He had ended by telling him to watch out. All very Stieg Larsson.

The minister had offered to help. I suggested that Rusbridger ask him to appoint a middleman, some trusted official who would meet me and become a point of contact in the hope that I could give them information which might be of use and (far more important for a selfish reporter) that they could squeeze information for me out of the police or even out of the Security Service, MI5. This happened very fast.

Within forty-eight hours, I was sitting in the coffee lounge of the Thistle hotel next to Victoria station with the middleman, a very bright and likeable character whom Rusbridger and I took to calling the Emissary. Our meeting was highly discreet, secret even, not because we were doing anything wrong but because, if News International found out that the *Guardian* was linking up – even indirectly – with a government minister, they would make propaganda and claim that we were part of a political plot. We might as well paint bullseyes on our backsides and invite them to kick us. I gave the Emissary a two-hour tutorial on crime at News International during which his phone rang two or three times, as the senior minister with whom he worked called in to check on progress. 'He's very excited about me seeing you,' he explained to me.

I gave him a short shopping list of questions to try to answer via his own contacts in government.

We were getting stronger.

While this was going on, I had decided to write a pamphlet, to be published in the run-up to the general election, which was widely predicted to happen in May 2010. It was to be called *Hack Attack* and it would summarise all of the evidence that Andy Coulson must have known that his journalists had been breaking the law and, therefore, that the man who looked set to be the next prime minister's close aide must have lied to Parliament when he gave evidence to the media select committee in July.

With the help of a researcher, I now had material from more journalists who had worked for the *News of the World*, each of whom independently agreed that, while the hacking might have been a secret from the outside world, inside their office, plenty of people knew, including Andy Coulson.

I got to know a couple of these journalists quite well. There was a lot of mutual suspicion at first. I heard from the *Guardian* that a former *News of the World* journalist called Paul McMullan had written a book which might disclose evidence of illegal activity and which he might want to publicise in the paper. I called him, and he was a model of surly resentment. He suggested I was taping the call. Legally, I would be allowed to; in fact, I was not. He said the *Guardian* was wrong to chase after journalists. Journalists were heroes, he said. Privacy was for bad people, a way of hiding their badness. That was all. He hadn't finished writing the book, he didn't know what it would say, he ended the conversation. For all his sullen resistance, McMullan was interesting:

if he really believed all that about privacy, he might well decide that there was no reason to hide what had been going on at the paper. So I stuck with him.

Over the weeks, I had several more phone calls with him, each a little longer than the last, each a little more relaxed. Then we met up and spent an afternoon in Brighton and – on the strict condition that this was all off the record – he opened up. McMullan had spent seven years on the paper, from 1994 when Piers Morgan was editor, through the next editor, Phil Hall, until he left in October 2001 when Rebekah Brooks was editor and Andy Coulson was her deputy. He was quite open about the fact that he had spent his time there swimming down a river of alcohol and cocaine and ended up in the Priory clinic, which had only reinforced his fundamentalist Fleet Street convictions: 'What I was taught in the Priory, is that you should confess everything, no such thing as privacy. Adolf Hitler wants privacy, Jesus doesn't.'

He was almost evangelical in his enthusiasm for the dark arts. He had risen from being a reporter to a deputy features editor under Brooks, and in that role, he had dealt routinely with Steve Whittamore and a couple of other PIs: 'I must have authorised hundreds of technically illegal operations. I say it's for the greater good.' He gave me the example of an actress whose medical records he accessed in order to be able to expose the fact that she had had an abortion.

Coulson, he said, knew all about it. As deputy editor, one of Coulson's tasks had been to set up a new investigations unit, built around McMullan and Mazher Mahmood, who specialised in dressing up as the 'fake sheikh' and tricking people into embarrassing revelations which he covertly recorded. 'How can Coulson possibly say he didn't know what was going on with PIs? He was the brains behind the investigations department, that was his first task. How can he say he had no idea about how it works?'

This was all very strong; but he refused to say anything on the record. I could quote it as the claims of an unnamed source, which would be interesting but it would have no impact. I needed evidence which nobody could deny. Which was why I spent a lot of time with a former *News of the World* reporter I traced, whom I will call York. She knew plenty about Glenn Mulcaire.

She explained that while Mulcaire was not much of a secret in the newsroom and even turned up to Christmas parties, there was only a limited number of people who could actually commission him. She named Greg Miskiw, Neville Thurlbeck, Jimmy Weatherup and Ian Edmondson. I knew enough now about the *News of the World* to see the pattern: all four of them had been news editors. If that was correct, it put Mulcaire right at the heart of the newspaper's work: it was part of the news editor's job to tell him what to do.

York also made sense of something which had been said by Mango, the anonymous source who had called the *Guardian* after the Gordon Taylor story. He had claimed that Greg Miskiw's network of dark arts involved a private investigator called 'Boyle' who had been paying off police officers. Wrong spelling. It was 'Boyall'. I knew John Boyall had been part of Steve Whittamore's network and had ended up in the dock alongside him, but what York explained was that Boyall was yet another PI who had worked direct for the *News of the World*: in the late 1990s, she said, Boyall had been Greg Miskiw's main man until he made the mistake of introducing Miskiw to his assistant, Glenn Mulcaire, who had then replaced him as the *News of the World*'s favourite gumshoe.

York seemed determined to help and agreed to talk to some of the key suspects – Greg Miskiw, Neville Thurlbeck, Ian Edmondson and others – and to tape the conversations in the hope that they would disclose evidence. It didn't work. She fed back a few useful titbits, but she fell into a frustrating pattern, reporting that she had spoken to key people yet always apologising that they had failed to say anything of interest.

Around that time, I found a sports report in the *News of the World*, dated 18 August 2002, which harked back to Mulcaire's early career as a footballer, describing the first game ever played by one of his teams, AFC Wimbledon: 'Glenn Mulcaire – the man they call Trigger – had been seemingly ruled out of the club's Combined Counties Premier Division debut with cracked ribs. But Trigger, part of our special investigations team, was steam-rollered into action just ten minutes before kick-off.' So the humble sports reporter knew about Mulcaire's work for the paper, even though the then deputy editor – Coulson – reckoned he had never heard of him.

Similarly, I came across an interesting paragraph in an unpublished book which had been written by a keen fan of AFC Wimbledon (locally known as 'the Dons'). It took the form of a diary. This was the entry for 4 March 2003, shortly after Coulson had become editor of the paper, describing how Mulcaire turned up to watch a game with his family in tow: 'He was getting back to a bit of Dons reality after being wined and dined at the Pont de la Tour by Murdoch executives the previous evening to plan some News International skulduggery. Not a good man to give your mobile number to isn't our Trigger. One call and he'll tell you everyone you've spoken to in the last couple of months.' So this ordinary football fan knew what Mulcaire was up to with Murdoch's team, yet still we were expected to believe that Coulson succeeded in knowing nothing.

It was steaming, screaming obvious that Coulson must have known, but the frustrating fact was that I had no smoking gun. The case against him was compelling yet not conclusive and, since UK libel law remains a relentless enemy of truth without proof, I decided that my planned pamphlet would simply provoke another blizzard of lies from Coulson and News International and achieve nothing, and so I abandoned the project. I would have to find proof which they could not deny.

I had known 'Karl' for nearly fifteen years. He was a seriously good detective, whom I had met when I was covering a murder trial. He was also a reporter's dream – strong and confident and blessed with a dramatic shortage of respect for anybody who did not match up to his standards, which happened to include some of his bosses. If he thought the public needed to know something, he would tell a trusted reporter even if that did mean defying official policy (which is why I'm not using his real name). And, as Murdoch's bad luck would have it, Karl happened to be in a position to help with the hacking scandal.

Meeting one day by arrangement, at a bus stop on the banks of the Thames, he told me that he knew a lot about Jonathan Rees of Southern Investigations. Now, simply because Karl did not think that a thug should be using bent officers to invade people's privacy for a tabloid newspaper, he undertook to help me to find out more.

With his guidance, I was able to accumulate a mass of detailed evidence about the work which Rees and his business partner, Sid Fillery, had been doing for journalists, particularly for Alex Marunchak at the *News of the World*. More important, I got hold of something which had real political punch – copies of invoices from News International, which showed that, in spite of Rees being jailed for a seriously vile conspiracy to take a woman's child away by planting cocaine on her, Andy Coulson's *News of the World* had started hiring him again after he emerged from prison. I also found that Rees had been involved in hacking into a target's email messages.

Clearly, this would put real pressure on Coulson's story. I got ready to write. In the meantime, reinforcements arrived from the House of Commons.

On 24 February 2010, the media select committee released its much-delayed report, unanimously attacking key players. They criticised the Press Complaints Commission for accepting News International's version of events at face value and described the conclusions of their report on the affair as 'simplistic and surprising'. They criticised the Metropolitan Police for their failure even to attempt to question anybody about the email for Neville Thurlbeck. 'It is our view that the decision was a wrong one. The email was a strong indication both of additional lawbreaking and of the possible involvement of others. These matters merited thorough police investigation, and the first steps to be taken seem to us to be obvious. The Metropolitan Police's reasons for not doing so seem to us to be inadequate.'

The committee reserved its strongest words for News International. There was no doubt, they said, that a 'significant number of people' had been hacked. They recorded that they had no evidence to show that Andy Coulson was involved but said it was 'inconceivable' that Clive Goodman was the only person on the paper who knew about it. 'A culture undoubtedly did exist in the newsroom of the *News of the World* and other newspapers at the time which, at best, turned a blind eye to illegal activities such as phone-hacking and blagging and, at worst, actively condoned it. We condemn this without reservation and believe that it has done substantial damage to the newspaper industry as a whole.'

The *News of the World*'s internal inquiry had been far from 'full' and 'rigorous' as its executives had claimed. It had kept secret its settlement with Gordon Taylor 'to avoid further embarrassing publicity' and had been wrong not to inform the PCC and the select committee of the settlement. The committee complained of the 'collective amnesia' of News International witnesses and continued: 'Throughout, we have repeatedly encountered an unwillingness to provide the detailed information that we sought, claims of ignorance or lack of recall, and deliberate obfuscation. We strongly condemn this behaviour which reinforces the widely held impression that the press generally regard themselves as unaccountable and that News International in particular has sought to conceal the truth about what really occurred.'

They left no doubt that they believed they were dealing with a cover-up in which the *News of the World* had enjoyed significant assistance: 'We are concerned at the readiness of all those involved – News International, the police and the PCC – to leave Mr Goodman as the sole scapegoat, without carrying out a full investigation at the time.'

This was strong – just about as strong as a report from a select committee can possibly be. And yet it made no difference. There was no sudden roar of indignation from MPs or from the government, not even a hint of irritation that this powerful corporation could commit crime and rely on the authorities to fail to do anything about it and then to come before a select committee and engage in a display of 'collective amnesia'.

The Murdoch papers played out a parody of bent reporting.

At the press conference, the *Sun*'s political correspondent, Tom Newton Dunn, swooped like a buzzard on the one paragraph in the report where the MPs had split. Tom Watson and other Labour members had written a paragraph about Matt Driscoll, the former *News of the World* sports reporter who had been given £800,000 compensation for the campaign of bullying led by Andy Coulson. Conservative members saw this as a political stunt, aimed at distracting attention from newspaper stories about the bullying of staff in Downing Street by the Labour prime minister Gordon Brown. The committee split in its vote on whether to include the point. One of the Conservative MPs, Philip Davies, was quick to give Newton Dunn a quote and so it came to pass that in the *Sun* the next day, the committee's report was covered in a short story on page 2 under the headline 'Report Hijack'. In its entirety, this read:

> A key Commons committee report on the press was hijacked by Labour MPs for political gain, one of its members has alleged. It was supposed to concentrate on issues of freedom of speech, privacy and libel 'tourism'. But Labour MPs tried to link the Tories with bullying allegations that shamed Downing Street.
>
> The committee also spent seven months probing a phone-tapping scandal for which a *News of the World* journalist was jailed but uncovered no new evidence. Tory MP Philip Davies said: 'There was a feeling the report was being abused for narrow, petty party political advantage. The main purpose was to defend freedom of speech.' Labour MPs wanted to smear Tory communications boss Andy Coulson, an ex *News of the World* editor. But the report found 'no evidence' he knew phone-hacking was taking place.

On page 8, the *Sun* also ran a leader comment, headed 'Cheap, pathetic and worthless', explaining to its readers that this was another dark day for Parliament, as the media select committee had abandoned fairness and independence and shamefully wasted seven months on unfounded claims by the *Guardian*. Since they had found no new evidence to support the *Guardian*, the committee had fallen back on 'familiar Labour tactics of smear and innuendo' by trying to link the Conservative Party to allegations of bullying. 'Its report is accordingly worthless.'

Murdoch's *Times* managed a grand total of six paragraphs at the bottom of page 15 on the committee's comments on the hacking scandal, matching the committee's view that News International had displayed 'collective amnesia' with a claim from the company that some members of the committee were guilty of 'innuendo, unwarranted inference and exaggeration'.

And on Sunday, the *News of the World* informed its readers: 'Your right to know is mired in MPs' bias. But a free press is too precious to lose.' After accusing the committee of a 'descent into bias, spite and bile' they went on to declare that 'We'll take no lessons in standards from MPs – nor from the self-serving pygmies who run the circulation-challenged *Guardian*.' No spite or bile there, then.

Rusbridger contacted the leader of the Liberal Democrats, Nick Clegg, and sent him a detailed summary of the story so far, suggesting that his party might call for a public inquiry. They didn't. I contacted a senior official at the Information Commissioner's Office and asked if they would consider running a new inquiry. They wouldn't.

Still, we had more ammunition. I was ready to publish all I had found about Jonathan Rees and his corrupt activities for the *News of the World*.

I had drafted a front-page story with a long feature to go inside the paper, revealing that Rees had been re-hired by Coulson's paper in spite of his prison sentence. It disclosed that three other private investigators – Glenn Mulcaire, Steve Whittamore and John Boyall – also had worked under Coulson at the *News of the World*, gathering information by illegal means. And yet, on Coulson's account, he had never known anything about any of them.

Drawing on Mango's information, the story also pointed out that during this time, Coulson's assistant editor, Greg Miskiw, had been arrested and questioned about his involvement with John Boyall and with the payment of bribes, and yet Coulson apparently had never known anything about that either. I had got fed up with calling Greg Miskiw and listening to his heavy breathing while I attempted to persuade him to talk to me. So I simply emailed him and told him that I was going to report the fact that he had been questioned by police unless he told me otherwise. He didn't reply. Fine.

However, there was a problem. As a result of Detective Chief Superintendent Dave Cook's work, Rees was now awaiting trial with several other men for the 1987 murder of Daniel Morgan. We could possibly be accused of being in contempt of court if we published such powerful material before the trial had taken place. We decided to run the story but to hide Rees's identity behind the unimaginative name,

Mr A. With the draft story written, I emailed Coulson, pressing him over his claims of ignorance.

I reminded him of the conviction in April 2005 of Steve Whittamore, who had been working for his paper: 'This conviction was reported in national news media. Can you tell me whether you became aware of this at the time and, if so, what steps you took to investigate the involvement of your journalists in this illegal activity?'

I told him that I knew that when police were investigating John Boyall, they had questioned Greg Miskiw. 'Can you tell me what steps you took to investigate and prevent a recurrence?'

I confronted him with the very public history of Jonathan Rees's crimes – not only his prison sentence for the cocaine plot but a long story in the *Guardian* in September 2002 which had detailed Rees's activities for the *News of the World*, and I asked him 'whether you were aware that, in spite of all of the above, Rees was hired again by the News of the World, after his release from prison, when you were editor, and paid from your editorial budget to carry out more work for the paper and that this work continued to involve the use of illegal methods?'

I ended the message:

Finally, the thrust of the piece as a whole is that your statement to the select committee, that you had never had any involvement at all in any form of illegal activity at any stage in your career as a journalist, is one which remains in doubt, largely as a result of the sheer scale of the illegal activity which was being conducted by private investigators in the pay of the *News of the World* during your time as deputy editor and editor. The core of this is whether it is conceivable that you were unaware of the explicit invoices which were being submitted, the considerable amount of money which was being spent, the considerable amount of information which was being supplied for stories which you were supervising, the number of your journalists who were directly involved in handling this information.

If it is possible to come back to me before four o'clock in the afternoon, that would be helpful.

Many thanks.

Nick.

He replied simply: 'I have nothing to add to the evidence I gave to the select committee.'

On 25 February 2010, the *Guardian* published a front-page story, headed 'Coulson hit by new charges: Paper hired convicted private eye while Tory PR chief was still in charge'. Inside, the feature was headed 'The strange case of Mr A and the editor who saw nothing'. Rusbridger ran a leader comment, summarising the refusal by the Murdoch papers and most of the rest of Fleet Street to report the findings of the media select committee, and, once more, he contacted the leader of the Liberal Democrats, Nick Clegg, and alerted him that he had published significant new information. Rusbridger's deputy, Ian Katz, also contacted Steve Hilton, the closest adviser to the Conservative leader David Cameron, in whose office Coulson was working, to warn him. Later, Katz repeated the warning to Ed Llewellyn, Cameron's chief of staff. As far as we could tell, neither political leader took any significant step as a result of this.

It was not clear that any of this information was having any appreciable effect on anybody outside the *Guardian* office.

At last, the big gun was ready to fire. Max Clifford's case was heading for court. And Clifford was clear: his silence was not for sale. He wanted the truth. He was a lifelong Labour supporter who wanted to expose Andy Coulson. All we needed was for the court to order the police to hand over the evidence in his case.

For months, Scotland Yard had been dragging their heels. Finally, under orders from a High Court judge, they had handed over Mulcaire's notes about Clifford – but they had redacted key parts of the document, blacking out anything which would have identified the *News of the World* journalists who had commissioned the hacking. This smelled bad: the police had not redacted anything when they disclosed paperwork for Gordon Taylor's case, so why start now? Charlotte Harris had also asked for an order for News International and Glenn Mulcaire to hand over relevant evidence. Now, she went back to court for yet another order, for the police to disclose the blacked-out parts of their paperwork.

In the background, one highly reliable source claimed to know that the name which Mulcaire had written on his notes about Clifford was 'Ian'. If that turned out to be the name behind Scotland Yard's redactions, that would be a stick of dynamite in News International's castle wall. 'Ian' would be no rogue reporter. 'Ian' would be Ian Edmondson – the assistant editor (news) since December 2004.

Everything stalled for Christmas and stalled again when Charlotte Harris was rushed into hospital for an operation. However, by mid-January, I was picking up reports that Rebekah Brooks had struck some kind of deal with Max Clifford and also that she was spreading a little smear that 'Nick Davies has been throwing money around left, right and centre to get people to talk.' There was also a nasty suggestion that the *News of the World* were digging into Clifford's private and financial affairs, trying to find something embarrassing that they could agree to keep quiet, just in case they needed a little whitemail.

And yet the case was still alive. On 3 February 2010, Mr Justice Vos issued new orders. He told News International that within one week, they must hand over copies of the *News of the World*'s original contract with Glenn Mulcaire; and of their secret settlement with him after he came out of prison; and of their secret settlement in the case of Gordon Taylor. The judge went on to tell Glenn Mulcaire that within two weeks, he must produce a sworn affidavit naming all those who had instructed him to hack Clifford's voicemail and all those to whom he had passed Clifford's messages. Finally, the judge also ordered the Information Commissioner to hand over Steve Whittamore's blue book, recording all the requests he had handled from News International journalists (the same document which had already been disclosed and then sealed in the Gordon Taylor case).

Charlotte Harris was now almost ready to go back to court to force the police to disclose Mulcaire's notes about Clifford in unredacted form. She had also taken a statement from the ICO's chief investigator, David Clancy, that there was 'a widespread and unlawful trade in confidential information commissioned by journalists of the *News of the World*'.

If all this came out in court, it would blow a gaping and irreparable hole in the Murdoch defences. And yet, as the days ticked by towards the judge's deadlines, I heard again that Max Clifford had agreed some kind of deal with News International, and that the *News of the World*'s lawyer, Tom Crone, had been called in to finalise it.

The first deadline, 10 February, came and went with no sign that News International had handed over the documents which the judge had called for. On 16 February, we ran a story warning that 'the *News of the World* is believed to be planning to settle a court case which threatens to disclose further evidence of the involvement of its journalists in illegal information-gathering by private investigators'.

The second deadline, 17 February, came and went with no sign of Mulcaire providing the affidavit which the judge had called for. But also there was no sign of a final agreement between Clifford and News International. I spoke to Max Clifford and then sent him an email, urging him not to give in, attempting to appeal to his long-standing support for the Labour Party: 'It is no exaggeration to say that some of the most powerful people in Britain are hanging on your next move, hoping you'll stick with it, because they know the size of the scandal that is waiting to emerge . . . You've ended up being the man with the future in his hands. You can settle, and the whole thing gets covered up for the foreseeable future. You can stand firm and be the man who made the difference.'

It was too late. The rumours were right. In spite of all his claims to want to expose the truth, Clifford had agreed to back off. On 25 February, Mr Justice Vos issued a new order, closing down the case because Clifford was no longer pursuing it. The truth would remain concealed. As flimsy compensation, I set out to discover exactly how News International had engineered this cover-up.

On 9 March, we disclosed that the Murdoch company had agreed to pay Clifford more than £1 million. Some of this was to cover his legal costs. Most of it was in the form of guaranteed income for stories which he would sell them over the next three years. This meant that it could be presented as something other than the payment of damages. Nobody was fooled. But it was clever. Our biggest gun was spiked and broken and, at least for now, we were beaten.

On Twitter, the comedian Stephen Fry reacted by asking for a definition of 'countryside' and providing the cryptic but aggressive answer – 'murdering Max Clifford'.

9. The mogul and his governments

Based on interviews with government officials and ministers; political biographies; and evidence disclosed to the Leveson Inquiry.

When he first arrived in the United Kingdom in January 1969, to buy the *News of the World*, Rupert Murdoch had no significant political muscle.

In the eyes of the UK establishment he was a young (aged thirty-seven), slightly plump, socially ill-at-ease businessman who had one supremely attractive characteristic: he was not Robert Maxwell, the ego-driven and corrupt millionaire whose lust for power was as subtle as snakebite and who had been closing in fast on the *News of the World*. Murdoch slipped in, offered a bigger buck and was warmly welcomed as the new owner.

For a couple of years, the worst that was said of him was that he was, well, a touch vulgar. The *News of the World* had never been acceptable in polite society. It specialised in the bawdy, a bit like the best kind of working man's pub – warm and cheerful, good for a laugh, with a flash of stocking top too. It picked up on obscure court cases, especially the ones where a doctor or a country parson was accused of fumbling with the undercarriage of some local widow. Murdoch soon started to push the boundaries.

Within months of taking over, he serialised the memoirs of Christine Keeler, the elegant young woman who had caused huge scandal by wrapping her long, slim legs around the then Secretary of State for war, the Conservative MP John Profumo, who had not only enjoyed an exciting affair with her but then lied to Parliament about it. This had all happened six years earlier: Profumo had resigned; the government had been disgraced. This was simply the inside story of what had gone on between the sheets. But it was good for sales.

A few years later, he did far more of the same when his journalists joined in exposing the Conservative peer Lord Lambton, who had found another elegant young call girl, Norma Levy, to play with, while a *News of the World* photographer peeked through a hole in the wall and captured the whole sweaty business on film. More sales, more money.

Even after he bought the *Sun*, later in 1969, he was still no kind of power-monger in the UK. He rescued a newspaper that was tottering towards the grave and once again increased its sales, with brash head-lines, sensational stories and all the nudes that were fit to print. *The Times* observed that 'Mr Murdoch has not invented sex but he does show a remarkable enthusiasm for its benefits to circulation.'

Still, the formula worked. By 1978, the *Sun* had become the most popular daily paper in the UK, and Murdoch finally began to become a serious player. Noisily, his two papers backed Margaret Thatcher all the way to Downing Street in April 1979 – and the great game of power began.

In 1981, two years after Mrs Thatcher became prime minister, Murdoch set out to buy *The Times* and the *Sunday Times*. The Thatcher govern-ment generously opened the way for him, choosing not to refer his bid to the regulator, the Monopolies and Mergers Commission, who would have had good grounds to block it. Government records that were finally released thirty-one years later, in 2012, disclosed that Murdoch secretly met Mrs Thatcher for a Sunday lunch at Chequers just as the deal was being put together. Murdoch and the government pretended that the two newspapers were exempt from monopoly law because they were on the verge of financial collapse. It wasn't true.

There was outrage in Parliament and bitter comment from rival newspapers, but Murdoch got what he wanted and, with that deal, established himself as the biggest newspaper proprietor in the UK, a man whom politicians now certainly wished to please.

So it was that in 1986, when Murdoch wanted to stop Robert Maxwell buying the *Today* newspaper, the Thatcher government referred Maxwell's bid to the Monopolies Commission, which blocked it; and in 1987 when he himself wanted to buy *Today* the government reversed its position and chose not to involve the Monopolies Commission, so he bought it; and in 1990, when he was nurturing his new satellite TV company, Sky, while Mrs Thatcher's government was passing a communications bill with a new framework of regulation for television, Sky was exempted from almost all of it.

Later that same year, Mrs Thatcher delivered one particularly graceful favour. Eighteen months after its launch, Sky TV was wallowing in failure, beaming four channels from the Astra satellite to the UK where just about nobody owned a dish to receive them, and losing some £2 million a week in the process. Murdoch wanted to save the company by merging with its only competitor, British Satellite Broadcasting, which was failing on an even grander scale but, as ever, this plan was clearly likely to run into trouble with the regulator, in this case the Independent Television Commission, which would object to the creation of a monopoly.

However, it so happened that the government was in the process of closing down the ITC and replacing it with a new regulator, to be known as the Independent Broadcasting Authority. There was a five-day gap between the death of the ITC and the birth of the IBA when there was simply no regulator in existence, and it so happened that during this brief moment of total non-regulation, the government looked away and quietly waved the merger through the legal fence: Murdoch was allowed to create BSkyB, with News Corp effectively controlling its board, owning 50% of the company (later reduced to 39% by a share flotation).

As ever, this was not the result of a formal deal. There was a natural and easy relationship between Murdoch and Margaret Thatcher. They saw the world through the same hardline neoliberal eyes – unfettered capitalism, deregulated markets, privatised everything. His subsequent relationship with Tony Blair, from 1994, when he became Labour leader, was more awkward. Blair was arguably the most conservative leader in the history of the Labour Party, but nonetheless, he and his closest advisers embraced Rupert Murdoch the way a trainer embraces a tiger, with great care and genuine anxiety.

Some of Blair's closest advisers privately looked on Murdoch and his crew with deep discomfort. Alastair Campbell once compared a lunch with senior Murdoch journalists to a meeting of the far-right British National Party. Certainly, they did not want to be pushed around by Murdoch; but Blair had seen how the *Sun* in 1992 had monstered the former Labour leader Neil Kinnock in order to help hand power to Murdoch's chosen candidate, the Conservative John Major. He had seen, too, how Murdoch had then lost faith in Major, reaching the point where the *Sun's* then editor, Kelvin MacKenzie, claimed to have answered an inquiry from Major about the following day's coverage by telling him: 'I've got a large bucket of shit on my desk and tomorrow morning, I'm going to pour it all over your head.' (In some versions of the story, Major replied weakly: 'Oh, Kelvin, you are a wag.')

With the simple aim of neutralising the threat, Blair and his advisers set out to finesse the relationship. Some of those involved say that their theory was that they would make no policy concession to Murdoch, but they would deliver three things: they would give his journalists stories; they would give him personal flattery and attention; and, every so often, when there was a policy which they themselves had chosen but which they knew would please him, they would wrap it up with a red ribbon and present it to him as though it were a gift. These same sources agree that it didn't work.

From the outset, they compromised. When Blair returned to London from his first bonding with Murdoch at News Corp's annual gathering, at Hayman Island, Australia, in 1995, one of his party's first acts was to change their media policy in Murdoch's favour – killing off their commitment for an urgent inquiry into foreign ownership of the news media, and withdrawing their plan to bring in a privacy law, to protect the victims of tabloid intrusion. It was not that Murdoch had threatened to monster them if they stuck to their policy, simply that they feared that he might and thought it prudent to send a signal which might placate him (although Blair continues to insist he had his own independent reasons for the change).

But this was a complicated relationship, and Blair's people did try to stand up to Murdoch. He wanted to buy Manchester United, and they stopped him. He didn't want them to create the new TV regulator,

Ofcom, but they did. He didn't want them to give the BBC new channels or to increase the licence fee, but they did both. However, the longer the game went on, the harder it was to keep the tiger in its place.

A senior figure who worked in Blair's Downing Street, speaking on condition of anonymity, described the obsessive preoccupation with what newspapers were saying and, in particular, with the *Sun*. The *Daily Mail* was important, and so was *The Times*, but it was the *Sun* which really mattered. The *Sun* journalists knew it and, according to several officials, learned to treat the government with a bullying contempt.

Sometimes, the officials say, the bullying would simply be a matter of the *Sun's* high regard for its own interests. A senior adviser at the Treasury recalls: 'We'd come out of the budget speech and do briefings with the press, and the *Sun* would stand there ostentatiously working on their calculators to find out how much extra tax Rebekah would have to pay – "How am I going to explain to my editor that she is going to have to pay all this extra money?"'

At other times, however, this behaviour became an attempt to interfere with policymaking – not simply through the legitimate journalistic activity of publishing news and comment but by bullying behind the scenes. In November 2001, Blair's Chancellor of the Exchequer, Gordon Brown, announced a big boost in spending for the National Health Service. It was a popular move, but the *Sun* saw it as an excuse to increase taxes and started monstering the chancellor: 'Taxer Brown . . . Chancellor's cure for the NHS is a massive gamble – using our money . . . Gord's bitter pill . . . If Gordon returns to tax and spend and hikes taxes, we will be gunning for him.' This evidently panicked Brown, who contacted the *Sun* and agreed to rearrange his diary so that he could go to their office that day in order to try to make peace. With his special adviser, Ed Balls, at his side, Brown sat down with the *Sun's* outspoken right-wing political editor, Trevor Kavanagh, for an interview which, according to one of those present, rapidly became a negotiation about policy. Kavanagh insisted that Brown should accept the advice in that morning's *Sun* for the NHS to start buying in services from private medical businesses. This was no part of Brown's policy, but Kavanagh won.

At the end of what Kavanagh himself described as 'a sometimes tense interview', Brown agreed that the NHS would receive not one penny of extra funding unless the service agreed to 'reforms' and 'modernisation'. The language was coded, but the meaning was clear: private health companies would be allowed into the NHS. One of Brown's then aides said: 'As a result, post 2001, we have Gordon held over the fire, backing "freedom hospitals", privatising dentistry. It became a barometer for whether the *Sun* thought he was strong enough to become prime minister.'

In the same way, after the abduction and murder of eight-year-old Sarah Payne in July 2000, Rebekah Brooks not only used the columns of the *News of the World* to campaign for a new 'Sarah's Law' but also repeatedly browbeat ministers behind the scenes, demanding that they give her newspaper a victory for which she could claim credit. She wanted a version of the American Megan's Law, which publishes the names and home addresses of convicted sex offenders. The government – supported by police and some children's charities – thought that was a very dangerous idea: at best, it would drive paedophiles underground, making life difficult for the police; at worst, it would provoke physical attacks on named child-abusers. They resisted. Rebekah insisted. The result was that an idea which would otherwise have been shelved was revived and finally introduced in a diluted form – more Rebekah's law than the government's.

Again, as editor of the *Sun* from January 2003, Brooks hectored ministers to support the newspaper's campaign to cure overcrowding in prisons by transferring inmates to prison ships. One former official recalls: 'Every Home Secretary she dealt with must have scars on their backs from her trying to whip them into line over prison ships. Several ministers gave in and agreed to do it, but then they'd check with officials who said "Are you off your rocker? This is a very expensive thing to do, the sums just won't add up."'

Beneath the recurrent effort to change government policy, some Murdoch journalists simply demanded – and received – special favours for their work. One official recalls Rebekah Brooks calling Downing Street in a rage after the *News of the World* was given a rare joint interview by Tony Blair and Gordon Brown during the 2005 election campaign. Another editor might have been fobbed off politely, but Rebekah demanded recompense.

First, Downing Street arranged for Brown to give an exclusive interview to the *Sun*'s Trevor Kavanagh, who has the brain of a fox and the strike of a viper. That ended badly when Brown refused to comply with Rebekah's requirement that he announce tax cuts. 'Kavanagh was looking at him with contempt – "Are you going to say anything that would make it into my paper?"' So then Downing Street offered up an exclusive interview for Rebekah Brooks and Kavanagh with Tony Blair and his wife, Cherie, during which they were required to discuss their sleeping arrangements, sex life and romantic moments.

It was not only in their dealings with Murdoch journalists that the Blair government found themselves sliding downhill. On a parallel track, they started conceding far more ground in their relationship with Murdoch himself. There are serious people who live and breathe Westminster politics who believe that Tony Blair's decision to back the invasion of Iraq in March 2003 was crucially influenced by his fear of Murdoch. On this reading, among his other motives, Blair was thinking ahead to the very real possibility that he would have to fight a referendum campaign over Europe (either joining its currency or adopting its new constitution); knew that the anti-EU Murdoch papers would throw all available ammunition at him; and calculated that he had to join forces with the US invasion to prove that he still stood by the 'special relationship' with Washington and had not simply fallen into the sweaty embrace of Paris and Bonn.

During March 2003, as he was poised to make the final decision to back the invasion without waiting for a UN resolution which could have made it legal, Blair made three phone calls to Rupert Murdoch, according to a disclosure under the Freedom of Information Act. Years later, at the World Economic Forum in Davos in February 2007, Murdoch was asked whether his newspapers had succeeded in shaping the agenda on the invasion of Iraq. 'No, I don't think so,' he answered, before adding: 'We tried.'

Similarly, there is some evidence that Tony Blair would have taken Britain into the euro if it had not been for the relentlessly threatening noises from Murdoch, who loathed the European Union with its thicket of regulation, and particularly loathed the idea of Britain joining the euro in case it pushed up the cost of his borrowing. In his diary, Alastair Campbell recalls Blair phoning him after a dinner with Murdoch and complaining that it was pointless trying to talk to Murdoch's people about Europe because Murdoch was so over-the-top. 'It was faintly obscene that we even had to worry what they thought,' Campbell adds. Campbell's deputy, Lance Price, has said he understood that Blair had given Murdoch an assurance that the government would not change its policy on Europe without talking to him first, which was effectively a veto. In practice, Blair opted to quietly shelve the problem simply by deciding not to decide whether or not to join the euro. That was in itself a significant shift in policy.

However, Murdoch destabilised that uneasy compromise by working on Gordon Brown. The chancellor was badly trapped: on the one hand, he wanted to be seen to be loyal to Blair and so his people briefed the press that he shared Blair's view of the euro; on the other hand, he didn't share Blair's view and wanted the Eurosceptic press, including Murdoch's papers, to know it, so his people also briefed the opposite. All of which turned into a cack-handed disaster.

In the autumn of 1997 Brown's media adviser, Charlie Whelan, spent an evening in the Red Lion pub, just across the road from Downing Street, where he was overheard briefing journalists that the government had made a firm decision not to join the euro before the next election. That would have pleased Murdoch, but it didn't please the prime minister, who heard what was happening on the Westminster grapevine and had to call Whelan in the pub to find out what the world was being told about his government's policy.

The pound crashed, Downing Street was furious, there was an emergency debate in the House of Commons, and Brown was forced to find a way of pacifying his prime minister, who wanted to stick with his 'no decision' decision, while also pleasing Murdoch, who wanted the euro tossed into a policy dustbin. Brown came up with a brilliant device, announcing that Britain would join the euro only if it passed five tests. Since each of these tests was more or less subjective, this allowed the prime minister to say that there was still no decision and Murdoch to believe that the tests would fail. Murdoch was right.

The prime minister may have been interested in joining the euro. He never came close.

There was a poignant and revealing incident one afternoon in November 2006.

Gordon Brown was still Chancellor of the Exchequer but clearly determined to replace Tony Blair as prime minister. Brown's press office took a call from a reporter at the *Sun*, who announced that they had discovered that Brown's four-month-old son, Fraser, was suffering from cystic fibrosis.

A senior aide recalled how Brown phoned his wife, Sarah, who was in the flat above his office with Fraser and their three-year-old son, John; how she came down so that the two of them could decide together what to do; and how both of them were soon close to tears of desperation. Their firstborn child, Jennifer Jane, had died nearly five years earlier, aged just ten days. Doctors had only recently confirmed that Fraser had cystic fibrosis and, since it is a genetic condition, they were waiting for all the children on both sides of their family to be tested to see whether any of them might also be afflicted.

How would those children feel if they learned they were at risk by reading about themselves in the *Sun*? How would Fraser feel if, when he was old enough to read, he came across stories on the Internet about his illness possibly meaning that he might die young? The aide recalled: 'Gordon really was near tears. He was absolutely clear that he was not going to have his son treated as press property.'

So they came to a decision: if they could not prevent the story coming out, they could at least try to make sure that it came out on their terms and not as the property of the *Sun*; they would put out a press release describing their son's condition for all news organisations. This was a dangerous act of defiance.

If Brown was to become prime minister, he needed Fleet Street – particularly the *Sun* – to support him. But the *Sun*, like Rupert Murdoch's three other UK titles, backed the rival Blair camp. Brown had done his best to throw right-wing meat to the *Sun*'s attack dogs, but they were reluctant to swallow it, observing that Brown was simultaneously offering left-wing treats to the Labour MPs whose support he also needed. Now, it was horribly obvious that if the Browns gave away the *Sun's* exclusive about Fraser's illness, they would be slapping the *Sun* in the face just as Brown most wanted to reach out and take its hand. Nevertheless, Brown stood his ground and insisted. And then Rebekah Brooks called.

According to the senior aide: 'She made it pretty clear that this would be a disaster for Gordon's relationship with the *Sun* if their exclusive was spoiled. She said it would mean that in future when the *Sun* had stories about Gordon, they would publish them without checking with him. She was putting on the thumbscrews. There were three or four calls from her that afternoon – "What are you going to do? You mustn't do this."'

Concern for the child, or for the parents who were supposed to be her friends, does not appear to have coloured her position. Another source close to Brown claims that Rebekah also called direct to Sarah Brown that afternoon, putting pressure on her to protect their exclusive: 'She was saying, "We do feel for you, we want to make it gentle."'

Brown stuck to his line, but his advisers were so worried about alienating the *Sun* that they engineered a discreet compromise. One of them called the *Sun* to tell them that they would delay releasing the Browns' statement until the early evening in order to give the *Sun* time to produce a mock-up of their next day's front page which they could send round to TV studios, so that the early evening bulletins might present the story as their exclusive. Rebekah had to be pleased.

Brown never managed to bend far enough to pull off Blair's trick of making peace with the Murdochs. Brown and Rupert Murdoch liked each other and got on well, meeting for private breakfasts at Claridge's hotel when the mogul was in London. The problem was that Brown's gut instincts were far more radical than Blair's. Furthermore, he thought James Murdoch was conservative beyond comprehension and he loathed much of News International's journalism, particularly the work of Trevor Kavanagh, who was happy to attack Brown in print and to his face for being too soft on migrants, criminals, 'benefit scroungers' and other *Sun* targets.

Brown spent years trying to get it right. Sometimes, his radical roots would break through. Then his fear of the *Sun* would take over and he would compromise his own beliefs. For example, in 2003, officials say he hatched a plan to impose VAT on newspaper sales to punish News International for its bullying – and then quickly saw the blood on the *Sun*'s teeth and dropped it. He was opposed on principle to Tony Blair's 'reform agenda', to model public services on private businesses by giving each school and hospital a budget and making them compete for students and patients. But the *Sun* liked Blair's plan and made its feelings very clear. At the News International party at the Labour conference in the autumn of 2003, according to one of Brown's staff, he was surrounded by hostile Murdoch journalists 'like a pack of dogs and they all started yapping and biting and chewing into him. Gordon was blocking foundation hospitals, and they didn't like it. There was a horrific exchange with them.'

The pressure to adopt the reform agenda continued, according to another former official who says: 'There were a lot of calls to Gordon's office from people like Trevor Kavanagh – "you're making a big mistake" kind of stuff.' One source says that Rupert Murdoch personally told Brown that he must support the 'marketisation' of the health service. Eventually, as the final clash with Tony Blair grew closer, Brown sidelined his principles and softened his approach to the whole subject.

In search of News International's backing, he spent months sending them signals which were so clear as to be clumsy. In June 2006, he reacted to news reports which said he was left wing by announcing that he would renew the Trident nuclear missile programme. Tony Blair's chief of staff, Jonathan Powell, later wrote that Brown was 'desperate to convince Rupert Murdoch that he was, in fact, a centrist in the hope of securing the support of his papers'. He made a series of speeches about terrorism which reflected the editorial hard line of the *Sun*, sweeping aside anxieties about human rights and due process, calling for detention without trial for terrorist suspects, and supporting the introduction of compulsory identity cards.

But the aggression from News International broke out again, in

September 2006, when Brown's close ally, Tom Watson, led a group of junior ministers in the 'curry-house plot' – all resigning and calling for Blair to announce a date when he would stand down so that Brown could take over. The Murdoch titles rushed to Blair's defence, damning the plotters and Brown too. They remained surly, further aggravated two months later by the clash over the story about Fraser's illness.

Brown lurched towards them again. In March 2007, he gritted his teeth and publicly visited one of Blair's hated new academy schools. That same month, he made his biggest gesture when he announced that he would cut the standard rate of income tax from 22% to only 20%. Three different advisers speaking independently say that Brown did this simply and solely to curry favour with Rupert Murdoch, who liked low-tax, low-spend governments. It worked. The *Sun* was delighted, welcoming it as 'A Reason 2p Cheerful'. It was also a total disaster. Looking for a way to pay for the tax cut, Brown ended up taking money from the poorest workers in the country, provoking an outcry from his own MPs.

Still, the lurching worked to some extent. Brown had one big advantage: it looked like sooner or later, he was bound to get Blair's job. The Murdoch papers wanted to be close to the winner, moved to embrace him and, in June 2007, with their support, Brown became prime minister as Blair stepped down.

By the time the *Guardian* published the first phone-hacking story two years later, in July 2009, the tricky relationship had collapsed into the kind of marriage in which the couple never touch each other but can just about manage a polite conversation at mealtimes. The question now was whether, having helped Gordon Brown into power, News International would be content to let him stay there.

Brown was still in contact with Rupert Murdoch. The day after his brief and clumsy appearance at Rebekah Brooks's lakeside wedding ceremony, in that summer of 2009, Brown had included Murdoch among his guests at a small dinner party in Downing Street in honour of the visiting US president, George W. Bush. The evening had gone well, with Brown far more at ease with older men in suits than with the young Cameron crowd in Oxfordshire, reaching a point of informality where, according to *Brown at 10* by Anthony Seldon and Guy Lodge, during a private meeting between Bush and Brown, the US president beckoned to one of Brown's advisers, asked if he could take a message to Bush's own staff outside the room and whispered: 'Can you tell them to kiss my ass?'

Through his previous two years as prime minister, Brown had continued to try to cuddle up to News International. He made a powerful speech, which could have been written by Trevor Kavanagh, warning of the threat from migrants, calling for 'British jobs for British workers'. He backed the *Sun's* controversial call for forty-two days of detention without trial for terrorist suspects, an idea which was so unpopular that it was thrown out before it could become law.

In private, he had been equally generous. When Rebekah Brooks became involved with her husband-to-be, Charlie Brooks, who was training racehorses, she personally told the prime minister that the government should abolish the horse-race levy, which raises tax income at the expense of the racing industry. Two Downing Street advisers say that Brown asked them to look into it and to speak to Charlie Brooks 'to make him feel involved'. At one point, he hired a new policy adviser, Kath Raymond, who happened to be the partner of the then chief executive of News International, Les Hinton. She was an experienced special adviser, but other Downing Street staff were not amused. 'She was not a policy person at all,' said one. 'She was like Posh Spice, who was in the band even if she couldn't sing.'

Following months of pressure from the Information Commissioner to deal with private investigators blagging confidential data, early in 2008 Brown's government agreed to toughen the law to make it an imprisonable offence. Brown was then visited by a delegation of Les Hinton from News International, Paul Dacre from the *Daily Mail*, and Murdoch MacLennan from the Telegraph Media Group, who persuaded the prime minister to shelve the plan (an interesting move from three newspaper groups who consistently denied that their journalists had ever broken the law).

The prime minister received some reward. At his party conference in the autumn of 2008, his leadership was challenged by the young Foreign Secretary, David Miliband. The *Sun* backed Brown. At a News International lunch, several *Sun* journalists confronted Miliband, ridiculing his support for a new European constitution. According to one who was there, this ended with Miliband asking Trevor Kavanagh if he had even read the draft treaty which he was attacking, and Kavanagh telling Miliband that he was stupid and rude. News of this reassuring clash was fed back fast to Brown's camp. When he made his keynote speech, Brown swatted Miliband aside by declaring that this was 'no time for a novice', a line that had been dreamed up for him a day or so earlier by Rebekah Brooks when dining with Brown's close ally, Ed Balls.

At the same time, however, Brown's first two years in Downing Street had seen News International become more and more demanding – in print and behind the scenes – calling for more hostility to migrants and to the European Union, more ferocity towards terrorists and other offenders, more resources for British troops in Afghanistan.

When the abuse and murder of the seventeen-month-old boy known as Baby P exposed the London borough of Haringey to keen criticism in 2007, the *Sun* had campaigned publicly for its head of children's services, Sharon Shoesmith, to be sacked. That was an uncontroversial act for a campaigning newspaper but, behind the scenes, Rebekah Brooks was phoning the Secretary of State for children, Ed Balls, and pushing hard for him to agree, if only to stop the *Sun* switching its fire on to him. 'She was pretty blunt with him,' according to an official who heard some of the phone calls. 'She was telling Balls he had to sack her [Shoesmith], and it was quite threatening – "We don't want to turn this thing on you."' On 1 December 2008, Balls used special powers to remove Shoesmith from her post, a decision which was later found in the court of appeal to have been 'intrinsically unfair and unlawful'.

When Brown planned a reshuffle of his government in October 2008, Rebekah intervened, privately lobbying for the prime minister to keep her friend Tessa Jowell in post even though she was clearly branded as an ally of Tony Blair, and to block her loathed enemy, Tom Watson, who was a keen supporter of Brown's. For whatever reason, Brown kept Jowell as a minister attending Cabinet meetings – but also kept Watson as a more junior member of government. Similarly, when Ian Blair stepped down as commissioner of the Metropolitan Police in January 2009, she is said by one source to have lobbied hard for him to be replaced by his deputy, Paul Stephenson, who duly got the job.

Beyond these high-handed interventions, the difficulty with the Murdoch organisation was that they were clearly moving very close to David Cameron. Murdoch's former editor, Andy Coulson, was installed in the Conservative leader's private office; Murdoch's UK chief executive, Rebekah Brooks, was Cameron's confidante; Rupert Murdoch dined with him; James Murdoch dined with him and met his closest political ally, the shadow chancellor, George Osborne, for late-night drinks.

By the time the long fuse of the phone-hacking scandal started to burn in July 2009, News Corp and Cameron's team were engaged in an energetic exercise in political semaphore, each side sending out signals – some in private, some very public – indicating what each might want from the other if they were to form a relationship. These signals were particularly loud and clear on the subject which was most important to Rupert and James Murdoch: the ambition for their business to become even bigger.

James Murdoch never liked the BBC.

In part, this was simply the wrestler's view of his rival. He had first worked in the UK, from 2003, as chief executive of BSkyB, where he had been forced to face the uncomfortable fact that the BBC was the only broadcaster in the country which was big enough to offer him any serious competition. Or, as he put it to shareholders in his own signature style in November 2005, after two years of disappointing results at BSkyB: 'We have been abused and opposed by everybody – the BBC and the papers. They are still against us.'

But it was also a matter of ideology. The idea of a publicly funded broadcaster simply repelled him. In an interview with the *Guardian* in 2000, James considered the subject of the licence fee which was then delivering four TV channels, fifty-seven radio stations and the busiest news website in Britain at a cost to each household of £139.50 per year, and released a burst of neoliberal invective, declaring that it was 'a subsidised, horrific – how shall I put it – evil taxation scheme'.

A senior BBC executive who often dealt with him recalls: 'He just could not accept that an intelligent adult could possibly believe that the BBC is anything other than an outrage. Listening to him talk about the BBC is like listening to Richard Dawkins talk about God – "Come on, snap out of it, you can't believe this stuff."'

Reflecting this commercial and ideological opposition, the Murdoch network engaged in a sustained campaign of attacks on the BBC, using various means which were perfectly fair and also on occasion apparently foul. The fair end involved conventional lobbying, using public speeches, formal meetings with ministers and social access to the power elite to argue persistently for the BBC to be cut back and for BSkyB to be spared from regulation. When the House of Commons media select committee in 2005 and again in 2008 needed a specialist adviser, on both occasions the job was filled by former heads of public affairs at BSkyB, Ray Gallagher and Martin Le Jeune. When the committee's chairman, John Whittingdale, needed funds for his local cricket club, BSkyB made a donation of £3,000.

All of that was within the bounds of standard lobbying practice, but there are signs of some fouler tactics. In 2004, when the BBC was teetering on the edge of a strike by staff, a political officer from the broadcasting union BECTU reported being approached by a lobbying agency with links to News Corp who had asked if they might be able to help in some way. This looked very much like an attempt at industrial sabotage. The union declined the offer.

At the heart of this campaign was News International's coverage of the BBC. Towards the end of March 2009, for example, a right-wing think tank, the Centre for Policy Studies, published a highly negative report which claimed that the BBC lacked originality in its programme-making. Fleet Street generally did not bother to report it, but the *Sun* ran an aggressive news story: 'The BBC is branded a parasite today for blowing the licence fee on copycat shows.' They failed to point out that the report had been written by Martin Le Jeune, the recently retired head of public affairs at BSkyB.

The *Sunday Times* launched into the BBC, with a sequence of hostile stories about spending on taxis. That paper and the *Sun* also ran a relentless campaign about the salaries of BBC executives which rose as high as £800,000 for the director general, failing to mention that James Murdoch himself was being paid $9.2 million for a year's work. A search of a database of Fleet Street stories suggests that during this assault on the BBC in 2009, the News International titles ran a total of 515 stories about the licence fee.

In August 2009, James Murdoch delivered the MacTaggart lecture at the Edinburgh TV festival. Although his own newspapers were engaged in what appeared to be a campaign of politically motivated assaults on the BBC, he insisted that news media must show 'independence of faction, industrial or political'. He went on to damn the BBC, accusing it of leading a 'landgrab' and of having ambitions which were 'chilling' in their scale. Its expansion must be stopped: 'In the interests of a free society, it should be sternly resisted.' More than that, he said, the BBC should have its public funding killed off or cut severely: the licence fee should survive 'if at all . . . on a far, far smaller scale'. He ended with a trumpet blast of belief in his own values: 'The only reliable, durable and perpetual guarantor of independence is profit.'

James Murdoch also never liked Ofcom. Like his father, he never liked any form of regulation which offered any kind of obstacle to the expansion of their business. He particularly disliked Ofcom, the Office of Communications, which had been involved in giving him the political equivalent of a public spanking. Twice. First, in November 2006, when he was chief executive of BSkyB, it was Ofcom which got in his way when he bought 17.9% of the ITV commercial television network. He did it to stop the rival NTL merging with ITV, creating a beast big enough to compete with BSkyB. And it worked: his raid initially pushed the ITV share price so high that NTL could no longer afford the deal. But then Ofcom investigated and reported that the share grab had given BSkyB too much influence over broadcast news bulletins in the UK. That triggered an inquiry by the Competition Commission, who told BSkyB that they must sell most of their ITV shares. BSkyB became embroiled in years of legal appeals, and the value of their ITV holding fell through the floor.

Just as Ofcom were landing that blow, in March 2007 they struck a second time when they announced an investigation into pay TV in the UK. This was a market worth £4 billion a year, dominated by BSkyB. The Murdoch company owned the rights to key sporting events and to a huge archive of films, all of which they sold to subscribers through their own satellite platform – and also to rival pay-TV outlets. These smaller rivals complained that BSkyB exercised a 'vicious circle of control', charging them extortionate rates to carry their output. Ofcom were clearly willing to consider ordering BSkyB to cut their prices so that consumers had more choice about which pay-TV channels to subscribe to.

James fought back hard. Ofcom faced what one of those involved called 'a barrage of disputation and aggression' as BSkyB used its financial strength to hire specialist litigators, corporate lawyers, consultants and expert witnesses, all of whom submitted a torrent of reports, attempting to find fault in the regulator's behaviour. In the background, the Murdochs used political lobbyists and their own direct access to ministers to complain bitterly about Ofcom's role. As with their campaign against the BBC, there were some indications that they may have been tempted to use fouler means. Ofcom's chief executive, Ed Richards, told colleagues he suspected he was the object of some surveillance. Neighbours at his home in Wales said somebody had been asking questions about him, and there were signs that someone might have been looking through his dustbins.

As with the BBC, so too with Ofcom, the assault came to a climax in James Murdoch's MacTaggart lecture on 28 August 2009. He called for 'a radical reorientation of the regulatory approach' to UK media and denounced his tormentor as 'a regulator armed with a set of prejudices and a spreadsheet'.

So it was that in the summer of 2009, with a general election due within the following twelve months, there was a special interest in a simple question: would News International be content to let Gordon Brown stay in Downing Street?

★   ★   ★

Gordon Brown's camp watched these manoeuvres sullenly from the sidelines, conspicuously failing to comply with the Murdochs' demands that the BBC and Ofcom be cut back. Some of those who were close to Brown claim that this was because they regarded the demands as illegitimate and wanted no part of them. Others say that by this time in his premiership, Brown had sunk into a mire of anxiety and dithering and that they failed to react simply because they failed to decide to do so.

It appears that Downing Street also failed to understand that Brown's personal link to Rupert Murdoch was counting for less and less as James Murdoch continued his grab for power inside News Corp. According to several sources, father and son were now frequently snarling at each other. In February 2009, James won an important battle when Murdoch's chief operating officer, Peter Chernin, announced that he was leaving. Michael Wolff's book, *The Man Who Owns the News*, describes how in 2005 Chernin and Roger Ailes, the president of Fox News, had 'ganged up' on James's older brother, Lachlan, forcing him to retreat back to Australia. James was not going to be pushed through the same door.

With Chernin clearing his desk, James moved aggressively against News Corp's head of marketing and corporate affairs in New York, Gary Ginsberg, an influential figure in the senior ranks of the company and an ally of his father. According to one senior executive: 'James went after Ginsberg in the most vicious way, denouncing his ideas as the most stupid he had ever heard, saying things like "I'll crush you if you make that happen."'

Although much of this was hidden from the outside world, nevertheless the gap in Gordon Brown's defences was easy to see, and David Cameron moved in quickly. At key moments during 2009, Cameron and his spokesmen simply picked up the signals from James Murdoch's camp and played them back, while the Murdoch team replied with their own signals of encouragement and desire, rather like two birds calling out to each other in the woods, moving closer and closer in harmony.

In March 2009, Cameron picked up the very loud call about the BBC licence fee, declaring in a speech that it should be frozen, adding a particularly seductive note that it would be difficult to keep the licence fee at all if the BBC did not make changes. The message was well received and understood by the Murdoch camp, who flashed back a response, through the *Sun*, with a news story which said nothing about the impact which a frozen licence fee might have on the BBC's ability to produce quality programmes but reported that 'Mr Cameron wants to curb the BBC's bloated bureaucracy and waste of cash. He plans to choke off the taxpayer funding that gives it an advantage over rivals such as Sky.' The *Sun* then listed the amounts which, they claimed, the corporation had spent on taxis and high salaries.

The two sides exchanged a chorus of other calls about the BBC. The Murdochs complained that the BBC now had more than half of all radio listeners and that more of the bandwidth should be given to commercial radio companies, many of whom bought their news bulletins from BSkyB. Cameron's junior media spokesman, Ed Vaizey, saw it the same way: 'There is a good argument for the BBC to be rid of Radio 1 and give the commercial sector a chance to use the frequency.'

The Murdochs accused the BBC of trespassing into new markets which had previously belonged to commercial providers, specifically 'providing magazines and websites on a commercial basis'. David Cameron similarly complained about 'the big boot of the BBC coming thumping into a new market and suddenly the Internet service, the education provider, the small publishing businesses are completely squashed'. The Murdochs also attacked the BBC Trust, which ultimately owns and oversees the BBC, for its 'recklessness . . . total failure . . . abysmal record'. Their primary complaint was that the trust had failed to stop the BBC's expansion into new commercial markets. Seven weeks later, Cameron's senior media spokesman, Jeremy Hunt, announced that a Conservative government would abolish the BBC Trust because it had allowed the BBC 'to crush media competition'.

And then there was Ofcom. On 26 June 2009, two years after it started its inquiry into pay TV, Ofcom announced that BSkyB should be forced to cut as much as 30% off the price of the material it sold to rival platforms. BSkyB said it would appeal. One well-placed source says that James Murdoch was furious at this judgement and was declaring with considerable anger that Ofcom must be abolished. Ten days later, on 6 July 2009, David Cameron announced that, if elected, he would abolish Ofcom.

On 9 July – the day after the *Guardian* ran its first phone-hacking story – *The Times* ran a story accusing Ofcom executives of having high salaries and expense accounts. On 15 July, James Murdoch and Rebekah Brooks met another Cameron ally, Oliver Letwin, who was in charge of drawing up the Conservative manifesto for the coming general election, specifically to discuss the future of Ofcom. On 23 July, the *Sun* ran a column by Kelvin MacKenzie which accused the Ofcom chief executive, Ed Richards, of 'brown-nosing' and described the Ofcom chair, Colette Bowe, as 'an elderly has-been'.

The two camps exchanged another short burst of signals on one of BSkyB's main sources of income. The Murdochs said there was too much regulation around advertising on television and that this was diverting valuable ad revenues into the bank account of the entirely unregulated Google. Jeremy Hunt saw it the same way: 'Google's advertising revenue in the UK surpassed that of ITV in the first half of this year . . . In such a climate, it is right to examine whether some of the regulations designed to ensure a level playing field are still appropriate.'

By late August, after James Murdoch's MacTaggart lecture, the manoeuvring was nearly complete. Immediately after the lecture, Jeremy Hunt travelled to New York where, according to the House of Commons register of interests, he had meetings with 'representatives of News Corp'.

In the background, according to two well-placed sources, Rupert Murdoch was growing increasingly tetchy about his son's hectoring insistence that they must abandon Gordon Brown. But Rebekah Brooks, who continued to command the older man's attention, acted as a peacemaker between the two and joined James in persuading Rupert that they must support Cameron. The sources claim that a key part of James's argument was that a Cameron government would be less likely to cause problems with their secretly planned bid to buy all of BSkyB, the most important move on News Corp's horizon. Reluctantly, the sources say, the father bowed to the son's pressure, though, according to one, 'he was very pissed off about it'.

On the evening of 10 September 2009, James Murdoch met David Cameron for a private drink at the exclusive George club, in Mayfair. There, the young mogul explained that he had held discussions with his father and Rebekah Brooks and with the new editor of the *Sun*, Dominic Mohan, and, as a result, he was able to tell Cameron that Britain's biggest-selling newspaper had decided to announce that they would be supporting the Conservatives at the next general election.

It was a night of doubletalk and drunkenness.

Nearly three weeks after James Murdoch and Cameron met at the George club, a teeming mass of Labour supporters gathered in the banqueting hall of the Grand Hotel in Brighton for the big fund-raising dinner which is always a central event in their annual party conference. Outside in the opulent white-panelled corridor, one of Gordon Brown's most senior ministers, Peter Mandelson, was pacing up and down with his mobile phone to his ear.

On the other end of the line was Rebekah Brooks. She had news. The *Sun* was changing sides. The doubletalk flowed like wine. Brooks pretended that this was a decision that she and a few senior staff from the *Sun* had made that day. Mandelson knew very well that the *Sun* had been playing footsie with the Conservatives for months. Mandelson, for his part, pretended to be worried that she was making a terrible mistake which would alienate her readers and told her gently that she really was a chump (although Brooks later said she heard a more abusive word).

Back in the banqueting hall, Mandelson reported to Brown and advised him to pretend to be indifferent to the news, and so he did. Mandelson cancelled a dinner he was due to have with James Murdoch. Brown and his entourage boycotted the News International reception which was being held that evening and did their best to avoid reading the copies of the first edition of the next day's *Sun* which were distributed all over the Grand Hotel with 'Labour's lost it' blasted across its front page. So they pretended that life would go on unchanged and, thus content, some of them ended the night in the small hours of the morning gathered around a piano in the ground-floor bar singing Abba songs with their arms wrapped around each other's shoulders.

But the biggest piece of doubletalk was that this was simply about journalism. Brown's advisers went along with the pretence, if only because it made it easier to bear the blow. When they met for their late-night debrief in one of the hotel bedrooms, they all agreed that they would deal with this by withdrawing all co-operation from the *Sun* – no stories, no briefings, no help at all for the paper's journalists.

Rebekah Brooks, too, pretended that her conversation with Mandelson was simply journalistic, that this was nothing more than a newspaper executive courteously reporting a change in the line which would be taken in the leader column. In reality, however, this was a deeply political act.

It was political in its staging. It was now nearly three weeks since James Murdoch had told David Cameron that the *Sun* would back him, and yet the readers of the *Sun* had not been told. The announcement had been held back to this particular evening, 29 September 2009, when it was likely to cause maximum political damage to Gordon Brown.

Earlier that day, the prime minister had delivered his keynote address to the conference. For a leader whose popularity was sagging danger-ously low, this was an important moment. Even a prime minister on his political deathbed is capable of producing a speech which will move the party faithful and which is calculated to strike some good notes with the electorate beyond the conference hall. Now, the news coverage of his speech was bound to be tainted or even swamped by the *Sun*'s announcement.

To make sure they dominated the TV bulletins as well as the news-papers, News International had set up an irresistible picture, flooding their headquarters in east London with blue light to match the official colour of the Conservative Party, and releasing blue smoke from the roof.

Above all, the move was political in its intent. By this time, Gordon

Brown's government had been weakened by two years of recurring crises and tumbling popularity, from a height of 42% support in the polls in October 2007 to only 25% now. It was clear to all observers and to the Labour leadership itself that they were unlikely to win the general election which was expected in about eight months, in the spring of 2010.

There was nothing unusual about a newspaper declaring its support for an opposition candidate during an election campaign, but to do so eight months in advance of an election was a declaration of war on a sitting prime minister. It may well be that Brown's government was dying but the coming months saw the political assassin, discovering that a chosen target was seriously ill, nonetheless sneaking into the sickroom, climbing on to the bed and delivering a kicking of fatal ferocity. This was the act of a newspaper engaged in something which went well beyond the boundaries of mere journalism. Internal emails show that Brooks had sent the draft of the *Sun* leader column which announced the change of political line to James Murdoch for his approval. While the *Sun* now advertised its wedding to the Conservative cause, it said nothing public about any views that News Corp might share with the Conservative leadership on the future of the BBC or Ofcom. It set out not simply to support the Conservatives in its leader comments, nor even simply to choose to cover news stories which showed the Conservatives in a good light, but to engage in a sustained campaign of distortion in its news stories. Its readers were now ballot fodder. The *Sun* started to monster the prime minister.

The day after the conference, amidst the furore about the *Sun's* announcement, other newspapers recognised that Gordon Brown had delivered an effective speech. They acknowledged his weakness, they questioned some of his claims, but they judged too that this was a well-crafted piece of work, delivered with power and passion. The new *Sun* which had spent the previous twelve years running news stories which showed Labour in a good light, suddenly turned on its heel and poured scorn on their recent ally.

They found no space to mention Brown's scorching attack on the Conservatives and on the 'bankrupt ideology' of unrestrained free markets which the prime minister blamed for the global financial crisis of the previous year. Nor did they mention the prime minister's plans to limit bankers' bonuses; to create a national investment corporation; to employ 10,000 young people in skilled internships and 10,000 more in 'green' jobs in the low-carbon economy; to tackle the antisocial behaviour of 50,000 chaotic families; to give more money for international aid; to hold a referendum on voting reform; to create programmes to help teenaged mothers; to make further reforms of the House of Lords; to guarantee annual increases in the minimum wage. Some commentators thought these ideas were too modest. Few believed they would be enough to revive Brown's fortunes. For readers of the *Sun*, they simply did not exist.

They did report some of his plans, but every positive was turned into a negative. Brown wanted change for a global age, but for the *Sun*, that was simply 'a tacit admission that New Labour has failed'. Brown hit a rhetorical peak when he spoke about the 'unsurpassed heroism' and courage of British troops in Afghanistan, provoking a standing ovation in the conference hall, but in the *Sun*, this was just another problem: 'Mr Brown spent only 35 seconds paying tribute to our servicemen and women.'

Brown said: 'Every change we make, every single pledge we make comes with a price tag attached and a clear plan for how that cost will be met.' In the *Sun*, this became: 'He drew up a wish list of policy pledges – without admitting Britain was broke or explaining where the cash would come from to pay for them.'

He announced free childcare for a quarter of a million impoverished children but, according to the *Sun*, this 'began to unravel immediately as middle-class parents reacted with fury'. He said tests for cancer would be completed within a week, but this 'appeared to be unfunded'. He promised tighter controls on immigration, but this was done in 'only 83 words'. He said the new twenty-four-hour drinking law had been a success in some places and a failure in others, so local authorities would have the option of limiting licences in trouble spots. This became: 'Mr Brown vowed to tear up Labour's own 24-hour drinking laws – clear recognition that they have added to the antisocial behaviour that plagues our streets.'

This was only the beginning. For months, the *Sun* laid into Brown. The monstering was most intense in its coverage of the British military presence in Afghanistan. This had been building up during 2009 with aggressive stories attacking the Ministry of Defence – but not generally the prime minister – for choosing not to send an extra 2,000 troops to Helmand province until the US government had sorted out its own plans, and for providing inadequate equipment which allegedly exposed British soldiers to unnecessary risk. But as Brown fell from News Corp's favour, the aim of these stories swung round and had started to target the prime minister himself. By mid-July 2009, the *Sun's* defence correspondent was allowed to report: 'Every new death in Helmand falls at No. 10's door. It is a stain from which Mr Brown will seriously struggle to recover, whatever he does to help now.' On 28 August, the *Sun* launched a vitriolic campaign under the banner 'Don't you know there's a bloody war on?', with pictures of all 221 British military personnel who had died in Afghanistan and powerful attacks from, among others, the mother of a corporal who had been killed. In the first few weeks of September, the *Sun* ran a letter from the stepfather of a young soldier who had died in Afghanistan, with the headline 'Dear PM, you killed our boy'. They followed up with stories which called Brown 'spineless', urged him to sack himself and warned readers that 'the PM will carry on spending YOUR cash to save his skin at the next election'.

After the *Sun* publicly switched their support to the Conservatives on 29 September, the assault became ferocious. The Ministry of Defence cut back on training for the Territorial Army. The *Sun* complained. Gordon Brown reversed the decision. The *Sun* complained – 'a humiliating U-turn'. On Armistice Day, 9 November 2009, Brown went to the Cenotaph, suited and sombre, to lay a wreath in memory of British soldiers killed in action, as prime ministers have done for years. The *Sun* complained that he failed to bow his head properly.

That same day, they discovered that in writing to the mother of a soldier who had been killed in Afghanistan the previous month, he had misspelled her name. The dead soldier was Jamie Janes. Brown had addressed the mother as 'Mrs James'. That one misplaced letter meant that his apparently kind act of writing to commiserate in his own hand became, in the words of the *Sun*, 'a disgraceful, hastily scrawled insult'. Coupling this with his supposed failure to bow deeply enough at the Cenotaph, the *Sun's* news story reported: 'His gaffes come despite the *Sun's* campaign to remind him there is a bloody war on.' When Brown tried to make peace with Mrs Janes by telephoning her personally to apologise, the *Sun* heard of his plan, advised her to tape the call and then turned that against him by quoting it in detail, shifting the stress away from Brown's apology and towards Mrs Janes's claim that her son had died because he lacked the right equipment.

An official who was close to Brown at this time says that the prime minister was deeply upset and contacted Rupert Murdoch to warn him that this kind of behaviour by the *Sun* could end their relationship. Murdoch suggested that he speak to Rebekah Brooks. The official says Brown did so, telling her: 'I want to express my disappointment over this. You are attacking me personally. It's totally outrageous . . . You are undermining the war effort.' Brooks defended the *Sun's* coverage, according to this official, adding: 'We reserve the right to disagree with you. It isn't personal.' Brown insisted that it was personal. Brooks attempted to mollify him, ending the conversation by expressing the hope that they would talk again, to which the prime minister replied 'I don't think so,' and cut the call.

With the *Sun's* attacks continuing unabated, Brown took a controversial step, arranging for Rupert Murdoch and Brooks to be given an off-the-record briefing by the then head of MI6, Sir John Scarlett. One of Brown's close advisers says that Sir John warned them that the Taliban were using *Sun* stories as propaganda and that they were damaging British military morale. Rebekah Brooks started to argue with Sir John, according to this adviser, and the conversation became tense, finally reaching a point where Murdoch cut across Brooks and told Sir John that he could expect to see a calmer tone in the *Sun's* reporting. It didn't happen.

His back to the wall, the prime minister talked to advisers about hitting back. When the hacking story first broke in the *Guardian* in July 2009, he had treated it as a mess to be avoided for fear of irritating Murdoch. According to one of his advisers, he asked Cabinet ministers who might have been victims to stay silent. By the time an election was in sight and News International had dumped him, he considered getting involved.

In March 2010, he asked the Cabinet Secretary, Gus O'Donnell, if he could call for a public inquiry into the hacking and was frustrated when O'Donnell replied that the available evidence would not justify it in law. Brown then asked his advisers to draft a speech in which he attacked the Murdochs full on, criticised James Murdoch for his MacTaggart lecture, defended the BBC licence fee and called for a new approach to regulation of the media. He never used it. The tiger was too dangerous.

While Brown was being attacked by the *Sun*, David Cameron was moving closer. Whereas Brown had seen his keynote speech to his party conference overshadowed and then misreported by the *Sun*, Cameron had made his the following month with the blessing of a text from Rebekah Brooks: 'I am so rooting for you, not just as a personal friend but because professionally we are in this together. Speech of your life? Yes he Cam!' The day after the speech, she texted him again: 'Brilliant speech. I cried twice. Will love "working together"', and the *Sun* reported that Cameron had 'the strength to get battered Britain back on its feet' and that he had made 'a power-packed speech'. It was hard to read that without regarding it as propaganda posing as journalism.

In November 2009, Cameron had announced his support for Rebekah Brooks's long-running campaign to use prison ships to create extra space for offenders. The *Sun* reported it. The following month, the Camerons marked New Year's Eve with Rebekah Brooks and her husband, Charlie, at a party hosted by the TV presenter Jeremy Clarkson, also attended by other senior Tories as well as Andy Coulson. In January 2010, Cameron announced his support for prison ships a second time. The *Sun* reported: 'The Tories have got the message. Using prison ships could help them sail to victory when the general election comes.' Jeremy Hunt held two meetings with James Murdoch, which included discussions about the future of Ofcom.

By the spring of 2010, it was clear that the prime minister would announce a general election for early May. It also finally became publicly clear that News Corp had one more very big iron in the political fire. The *Independent* disclosed that the Murdochs were planning a bid to take over the 61% of BSkyB which did not already belong to them. That would make them the dominant players not only in British newspapers but also in British television, significantly boosting their power as well as their profit – but only if the government and Ofcom let them do it.

More than ever, News Corp needed a friend in Downing Street.

10. March 2010 to 15 December 2010

Reporting is not a spectator sport (no matter what they teach in college). You can't sit and wait for the information to present itself like a postman knocking at your door – not if you're interested in doing something more than recycling press releases for a living; not if you can begin to understand why the best stories are the ones which someone somewhere doesn't want you to know. You have to get in there and make it happen; use every last devious ounce of imagination to find ways of forcing the miser to let go of the gold.

In the spring of 2010, Alan Rusbridger came up with a neat manoeuvre. Reversing the normal convention under which editors grab hold of stories and keep them for their own pages, he started contacting other journalists to give them our work to encourage them to take it further. Since Fleet Street was clogged with self-interest, he tried broadcasters, approaching senior executives at the BBC and Channel 4. Both decided to make documentaries, for *Panorama* and for *Dispatches* respectively; and I briefed the people involved. He spoke also to Peter Oborne, a conservative columnist on the *Daily Mail* who had a reputation for plain-speaking and who, Rusbridger calculated, was one of the very few conservative journalists who might be brave enough to take on Coulson. I met him in a wine bar in Victoria and tried to explain the background. He went off to do his own research.

Most important, Rusbridger spoke to Bill Keller, executive editor of the mighty *New York Times*. It can't have been hard to get him interested. It was not just that Rusbridger was offering him a story which involved the royal family, tabloid hacks and private investigators as well as politicians and police officers apparently colluding with power. Better than that, it was all about the man who had taken over the *Wall Street Journal* and who was attempting to use it as a weapon of mass-media destruction against Keller's beloved paper. Keller moved fast.

Three days later, on 15 March, three *New York Times* reporters arrived in London and came straight to the *Guardian* office. That evening, Rusbridger and I spent four hours briefing them. I then followed up a day later with another four-hour session in their London office. Rusbridger introduced one of them, Don Van Natta, to our source the Emissary. I introduced Van Natta to the detective Karl (a strange encounter, in the *haut bourgeois* surroundings of the piano lounge of the Grand Hotel in Brighton, where Karl unravelled the grubby world of Jonathan Rees and his circle of bent cops). I kept pumping them with background and contacts. It felt weird to be handing over reams of hard-won information to other journalists. It also felt dangerous: for all I knew, they would find that we had got the whole story wrong and publish something that would wipe us out; but we were isolated and we needed support. Plus Van Natta agreed that they would repay the favour by giving me their unpublished material once their story was done. Not a bad deal. Not a bad ally.

Meanwhile, attempting to recover from the collapse of Max Clifford's legal action, I remembered something I had read in *Good Times, Bad Times*, the memoir of Harry Evans describing his experience as editor of the *Sunday Times* between 1967 and 1981. He recalled how in March 1974, he had sent reporters to Paris to investigate the mysterious crash of a DC-10 passenger plane, which had killed all 346 of those on board. The initial evidence which they dug out suggested that there was a structural fault in the plane which meant that it was always likely to crash and that the manufacturers, McDonnell Douglas, should have recalled it; but they couldn't publish such an aggressive story without hard evidence. Evans described in the book how his reporters had intervened in the events they were reporting, acting as middlemen linking the bereaved families with highly effective lawyers in the United States, encouraging them to sue there because the US courts were most likely to order McDonnell Douglas to disclose internal paperwork. That worked. I decided to try to do the same.

So, instead of passively waiting for potential victims to see their way through the fog around Scotland Yard, I set out to discover who had been targeted by Mulcaire so that I could tip them off; encourage them to sue; hook them up with the right lawyers; ply the lawyers with back-ground information and advice; do whatever it took to help the lawyers get to court so that a judge could drag out the truth for us.

I was now sure that at least two more Cabinet ministers were among the victims, but I could not persuade them to sue. Months earlier, the former Secretary of State for the media, Tessa Jowell, had confirmed to me that during the original inquiry in 2006, police had told her that her messages had been repeatedly intercepted during the time when she was separating from her husband; but she had urged me not to publish this for fear of reviving press interest in her family, and I agreed. (I think I was wrong to agree this: as Jowell had been the Secretary of State responsible for the media, the fact that the *News of the World* had dared to hack her messages was probably too important to be withheld for personal reasons.)

A second Cabinet minister – David Blunkett's successor as Home Secretary, Charles Clarke – had been followed by Derek Webb. I asked a friend who knew Clarke to tell him that this meant that he had probably also been hacked, but the answer came back that he was not interested in pursuing it. Perhaps he did not want a fight with Murdoch, perhaps he did not want to revive whatever mad gossip had attracted the paper to him in the first place.

I identified about a dozen law firms who specialised in representing celebrities in their dealings with newspapers and contacted all of them, explaining about the evidence at Scotland Yard and offering to help. Most of these clients didn't want to know. Some were too busy. Some were worried about reviving an embarrassing story. Some were simply scared of provoking an attack by Murdoch's papers. But a few agreed to write to the police, following the small group of lawyers who were already preparing to fight.

Rusbridger had picked up a rumour that at some stage the Australian actress Nicole Kidman had been told by police that she was a victim. I found that Kidman was represented in London by a lawyer called John Kelly, a burly Liverpudlian who worked for the specialist media law firm Schillings (generally hated by journalists for their aggressive action on behalf of celebs). I called Kelly and, although he insisted that Kidman had had no such warning from the police, he was interested in what the police were doing. I went to see him at the Schillings office in Bedford Square, central London, and gave him a one-hour tutorial on how to hack phones and how to extract information from Scotland Yard. He took it all in and acted on it, writing to the Yard on behalf of seven clients to ask if their names showed up in Mulcaire's notes.

The police eventually admitted that two of them did. Both of them agreed to go to court to force police to hand over the notes. To begin with, Kelly kept their identities quiet but, as the cases proceeded, it became clear that he was acting for the comedian and actor Steve Coogan, whose relationship with the indie musician Courtney Love had made him a tabloid target, and Andy Gray, former international footballer turned TV commentator, whose relationship with anybody gave the tabloids an unnatural interest in the whereabouts of his trousers.

By this time, the spring of 2010, Mark Lewis had left his Manchester law firm; bleached his hair in punky spikes; fallen in and out of love with Charlotte Harris several times; fallen in and out of a working partnership with her; opened up a sideline as a stand-up comic; and ended up working on his own at a small law firm called Taylor Hampton with an office up a scruffy flight of stairs opposite the Royal Courts of Justice in central London. He soon picked up an important client.

In the backwash of Max Clifford's aborted legal action, it had become apparent that while the *News of the World* were targeting Clifford in order to try to steal the stories he was selling, they had also hacked the voicemail of his assistant, Nicola Phillips. I tracked her down and – in my new role as the supplier of ammunition for the legal guns – introduced her to Lewis. She was now working for herself as an independent PR and was worried about falling out with the Murdoch papers but, to her credit, she decided to fight.

I discovered that one of those who had been warned by the police in 2006 was the left-wing MP George Galloway. I hooked him up with Mark Lewis. Separately, Lewis was ratcheting up the pressure on Lady Buscombe, chair of the PCC, formally issuing a writ for libel for the speech she had made implying that he had misled Parliament.

Having had her case for Max Clifford diverted at the courtroom door, Charlotte Harris was now working with Sky Andrew, the football agent who was one of the eight victims named in court at the trial of Goodman and Mulcaire – again, no doubt that police had evidence he was a victim. News International clearly didn't want that to go anywhere. Andrew had had several discreet phone calls from lawyers attached to the *News of the World*, urging him to drop the idea. One of them had gone so far as to offer him a retainer of £25,000 a year for up to five years if he would withdraw – strange behaviour from an organisation which claimed to have nothing to hide. Andrew declined. Harris started pushing his case towards court.

I passed her the list of Steve Whittamore's victims which I had scribbled down from the computer of Alec Owen as he scrolled through his records from the ICO. These were people whose confidential information had been blagged by Whittamore's network. Harris started to approach some of the politicians on the list, guessing that if they had been blagged, they might also have been the victims of hacking. Soon, she was charming her way through the Palace of Westminster, forming an alliance with Tom Watson and, through him, with Gordon Brown, who became a client; writing to Scotland Yard on behalf of a dozen MPs who thought their details might show up in Mulcaire's paperwork; and acting for the former Liberal Democrat home affairs spokesman, Mark Oaten, whose sex life had been brutally exposed by the *News of the World* and who strongly suspected that his voicemail had been hacked in the process.

I had endless calls with Lewis and Harris, swapping gossip and trying to piece together the truth. Charlotte Harris on the phone is like a tornado in your ear. She talks very fast and creates a seamless confusion between her conversation on the phone and whatever conversation she is also holding in the background at her end, dropping instructions to taxi drivers or provocations to Mark Lewis into the middle of talking about News International. There was one Saturday when she seemed to be with her two young daughters in a supermarket: 'We're in court next week yesmummywillgetyouabiscuit but I don't know what time.' On that particular conversation, she was suddenly cut off in mid-storm. I kept trying to call back. I got more and more worried that she and her girls must have been hit by a car as they left the supermarket. Twenty-four hours later, I finally got through to her and discovered they were all fine. They hadn't been in a supermarket at all. She had been doling out biscuits in her kitchen and had then taken her youngest girl to the bathroom to change her nappy, with her phone jammed between her shoulder and her ear, until the phone had leaped sideways and dived into the toilet.

Like some kind of marriage fixer, I also introduced Lewis and Harris to Mark Thomson, who was still pressuring the police on behalf of his dozen clients, so that they could exchange information and plot tactics together. Thomson was driving me mad. He kept hinting that he had uncovered something special.

'I've got a dynamite case. Dynamite!'

'Who? What's it about?'

Then he'd grimace and shake his head apologetically: 'I can't comment.'

Thomson and I met often and, on the advice of a security expert, got into the habit – now evidently adopted by all well-informed gangsters – of removing the batteries from our mobile phones so that there was no power for 'roving bug' spyware, which could otherwise relay our conversation through the microphone on a handset. We worked out that, although the phone companies kept call data for only twelve months, their security departments might still have the data they had collected for Scotland Yard in 2006 as well as any history of blagging attempts which they had spotted. He applied for their records. I pointed out that, in the transcript of the original trial of Goodman and Mulcaire, the prosecutors said Mulcaire always wrote 'Clive' in the top left-hand corner of any work he was doing for him. Logically, he would have done the same for other journalists who commissioned him. Thomson, as he later put it, 'nearly puked with excitement' at the prospect of forcing the police to disclose these notes.

A couple of times he asked me if I thought that the *News of the World* were still hacking, and I told him about the private investigator who had claimed that one of the paper's feature writers, Dan Evans, was in fact a specialist hacker. He asked if I could get the investigator to make a statement, but that was impossible. Thomson didn't suggest that Dan Evans's name meant anything to him. Not just then.

I also knew that the police finally had admitted that at least two of Thomson's clients showed up in Mulcaire's notes. I established that one of them was Jade Goody, the former occupant of the Big Brother house whose wild ways had become a running story for the tabloids and who had died of cancer in March 2009, aged only twenty-seven. But the trustees of her estate were not interested in pursuing a case. Thomson was clearly following the second case. I guessed he must be going to court to force Scotland Yard to hand over evidence. I kept answering his questions and supplying him with information, hoping this would somehow yield a court hearing where some truth would emerge.

Tamsin Allen from the law firm Bindmans was putting together her case for a judicial review of the original police inquiry on behalf of Brian Paddick and Chris Bryant. The simple fact of a former officer as senior as Paddick taking Scotland Yard to court was stunning in itself. If he needed encouragement, it came in the form of the Yard's replies to Allen's letters asking if either Paddick's or Bryant's name showed up in Mulcaire's notes. The Yard's lawyers claimed there was no mention of Paddick there at all and no evidence that Bryant had been hacked. They didn't believe it, and nor did I – particularly when Chris Bryant's phone company revealed that their records showed three attempts to blag information about him from their staff in December 2003 when the *News of the World* and other papers had been busy exposing his sex life.

I hooked up Tamsin Allen with Brendan Montague, a freelance journalist who had contacted me because he suspected the *News of the World* had hacked his phone to steal a story. I also passed her a good-looking rumour that the former Home Secretary David Blunkett had been hacked when the *News of the World* were chasing his sex life. Since she was well connected in the Labour Party, she was able to approach him, but – like his colleagues Tessa Jowell and Charles Clarke – he showed no interest in taking on a fight. Perhaps it made a difference that News International had hired him as a well-paid columnist for the *Sun*.

That was our artillery, rolling slowly towards its target: Steve Coogan and Andy Gray with John Kelly at Schillings; Nicola Phillips and George Galloway with Mark Lewis; Sky Andrew and maybe some MPs with Charlotte Harris; some anonymous client and maybe some dynamite with Mark Thomson; Brian Paddick, Chris Bryant and Brendan Montague with Tamsin Allen. At that point, it didn't look like much.

★   ★   ★

By the beginning of April 2010 – with every political pundit predicting that Gordon Brown would lose the general election in May – Andy Coulson was poised to enter Downing Street at David Cameron's side, to become one of the most powerful people in Britain.

On 4 April, Peter Oborne published the column which he had discussed with me. It was noticeable that it was not in the *Daily Mail*, for whom Oborne normally wrote. The *Mail* evidently had taken fright at the idea of running anything critical of the Conservative leadership when there was an election in sight. Instead, it was published in the *Guardian*'s Sunday sister paper, the *Observer*. Oborne was forthright in his view.

He suggested that Coulson was the latest example of a 'behind-the-scenes fixer and thug' attached to a leading politician; noted that Fleet Street had ignored the hacking scandal 'under a system of *omertà* so strict that it would secure a nod of approbation from the heads of the New York crime families'; summarised the disclosures made by the *Guardian* and concluded: 'As deputy editor and then editor of the *News of the World*, [Coulson] was presiding over what can only be described as a flourishing criminal concern.' Oborne said it would be 'extremely worrying' if Cameron were to allow Coulson anywhere near Downing Street.

It was a brave piece and one which must have worried the Conservative leadership since it came from a conservative columnist, yet the column was greeted by silence. It was not just Fleet Street who were playing the *omertà* game. No leading politician would speak out against Coulson. No political party put the hacking scandal anywhere on their agenda.

I knew from the Emissary that there were senior figures in the Labour Party who were riveted by the affair. He said the Justice Secretary, Jack Straw, would call the commissioner of the Metropolitan Police and demand to know the truth; the Home Secretary, Alan Johnson, would check official files; the prime minister, Gordon Brown, was so worried that he himself might have been hacked that his wife, Sarah, had contacted Scotland Yard to find out. She had been told there was no evidence that she or Brown had been targeted by Mulcaire, the Emissary said, and I told him not to trust too much of what Scotland Yard told anybody about the hacking. He said the prime minister planned to go on television and make a big splash about the whole story. That didn't happen. No senior politician was going to pick a fight with the man who spoke to nearly 40% of Britain's newspaper readers, not in the run-up to an election.

The new editor of the *Independent*, Simon Kelner, got a taste of the danger when he promoted his paper with an advertisement declaring that 'Rupert Murdoch won't decide this election. You will.' James Murdoch reacted by storming into Kelner's office, with Rebekah Brooks at his side, to inform him loudly that he was a 'fucking fuckwit', threatening that the Murdoch papers would investigate Evgeny Lebedev, the son of the *Independent*'s owner. 'We thought you were our friend,' Brooks told the bewildered editor as they left.

This political inertia was unfortunate, because I was making a little progress. I had been working my way down several grapevines, one of which led me to a genuinely high-minded person who held a senior position in the criminal justice system. She had to work off the record so, in search of a memorable alias, I'll call her Lola. She agreed to meet me in her office, where we talked for a while and, once she had established that she was safe, she made a dream move. She produced a file, left it open on her desk, said she was going to be busy elsewhere for a while and left me alone with it. Her last words as she left the office were a polite apology that she was afraid there was probably not very much in there. She was wrong about that.

The file contained reports written by Scotland Yard during the original 2006 inquiry. One, dated 30 May 2006, contained a line which leaped off the page: 'A vast number of unique voicemail numbers belonging to high-profile individuals (politicians, celebrities) have been identified as being accessed without authority. These may be the subject of wider investigation in due course.' A vast number! Not a bloody handful, as the police had been claiming.

Some of these victims were even named in the paperwork – Max Clifford was there, and the former England football manager, Steve McClaren. And look at the timing. The police had written this memo in May 2006 – at least ten weeks before they arrested Goodman and Mulcaire, so this evidence of a vast number of victims was nothing to do with the material which they had seized during the arrests on

8 August. The police must already have had some big cache of evidence. Maybe they had collected data from the phone companies. Maybe they had been tapping Mulcaire's phone before he was arrested. Whatever, the fact was that clearly they had gathered a lot more evidence than I had suspected – and kept very quiet about all of it.

The scale of the hacking uncovered by police in 2006 was referred to again in a memo dated 8 August, the day of the arrests, when a senior prosecutor wrote: 'It was recognised early in this case that the investigation was likely to reveal a vast array of offending behaviour.' They might have recognised it, but they made very sure that they didn't mention it to the public in whose name they were supposed to be operating. The prosecutor then added something which began to explain the silence: 'However, the Crown Prosecution Service and the police concluded that aspects of the investigation could be focused on a discrete area of offending relating to JLP and HA and the suspects Goodman and Mulcaire.'

The initials clearly referred to Jamie Lowther-Pinkerton and Helen Asprey, two of the three Buckingham Palace employees who were named in court as Palace victims. What was important was that this paperwork showed that police and prosecutors had made a conscious decision to limit the inquiry. More than that, Lola's file revealed that they had made a second conscious decision 'to ring-fence the case to minimise the risk of extraneous matters being included'. The papers made it clear that that was a subtle bureaucrat's way of saying that they had decided not to have any public mention of particularly 'sensitive' victims such as members of the royal family. Evidently, it had been the police who had suggested this, doffing their helmets in the direction of Buckingham Palace; and the prosecutors had been only too happy to curtsy nicely before the throne and to agree – as one note put it – that the case should be 'deliberately limited' to 'less sensitive' witnesses. And they had never mentioned that either.

I thanked Lola profusely.

As I sat down to write this into a story, something else came through. After four months of obstruction, delays and several clear breaches of the Freedom of Information Act, Scotland Yard finally answered my remaining questions about the contents of the material which they had seized from Glenn Mulcaire. Apart from the ninety-one PIN codes and one document with transcribed emails which they had already admitted, they now disclosed that this material also contained 4,332 names or partial names of targets; 2,978 mobile phone numbers; and thirty cassette tapes containing voicemail. Yet more evidence that the scale of Mulcaire's crime – and of Scotland Yard's failure – was way beyond the official version of events.

In the vague hope that the police had decided to obey the law, I put in another Freedom of Information request, asking for the number of hacking victims they had warned in 2006 and in 2009. Their response – again – was to breach their legal duty to reply within twenty days and then to start making excuses for not providing the information.

On 5 April, the day after Peter Oborne's column had appeared in the *Observer*, I ran a story disclosing the contents of Lola's file and also revealing these numbers. The following day, as Gordon Brown formally confirmed that there would be an election on 6 May, I wrote again, summarising all that we now knew about the police behaviour: 'Something very worrying has been going on at Scotland Yard. We now know that in dealing with the phone-hacking affair at the *News of the World*, they cut short their original inquiry; suppressed evidence; misled the public and the press; concealed information and broke the law. Why?'

The Yard immediately demanded space to reply, and the *Guardian* published an article, under John Yates's byline, denying that police had been concealing evidence. 'Nothing could be further from the truth,' he wrote. The Yard's handling of the affair, he said, 'should be recognised for what it is – a success'. It irritated me that the *Guardian* had let Yates do this. Good newspapers believe in giving a balanced view of the world. Fine. Some people then exploit that belief and use it to balance truth with falsehood.

Lola's file had revealed one more secret. It disclosed that the original inquiry had been deemed so sensitive that a series of Scotland Yard reports were sent to the then Attorney General, Lord Goldsmith, who reviewed them in his capacity as the government's legal adviser. Surely those reports would still be sitting in a file in the Attorney General's office. If we could get hold of them, they would tell us still more about what the police had known in 2006, and maybe I could stop Scotland Yard scattering falsehood around the place. It might also tell us more about Andy Coulson.

Like scrambling up a muddy hill, always slipping down.

I contacted the Emissary, who was immediately alert to the political potential of these reports. Normally, he said, he could have tried to arrange for a government minister to retrieve the file, but because Gordon Brown had formally called the election, members of the government were now banned from their own offices. The only alternative was to persuade a civil servant to hand them over. He agreed to try it. For forty-eight hours, I sat with my fingers crossed, hoping that the Emissary would be able to retrieve the police reports. But he couldn't: the officials in the Attorney General's office refused to co-operate, so the reports stayed hidden. This was so frustrating – if I had seen Lola's file just a week earlier, I could probably have found a friendly Labour minister to dig out the treasure. As it was, all I could do was practise my swearing.

Separately, I contacted the Crown Prosecution Service and David Perry QC, who had been the prosecuting counsel at the trial of Goodman and Mulcaire, and tried to get them to admit that they had been wrong to say that it was an offence to hack voicemail under the RIPA law only if the message had not been heard already by the intended recipient. The CPS stood by their story and told me they would not answer any more questions. David Perry never replied.

At the same time, I had been working my way down a very different grapevine, of people who knew Glenn Mulcaire, particularly those who shared his passion for AFC Wimbledon. It felt like a waste of time; but then, in late April, I called a friend of Mulcaire, whose job means he cannot be identified, so I will call him Ovid. I asked him some tired question, just going through the motions, and to my surprise, he replied: 'You've just struck gold.'

He explained that Mulcaire used to run the reserve team at AFC Wimbledon and had had to write notes for the match programme, which he had found difficult, so Ovid had helped him. When Mulcaire came out of prison in May 2007, he had decided to write two books

– the boring one which I had already heard about, advising people how to improve their personal security, and a second one about the whole history of his illegal activity at the *News of the World*. And for this second book, he had asked Ovid to be his ghostwriter. Mulcaire had spent several days pouring out his heart and memories to Ovid, who had written a synopsis for both books. And yes, if I would come to London to meet him, he would be happy to hand over the synopsis for the tell-all book as well as the notebooks in which he had recorded all the detail. I agreed. Quickly.

When I met him the next day outside Holloway Underground station, as arranged, his opening line was worrying. 'Good news and bad news,' he said. The good was that he had found the synopsis and he had a copy of it for me. The bad news was that he had a young daughter and she had needed a new bedroom and so a few months ago he had cleared out his study and he had thrown out a lot of old notebooks . . .

There are times when you just want to chew through your own arteries. The synopsis was interesting, but it had been written as a tease, to provoke a publisher into commissioning the whole book, and deliberately it held back on all the important detail. It said an editorial executive had ordered Mulcaire to hack the royal phones, but it didn't name the executive. It said somebody had approached Mulcaire before he was put on trial and had persuaded him to 'change his story', but it didn't name the persuader or explain what Mulcaire's story would have been. It made it very clear that this was no 'rogue' operation. Indeed, the synopsis claimed that the *News of the World* had pressurised Mulcaire against his will to target the royal household: 'I was told in no uncertain terms – "stop now and you will never work in the media again". What choice did that give me? My loyalty cost me.' But who had pressurised him? Coulson? Some other executive? The synopsis did not say, and Ovid could not remember.

Ovid said the notebooks would have answered all these questions and more, that Mulcaire had gone into great detail about what he had done and who he had done it for. He remembered a few of the targets – the TV presenter Chris Tarrant, the Russian oligarch Roman Abramovich and Prince Charles. All very interesting, and certainly, where Tarrant and Abramovich were concerned, I could try to alert them.

Ovid also reckoned that Mulcaire had had seriously good contacts among the police and that he had been tipped off that he was being investigated before he was arrested in August 2006, and that this tip-off had included a warning that the Security Service, MI5, were looking at him; but Ovid wasn't sure, and the notebooks were gone – all that lovely detail, all those powerful facts. And, of course, the book had never been written, because Mulcaire had done a deal with the *News of the World*. They might still be denying it but I had no doubt that they had paid Mulcaire money in exchange for a binding undertaking not to tell what he knew.

I wrote a story based on the synopsis which Ovid had given me and I extracted a quote from one of the most influential members of Gordon Brown's government, Peter Mandelson, who was more willing than some of his colleagues to fire a shot at Rupert Murdoch: 'The idea that as editor of the *News of the World*, Andy Coulson was not aware of this activity beggars belief. If the election in less than a week goes the Tories' way, we would see this man taking on a major role in the British government. People should think long and hard before considering voting Conservative.'

It had no impact at all. People were too busy electing a government to start worrying about stuff like that.

There was a pause. David Cameron emerged as victor from the election and moved in to Downing Street, with Andy Coulson at his side. A few weeks later, on 15 June, James Murdoch announced that News Corp were bidding to take over BSkyB. I could see as clearly as anyone else that this would make them more powerful than ever but there was not much I could do about it. I had run my best stories before the election and, just as News Corp were announcing their bid, I veered off sideways when I read a story on the foreign pages of the *Guardian*, about an American soldier called Bradley Manning who had been arrested and accused of giving a massive tranche of secrets to an organisation called WikiLeaks.

I persuaded the WikiLeaks founder, Julian Assange, to release the secrets to an alliance of news organisations led by the *Guardian* and spent several months working with him until August when I realised I had to return to the hacking: after some five months of research, the *New York Times* were getting ready to publish.

On the afternoon of Wednesday 1 September 2010, fourteen months after we published the Gordon Taylor story and began the battle, the US paper finally posted their hacking story on their website – and we breached the outer walls of Murdoch's castle. Most of their long story simply confirmed what the *Guardian* had been saying – on one level it was simply a relief that they had not concluded that we really were wrong. This way, we had a lot of extra muscle to support the things we had said. But, on several critical points, they went further. Above all, they had managed to find a former *News of the World* journalist who was willing to come out on the record and put his name to serious claims about phone-hacking – and to put Andy Coulson in the middle of the action.

Sean Hoare, the paper's former show-business correspondent, told the *New York Times* on the record that he personally had played recordings of hacked voicemail messages to Coulson when they worked together at the *Sun* and that later, when he worked for him at the *News of the World*, he had continued to tell him about stories which were based on hacked messages. Coulson 'actively encouraged me to do it', Hoare said. That was reinforced anonymously by a former executive from the *News of the World* who was quoted claiming that Coulson had talked freely about illegal news-gathering techniques, including phone-hacking, and that the subject had come up at 'dozens, if not hundreds' of meetings with Coulson. 'The editor added that when Coulson would ask where a story came from, editors would reply "We've pulled the phone records" or "I've listened to the phone messages."'

Beyond those two sources who specifically named Coulson, others had told the *New York Times*, as they had told me, that phone-hacking was 'pervasive' in Coulson's newsroom. 'Everyone knew,' according to one unnamed senior reporter. 'The office cat knew.' Most of these former reporters were unnamed, but one, Sharon Marshall, was quoted as having witnessed hacking when she worked at the paper under Coulson between 2002 and 2004. 'It was an industry-wide thing,' she said. It was now simply unbelievable that Coulson had not known his reporters were breaking the law.

All this clearly crashed through News International's defences, but the story was embarrassing too for the Metropolitan Police. It quoted several unnamed police sources who suggested that the original 2006 inquiry had been hampered by a desire to avoid upsetting Britain's biggest-selling newspaper: 'Several investigators said in interviews that Scotland Yard was reluctant to conduct a wider inquiry in part because of its close relationship with the *News of the World*.' And, in that context, they produced the beautiful nugget that Dick Fedorcio's then deputy, Chris Webb, allegedly had approached one of the Caryatid detectives, waving his arms and urging him to stop and think about whether to pursue the inquiry.

Finally, they had managed to get hold of the mysterious tape I had heard about when I was researching the original Gordon Taylor story, on which Mulcaire could be heard explaining how to hack voicemail to a journalist whose name sounded like Ryan or Ryall. One of the *New York Times* reporters, Jo Becker, had performed a brilliant investigative trick, by feeding the dialling tones at the beginning of the tape into specialist software which converted them back into a phone number. She had then phoned that number and identified the mysterious 'Ryan' or 'Ryall', but he refused to speak and, to avoid the risk of error, the paper had held back his name.

News International and Scotland Yard denied everything, and various Conservative MPs said this was all old stuff and anyway Sean Hoare had had drink and drugs problems (which was true but not exactly relevant). None of that could prevent the eruption of a small but very loud chorus of protest. A few politicians rushed through the gap in Murdoch's defences, looking for Coulson, worrying out loud about News Corp's bid for BSkyB. The media select committee said it would take more evidence. Two other select committees – on home affairs, and on standards and privileges – announced their own inquiries. Tom Watson, who had become increasingly active since the election, called on Scotland Yard to reopen their failed investigation. He also called on the prime minister to set up an inquiry into the relationship between the police and the *News of the World*.

The *Guardian* followed up with a barrage of stories. We disclosed that the then Metropolitan Police Commissioner, Sir Ian Blair, was one of those whose details had been found in Mulcaire's paperwork, 'raising questions about whether officers who were directly involved in the investigation had discovered that they, too, had been targets of the newspaper'.

We reported that after our Gordon Taylor story in July 2009, the Home Office had considered calling in the Inspectorate of Constabulary to investigate Scotland Yard's failure but had rejected the idea – because they did not want to upset Scotland Yard. We disclosed that the former deputy prime minister, John Prescott, was poised to sue. When Prescott then gave interviews about this, he was answered by the former assistant commissioner of Scotland Yard, Andy Hayman, who went on the radio and bluntly declared: 'We have to get real over this. This is just another episode of Lord Prescott's rants.'

John Yates was hauled in front of the home affairs select committee where he repeated the RIPA bollocks and explained: 'There are very few offences that we are able to actually prove that have been hacked – that is, intercepting the voicemail prior to the owner of that voice-mail getting it him or herself.' He then noticeably failed to tell the committee what he had acknowledged to Alan Rusbridger behind closed doors, that regardless of this strange interpretation of the law, there had been 'a mass attempt at penetrating people's voicemail systematically'.

Having diminished the scale of the *News of the World's* hacking, Yates went on to make a very bold claim about Scotland Yard's efforts to warn the victims. Detectives had acted, he said, 'out of a spirit of abundance of caution'. He went on to tell the MPs: 'We have taken what I consider to be all reasonable steps in conjunction with the major service providers – the Oranges, Vodafones – to ensure, where we had even the minutest possibility they may have been the subject of an attempt to hack, we have taken all reasonable steps in my view.' Asked to define 'reasonable steps', Yates said: 'Speaking to them or ensuring the phone company has spoken to them.'

Really?

We followed up an obscure paragraph at the end of the *New York Times* story which suggested that a *News of the World* reporter had been suspended for a recent attempt to hack into the mobile phone of a

TV personality. Neither the reporter nor the alleged victim was named, but I established that this was a reference to the 'dynamite' case which Mark Thompson had been nursing since earlier in the year and that the suspect reporter was none other than Dan Evans, the feature writer whose skill as a hacker had been flagged up to me by a private investigator.

I was amazed at Mark Thomson's self-control: he had said nothing when I dropped Evans's name on him months earlier even though, I now understood, he had obtained some kind of evidence from his unnamed client's phone company that her alleged hacker was using a phone which was registered in the name of Dan Evans from the *News of the World*. We ran the story, reporting also that Evans had been suspended since April when Mark Thomson evidently had confronted News International with his evidence.

In response, the Press Complaints Commission went into a spin. Their new chair, Lady Buscombe, had been on the radio in May, declaring that 'if there was a whiff of any continuing activity in this regard, we would be on it like a ton of bricks'. But now, six months later, it emerged that they had done nothing to investigate the allegations about Dan Evans on the strange grounds that his alleged victim was suing. The *News of the World* put out a statement claiming to have played straight by telling the PCC all about Evans. In reality, we found, they had said nothing at all when they suspended him in April and had finally told the PCC in June – just after the *New York Times* had started asking them questions about it.

We also ran quotes from our own sources among former *News of the World* journalists, including Paul McMullan who, after nine months of doubt, bravely agreed to talk on the record. He said that as deputy features editor under Rebekah Brooks, he had commissioned hundreds of illegal acts from private investigators and that senior editors including Coulson were aware of phone-hacking by reporters. 'Coulson would certainly be well aware that the practice was pretty widespread. He is conceivably telling the truth when he says he didn't specifically know every time a reporter would do it. I wouldn't have told him. It wasn't of significance for me to say I just rang up David Beckham and listened to his messages. In general terms, he would have known that reporters were doing it.' Five other former *News of the World* journalists, speaking off the record, agreed with him in the same *Guardian* story.

Later that day, there was a hacking debate in the House of Commons, and Tom Watson made a powerful speech. There was a shame, he said, which all of them shared:

> The truth is that, in this House, we are all, in our own way, scared of the Rebekah Brookses of this world. It is almost laughable that we sit here in Parliament, the central institution of our sacred democracy, yet we are scared of the power that Rebekah Brooks wields without a jot of responsibility or accountability.
>
> The barons of the media, with their red-topped assassins, are the biggest beasts in the modern jungle. They have no predators. They are untouchable. They laugh at the law. They sneer at Parliament. They have the power to hurt us, and they do, with gusto and precision, with joy and criminality. Prime ministers quail before them, and that is how they like it. That indeed has become how they insist upon it, and we are powerless in the face of them. We are afraid. That is the tawdry secret that dare not speak its name.

Channel 4 broadcast the *Dispatches* programme, which Rusbridger had suggested they make, rehearsing the familiar story and adding one new anonymous source who said Coulson knew about the hacking. The Channel 4 crew saw signs that their own phones might have been hacked during production, and I put them on to Tamsin Allen. The *Independent*, after fifteen months of hostility to the story, were beginning to change sides. They finally disclosed that Tessa Jowell had been hacked, at least twenty-eight times, provoking a minor backlash from Rebekah Brooks who ran into the *Independent* editor, Simon Kelner, at a party in Oxfordshire and refused to talk to him before loudly telling another guest that 'the *Independent* is a perfectly ridiculous newspaper'. One of the guests told Kelner to be careful that his phone was not hacked. Kelner said he was sure it wasn't and, to prove the point, called into his voicemail, entered his PIN – and discovered that it no longer worked. A few weeks later, Brooks gatecrashed a lunch between Jowell and *Sunday Times* journalists and denounced her to her face, accusing her of making comments which had allowed the *Guardian* to stoke up the hacking story.

The *Independent* ran another useful story, revealing that the reporter on the 'Ryall' tape had been working on the *Evening Standard* when Mulcaire coached him on how to hack voicemail and was now at *The Times*. A journalist I did not know contacted me to explain that it was not 'Ryan' or 'Ryall' but 'Raoul' – Raoul Simons, who had indeed been a sports writer on the *Evening Standard*. After one of the occasions when the sex life of the England football manager Sven-Göran Eriksson was exposed by the *News of the World*, Simons had written a piece about Mulcaire as a specialist who could protect the security of football celebs like Eriksson. This was ironic, to say the least, since it was Mulcaire himself who had hacked Eriksson's phone. But Mulcaire was pleased with the story and had returned the favour to Simons by giving him a brief tutorial on hacking – a gift that would have been less poisonous if Mulcaire had not recorded it and then allowed the recording to fall into the hands of police.

By the time we finally identified him, Raoul Simons was working for *The Times*. They suspended him, and later I heard that he had slumped into a deep depression. It did seem highly unfair that News International were suspending a reporter who had had a minor involvement on a paper that did not belong to them while they lied and paid out a fortune to protect those from their own stable who were up to their elbows in crime.

In the face of this new storm, the opposition fell back. Senior Tories started muttering to journalists that Coulson might have to go, and one of the *Guardian's* political correspondents heard that Rupert Murdoch and Rebekah Brooks had agreed a new strategy and were urging Coulson to step down in order to kill off the Labour Party's political interest in the affair. This was bolstered by a leak to the effect that Rupert Murdoch had called the former prime minister Tony Blair and asked him to persuade the Labour MPs to go quiet, and that Blair had called his successor, Gordon Brown, and asked him to pass this on. The Blair camp later denied this.

More important, John Yates agreed to reopen the police investigation. For a brief moment, that looked like another significant breakthrough and then we discovered a little more about it. First, this inquiry was to be run by Yates's staff officer, Detective Superintendent Dean Haydon, who might be a good and honest man but who was unlikely to be allowed to break out of Yates's very limited view of the affair. Second, as if to confirm our worst fears, it turned out that the inquiry would look only at 'new' evidence, so it would interview Sean Hoare and Paul McMullan and any other new witnesses, but specifically would not go back and look at the mass of evidence which had been sitting in Scotland Yard for four years now. And third, when Haydon's officers approached Sean Hoare, they told him they would interview him 'under caution', i.e. not as a witness who might help them but as a suspect who could be charged with a criminal offence as a result of what he told them. Hoare could see no reason why he should offer himself up as Scotland Yard's victim and answered 'No comment' to all the questions put to him.

Paul McMullan, who was a more confrontational character, publicly refused to have anything to do with being questioned under caution and defied Scotland Yard to come and arrest him. They stayed away. They interviewed Matt Driscoll, who spent three hours with them in a suite of the Hilton hotel near Tower Bridge, telling them everything he knew about illegal information-gathering at the *News of the World*. They also questioned Coulson, who denied everything.

The Murdochs seemed unmoved. As the hacking story bubbled and boiled through that September, Pope Benedict XVI visited the UK – and held a private meeting with James Murdoch, who had donated a reported £100,000 to fund the visit. Somewhere in the corridors of power, their bid for BSkyB was quietly moving forward.

By now, the legal artillery was getting close to the front line. Certainly, News International could see the threat and were trying to stop it in its tracks. They didn't understand quite what they were dealing with. We had a secret weapon.

Back in May, I had been asked to go to a private meeting to talk about the future of the media. It was in a posh restaurant in South Kensington. There was just a small group of us around a table – some lawyers, a High Court judge, the *Channel 4 News* anchor Jon Snow and the man I was sitting next to, Max Mosley.

Mosley, I knew, had been a victim of the *News of the World* on an eye-watering scale of viciousness. They had, as he put it now, 'tried to destroy my life' by posting on their website video extracts of him naked with prostitutes. Talking to him, it was clear that the £60,000 damages he had then won had done little to heal his emotional wound.

Mosley, who was seventy when I met him that evening, has a quiet, deferential manner, but he is obviously also a very determined man. He told me that his family had warned him not to fight the Murdoch organisation because he could never win, but he had made up his mind that he was going to challenge the *News of the World* and the press generally over their invasion of privacy. Indeed, he made it clear that he was willing to spend the rest of his life doing it. He would also spend money, although at first I did not understand quite how much he had in the bank. Very quickly that evening, we agreed to work together.

Already, he had one very interesting plot. He had opened up a line to Glenn Mulcaire through his own private investigator, a former police officer who happened to live near Mulcaire in south London and who had befriended Mulcaire at AFC Wimbledon games. It was clear that Mulcaire was very worried about money, and Mosley was thinking of coaxing him into a direct conversation in which he could offer to hire him as his own security consultant, on the understanding that he would make a clean breast of his role at the *News of the World*. I encouraged him, and we agreed that I might supply questions for these conversations and check the answers to make sure Mulcaire was telling the truth.

Within weeks, however, a second plot emerged. I was talking to Mark Lewis, who was complaining that he might have to drop his libel action against the PCC chairwoman, Lady Buscombe, simply because he could not afford the costs. That case was important. She had implied that he misled Parliament in repeating what a police officer had told him about the number of people whose messages had been intercepted by the *News of the World*. If the case went to court, it might flush out more of the evidence which the police were still busily concealing about the true number of victims. It might also underline the failure of Buscombe and the PCC to play fair with the evidence in the hacking scandal. On 9 June, I emailed Mosley and explained the problem and asked if he might underwrite Lewis's costs. He agreed.

Within days, Mark Lewis had introduced Mosley to Tamsin Allen, and Mosley soon was also underwriting the costs of the judicial review which she was organising for Brian Paddick and Chris Bryant, which threatened to force Scotland Yard to reveal the history of its decision-making in the 2006 inquiry. With Mosley's help, our artillery was bigger and faster than ever.

Mosley and I took to meeting in the quiet corners of an upmarket café near his home in Knightsbridge, plotting amongst cream cakes and chocolate croissants. By the time the *New York Times* published in September, Mosley was reporting that Mulcaire had agreed to become his security adviser on a two-year contract on the condition that he told the truth about his work for the *News of the World*. I wrote a seven-page briefing memo for Mosley's lawyer, identifying key facts and key questions to put to him. By October, Mulcaire had signed his new work contract and was beginning to talk. He was not necessarily telling the truth.

I knew from my sessions in Mulcaire's home that talking to him was like grabbing handfuls of mist. There was nothing threatening or unpleasant about the man, but he would never give a straight answer if a bent one came to mind. For example, Mosley reported, Mulcaire was claiming that 70% of his commissions had come from Ian Edmondson. That might have been true for the last twelve months of Mulcaire's work for the *News of the World*, but for the four or five years before that, all the former *News of the World* sources agreed that Mulcaire had done most of his work for Greg Miskiw. Mulcaire, however, was claiming that Miskiw had given him only 5% of his commissions. Since Miskiw was his close friend and since Edmondson seemed to be nobody's close friend, that looked very much like a neatly bent line. So, when he went on to say that Ian Edmondson had made some kind of threatening phone call to his home after he came out of prison in the spring of 2007, it was hard to take it at face value. Similarly, when he claimed that he had only ever hacked a grand total of a hundred public figures, I remembered all that I had been told by former *News of the World* journalists and reckoned that Mosley and I were being served up with more mist.

At one of the meetings in the posh café, Mosley explained that, apart from earning very good money running Formula One racing, he had also inherited a fortune. He wasn't specific about its size but he explained that there was a very large amount of money which had been held in a family trust in Liechtenstein, and he had made a big decision. He was considering asking the trustees to move all of it onshore, paying whatever huge taxes needed to be paid, so that he had access to it as a fighting fund. He was happy for me to mention that to others who might need help in their legal actions.

By that autumn, following his support for Mark Lewis's libel action against Lady Buscombe, he was helping several hacking victims, agreeing that he would pay the potentially very large legal bills if they lost a case and had the costs awarded against them. My researcher, Jenny Evans, had told me she happened to know a young woman who had been the key witness in the aborted trial of a TV presenter, John Leslie, who had been charged with rape and then cleared. This alleged victim had seen signs of her phone being hacked at the time of the trial, back in July 2003 – a particularly disgusting intrusion, if true. Through Jenny, I passed her on to Charlotte Harris, who took on her case, shielding her identity by calling her Miss X. Again, Mosley agreed to cover the costs if they lost.

I heard of another lawyer who had clients who appeared to have been victims. Gerald Shamash was representing John Prescott and also the former England footballer Paul Gascoigne who had seen so much of his private information turning up in the *News of the World* that it had begun to make him mentally ill, breeding a paranoia that the press were spying on him, but he was worried about suing in case he lost and could not pay the bill. Mosley stepped forward to help.

One way and another, word was spreading among the *News of the World*'s victims that the police were sitting on evidence which might include their names. Charlotte Harris was doing a brilliant job of procuring informants among former and current *News of the World* executives and was coming up with more names of possible victims. I was working with more former *News of the World* journalists and I had also opened a line to the private detective Derek Webb, who had specialised in physical surveillance for the paper and who now saw that almost certainly it was phone-hacking which had allowed the news desk to be able to tell him where to find his targets.

Whenever I found a new victim – actors from TV soap operas, a couple of film stars, a TV presenter – I tried to connect them with the lawyers who were suing. For months I had been in touch with David Law, a friend of the family of Paul McCartney's former wife, Heather Mills. Law had eventually wrung out of Scotland Yard an admission that Heather Mills's name and three of her mobile phone numbers were in Mulcaire's notes. I steered her towards Mark Thomson, who was not fooled by the line at the end of the police letter which added that there was no evidence that any messages on these phone numbers had been unlawfully intercepted. Then I introduced Thomson to Max Mosley, who agreed yet again to act as a safety net, this time for Heather Mills's costs.

In addition to the victims I sent them, the lawyers were finding more of their own. Other lawyers were joining in. By the end of October 2010, 194 people had asked Scotland Yard if their details showed up in Mulcaire's material. That same month, after more than a year of behaving like a sulky toddler, replying to potential hacking victims with the legal equivalent of a grunt, the police came out with a new ruse. In addition to waiting for victims to guess that they might be victims, and providing only the minimum of information, and couching it in language which suggested that the information was not evidence of crime, they started replying to lawyers that they would provide information only 'if your client has grounds for a reasonable suspicion that his mobile telephone voicemails were unlawfully intercepted'.

The lawyers were furious. As Mark Lewis put it in a story which I ran in the *Guardian*: 'It's a bit like the police discovering that your house has been burgled, but you don't know that it's happened – and they won't tell you anything about it unless you can come up with your own evidence to show you've been a victim of the crime. It's a transparent attempt to stifle legal claims by concealing evidence. The police are obstructing justice.'

Only six victims had broken through to the point where they had formally issued proceedings but, with Mosley in the background and the group of lawyers pushing hard, they were beginning to look powerful. Three of them – Andy Gray, Steve Coogan and George Galloway – were still at an early stage, and News International had simply served defences in which they denied everything. The other three were becoming more of a threat, and News International were being a little more imaginative in their efforts to get rid of them.

Sky Andrew, having already ignored an offer of £25,000 a year to drop his case, was working his way through the courts. Guided by Charlotte Harris, he was starting to ask for an order to force News International to disclose internal email, which could prove powerful. If Andrew ended up with evidence which identified the person who had told Mulcaire to hack him, the *News of the World* would be in trouble: Mulcaire had admitted this hacking at the original trial, so they would have no room to deny it.

News International reacted by dangling more money in front of him. How about £200,000 to go away, they said. No. Well how about £200,000 plus another £1.2 million in free advertising for a charity of his choice and how about accepting this money directly from them, without going through Charlotte Harris, so that he wouldn't have to pay her costs? The answer was still no. Sky Andrew was not for sale. Good man. It was at about this time that Vodafone told him that right now – not way back in 2006, but right now, while he was suing the *News of the World* – somebody had been trying to access his voicemail. We never established who was responsible.

One of Mark Thomson's anonymous clients – identified only as AZP – had been to court in June and had won an order for the police to hand over all relevant evidence in their possession. By September, the reporting restriction was lifted to reveal that AZP was, in fact, the actress Sienna Miller. Thomson was hinting that the case was going to be important but, discreet as ever, was refusing to explain what he meant. Clearly, her case was worrying News International. If a garbled rumour from New York was to be believed, Rupert Murdoch had heard about the threat and tried to neutralise it.

According to this version of events, Murdoch had approached the editor of *Vogue* magazine, Anna Wintour, and had gently suggested that Miller was making a mistake and that it might be helpful if Wintour had a word with her, and perhaps arranged for her and Rupert to have tea together, 'to tell her to be sensible'. Nothing threatening, of course, but it was a fact that Miller was an actress and, among Murdoch's many properties, he did happen to own one of the biggest film studios in the world, Twentieth Century Fox. That rumour certainly reached London and certainly made Sienna Miller pause and worry and wonder about whether to go on. Like several others in this story, she had more courage than the opposition and decided to stick with it.

Nicola Phillips, aided by Mark Lewis, was also suing, threatening to force police to expose the same paperwork which had been concealed in the case of her former boss, Max Clifford – paperwork which, we believed, would expose the role of Ian Edmondson. Phillips reported a series of calls from Edmondson himself who said he just wanted to talk to her 'as a mate' and then pressured her to drop her case. Since she was now an independent publicist, she found this alarming, particularly when she received a call from another *News of the World* executive who suggested that they could dig out and publish a damaging allegation about her. Bravely, she stood up to this. Then she made an even more threatening move.

On 27 October 2010, she went back to court to ask the judge to order Glenn Mulcaire to name all those at the *News of the World* who had instructed him to hack her phone. The judge wanted three weeks to come to a decision. It was clear from the argument in court that, even if the judge agreed to grant the order, Mulcaire would want to appeal, in which case News International could fire their biggest weapon – money. They could pay Mulcaire's legal fees, knowing that Phillips would not be able to afford to pay hers, so they would win. Except that we had our secret weapon: on 3 November, Mark Lewis contacted Max Mosley who readily agreed to underwrite her costs. Murdoch was not the only one who had cash on his side.

Then there were signs of News International using another familiar tactic. On 10 November, somebody contacted Nicola Phillips on her mobile and, using a false name – Lee Jennings – attempted to tie her up on the line in a way which would have allowed a second person to dial her number and get access to her voicemail. Certainly, that was how the police later interpreted this. But Phillips was instantly suspicious as 'Lee Jennings' babbled about having seen her at a club, and she quickly got off the line.

On 17 November, Mr Justice Mann ordered Mulcaire to tell all about the hacking of Nicola Phillips's phone. As we had predicted, Mulcaire immediately appealed. I reported that on the front page of the *Guardian* and included a line which identified Ian Edmondson as a person about whom Mulcaire would be questioned. Nine days later, on 26 November, Nicola Phillips was in tears after receiving what she took to be a direct threat to her new career as a publicist. It had come in a phone call from a third party, who was in touch with News Corp, and the thrust of it was: 'We didn't like that about your case on the front page of the *Guardian* – you have to decide whether to pursue the case or your career.' Once again, with real backbone, she stuck with it.

On 19 November, Andy Gray went to court to ask for a similar order for Mulcaire to name the person who had instructed him to hack his voicemail. Our best sources on this suggested that that would expose the name of Greg Miskiw, one of Edmondson's predecessors as head of news. Andy Gray went further than Nicola Phillips, asking for an order for Mulcaire to disclose a range of other information about those he had worked for. On 6 December, Steve Coogan applied for a similar order.

In the meantime, on 23 November, Mark Lewis won his libel action against the PCC chair, Lady Buscombe, forcing the PCC to pay damages and Lady Buscombe to apologise for her misleading comments about him – an embarrassing move for the leader of an organisation which was supposed to uphold standards of accuracy and fairness.

The pressure on News International's inner walls was becoming severe, but they showed extraordinary resilience, dealing out denials in court paperwork as though the truth could always be repelled. Then the pressure increased – Andy Coulson was ordered to appear in court.

★   ★   ★

This move came from the side of the picture, from the radical Scottish politician Tommy Sheridan. He had been the victim of a *News of the World* exposé in October 2004, when the paper had accused him of enjoying orgies. Sheridan had sued for libel and, in August 2006, won £200,000 damages. However, the newspaper claimed that he had lied on oath in order to win the damages. The Scottish police had investigated and now, in December 2010, Sheridan was on trial for perjury at Glasgow High Court. He had sacked his barrister and was putting his own case to the jury and he had called Coulson as a witness.

I had been passing information to Sheridan's solicitor, Aamer Anwar, who had followed up by getting a court order to force Scotland Yard to hand over the notes which Mulcaire had scribbled while he was hacking Tommy Sheridan. These were then displayed in open court – the first time that we had succeeded in flushing the hidden paper- work out into the public domain – and there, in the top left-hand corner, just as we had suspected, was a single word identifying the person who had commissioned the hacking – 'Greg', the former assis- tant editor, Greg Miskiw.

Coulson had consistently refused to answer any of the questions which I had sent him and so, on the eve of his appearance, I gave Aamer Anwar a nine-page memo identifying questions which Sheridan might put to him.

It was an interesting day in court. I had a brief encounter with Coulson at the doorway, during which he informed me quietly that I was a traitor. Sheridan did his best to confront him with allegations of his knowledge of crime, but Coulson was sharp and confident and conceded nothing. Faced with the paperwork which suggested that his assistant editor, Greg Miskiw, had ordered the hacking of Sheridan's phone, he said: 'I'm saying that I had absolutely no knowledge of it.' He agreed that he had been on 'not unfriendly terms' with the former assistant commissioner Andy Hayman but he denied that the *News of the World* had been holding information about Hayman's sex life which might have prevented him running a thorough investigation. He denied asking Clive Goodman to take the blame for the sake of the paper. He repeated his claim that he had never heard of either

Mulcaire or Steve Whittamore while they were working for him. Asked about Sean Hoare's allegations in the *New York Times*, he said he had spoken voluntarily to the recent Scotland Yard inquiry.

And by good chance, on the very day that Coulson appeared at Glasgow High Court, somebody had leaked to the *Daily Telegraph* the fact that the Crown Prosecution Service had reviewed the evidence collected by John Yates's staff officer, Detective Superintendent Dean Haydon, and concluded that it provided no basis for charging anybody with any offence. No surprise considering he had been told not to look at the best of the evidence.

News International were holding their line. And why would they do anything else? They had never had to obey the rules which bound the little people. I was beginning to wonder when we would ever break through. And then we did.

Mark Thomson told me that he had lodged a detailed account of Sienna Miller's case with the High Court. That was a public document. It took a small amount of sweat and hassle but on 14 December, the court handed over the twenty-page 'particulars of claim' which Thomson had prepared with his barrister, Hugh Tomlinson QC, on her behalf.

Thomson's hints had been correct. He had done an enormous amount of work, analysing Sienna Miller's itemised phone bills, forcing the police to hand over records of calls made by Mulcaire, linking them to Mulcaire's hacking notes, cross-referring them to *News of the World* stories, extracting data from Sienna Miller's phone company, linking that back to Mulcaire's notes. The resulting document was powerful.

First and most important, it disclosed the name which had been written by Mulcaire in the top left-hand corners of the notes which he had made as he hacked Sienna Miller's phone – Ian, 'which the claimant infers to be Ian Edmondson', as the legal document put it. That was strong. After Ross Hindley, Neville Thurlbeck and Greg Miskiw, this was the fourth *News of the World* journalist to be firmly implicated in activity which was supposed to have involved only the rogue Clive Goodman. And this was the current assistant editor (news), who had been in post for six years.

Second, it disclosed the sheer scale of the operation against Miller. She had feared somebody was listening to her phone and changed it twice, but Mulcaire had pursued her, blagging his way to her new numbers as well as the account number, PIN code and password for all three. And then he had blagged similar details for nine other numbers used by those close to her – for her mother; her former partners Archie Keswick and Jude Law; Keswick's girlfriend; Law's assistant; and three numbers belonging to her publicist Ciara Parkes.

Third, it claimed that the hacking of Miller was part of a wider scheme, hatched early in 2005, when Mulcaire had agreed to use 'electronic intelligence and eavesdropping' to supply the paper with daily transcripts of the messages of a list of named targets from the worlds of politics, royalty and entertainment.

The damage to the *News of the World*'s defences was catastrophic. And it was just as bad for Scotland Yard. They had been sitting on all this evidence for more than four years. Why had they never warned Sienna Miller or any of the other victims around her? Why had they never interviewed Ian Edmondson? Why had they not passed this paperwork to the Crown Prosecution Service? Why had they not done anything about it even in the last three months when John Yates's staff officer was conducting a new inquiry?

The castle wall was quaking.

11. The biggest deal in the world

Based on interviews with government ministers, officials and advisers; with sources in News Corp and other news organisations; and on sworn evidence and internal documents, emails and texts from the Leveson Inquiry.

On the afternoon of Tuesday 18 May 2010, a week after David Cameron became prime minister, a chauffeur-driven car prowled across the wide tarmac of Horse Guards Parade in Whitehall, central London, to deliver a visitor to the side alley which leads to the back of 10 Downing Street.

Over the previous seven days, various senior politicians and foreign leaders had arrived with some fanfare at the front of the building, waving at the photographers and stepping through the famous black door. This visitor had been asked to avoid the watching eyes of the media. This was an important visit – the first official meeting between the new prime minister and a person who held no government post – but it was secret. This was Rupert Murdoch coming for tea, to give the Conservative leader a chance to thank him for his support during the election campaign. As he came in from the side alley, he was greeted by one of Cameron's closest advisers, Andy Coulson.

This was a sociable time for Murdoch's men and women. On the following weekend, down at the Hay literary festival on the Welsh borders, his executives from BSkyB entertained three Conservative MPs and five members of the new Conservative Cabinet, including the new junior minister responsible for the media, Ed Vaizey. They also entertained one former Labour minister, Tessa Jowell, who pointedly asked Vaizey if his private office knew that he was accepting hospitality from BSkyB while holding a brief for government policy on the media. Vaizey, according to one witness, 'went a bit pale'.

The end of the World, 10 July 2011. The final edition of the paper that hacked for stories

Actor and hacking victim Hugh Grant on his way to give evidence at the Leveson Inquiry, November 2011

Actress Sienna Miller arrives at the Leveson Inquiry with her legal team to talk about her life as a tabloid target

Above: Professional Footballers Association chief executive Gordon Taylor – hacked

Right: England footballer David Beckham – hacked

Celebrity PR Max Clifford sold scandal to Fleet Street and was then destroyed by scandal, here on his way to the trial which ended in May 2014 with an eight-year jail sentence for sex crimes

Trial by media. Andy Coulson on the receiving end of press photographers as he walks into the Old Bailey, November 2013

Stuart Kuttner, veteran managing editor of the *News of the World*, on his way to court

The man who ran the 'dark arts' at the *News of the World* – assistant editor Greg Miskiw

Above: Award-winning chief reporter Neville Thurlbeck on the wrong side of the law

Left: James 'Whispering Jimmy' Weatherup, former news editor of the *News of the World*

Right: Labour MP Tom Watson who took on the *News of the World*. The paper put a private investigator on his tail

Below: The hacker: Glenn Mulcaire outside court with a TV crew on his heels

Out of court: Rebekah and Charlie Brooks leave the Old Bailey after the jury acquitted them on all charges

A guilty man: Andy Coulson leaves the Old Bailey after being convicted of phone hacking, June 2014

Very soon, Murdoch's UK chief executive, Rebekah Brooks, was a guest at the prime minister's official rural retreat at Chequers, forty miles north of London. His editor at the *Sun*, Dominic Mohan, became the first editor to be allowed in to meet Cameron; his editor at *The Times*, James Harding, was the second; his editor at the *News of the World*, Colin Myler, was the first Sunday newspaper editor.

It is a rule of life in the power elite that there is no such thing as a purely social act.

The following month, on 15 June 2010, James Murdoch confirmed the rumours that had been bouncing around the media world for months when he announced the biggest deal in the history of his father's global corporation: News Corp would buy the entire remaining shareholding of BSkyB, to go with the 39% which they already owned. This was big. With an opening offer of 675p a share, which rose eventually to 850p, News Corp had set aside £8.2 billion for this one project. Thomson Reuters, who specialise in financial data, rated it as the year's most expensive single cross-border deal, not just in the UK but anywhere in the world.

News Corp had spent more than two years nursing their plan, gathering cash and waiting for the right political moment to make their move. That moment had arrived, albeit with an unforeseen complication. The election on 6 May had seen the Conservatives win the most seats, but not enough to have an outright majority in the House of Commons. For five days, Gordon Brown had remained in post while he and Cameron separately attempted to link up with the Liberal Democrats, whose seats now held the balance of power. Finally, with the *Sun* baying for Brown's blood and accusing him of being a squatter in No. 10, Cameron had won the day and formed a coalition government with the Lib Dems.

Now, with the unpredictable Brown ousted, News Corp were ready. For Rupert Murdoch, this was a chance to take complete control of the richest broadcaster in Britain, with an annual income of £5.9 billion, compared to the BBC's £4.8 billion, with all that that meant for his commercial power. It was a chance, too, for him to become not only the biggest newspaper player in the country but also the dominant broadcaster, one of only three TV news providers (along with the BBC and ITN), one of only two radio news providers (along with the BBC) and the giant of pay TV with 67% of viewers, with all that that meant for his political power. More than that, it was a chance to use BSkyB's massive operating profit, then running at £855 million a year, to borrow even more money and to take over one of the few remaining global media groups which was still bigger than his. Time Warner or Disney were the favoured targets. Then, finally, nearly sixty years after Rupert Murdoch inherited his father's share of a single newspaper in Adelaide, News Corp would be the biggest media business in the world. As if to mark his rise into the final heights, the mogul had recently baptised his daughter, Grace, in the Holy Land waters of the River Jordan, with his guests, including Tony Blair, all dressed in white. If all went well, the deal would be done in time for his eightieth birthday in March 2011.

For James Murdoch, however, there was an extra attraction. If News Corp controlled BSkyB, its cash flow would make it the company's biggest single earner, tilting the balance of power from New York to London, from father to son. According to two News Corp sources, Rupert Murdoch knew very well that the bid was another round in James's power-grab but thought that he could control him. That illusion was quickly shattered when James upset News Corp's plans to run the bid from New York by giving the job to Deutsche Bank in London before his father had made a move. 'We were left at the gate,' according to one senior executive in New York.

However, to seal the deal, the Murdochs first had to do what they least liked doing: they had to handle the media regulators, particularly the hated Ofcom. News Corp was armed with the weapons of passive power: a special relationship with government, based on the privilege of access and the advantage of fear. It also had problems: all the irritations of democracy and a great many silent enemies.

On 15 June, James Murdoch telephoned the new Secretary of State for business, Vince Cable, to give him formal notice of the bid. Cable was potentially a problem. He had never been part of the plan – a Liberal Democrat with whom News Corp had no relationship, thrust into government by the need to form the coalition. Worse, Cable was clever and one of the few British politicians who genuinely understood the world of high finance. Worse still, he had a track record of tough and outspoken criticism for capitalists who abused their power. It would be up to Cable to decide whether to refer the bid to Ofcom.

James Murdoch, however, was sure he was on to a winner. Without irony, he glanced back to his study of ancient history, to the moment when Julius Caesar risked everything to seize absolute power for himself, and decided that the internal code name for the bid should be 'Project Rubicon'. In Caesar's case, the politicians who held power in Rome turned and fled when they heard that the mighty general had marched his army across the River Rubicon to attack them. In James Murdoch's case, he looked down on those who now held power in London and evidently expected an equally easy adventure.

There were two key players on the small team which James Murdoch had assembled in London to pilot the bid: Matthew Anderson, head of communications and strategy, known as Rasputin to some senior executives in New York who openly loathed him as James's Yes Man; and Fred Michel, head of public affairs, a very English Frenchman, clever and charming, who had settled in the UK to specialise in the lobbying of politicians. From the outset, Vince Cable was hard to handle.

Simply, he refused to have anything to do with them. Following his phone conversation with James Murdoch on 15 June, Cable's officials warned him that, in deciding how to react to the bid, he was required to act in a 'quasi-judicial' role, applying the law without any form of political consideration. Cable duly cancelled his plans to go to News Corp's annual summer party the next day and closed his door to the Murdochs.

At first, this caused only a little worry to the News Corp camp. James was convinced that Cable could not possibly call in Ofcom and ignored close advisers who implored him to make a public case for the bid. 'They have no right to review this,' one adviser recalls him declaring. 'If they do refer it, we'll sue them in court.'

For a while, he seemed to be right. Fred Michel bypassed Vince Cable's closed door by speaking to Cable's colleagues and officials, reporting back that all seemed well. Indeed, it emerged, Cable's officials had written Cable a briefing paper which advised that he had no grounds to intervene. James Murdoch visited the new Secretary of State for the media, Jeremy Hunt, who had remained close to News Corp. Hunt was coy about the relationship. On his way to meet James for dinner after a reception in May, he had tried to hide behind a tree to avoid a group of journalists. Now – just as Cameron had met Rupert Murdoch in secret – he chose to meet James without any officials to record a minute. In New York, Rupert Murdoch dined with David Cameron and found him as amiable as ever. Cameron may well have noticed that Murdoch's Australian newspapers had just engaged in an aggressive campaign which had helped to oust his opposite number in Canberra, Kevin Rudd.

It was early in August when the mood began to change. Vince Cable received a twenty-page brief from Enders Analysis, a specialist media consultancy in London run by a sharp-witted American, Claire Enders. She warned that the bid would not only reduce the number of news owners but would also allow News Corp such a powerful commercial advantage – merging their news operations, outbidding rivals for the rights to sports and films, offering cut-price deals for advertisers – that they could squeeze the life out of other media companies, thus further reducing the number of news owners. She urged him to ask Ofcom to review the bid. Cable – as he later explained to the Leveson Inquiry – began to worry.

By mid-September, with some encouragement from Claire Enders, a group of media organisations had formed a loose alliance to oppose the bid. Fear of retribution from the Murdochs made this difficult. Virgin Media, who had just signed a new deal to swap output with BSkyB, refused to join. Channel 4 nearly joined and then backed out. The BBC joined and then found themselves on the receiving end of such a caterwauling scream of protest from the Murdoch papers, that they backed out. The *Guardian*, the Mirror Group, the *Financial Times* and British Telecom (who were involved with pay TV) all joined the alliance, with the *Mail* and the *Telegraph* nervously agreeing to help as long as they did not have to say anything in public.

Fred Michel began to pick up worrying signals. The *New York Times* had published its big story about phone-hacking, and Tom Watson and other MPs, including some of Vince Cable's Lib Dem colleagues, were beginning to link the scandal with the BSkyB bid. The new media alliance were sending letters to Cable, who decided to commission an independent lawyer to tell him whether he had the power to bring in Ofcom.

News Corp turned up the temperature. The owner of the *Daily Mail*, Lord Rothermere, found himself on the end of an angry phone call from James Murdoch. One of Vince Cable's fellow Lib Dem MPs, Norman Lamb, had a conversation with Fred Michel which so alarmed him that he immediately wrote a note about it: 'An extraordinary encounter. FM is very charming . . . They have been supportive of coalition. But if it goes the wrong way, he is worried about implications. It was brazen. Vince Cable refers case to Ofcom – they turn nasty.' Michel later told Leveson that, while Lamb may have felt a threat, he had not intended to deliver one. The power of fear.

Fred Michel started trying to find ways to get round Vince Cable's closed door. He suggested that they ask the editor of *The Times*, James Harding, and the European editor of the *Wall Street Journal*, Patience Wheatcroft, to speak to Cable's close ally, Lord Oakeshott – a potentially improper abuse of the journalists as political agents. Alternatively, he suggested, *The Times* editor might interview Vince Cable himself and then he – Fred Michel – could 'pop in at some stage to give him an update' on the bid. The fact that Cable had made it very clear that this would be a breach of his quasi-judicial role made no apparent difference. At the Conservative Party conference, early in October, Michel and Rebekah Brooks lobbied senior ministers, including Jeremy Hunt, whose office continued to send News Corp signals of encouragement. Rebekah Brooks, staying close to David Cameron, was a guest at his private birthday party on 9 October.

The power of News Corp's lobbying briefly became public in mid-October as Cameron moved against the Murdochs' old enemies, Ofcom and the BBC. The government took away 28.2% of Ofcom's budget for the next four years, nearly a fifth of its staff and some of its most important legal powers. They then froze the BBC's licence fee for six years, effectively cut its budget by 16%, removed 25% of the funding for its website (which was particularly disliked by News Corp) and made it close most of its magazine business. Both of the Murdochs' target organisations were deeply weakened.

But there were limits to News Corp's power. They had no formal deal with Cameron, only their special relationship which allowed them to push hard for what they wanted but which was countered by other pressures. Ofcom lobbied energetically against them, warning that the attack on them was too brazen to be accepted by the public, and succeeded in persuading Cameron not to fulfil his promise to abolish the regulator altogether. James Murdoch had loudly demanded Ofcom's death and is said to have been furious at Cameron's compromise.

The BBC had originally been confronted by Jeremy Hunt with the threat of even deeper cuts in their spending, but Hunt had to recognise the popularity of the BBC and had been forced to give ground when he was told that the director general, Mark Thompson, the chair of the BBC Trust, Sir Michael Lyons, and every other member of the trust would resign together in protest if he persisted.

Then Vince Cable moved. The independent lawyer to whom he had gone for specialist advice had given him clear advice that he had the right to intervene and, on the evening of 3 November, he announced that he was asking Ofcom to review the bid for BSkyB on the grounds, as he later told Leveson, that 'the Murdochs' political influence had become disproportionate'. Ofcom had to report back by 31 December, and, if they said there was a problem, Cable could then refer the bid to the Competition Commission for an investigation which would be slower, deeper and far more expensive for News Corp to deal with.

Cable received loud support the next day from numerous members of the House of Lords, including the former director general of the BBC, John Birt, who recalled how he had once met a government minister who was due to go to see Rupert Murdoch and 'I do not exaggerate: the minister was actually shaking at the prospect.'

James Murdoch again was furious. He instructed lawyers to try to sue the government but then dropped the plan. He went to the prime minister at Chequers, and complained bitterly. Soon afterwards, Rebekah Brooks called the executive director of the *Telegraph*, Guy Black, told him he was an 'arch plotter', angrily insisted that he must disband the media alliance opposing the bid and claimed that Cameron had told

James that the bid would go through. Black checked, found this was not true and resisted the instruction.

James's troubles were deepened by the fact that he was now effectively at war with his father. After months of vilification, he had succeeded in forcing Gary Ginsberg, the director of communications in New York, to resign. But when James tried to engineer his right-hand man, Matthew Anderson, into Ginsberg's position, his father angrily blocked him.

There was another round of friction over a bizarre project to spend $30 million on a poultry and cattle business in Western Australia. Rupert was backing it because the business belonged to an old friend and ally, Ken Cowley. In the beginning James also backed it: he is politically green around the edges and planned to turn the land into forest, to sell carbon credits to improve the company's environmental record. His father's advisers derided what they called the 'chicken farm' and, when finally James recognised that the project was a non-starter, he agreed to go to his father to urge him to abandon it. Told of this, the older man refused to see him. 'Fuck James,' he said, according to one of his closest advisers.

Two sources who were close to the Murdochs say that at around this time, the feud between the two men became so bad that advisers from both camps persuaded them to hold a summit meeting. This idea itself rapidly became part of the dispute. They say Rupert reluctantly agreed to a meeting but said James must come to him in New York. James also agreed to meet – but insisted that his father come to his HQ, in London. The advisers moved in like a flock of nannies dealing with kids fighting over a toy and are said to have finally succeeded in persuading the two men to meet in the middle – literally in the middle, of the Atlantic. In the Azores.

So it was, according to the two sources, that the old man and the young pretender flew in to the remote islands from their respective encampments, and the old mogul took charge and dictated his terms: 'You're coming to New York. Nobody else is going to run Europe and Asia. It's being disbanded. And if you don't agree, you're fired.' James, they say, decided he had overplayed his hand and agreed to be simultaneously promoted and brought to heel, accepting that in the following year, he would be given the new title of deputy chief operating officer and that he would move to his father's side in Manhattan.

Meanwhile, New York executives noticed 'a smiley man' who suddenly started turning up at some of their meetings, sitting, observing, noting and saying nothing. This proved to be a family therapist, hired to attempt to disentangle the emotional knots which bound together Rupert Murdoch and his children.

There was one other problem bubbling in the background: the hacking scandal. By sheer fluke of timing, at the same time as Vince Cable called in Ofcom in November 2010, Mr Justice Vos in the High Court was ordering News International, the police, and Glenn Mulcaire to disclose more and more material. This ran into a potentially significant problem. For several years, the IT department at News International had been warning that their servers were overloaded and suggesting that a mass of old emails must be deleted from the company's vast electronic archive. From December 2007, some 9 million messages were purged in batches as part of scheduled maintenance. In 2009, it was agreed that there would be a major clear-out of hardware and software in the autumn of 2010 when News International were due to move into their new office in Thomas More Square, known internally as TMS.

Then the policy shifted. Some tens months before the move to TMS, on 20 November 2009, an internal email recorded that 'the senior executives are looking to introduce a more aggressive purging policy'. This message went on to list the aims of the policy, which included: 'To eliminate in a consistent manner across NI (subject to compliance with legal and regulatory requirements) emails that could be unhelpful in the context of future litigation in which an NI company is a defendant.' This was written four months after the *Guardian*'s story about Gordon Taylor, while Max Clifford was still suing the company for hacking his phone and insisting that he would flush the truth out into the open.

In the event, nothing was done to delete the emails, although by the following spring, May 2010, it had been agreed that when they moved to TMS in the autumn, News International would clear out all emails which had been sent or received before December 2007. Again, this decision flowed from a genuine need to unblock the company's sagging computer system, but, if it were put into effect, the result would be to obliterate the email records covering the entire period of Mulcaire's employment and the efforts to deal with him and Goodman leading up to their jailing in January 2007.

Nothing was deleted at that point, but the policy shifted again. In August 2010 as the move to TMS approached, Rebekah Brooks, as chief executive, asked for the deletion to cover a further two years. 'Everyone needs to know that anything before January 2010 will not be kept,' she wrote. When the IT department queried the new date, she wrote: 'Yes to Jan 2010. Clean sweep.' One internal email suggests that she had discussed this with James Murdoch: 'Rebekah. . . adamant on Jan 2010 and has discussed it with JRM who wants to draw a line as per 2010.' This would not appear to have had any potential impact on the time frame in which the High Court was then interested.

Still, there was little action, apart from the purging of some 1.1 million emails that August as a result of a disk failure corrupting the data. While the move to TMS was taking place, it so happened that Mark Thomson was moving forward with Sienna Miller's case. On 6 September, he wrote to News International to ask them 'please to confirm by return that you will preserve all the documents in your possession relating to our client's private life'. Three days later, on 9 September, an internal email from the IT department recorded: 'There is a senior NI management requirement to delete this data as quickly as possible but it needs to be done within commercial boundaries.' On 30 September, a contractor working for News International deleted all emails dated up to the end of 2004, a total of some 4.5 million messages. This covered a significant part of the period when Mulcaire was hacking, but it is not clear that this destroyed any messages relating to Sienna Miller: her private life became a central focus for the *News of the World* during the following year, 2005. Only 1.5 million of these messages were eventually recovered by police.

By October, with hacking victims pushing hard in the High Court, there was some anxiety within the company. On 7 October, Brooks emailed the company's commercial lawyer, Jon Chapman: 'How are we doing with TMS email deletion policy?' Chapman forwarded this to an IT executive, adding his own thoughts: 'Should I go and see [sic] now and get fired – would be a shame for you to go so soon?!!! Do you reckon you can add some telling IT arguments to back up my legal ones.' Two days later, Chapman wrote again to the IT executive that, 'given the current interest in the *NoW* 2005/6 voicemail interception matter', they should preserve the email archive of any current employee who had been working for the paper at that time. He went on to add, 'from an abundance of caution', that this should include any messages between Andy Coulson and seven named individuals including Alex Marunchak, Greg Miskiw and Neville Thurlbeck.

Giving evidence years later, Brooks said that she had approved the preservation of emails which might be related to the hacking and that, when earlier she had given the order for a 'clean sweep', she had not intended that to include anything which might be linked to the hacking. The policy of email deletion remained unchanged as the hacking cases moved through the High Court. Separately, in October 2010, as the move to TMS took place, the company destroyed all of its journalists' old computers, including that of Ian Edmondson, who had been named by Mark Thomson in his letter to News International the preceding month.

In court, News International challenged Mr Justice Vos's orders for disclosure, claiming falsely that their archive held emails for only six months, but the wall of concealment which had stood for four years was clearly beginning to leak. Sources close to James Murdoch say he was increasingly anxious to complete the BSkyB deal quickly.

His team began a frantic new round of lobbying, with limited success. Fred Michel persuaded the Scottish First Minister, Alex Salmond, to tell newspapers in Scotland that the bid was important to protect jobs. But when Michel tried once more to breach the quasi-judicial boundary and get James through Cable's door, he was rebuffed by Cable's special adviser, Giles Wilkes, with the memorable line that a meeting would be acceptable 'when a Google of Vince Cable, News International and Sky doesn't turn anything up'. Michel tried to get James in to see one of Cable's most senior colleagues, the chief secretary to the Treasury, Danny Alexander, and was locked out again. Even Jeremy Hunt had trouble seeing them.

In spite of everybody else's caution, Hunt agreed to meet James to discuss the bid. However, his own departmental lawyers then gave him 'strong legal advice' that he should not do so, because of the quasi-judicial boundary around the subject. When Fred Michel texted the news to his boss, James replied: 'You must be fucking joking.' James then exchanged texts with Hunt, who – in spite of the legal advice – then agreed to talk to him on the phone. He agreed to do this on 15 November, and to do so on their mobiles, which would not be monitored by officials with the result that – as with their meeting in January – there would be no record of what they said. (Lord Justice Leveson later concluded that this kind of 'off the record' contact was 'corrosive to public trust and confidence'.) That phone call evidently had the desired effect on Hunt, who went back to his departmental lawyers to ask if he could 'make representations' to Cable. Four days later, on 19 November, the lawyers told him that it would be 'unwise' to do so. That did not stop Hunt.

That same day, in spite of the repeated legal advice, he drafted a memo to the prime minister, suggesting that the two of them should meet Cable and his party leader, Nick Clegg, to discuss the bid: 'James Murdoch is pretty furious at Vince's referral to Ofcom. He does not think he will get a fair hearing from Ofcom. I am privately concerned about this because News Corp are very litigious and we could end up in the wrong place, not just politically but also in terms of media policy.' In the final version of the memo which he sent to David Cameron that evening, Hunt tactfully deleted the idea that he was concerned 'politically' but made his view very clear, adding that he thought it would be 'totally wrong to cave in' to opposition to the bid.

All this was done behind the scenes, hidden from the public. When Hunt's memo to the prime minister was revealed more than a year later at the Leveson Inquiry, Hunt conceded that in retrospect he realised that 'it would not have been possible for Vince Cable to attend such a meeting'. As it was, the meeting which Hunt suggested never happened, but James Murdoch raised the level of fear, with a speech in Barcelona which carried a clear threat to pull BSkyB's business out of the UK, taking 30,000 jobs with him: 'From our perspective – from

India to Italy to Germany – countries are becoming more welcoming of investment and more welcoming of what we can bring.'

Regardless of the legal restraint on interfering with the quasi-judicial process, Fred Michel and/or James Murdoch continued to lobby not only Hunt but also coalition MPs, special advisers and at least four Lib Dem members of the House of Lords. They also became more aggressive. On 15 December – the day the *Guardian* broke the story of the hacking of Sienna Miller and her friends and family – the All-Party Parliamentary Group of MPs who had a special interest in the media invited News Corp to send a representative to a breakfast meeting to debate the bid with somebody from the opposing alliance. News Corp refused to send anybody. Later that day, when they heard that the MPs had gone ahead and met with the alliance, News Corp withdrew all their funding from the group.

Meanwhile, Claire Enders, who was still centrally involved with the alliance, was told that News International would no longer co-operate with her, which threatened her ability to produce accurate reports on the media world. News International followed up by indicating that they were considering cancelling their £45,000 annual contract to receive her reports. Enders refused to back down. They cancelled the contract. Clearly, James Murdoch's team were worried.

Then, suddenly, it all changed.

At 2.30 in the afternoon on 21 December 2010, the BBC business editor, Robert Peston, posted a stunning story on his blog. This disclosed that on 3 December, two women who were working for the *Daily Telegraph* had approached Vince Cable pretending to be mothers from his constituency and secretly recorded their conversation. Over the previous few days, the *Telegraph* had printed several stories about it – but had not published the stick of dynamite which Cable had produced. Peston now reported that Cable had told the two women how he had blocked the BSkyB bid, saying, 'I have declared war on Murdoch, and I think we're going to win . . . I can't politicise it, but, for the people who know what is happening, this is a big thing. His whole empire is now under attack.' With one brief outburst, Cable had blown a hole in the neutrality which was essential for his quasi-judicial role.

Peston's story hit the power elite like a fan dancer at a funeral: some were amazed; some were alarmed; everybody noticed. James Murdoch was so excited that he was physically jumping with joy, according to one News Corp source. Up and down Whitehall, ministers and officials called emergency meetings: this was a threat not just to Cable's job but, by extension, to the stability of the coalition government itself.

In the Department of Culture, Media and Sport, Jeremy Hunt spoke by phone to James, who complained that Cable was clearly biased and revived his threat to sue the government. Hunt texted the Chancellor of the Exchequer, George Osborne: 'Cld we chat about Murdoch Sky bid? I am seriously worried we are going to screw this up.' And then again seconds later: 'Just been called by James M. His lawyers are meeting now and saying it calls into question legitimacy of whole process from beginning, "acute bias" etc.'

In Downing Street, the prime minister met with Osborne and officials. Rapidly, they agreed that Cable could keep his job, which would stabilise the coalition, but he must hand over responsibility for the BSkyB deal to another minister. And they chose . . . Jeremy Hunt. Fully aware that Hunt was sympathetic to the bid, Cameron asked the Treasury Solicitor, Sir Paul Jenkins, to advise whether Hunt had said anything public which might cause a problem. Sir Paul checked and reported that he could see no fatal problem.

However, Cameron's request that Sir Paul review Hunt's 'public' comments meant that he did not consider the memo which Hunt had sent to Cameron four weeks earlier, in which he had ignored legal advice by attempting to organise a meeting with Cable and declared that he thought it 'totally wrong' to give in to opposition to the bid. Nor did Sir Paul consider any of Hunt's discreet encouragement for the takeover in his contacts with News Corp, including the fact that earlier that same day, less than two hours before Robert Peston posted his story, Hunt had heard that the European Commission had ruled that they had no objection to the bid and had texted James Murdoch: 'Congrats on Brussels. Just Ofcom to go!'

At 5.45 that afternoon, a little more than three hours after Peston's story broke, Downing Street announced that Vince Cable would pass over all responsibility for the bid and for all media mergers to Jeremy Hunt. Within ten days, Hunt would receive the report from Ofcom and decide whether to wave the deal through or to refer it to the Competition Commission. Shares in BSkyB rose sharply.

One intriguing question remained. Since the *Daily Telegraph* had not published Cable's destructive comments, how had Robert Peston from the BBC managed to get hold of them, including the recording of Cable's voice? The *Telegraph*, although embarrassed by the clear implication that they had suppressed the story because they opposed the bid, responded by hiring the upmarket security company Kroll to investigate the leak. Six months later, Kroll reported their 'strong suspicion' that the whole affair had been orchestrated by a former editor of the *Daily Telegraph*, Will Lewis, who had left the paper under unhappy circumstances seven months earlier . . . and was now working as right-hand man to Rebekah Brooks at News International.

Kroll found evidence of texts and phone calls between Lewis and a computer specialist at the *Telegraph* during the twelve days before the story broke. They also found that that specialist had since left and gone to work at News International. And it was a matter of record that Lewis and Robert Peston had worked together years earlier at the *Financial Times* and remained close friends. Giving evidence to the Leveson Inquiry, Lewis declined to answer questions about whether he had organised the leak. It really didn't matter. The breakthrough was clear.

Two days later, on the evening of 23 December 2010, a triumphant James Murdoch and his wife, Kathryn, sat down for an informal private supper with Rebekah and Charlie Brooks. They were joined by the prime minister and his wife, Sam. Caesar was in sight of Rome. What could possibly stop him?

12. 15 December 2010 to 28 June 2011

The Sienna Miller story hit them hard. On 16 December 2010, the day after we had published her devastating submission to the High Court, News International suspended Ian Edmondson. They made sure that they said nothing in public, but it was a very significant moment, the first sign of a new strategy, of selective sacrifice. Edmondson might have worked for them for years, might have thought they would protect him, might have guessed they felt some loyalty, but as soon as his presence became a threat, they were ready to toss him over the wall to the enemy.

Christmas and the New Year holiday intervened, with the press feasting on Vince Cable's removal from the BSkyB bid. On 5 January 2011, the *Guardian* disclosed Edmondson's suspension. On 7 January, News International got hold of the fat file of Mulcaire paperwork which Mark Thomson had forced Scotland Yard to disclose. It traced in horrible detail how their full-time private investigator, acting on instructions from their long-standing head of news, had repeatedly and unlawfully eavesdropped on the voicemails of Sienna Miller and her friends and family.

They reacted by adding a little more weight to their new strategy, announcing that they were conducting an internal inquiry to find out what had been happening. This was all too like the scene in *Casablanca* where the corrupt police captain declares that he is 'shocked – shocked – to discover that gambling has been going on' in the casino where he has just been placing his bets. The internal inquiry was headed by Rebekah Brooks.

Edmondson tried a little psychological warfare on his former commanders, leaking to the press the fact that he had 'had a cup of tea' with Max Clifford, with the clear implication that he might just decide to use the celebrity PR agent to tell all. He also hired himself a tough lawyer, Eddie Parladorio. (It isn't clear whether Edmondson noticed the oddity that Parladorio was highly likely to have had his own messages eavesdropped by the *News of the World* in July 2002 when he had a relationship with the eternal tabloid target Ulrika Jonsson, whose phone certainly was hacked; and that Max Clifford also certainly had had his phone hacked in 2005/6 – on Ian Edmondson's instructions.) Edmondson remained suspended.

However, the real problem for the Murdoch commanders was that while they were busy reinforcing their defences against the evidence uncovered by Sienna Miller, another big gun was finally rolling into position. Sky Andrew's case was ready to blow another hole in News International.

On 12 January, the police belatedly obeyed a court order to hand over evidence which they had been holding for more than four years on the hacking of Andrew's phone. However, repeating the pattern from Max Clifford's case a year earlier, the police took it upon themselves to redact all of the material so heavily that Andrew's lawyer, Charlotte Harris, had to submit a new application to the High Court for an order to compel the police to disclose the evidence so that it could be read properly.

This had bought News International some time, but clearly the Murdoch team were nervous and they repeated that they were holding a 'comprehensive internal inquiry'. The *Guardian* discovered that all they were doing was searching Edmondson's computer and emails, apparently checking to see what would happen if the court accepted Charlotte Harris's request for internal email to be handed over. More important, Sky Andrew had another shot to fire.

Weeks earlier, a judge had ordered Glenn Mulcaire to name the person who had told him to hack Andrew's phone. In the case of Nicola Phillips, he had been able to block a similar order by appealing on the grounds that he could not be ordered to disclose information which might incriminate him. We strongly suspected that News International were funding him to do so. But with Sky Andrew, they couldn't do that: Mulcaire had already been convicted of hacking Andrew, back at his original trial in January 2007. He had no way out. He had to name the name.

On the afternoon of 17 January 2011, after more than four years of silence, the *News of the World*'s former private investigator lodged an affidavit with the High Court. The following morning, the *Guardian* reported that this was understood to have named the person who had commissioned the interception of Sky Andrew's voicemail – Ian Edmondson. Nicola Phillips's case had hinted at him, Sienna Miller had named him and now Sky Andrew had nailed him. A rogue reporter was an embarrassment. A rogue news editor was devastating – not only for News International, but also for the police and the prosecutors who had done nothing about this evidence for years, and, beyond them, for the prime minister's right-hand man, whose credibility was draining away like old bath suds.

Within twenty-four hours, the crisis for Coulson got worse. A hearing in the case of Andy Gray disclosed that the name which Mulcaire had written in the top left-hand corner of his notebook as he hacked the football commentator's phone was Greg Miskiw. Miskiw had already been named in the case of Tommy Sheridan, and here was confirmation. Miskiw had been one of Edmondson's predecessors as news editor. A rogue reporter perhaps could have slipped under the newspaper's radar. But this was two rogue news editors – spending the lion's share of the editorial budget, providing the paper's most important stories and reporting directly to their editor (Coulson in the case of Ian Edmondson) and their deputy editor (Coulson in the case of Greg Miskiw). How could he not have known that the budget and the stories were tied up with hacking? Forty-eight hours later, on Friday 21 January, Andy Coulson quit.

He announced his resignation as the prime minister's spokesman without admitting a thing. He came out with a nice sound bite, that when a spokesman needs a spokesman, it's time to go; and he left the stage in the role of an innocent man who had become a distraction for government. This may or may not have been a move which was urged on him by Rebekah Brooks, trying to relieve the political tension. (It emerged later that on 14 January, she had asked her secretary to find 'somewhere discreet' for her to meet him and had done so at 7.45 the following morning, at the Halkin hotel in Belgravia.) As it was, the political reaction followed a familiar path – loud, brave protest from a small number of MPs such as Tom Watson, Paul Farrelly and Chris

Bryant; the traditional safe silence from most of them, including the front bench of the Labour Party.

The new Labour leader, Ed Miliband, complained that Cameron had made a serious error of judgement in appointing Coulson in the first place, but noticeably did not complain that Cameron's real problem was that he had felt it necessary to appoint a Murdoch journalist as his media adviser. Miliband had just done exactly the same thing, hiring the former *Times* reporter, Tom Baldwin, straight from the Murdoch stable. A few days later, on 27 January, Baldwin emailed every member of Miliband's shadow Cabinet, urging them not to use the phone-hacking scandal as a means of attacking News International: 'We must guard against anything which appears to be attacking a particular newspaper group out of spite.'

Meanwhile, there were reports and rumours that, with Jeremy Hunt now handling the BSkyB bid instead of the troublesome Vince Cable, News Corp were secretly negotiating some compromise with the Cameron government which would allow them to seal the deal without facing an inquiry by the Competition Commission.

But if anybody in the Murdoch empire thought that Coulson's departure would end the hacking scandal, they were wrong. It kept getting in their way, like some small dog yapping at their ankles. Now it was getting ready to bite them. Two of their most powerful allies were about to desert them.

It had been brewing for a while. On the day that we published the paperwork in Sienna Miller's case, 15 December 2010, I had emailed the Director of Public Prosecutions to ask whether this clear evidence of crime against the actress and her friends had been passed to prosecutors by the original Scotland Yard inquiry. I was sure it had not been. The DPP simply failed to reply. I emailed again. He said nothing. Tom Watson wrote to him to urge him to reply to my question, and still he stayed quiet – until 15 January, when suddenly he announced that he was commissioning a senior barrister, Alison Levitt QC, to conduct a 'comprehensive review' of the material which Scotland Yard had in its possession.

Looking in from the outside, it was hard to read exactly what was going on behind closed doors, but big wheels must have been turning within the DPP's office and probably the Home Office too, to produce a decision like this. Effectively, it meant that finally the DPP was willing to expose the failure at Scotland Yard. It seemed unlikely that John Yates and his friends at the top of the Metropolitan Police would have encouraged that.

I had a small practical difficulty, that I had chosen this moment to head off to east Africa to rest and get my breath back. I was trying to follow events from under a mosquito net with a mobile phone which stopped working in a house that had no Internet link. I ended up filing a story on my laptop from a roadside café. But I had the consolation of knowing that the Murdoch camp faced far worse problems.

Knowing that the civil actions by Sienna Miller and Sky Andrew would expose more hard evidence about Ian Edmondson if they came to court, News International chose to try to get ahead of the game, by exposing Edmondson themselves. This might have worked if he truly had been a 'rogue' news editor, so that he could be sacrificed without jeopardising others. But the reality wasn't like that.

On Monday 24 January, three days after Coulson's resignation, Rupert Murdoch flew into London, cancelled his planned visit to the World Economic Forum in Davos, Switzerland, and attempted to sort out the mess. On Wednesday, News International passed to police three email messages which they said they had found in Ian Edmondson's computer. They refused to say what they contained but clearly there was some kind of strong evidence of crime in there – evidence which was likely to emerge anyway in Sky Andrew's case.

That afternoon, as I prepared to fly back early to London, the *Guardian* learned that Ian Edmondson was no longer suspended: he had been sacked the previous day, simply abandoned to the enemy, as though he had never been part of their army. And far, far more important, Scotland Yard announced that, having seen the three emails, they were setting up a new inquiry into the phone-hacking affair, and that this would not be run by John Yates's Specialist Operations but would be handed over to a deputy assistant commissioner from the Serious Crime Directorate, Sue Akers.

In any revolution, it's a turning point if the military desert the government and allow the rebels to take power. This was no revolution, but the idea was the same. Scotland Yard didn't need a weatherman to know which way the wind was blowing: like the DPP, they were changing sides.

For News International, pursuing their new strategy of selective sacrifice, the decision to hand three damning emails to the police was an attempt at an orderly retreat: admit that Ian Edmondson had been up to no good; chuck him over the battlements to join Clive Goodman; if necessary, chuck Greg Miskiw too (he had left the paper years ago, he was expendable); and then fall back to a new position to try and defend the rest of the outfit. It was a doomed move. They had lost Andy Coulson from government, with whatever cracks that left in their relationship with the prime minister; they had lost the benefit of inaction by Scotland Yard and the DPP's office; and, more than that – most unusual for the Murdoch organisation, most uncomfortable – they had lost control of events.

Scotland Yard called the new inquiry Operation Weeting. In the beginning, none of us trusted it. This was surely just a PR move, bound to fail.

But two weeks after it was launched, on 9 February, Operation Weeting released a statement which contained the following solid-gold sentence: 'The new evidence recently provided by News International is being considered alongside material already in the Metropolitan Police Service's possession.' At last! Such a simple move and so absolutely vital – finally, they were going to investigate the evidence they had been sitting on for more than four years. And then another gold bar, which must surely have struck Andy Hayman and John Yates like a fist in the face: 'All actions and decisions by the previous investigation are being reviewed.' Quite right, too. Finally, there were also clear clues about a total reversal of the bad-faith treatment of victims: 'Adopting a fresh approach towards informing victims and potential victims . . . identified some individuals who were previously advised that there was little or no information held by the MPS [Metropolitan Police Service] relating to them . . . will make contact with everyone who had some of their personal contact details found in the documents seized in 2006.'

Within minutes, I was swapping phone calls with allies. I was still inclined to be suspicious, but they knew more. During the previous forty-eight hours, Weeting officers had already started approaching some of those public figures who had tried so hard to get the truth out of Scotland Yard and who had been so ruthlessly frustrated. They had been to see the former deputy prime minister John Prescott – now Lord Prescott – and, instead of mucking him about and publicly declaring that he had never been hacked, they had simply shown him paperwork which revealed beyond doubt that in the spring of 2006 – just as we had always said – he had been a prime target for Glenn Mulcaire who had succeeded in listening to at least forty-five messages which he had left on the mobile phone of his special adviser, Joan Hammell; and that Mulcaire had then emailed Ian Edmondson to tell him about them.

Prescott was furious, both with the police and with News International. And truly it was breathtaking that the police had had evidence of this scale of interception of the communications of the second most powerful politician in the land, handling all kinds of sensitive government secrets – and they had chosen to do nothing, not even to mention it to him, not even when he and his lawyers spent months asking them. Instead, they had chosen to deny it and, in the case of Andy Hayman, to accuse him of ranting.

Over the next few days, I heard that the former Media Secretary Tessa Jowell was 'absolutely furious' after being told by Weeting that Scotland Yard had previously let her know about only a fraction of the illegal eavesdropping which she and her family and friends had suffered; that the former deputy assistant commissioner Brian Paddick was similarly shocked to be shown paperwork which revealed that his private life had been a special project for Mulcaire, even though Scotland Yard originally had told him that there was no sign of him at all in Mulcaire's records.

Weeting officers also had been to see the former Europe minister, Chris Bryant, whose suspicions previously had been airily dismissed by John Yates's men. Now, Weeting showed him how Mulcaire had made copious notes about him, including the phone numbers of twenty-three people who were close to him.

This became a tale of two battlefields. One was a dreary office block next to a cinema in a busy high street in Putney, south-west London, an old police building which for years had been used by anti-corruption squads and which now became the base for Operation Weeting. This was where a group of forty officers now gathered to force their way inside Murdoch's empire. The fight in Putney was often hidden, though we could always pick up the distant sounds and rumours of action.

The second battlefield was far more visible. The Royal Courts of Justice in the Strand, home of the High Court, looks like something out of a fairy tale: outside, a confusion of antique turrets and archways; inside, a vast flagstone hall like a cathedral with a labyrinth of corridors and twisting stairs leading off to oak-lined courts and dusty back rooms full of forgotten files and half-forgotten functionaries. The half-dozen public figures who had dared to sue the Murdochs had already found their way here with important results. In the background, more had been approaching the hacking lawyers, because they had found their courage and/or because they had been approached by Operation Weeting and shown solid evidence that they had been targets.

Mark Lewis was about to sue on behalf of the former champion jockey Kieren Fallon, who in 2009 had been sent a letter by Scotland Yard which gulled him into thinking they had no evidence that he had been hacked: now he had been shown extracts from Mulcaire's notebooks which clearly suggested that the *News of the World* had been listening to his voicemail in the autumn of 2004 when he was in the midst of suing the paper for libel, a particularly serious matter if it involved cheating to win the court case.

One of the lawyers whom I had approached in my efforts to generate legal actions was Graham Shear. He was now suing on his own behalf. Shear had acted for a string of public figures including footballers who had been the targets of attempted entrapment for the tabloids by professional kiss-and-tell girls. Over the years, Shear had found himself being physically followed by journalists and had suspected that his phone was being monitored. After I contacted him in 2010, he had written to Scotland Yard who told him that there was no trace of him in Mulcaire's notes. Now he discovered that this was not true: the *News of the World* had been able to listen not only to his personal voicemail but also to legally privileged messages from clients.

Some of the hearings in the High Court were landmarks. On 17 February, an open court finally dealt with Mark Thomson's mysterious 'dynamite' case which had already led to the suspension of Dan Evans, the *News of the World* feature writer who was also a specialist hacker. The anonymous victim who was suing turned out to be Sienna Miller's stepmother, Kelly Hoppen, who was a tabloid target not only because of her link to Miller but also because she was an interior designer with various celebs among her clients and had made TV programmes.

Her counsel, David Sherborne, made very clear the significance of Hoppen's complaint. Since Dan Evans was alleged to have tried to hack her voicemail in June 2009 – nearly three years after the arrest of Goodman and Mulcaire – it 'drives a coach and horses' through News International's claim that the hacking was all in the past.

Sherborne told the court that telephone billing records showed that on the morning of 22 June 2009, on the day after a Sunday newspaper had made Hoppen newsworthy by claiming that she was in a new relationship, Dan Evans had dialled her number twice: on the first occasion, she had answered, and he had hung up; on the second occasion, she had not answered, and yet he had stayed connected for twenty-five seconds, allegedly trying but failing to listen to her voicemail. News International and Evans insisted that it had all been a mistake, that the keys on his phone had got stuck and accidentally dialled her and stayed connected. It was, according to News International's counsel, Michael Silverleaf QC, in an unfortunate choice of words, simply 'one rogue call'.

The bad news for News International was matched by equally bad news for Scotland Yard. The hearing revealed that in the last few days, Operation Weeting had presented Kelly Hoppen with three different sheets of notes from Mulcaire's records which showed that – quite separately from any activity by Dan Evans in the features department – Mulcaire himself, working for the news desk, had been monitoring and attempting to intercept her mobile telephones during 2005. Weeting had also disclosed a sheet from the original police investigation in 2006 which showed that even then detectives had seen and understood the meaning of those records and had linked one of the phone numbers in Mulcaire's notes to a former boyfriend of Hoppen's, believed to be the England footballer Sol Campbell. And yet, as the hearing revealed, Scotland Yard on two occasions had then told Kelly Hoppen that they had 'no evidence to suggest that [she] was subjected to unlawful monitoring or interception of [her] mobile telephones'.

On 25 February, the High Court administrators appointed a specialist 'hacking judge' to handle the impending torrent of cases. They chose Geoffrey Vos. It was a popular decision. Vos had already sat on several of the early hearings and shown that he was quick and clever but also that he had a waspish sense of humour which made his hearings more enjoyable than most. He also clearly saw the big picture and understood what News International and the police had been doing. Most important of all, he showed absolutely no sign of being frightened of them.

A week later, in a further hearing about whether Glenn Mulcaire should answer questions about the hacking of Andy Gray and Steve Coogan, Vos made a simple, strong background point: 'The documents from Mr Mulcaire's own handwritten notes are more than enough to satisfy me that interception of Mr Gray's voicemails was something that Mr Mulcaire was undertaking regularly . . . What possible other inferences could be drawn from the fact that Mr Mulcaire set up the procedures and obtained the necessary numbers to intercept Mr Gray's messages? . . . Mr Mulcaire clearly intercepted Mr Gray's voicemail . . . It is a fair inference from the fact that Mr Mulcaire had the wherewithal to intercept Mr Coogan's telephone that he is likely to have done so.'

This was very important. For four and a half years, Scotland Yard had pretended that this paperwork was not worth investigating, and now here was a High Court judge kicking that claim into the long grass with a large boot mark on its backside – and thus inviting all those who were named in Mulcaire's notes to think about suing.

The judge ruled that Mulcaire must answer a list of questions about those at the *News of the World* who had commissioned his hacking, echoing the earlier order that he must answer questions about who had told him to hack the phones of Nicola Phillips and Sky Andrew.

This order went wider and instructed him to answer questions about his work generally for the paper, including the names of those who had told him to hack the royal household and the means by which he had obtained internal passwords from the mobile phone companies. He appealed against this – and, again, we suspected that it was News International who were paying him to do so.

On 25 March, there was another landmark hearing when News International admitted that, contrary to their earlier claims, they had access to a vast archive of their email traffic going back to 2005. Sienna Miller and Sky Andrew had been asking for disclosure of messages about them and had been told repeatedly that the company stored email for no more than six months. Now, their solicitor, Julian Pike of Farrer & Co., formally apologised for previously misleading the court and explained that he himself had been misled by News International.

Pike now told the court that he estimated the archive contained some 500 billion bytes of data. In the single case of Sienna Miller, there were at least 11,000 email messages. And the whole archive was to be searched for information on anybody who was suing. For the police who for years had failed even to ask for this trove, this was another damning revelation. For all of the executives, editors and journalists at News International, this was terrifying: who could remember what they had said in emails over the last six years; who could say where this would end?

Vos ordered disclosure of all News International's relevant electronic records. Over in Westminster, Jeremy Hunt's office had been inundated with so many hostile public comments on the BSkyB bid that he was forced to delay announcing his final decision.

Around the corner from the Royal Courts of Justice, in the criminal courts of the Old Bailey, Jonathan Rees got himself a break. After a gruelling series of pre-trial hearings, the judge threw out the case against him and others for conspiring to murder his former business partner, Daniel Morgan. He was free. And so at last, we were free to name him.

We did so in a long story which pulled together all we now knew about his crimes for the *News of the World* and the very public signs that he was committing them. The point was not simply that, as editor, Andy Coulson would have to have been suffering from profound brain failure to remain ignorant of the crime in his newsroom, but that David Cameron wanted us to believe that with all the political antennae of the Conservative Party at his disposal, and with all the investigative might of the police and the intelligence agencies on his side, he too knew nothing at all about Andy Coulson's indifference to the law – a very convenient ignorance for a man who had reason for wanting to enjoy the benefits of having Murdoch's former editor on his team.

The idea that Cameron knew nothing became even more acutely difficult to believe when Alan Rusbridger revealed publicly that, back in February 2010, when we had written about Rees as 'Mr A', the *Guardian*'s deputy editor, Ian Katz, had drawn the story to the attention of Cameron's director of strategy, Steve Hilton, and later to Cameron's chief of staff, Ed Llewellyn. Rusbridger also disclosed that he personally had discussed the story with the Lib Dem leader, Nick Clegg, who had gone on to become Cameron's deputy prime minister.

Now, the BBC's *Panorama* programme revealed the first hard evidence that Coulson's paper had commissioned the hacking of email as well as voicemail. The BBC had been working on this for months, after Rusbridger encouraged them to look at the story. At Rusbridger's request, I had given them information and advice, but they had succeeded in breaking significant new ground. They got hold of the contents of a fax which had been sent to the *News of the World* in July 2006, containing information which appeared to have been obtained from the computer of Ian Hurst, who had worked with British Intelligence in Northern Ireland where he had had access to highly sensitive material.

Panorama found a source who tipped them off that Hurst's computer had been hacked by a specialist called Philip Campbell Smith who, by chance, had worked in British Intelligence in Northern Ireland along-side Hurst. *Panorama* approached Hurst, showed him the fax and persuaded him to meet Smith in a hotel and to confront him while

the BBC secretly filmed them. It went beautifully. Smith casually admitted that he had hacked Hurst's computer: 'It weren't that hard. I sent you an email that you opened, and that's it . . . I sent it from a bogus address . . . Now it's gone. It shouldn't even remain on the hard drive . . . I think I programmed it to stay on for three months.' When Hurst then asked who had commissioned him to do this, Smith said: 'The faxes would go to Dublin . . . He was the editor of the *News of the World* for Ireland. A Slovak-type name. I can't remember his fucking name. Alex, his name is. Marunchak.'

Marunchak thus became the sixth of Coulson's journalists to be named in connection with the scandal, after Clive Goodman, Ross Hindley, Neville Thurlbeck, Ian Edmondson and Greg Miskiw. Marunchak was the most senior. He had risen to be senior executive editor at the paper. He was also in a sense the most important since, on the basis of all that I had heard from his former colleagues, I believed he was the grandfather of the dark arts at the *News of the World*.

The opposition were fighting for every yard of territory.

News International were still doing all they could to suppress the truth. *The Times* reacted to the *Panorama* programme about Philip Campbell Smith by smearing the BBC, accusing them (wrongly) of having hired Jonathan Rees in the past. Their lawyers were opposing all of the civil actions in court. More than that, I confirmed – courtesy of Max Mosley and his new employee, Glenn Mulcaire – that it was indeed News International who were paying Mulcaire's legal fees to appeal against the orders that he answer questions about his work for them.

Some of the lawyers also strongly suspected that News International may have been spying on us. On one occasion, Mark Thomson had a conversation with friends in which he mentioned that there was a Sienna Miller hearing coming up and, within an hour, he had calls from reporters at Sky and *The Times* asking if this was true. His law firm's technology specialists strongly suspected that somebody was monitoring the activity on his phone and those of other lawyers and of myself. Rusbridger and I both contacted our phone companies and asked them to check for any sign of anybody trying to access our voicemail.

There was also considerable suspicion that News International might destroy evidence. Having finally forced the Murdoch team to admit that they held an archive of emails, Mark Thomson feared they might now be deleted, and went to court for a preservation order.

The Press Complaints Commission continued to live in denial. In spite of losing the libel action brought by Mark Lewis for her thoughtless and one-sided remarks about him, Lady Buscombe turned up on the BBC *Today* programme and, instead of withdrawing the PCC's report which had upheld the *News of the World's* story about itself, she confronted the evidence that was now flowing into the public domain by claiming that 'we just don't know' the facts.

Although Operation Weeting looked like a thorough inquiry, the leadership of Scotland Yard showed no signs of acknowledging the scale of their failure. It was at this moment that they were compelled by their own police authority to disclose details of their senior ranks' intimate social contact with News International. It was clear what Scotland Yard would have to do. They would call in their Directorate of Professional Standards to run a parallel inquiry alongside Operation Weeting, urgently to establish a) why the original inquiry had failed, and b) why John Yates subsequently had also failed and been allowed to make a sequence of misleading statements to press, public and Parliament. Of course they would. No, they didn't. Weeting would finally investigate the *News of the World*, but, as things stood, nobody would investigate Scotland Yard.

And John Yates was making threatening noises towards the *Guardian*. As Operation Weeting began to uncover the truth, I had quoted Mark Lewis in the paper, accusing Yates of misleading Parliament by telling select committees that there had been only ten or twelve victims. Yates wrote to Rusbridger demanding that we withdraw this, publish a correction and undertake not to repeat it. Then he hired London's most notoriously aggressive law firm, Carter Ruck, to repeat his demands. The *Guardian's* in-house lawyer, Gill Phillips, sent back the legal equivalent of a Scud missile, a fourteen-page summary of the very good reasons for saying that he had indeed misled Parliament – and Yates dropped every demand.

Yates then became embroiled in a most unusual public bitchfest, with the Director of Public Prosecutions. This was provoked by Yates continuing to try to justify police failures by relying on the RIPA bollocks. After months of troubling silence, the DPP, Keir Starmer, finally stepped forward and directly and loudly challenged Yates. In a letter to the home affairs select committee, Starmer rubbished the claim that the original inquiry in 2006 had been told to adopt this narrow interpretation of the law: 'The prosecution did not in its charges or presentation of the facts attach any legal significance to the distinction between messages which had been listened to and messages which had not . . . The issue simply did not arise for determination.' This was very welcome.

And yet Yates persisted. In letters to the *Guardian* and then in evidence to select committees, he recycled the same old claims about RIPA, which succeeded only in provoking Starmer to come back at him, passing a detailed record of contacts between Caryatid and prosecutors to the home affairs committee. Its chairman, Keith Vaz, said the DPP's evidence was 'astonishing' and that Yates's version of events 'was clearly not what happened'.

I decided to check another of the claims which Yates had been making, that during the original Caryatid inquiry, they had ensured that the four mobile phone companies warned all of their customers who had been identified as victims of hacking. I already knew that they had done so only patchily. Now I discovered that the police had never told any of them that they were supposed to contact anybody. Worse, I found that two of the companies – Orange and Vodafone – had written to the police to explain that Yates's story was wrong. And yet now, more than four months after that warning, the Yard had still not told the select committee that Yates had misled them. Indeed, none of this seemed to register at all with his bosses, who allowed him to remain in post and even promoted him to take over as acting deputy commissioner.

★ ★ ★

On the morning of 5 April 2011 – sixty-four months after Buckingham Palace first complained to the police that there was something wrong with their voicemail – the *News of the World*'s former assistant editor Ian Edmondson and the current chief reporter Neville Thurlbeck were arrested on suspicion of illegally intercepting messages. Officers from Operation Weeting went to Wimbledon in south-west London to search Edmondson's home, and to Esher in Surrey to search Thurlbeck's. They removed paperwork and computers, and they searched Thurlbeck's desk at the *News of the World*. News International, wearing a straight face, put out a statement declaring that the company 'has consistently reiterated that it will not tolerate wrongdoing'.

That evening, all of Fleet Street's finest gathered in their dinner jackets and their ankle-length gowns for the annual press awards, under the chandeliers of the banqueting room at the Savoy hotel. There was enough tension to start a small war.

The organisers had arranged the room so that the *Guardian* table was at the maximum distance from the *News of the World*'s. I had been nominated twice for 'Scoop of the Year', for the WikiLeaks stories and for the hacking scandal. The awards are decided by the votes of Fleet Street executives. It went to the *News of the World* for their exposé of corruption in the Pakistani cricket team. Across the room, I could see the *News of the World* editor, Colin Myler, standing in front of his staff, leading their cheers, and it seemed to me that they had learned nothing.

On 8 April, News International came up with a cunning move. They admitted defeat. At least, they pretended to.

In a 'mea culpa' statement, which had been rumoured for weeks, the company announced that, following 'an extensive internal investigation', they would be offering an unreserved apology and an admission of liability to some of those who were suing and that they would set up a compensation scheme for any other justifiable claims. 'Past behaviour at the *News of the World* in relation to voicemail interception is a matter of genuine regret. It is now apparent that our previous inquiries

And, week by week, more public figures were coming forward to reinforce those who were willing to stand up and throw the ammunition. For months there had been only six people suing (Sienna Miller, Sky Andrew, Nicola Phillips, George Galloway, Andy Gray, Steve Coogan). By 15 April, there were twenty. By 26 May, there were thirty-one.

Some of what was emerging from Mulcaire's paperwork was genuinely shocking. It now appeared that the wife and at least one child of the former prime minister, Tony Blair, had been targeted; and the former wife of Prince Andrew, Sarah Ferguson, and her two daughters, Princess Beatrice and Princess Eugenie; and the former prime minister, Gordon Brown. The police had not bothered to warn any of them. And there was the Lib Dem MP Mark Oaten, whose sex life had been a target for the *News of the World*. Scotland Yard originally had replied to his request for information by telling him that Mulcaire's

she wants is a public inquiry, and that goes
t civil law provides.' The judge indicated his

ered in Miller's favour. She won – and News
hted. In principle, there was nothing to stop
with just about any case which any of the
Murdoch's company could start by opposing
et some of them thrown out. But any case

their voicemail, Harris realised that some of the notes were about a different Chapman, and that the police had misread a scribbled address. They thought it referred to Fulham in west London. Harris realised that what it really said was 'Soham' – home town of two ten-year-old girls, Holly Wells and Jessica Chapman, who had been abducted and murdered in August 2002. If the *News of the World* had hacked the phone of Jessica Chapman's family . . .

There was a real struggle now taking place in the High Court. News International won some important skirmishes. Armed with their new strategy of admitting liability, they faced Sienna Miller's case head on – and stopped it. Essentially, they forced her to admit that she had won. News International's barrister, Michael Silverleaf QC, said they were admitting liability for all the wrongs which Miller

failed to uncover important evidence, and we acknowledge our actions then were not sufficiently robust.'

This was huge. After all the lies and all the obstruction, all the aggression and all the claims about the rogue reporter, they were admitting that they had been wrong. But also this was clever. They appeared to be putting up their hands, admitting their crime and promising to tell the truth. In fact, what they were doing was to find a new device for concealing the truth. By conceding the general point that there had been crime, they could settle the cases much more cheaply, paying standard-rate damages instead of million-pound hush money – and they would stop any case coming to full trial with all its threat of public disclosure. They had abandoned another outer wall, in order to defend the castle itself.

The lawyers for those who were suing had taken to meeting in a Japanese sushi restaurant in Bloomsbury, where they would sit cross-legged on floor cushions, round a low black table, pull the batteries out of their phones and plan their next move. They saw News International's statement for exactly what it was – a means of concealment disguised as a policy of openness.

They had found a grand strategist in Hugh Tomlinson, a particularly clever barrister who had begun his working life as an expert in post-structuralist philosophy, translating the works of Gilles Deleuze, before becoming a lawyer. He specialised in media law – he had acted for numerous public figures who had crossed newspapers, including Prince Charles when he sued the *Mail on Sunday* for publishing a stolen journal – but he was also one of the leading exponents of the UK's emerging human-rights law. As News International fell back to their new position, Tomlinson and the other lawyers emerged from their sushi meetings with a straightforward response: they would bring up more weapons and intensify their attack.

Charlotte Harris had been forcing the police to hand over records which they had seized in 2006 of the numbers dialled from Glenn Mulcaire's phones. But, as ever, they had chosen to redact them heavily, so that all she could see were the times when Mulcaire called numbers belonging to her client, Sky Andrew. She strongly suspected that the unredacted version would reveal a pattern: that before he hacked Sky

Andrew, Mulcaire would have spoken to the *News of the World* to get his instructions and then would have spoken to them again afterwards to pass on the messages he had intercepted. To test her theory, she contacted a senior figure from the original case, who was not authorised to speak to her. Harris drenched him in charm but, even so, he was worried about saying anything. 'Well,' she said. 'If I'm wrong about this, cough.'

She paused. He didn't cough. She thanked him.

Then she went back to court to get an order to force the police to hand over unredacted versions of all the data they held for all calls made from all of Mulcaire's phones.

That became part of the new strategy – not simply to ask for bits of information for current clients but to get hold of everything – every surviving record of every phone call, text, email and invoice, all the links in the web of conspiracy for every possible victim from both the police and News International. This drive for information was coupled with a second new strategy, being guided by Hugh Tomlinson, to increase the flow of cases by identifying a set of 'generic issues', i.e. the underlying questions about Mulcaire's work. By putting it in this way, the lawyers would save everybody's time because the answers in one case would help to clarify all the others. More than that, it would be a good argument to persuade the court that they must be allowed to see everything. This 'generic disclosure' of material could then be examined by all of the lawyers who could create a 'confidentiality club' agreeing not to disclose anything about each other's clients. At last, they would be able to see the whole picture.

It worked. In a series of hearings in April and May, before Mr Justice Vos, the police finally were instructed to hand over to the confidentiality club in virtually unredacted form every single one of the pages of Mulcaire's notes; and to hand over in unredacted form all of the phone records which they had received; and News International were instructed to search all of their email records for any reference to any of those who were now suing and to any activity which could be related to it. This amounted to the most powerful possible arsenal with which to attack News International's claim to be telling the truth.

notes incl
Oaten dis
about him
word, tran
eight-year-
    Charlott
husband, L
officers co

alleged, and this included not only hacking her voicemail but also hacking her email. They undertook never to repeat any of the intrusions. And they offered her £100,000 in damages, an amount that was carefully calculated to exceed anything that she could possibly be awarded if she went to trial. That was the end of the case, Silverleaf argued: 'We accept liability. We have given her all the undertakings that she could possibly obtain, and we have offered to pay the amount of damages claimed.' It would be an abuse of process, he said, for Miller to continue.

For her part, Miller was not interested in the damages; she wanted the police and News International to disclose all that they held on her, for the truth to come out in open court. Silverleaf, however, told Mr Justice Vos that she must admit that she had won and stop. 'The civil justice system exists in order to adjudicate upon and remedy wrongs. It is not to allow people to vent their feelings or just to obtain information . . . What
beyond the remedies th
agreement.

So judgement was en
International were delig
them doing the same
lawyers might bring.
them and might well g
which appeared to have a real chance of coming to trial could be killed simply by surrendering. With dozens of cases queuing up in the background, this could cost a great deal of money, and the newspaper might suffer a large dent to its reputation, but its individual journalists and executives (and owners) need no longer fear exposure in the civil courts.

There was a similar problem with Tamsin Allen's application for a judicial review of the original police inquiry. It was going too well to succeed. In the High Court on 23 May, there was an extraordinary hearing, which I tried to describe in the *Guardian*:

The Royal Courts of Justice have heard hundreds of professional criminals claim that the police are bent. Yesterday, however, it was a respectable group of public figures including three Cabinet ministers and a former police chief who claimed that Scotland Yard had twisted the truth and buried the evidence in their case. In a series of withering attacks, the Metropolitan Police were accused of misleading the High Court, Parliament and the public over the phone-hacking scandal; and of keeping hundreds, possibly thousands of victims in the dark in a way which shielded Rupert Murdoch's News International from embarrassment and expensive legal settlements.

The former deputy prime minister, John Prescott, and the former Media Secretary, Tessa Jowell, had joined the former Europe minister, Chris Bryant, and the former deputy assistant commissioner, Brian Paddick, in asking the court to agree that High Court judges should review the original police inquiry. The real sting for the police was that in the face of this unusually prestigious attack on their behaviour, they were forced to admit what their barrister gently described as 'some operational shortcomings'.

It emerged that when finally (and very quietly) John Yates's crew had searched the material seized from Glenn Mulcaire in August 2006, they had overlooked numerous documents and scanned others on to their database in a form which was not searchable, with the result that Operation Weeting were having to start the job all over again. And not only had they sent completely misleading letters to those who suspected they were victims, according to Hugh Tomlinson, they had also submitted a formal response to this judicial review which contained 'patent factual inaccuracies'. In a written submission to the court, Tamsin Allen wrote that the effect of Scotland Yard's failure had been to protect News International from expense and embarrassment: 'We share the disquiet of the public about the police's motivation for playing down the scale of unlawful behaviour and the way in which News International has, as a result, been shielded.'

For me, sitting at the back of the court and scribbling notes, certainly it was reassuring to hear the *Guardian*'s coverage being vindicated (and to hear John Yates's threats and denials put firmly in their place). But it was also frustrating. The real value of the judicial review for me was that it would force the police to hand over exciting bundles of internal paperwork which might reveal what had gone on behind the scenes. Why had they behaved like this? Had they had any kind of secret contact with News International? Who exactly had been involved in all these lousy decisions? And now it looked like this paperwork would never come out in open court because, even though this particular hearing agreed that the judicial review should happen at some point, we all knew that it would not. The purpose of a judicial review is to seek a remedy for some failure in public administration. In this case, the remedy would be a new investigation – and we already had that, in Operation Weeting. At the next stage, the police would surely and easily be able to argue that there was no longer any justification for the courts to hold the review.

Just as the victory in the civil actions meant that cases like Sienna Miller's would never actually be heard in open court, our success in forcing Scotland Yard to run a real inquiry ironically also meant that they would not now have to disclose the inner history of their failure.

Meanwhile, I knew, News Corp were waiting impatiently for Ofcom to decide whether the BSkyB deal could be completed.

We still had two big shots to get to the truth – Operation Weeting, and whatever else we could come up with at the *Guardian*.

Weeting were going strong. On 14 April, they made their third arrest, of the former news editor, Whispering Jimmy Weatherup. This produced a couple of interesting sidelines.

First, I discovered that a reporter in the *Guardian* newsroom, Amelia Hill, had a brilliant source who knew exactly what Weeting were up to. As a result, she was able to report that, while News International were claiming to want to co-operate with police, the reality was that, as soon as they heard that Weatherup had been arrested, several executives went to his desk in the office, shovelled everything they could find into bin bags and then handed them over to Burton Copeland, the same law firm which Andy Coulson had hired five years earlier after the arrest of Clive Goodman.

Weeting officers had then turned up to search Weatherup's desk and were furious at this blatant obstruction. There had been a showdown during which, according to Amelia Hill's source, the police made it clear that they regarded this as a criminal offence and they would arrest those responsible and even search the offices of Burton Copeland if the contents of Weatherup's desk were not returned. News International blinked and told the lawyers to hand back the bin bags.

I had never met Amelia Hill, but clearly she was in touch with somebody very useful. I contacted her. She agreed to work with me. I didn't ask her who the source was. I guessed it was either an officer on Operation Weeting, or somebody so senior at Scotland Yard that they knew what Weeting were up to. We'll call him Jingle.

Immediately, he proved his value on a second sideline. Speaking to another officer from Weeting, Mark Lewis had picked up a hint that there was something odd about the place where Weatherup had been arrested, something which we needed to be aware of. This was a mysterious tease, which might have led nowhere, but Lewis asked me if I could find out more. I asked Amelia Hill to ask Jingle, who explained that Weeting had gone to Weatherup's marital home to arrest him and been told that he no longer lived there. They had gone to the flat which was his new base and found that this was not much more than a place where he stored some belongings. Finally, they had traced him to the home of a young woman, with whom he was having a relationship – and this young woman happened to work for Mishcon de Reya, the law firm where Charlotte Harris was now acting for several dozen hacking victims. I could see why a police officer would be worried and I warned Harris, who was able to establish that the young woman posed no threat to her work.

Over the weeks, I stayed in touch with Amelia Hill, who is tall and dark with a husky voice from the school of Marlene Dietrich, and, through her, Jingle supplied a stream of invaluable intelligence. Its first effect was to encourage us to trust Operation Weeting. Jingle said that they had been told not to worry about causing damage to the reputation of Scotland Yard and that there were officers in Weeting who thought John Yates had behaved so badly that he should resign. He said they had no doubt that Andy Coulson had known all about the crime in his newsroom, that 50% of the hacking had been done from phones belonging to the *News of the World*. They had seized masses of new material during the arrests of Edmondson, Thurlbeck and Weatherup; they were consulting prosecutors about the possibility of busting somebody at News International or Burton Copeland for obstructing them in the search of Weatherup's desk; they were thinking of prosecuting Glenn Mulcaire for a second time.

At one meeting, in a café near the High Court, Hill told me that Weeting were having trouble dealing with Greg Miskiw who, according to their analysis of Mulcaire's notes, had commissioned some 68% of the hacking. They wanted to arrest him, but Miskiw – who was often short of morals but never short of cunning – had left the country. He had sent police a message that he would return in August, but they didn't trust him. They put Miskiw's name on a national database as a wanted man.

Jingle also made it very clear that News International were not helping Weeting. What most worried them was that it looked like somebody in the Murdoch team had been systematically deleting their archive of emails. They had stumbled on this when a detective was talking to a technician working for News International, who mentioned an occasion when an executive had told him to delete a vast tranche of messages. According to Jingle, the technician had refused to do so, and the executive had then reached round to the keyboard of the technician's computer and deleted the messages himself. Jingle said that they believed that one particularly enormous deletion had taken place in January, just as News International were handing over three of Ian Edmondson's old emails and claiming to be helping the police, just as Operation Weeting were beginning their inquiry.

But in March, Weeting had brought in IT wizards who reckoned they could retrieve them. Jingle said they now believed that the total number of emails which had survived the programme of deletion was less than the total number which should have been available for the account of just one senior journalist. He was talking about the destruction of tens of millions of messages, maybe hundreds of millions. That explained why later that month News International's lawyers had had to grovel in court, admitting that contrary to all the company's previous claims, they did store messages for more than six months.

For my part, I kept throwing whatever I could find at Murdoch's walls. We disclosed that Weeting wanted to question Rebekah Brooks and that her phone had been tapped back in 2003/4, when Operation Glade were investigating her claim to the media select committee that her journalists had paid police in the past. This coincided with an interesting contribution from the actor Hugh Grant.

Grant's car broke down in Kent and, by sheer fluke, he was spotted by Paul McMullan, formerly of the *News of the World* and now running a pub in Dover. McMullan grabbed some pictures and then offered Grant a lift, which he reluctantly accepted. As they drove, McMullan chattered on so much about his work as a tabloid journalist that Grant, whose private life had been ransacked by the tabloids over the years, decided to try a little stunt.

Some weeks later, he turned up in McMullan's pub with a concealed recorder and, using a tabloid method to catch a tabloid man, he got McMullan talking and secretly taped him insisting that Rebekah Brooks must have known about the hacking. It didn't amount to serious evidence, but a transcript of the conversation was published by the *New Statesman* magazine in the same week that we ran our story about Scotland Yard planning to question her.

This had no impact at all at News International, where Brooks remained in charge of their internal investigation.

We disclosed that finally, twelve months after I had first asked under the Freedom of Information Act, Scotland Yard were admitting that during their original inquiry they had warned only twenty-eight of Mulcaire's victims; and, since our Gordon Taylor story, they had warned only eight more. By contrast, Weeting were now contacting hundreds. My remaining small respect for Andy Hayman and John Yates disappeared down a drain. I don't know whether it was a coincidence that at about this time, a friendly police contact told me of an email written by a senior Scotland Yard press officer, describing me as 'a man without compassion or a soul'.

Politically more important, we also disclosed the extraordinary case of Dennis Rice, a veteran Fleet Street reporter who had been shown evidence by Weeting that, when he was working for the *Mail on Sunday*, filing stories from the 2006 football World Cup in Germany, the *News of the World* were hacking his phone, apparently trying to steal his work. Evidently Mulcaire had also obtained the password which Rice used to access the *Mail on Sunday*'s internal computer system, potentially allowing the *News of the World* to monitor all of their email traffic and all of the stories they were preparing to publish.

Our story noted that this was a particularly sensitive claim since it could start to break the alliance of silence which had seen most Fleet Street papers refuse to investigate the scandal. We recorded that former journalists from the *News of the World* were claiming that the paper had also tried to steal stories from the *Sun*, the *Daily Mail*, the *Daily Mirror*, the *Sunday Mirror* and the *Sunday People*. In the same vein, I was hearing rumours that Rebekah Brooks had approached a private investigator and commissioned him to dig out evidence that other Fleet Street newspapers had been hacking voicemail in an apparent attempt to divert fire from News International.

I had several other plots running. Pursuing them, I kept coming across the footprints of a BBC journalist called Glenn Campbell, who had worked on the *Panorama* programme which exposed Alex Marunchak and the hacking of Ian Hurst's computer. We decided to pool resources. We started to collect information about News International's targeting of Gordon Brown. I already had the tape of Barry Beardall, the fraudster who worked for the *Sunday Times*, blagging confidential details about Brown from a London law firm, which Rusbridger had used to stop the *Sunday Times* publishing their smear story back in July 2009. Through Tom Watson, who was in regular contact with Brown, we started to get more examples, and we began looking into the controversial occasion in November 2006 when the *Sun* had breached the medical confidentiality of Brown's infant son, Fraser, by splashing across their front page the fact that he had been diagnosed with cystic fibrosis.

Campbell and I also worked together to bring out more of the activities of Jonathan Rees. It made no sense that Weeting were digging into Mulcaire's work but ignoring Rees's years of crime for Fleet Street – and the mass of paperwork, computer records and bugging transcripts which had been collected over the years by various inquiries into the murder of Daniel Morgan. Campbell had much better police contacts than I did. Between us, we started to assemble more and more detailed evidence of Rees's activity. The two of us held several meetings with Tom Watson who sent a summary of Rees's activity to the head of Operation Weeting, Sue Akers. On 17 May, she wrote back to him, to say that they were 'assessing your allegations along with others we have received to consider a way forward'. She added that Rees might be outside Weeting's official terms of reference. We translated that to mean that she was willing to investigate Rees if Scotland Yard would allow her to. We decided to give her bosses a couple of helpful nudges.

First of all, Campbell and I prepared stories. Together we had identified a whole raft of new people who had been targeted by Rees – politicians, senior police and more members of the royal household. Perhaps the most eye-catching was Kate Middleton, who had been Prince William's girlfriend when Rees targeted her but who was now married to him and in line to become queen. The oddest was John Yates, who had somehow wandered into Rees's field of fire.

And with all of this, the really crucial point was that Scotland Yard already knew it. More than that, just as they had sat on the Mulcaire evidence and failed to act, Campbell and I knew that they were sitting on several hundred thousand pages of evidence which had been seized from Rees by the various investigations into the murder of Daniel Morgan. Knowing all this, we made two other moves.

First, we agreed that the day before Campbell and I put out our stories, Tom Watson would stand up during Prime Minister's Questions in the House of Commons and pitch David Cameron a question about this. Second, we decided to share the story with a rival newspaper, the *Independent*. Although they had spent the first fifteen months of this saga attacking the *Guardian*, there had been a change of editor and a change of line, and now it looked as if they were willing to try to dig out the truth.

On 7 June, Tom Watson arranged for me to meet Martin Hickman, one of the *Independent*'s senior reporters and an old university friend of his. Not for the first time in this affair, I found myself handing over information to a rival reporter. Hickman was good – attentive and sharp – and he agreed that he would hold back until Campbell and I were ready to fire.

On 8 June, in the House of Commons, Watson stood up and gave the prime minister a summary of what we had found, adding: 'Yet the head of Operation Weeting has recently written to me to explain that this evidence may be outside the inquiry's terms of reference. Prime Minister, I believe powerful forces are involved in a cover-up.'

Cameron had little choice. He replied – in this most public of venues – that the police were free to go wherever the evidence might take them. 'There are no terms of reference as far as I am concerned. The police are able to look at any evidence and all evidence they can find.'

On 9 June, the *Guardian*, the BBC and the *Independent* all ran stories disclosing the detail behind Tom Watson's question. 'Pressure is building on the Metropolitan Police to expand their phone-hacking inquiry to include a notorious private investigator.' Within days, we heard that Scotland Yard had set up a small team, to be known as Operation Tuleta, and they had been told to search through the vast reservoir of material they held on Jonathan Rees so that they could decide whether to launch a full inquiry into his activities.

Ten days later, Scotland Yard was forced to set up a third operation. This one was called Elveden and its object was to investigate the alleged payment of bribes to police officers and other officials by journalists from the *News of the World*. According to News International's version of events, this was all their achievement. They claimed that they had discovered emails which appeared to contain evidence of corruption and dutifully had passed them to Scotland Yard. So, News International were on the side of law and order. Jingle told a different tale.

According to him (and to other friendly sources), it was the police who had forced these emails out of News International's hands. Like me, Weeting detectives had read on the media select committee's website the letter from the posh London law firm Harbottle & Lewis who had reviewed 2,500 internal *News of the World* emails and found they contained no evidence to support Clive Goodman's allegations of crime in the newsroom. As Jingle told it, detectives had guessed that the lawyers' copies might have survived the mass deletion of emails and had told News International to hand them over, which eventually they had done on the morning of 20 June. They appeared to show Andy Coulson authorising the payment of cash to police officers, and so Sue Akers had another inquiry to manage.

The pressure on News International was intense. They replied by pretending that nothing had changed. And in a way, they were right. A few weeks earlier, the US pressure group Media Matters had caught Rupert Murdoch in the street and asked him to comment on the hacking scandal. He had refused to say anything, explaining, 'I don't have to.' He was right. Who could force him?

On 16 June, News International held its annual summer party in a marquee in Holland Park, central London – and politicians of every colour and others from the power elite queued for an audience with the mogul, who was guided through the event by Rebekah Brooks. The traditional aggression was there too. Murdoch's former friend and business ally, Lord Sugar, had said earlier that day that journalists who had hacked phones should be jailed. When he then turned up at the party, he was confronted by an angry James Murdoch, who made it very clear that his invitation had been withdrawn – he was not welcome among them. When a News Corp executive ran into a Labour Party figure, he asked for a message to be sent to Tom Watson, that he would meet Watson and help him send Andy Coulson to prison, but Watson must leave Rebekah out of it. Still the same old power game.

As the end of June approached, there were reports that Ofcom had finally given their blessing to News Corp's bid for BSkyB. The Murdochs were about to become bigger players than ever, potentially the biggest media players on the planet. Who could possibly stop them?

On 28 June 2011, as I walked through central London in the sun, my phone buzzed in my pocket, and, when I answered, a familiar voice told me that the *News of the World* had hacked the voicemail of a murdered schoolgirl called Milly Dowler.

13. The last ditch

Based on interviews with government ministers, officials and advisers; with sources in News Corp and other news organisations; research by Sarah Ellison for Vanity Fair *magazine; and sworn evidence and internal documents, emails and texts from the Leveson Inquiry.*

Tuesday 25 January 2011 – a big day.

The previous evening, Rupert Murdoch had flown into London with one overriding objective: to clear the path for Operation Rubicon, the bid for BSkyB. This thrust him into a world he loved, of political manoeuvre; but the politics were getting complicated.

The Cameron government's loyalty was clearly divided, firstly by its coalition with the Lib Dems, who had no affection for Murdoch; and secondly by the uncomfortable fact that while Murdoch's newspapers all wanted the bid to go through, two other powerful right-wing newspaper groups, the *Telegraph* and the *Mail*, were opposing it, causing splits in the Conservative ranks.

Worse, Murdoch's own house was divided. Although father and son had struck a peace deal at their meeting in the Azores, senior executives in New York remained deeply sceptical of James's judgement. They had caught up with his early flanking operation, when he hired Deutsche Bank in London to run the bid, by hiring JP Morgan to do the same from New York. But the wrestling match continued, with James, as the man on the spot in the UK, tending to win – at least until today.

As a further complication, Rebekah Brooks was building her own mini-empire in London, with her News International camp bristling with mutual dislike for James's London News Corp people. Brooks's line to power was her relationship with Rupert Murdoch: while technically she reported to James, she spoke far more frequently to his father and appeared to be trying to score points with him by showing that she, not James, was the person who could save the bid.

Worst of all, the hacking scandal had gatecrashed the political party. The sacking of Ian Edmondson, the resignation of Andy Coulson: the sudden chain reaction of events was clearly threatening to damage News Corp's standing in the UK and potentially to undermine its political credibility with government. The rival factions in London disagreed over how to handle the crisis. Brooks had squabbled with James's head of communications, Matthew Anderson, about whether to say anything public when Edmondson was suspended in December. She had argued by email that it would not make Vince Cable any more sympathetic to the BSkyB bid – 'it's not going to change the Cable view of us' – while Anderson argued back that silence left them 'to live with a damning storyline that an organiser of hacking is still employed by the *News of the World*'. Brooks ignored him and kept the suspension secret until it leaked to the *Guardian*.

That friction was then significantly complicated by a dangerous split in Brooks's own camp. Her new right-hand man, Will Lewis – who appeared to have played such a key role in the removal of Vince Cable – was managing her internal inquiry. He was already unhappy that he had not been told that Edmondson had been suspended, learning of it only when he read it in the *Guardian* on 5 January.

As he dug into Edmondson's history, he came across the allegations of crime which Clive Goodman had made when he came out of prison; and the damning verdict of Michael Silverleaf QC in the Gordon Taylor settlement, that 'there is or was a culture of illegal information access' in the papers. In the background, Neville Thurlbeck had been making threatening noises, insisting that Ian Edmondson had been directly involved in the phone-hacking.

Lewis told friends he felt he was trapped on a ship of fools and was determined not to sink with it. He had persuaded Brooks to hire two close allies: a childhood friend, Simon Greenberg, as director of corporate affairs; and a former *Telegraph* computer specialist, Paul

Cheesbrough, as head of IT. The three of them were untainted by the history of crime and secretly they started making moves to expose it.

Crucially, with one eye on the company's email deletion policy, they set about safe-guarding the messages which police might need. On 10 January 2011, Lewis instructed Paul Cheesbrough in writing to preserve all emails sent and received by Ian Edmondson and twelve other key players. Over the next ten days, as his suspicions grew, he progressively added more names until by 20 January, the messages of 105 News International employees were being wholly or partially copied on to the safety of a laptop before being deleted from the main archive. At some point, Cheesbrough also removed the hard drive from Brooks's computer with the intention of storing it safely. All this was nitro-glycerine in Murdoch's London HQ.

It was while this was happening that the legal director, Jon Chapman, found in Ian Edmondson's hardware three emails which appeared to be evidence of crime.

Now Lewis and his allies insisted that these emails be handed to Scotland Yard. The old guard at the *News of the World* resisted. Brooks stalled. There was a tense meeting. Tom Crone arrived with Ian Burton, the senior partner of Burton Copeland. According to one of those who was at the meeting, Lewis made it clear that he thought Burton was 'a bullshitting twat' and when Burton told the meeting that they should hold back the emails and merely talk to police, Lewis told him he was not prepared to get dragged into the shit by him. Since the emails were very likely to be disclosed in open court to Mr Justice Vos, Brooks agreed that they be handed to police. That evening, she could show them to Rupert Murdoch.

Lewis's group also wanted Edmondson sacked. So, too, did some of James's camp. His chief press aide, Alice Macandrew, became embroiled in a half-hour shouting match with Brooks: Brooks wanted Edmondson to stay, Macandrew wanted him to go and for the company to run a real internal inquiry. Brooks agreed to sacrifice Edmondson but failed to set up a rigorous internal inquiry. When Lewis suggested they call in an outside law firm, Clifford Chance, to run a full investigation with independent accountants, she gently pushed the plan away, saying that it was an interesting idea but she would need time to think about it.

James Murdoch emerged from this confusion claiming to his father's advisers in New York that – as one of them recalled – 'he had put the hacking into a box'. London would handle the hacking; he would cross the Rubicon. Even from faraway Manhattan, it didn't look like that. There, News Corp executives recalled how repeatedly James and Rebekah had told them that the *Guardian* stories were nothing more than fiction and spite from a newspaper which hated News International. Now, however, their alarm bells were ringing loud. Now what they saw was James – whom they disliked and distrusted – losing his way and leaning for advice on Matthew Anderson who, in their eyes, thought all problems could be handled by making PR moves to tweak public opinion. 'If you're a hammer, everything looks like a nail,' as one New York executive put it. Tossing out Edmondson, they warned, was simply a short-term gesture to score them a law-abiding point, but it was not nearly enough if there was still more dirt to be uncovered in News International's stable.

Murdoch's in-house counsel, Lawrence 'Lon' Jacobs, was insisting that they must root out the whole scandal, even if that meant sacrificing Rebekah. Jacobs' problem was that he had lost favour with his chairman, apparently because he had led the opposition to Murdoch's plan to buy the $30 million 'chicken farm' from his friend Ken Cowley. Rupert Murdoch was not speaking to him or listening to him. He was listening to Brooks. And what really interested him was the bid for BSkyB.

It was like two bare electrical wires slowly coming together: the *Guardian* stories that had been swatted away with such indifference for the past eighteen months; and the big deal that had been planned for more than three years. If the scandal came to a head while the deal was still unsealed, there was going to be a white flash and a mighty explosion. The best way forward was clear: that the scandal would emerge only slowly while James's team hit the accelerator hard to speed up the bid. For Rupert Murdoch, it was all about timing.

★   ★   ★

As he took a grip on events on 25 January, Rupert Murdoch had good reason to be grateful for his special relationship with the government.

With Vince Cable ousted, the BSkyB bid was in the hands of the far more amiable Jeremy Hunt. The immediate problem, however, was that on 31 December, Ofcom had backed Cable's judgement, reporting to Hunt that the bid could jeopardise the public interest by reducing the number of independent news outlets. James Murdoch once again had been furious, not only at the content of the report but by the reaction of Jeremy Hunt who returned from his Christmas holiday on 5 January, met James's team the following day and appalled the young Murdoch by saying that he accepted the report and was intending to call in the Competition Commission – a move which, at worst, might kill the deal and, at best, would stall it for many months. One News Corp adviser cynically suggested that Hunt was frightened of being accused of being pro-Murdoch and was now hiding behind the regulators just as the previous year, on his way to dine with James Murdoch, he had hidden behind trees. Hunt said he was simply following the law.

But Hunt was no enemy. Where Cable had refused even to speak to News Corp for fear of jeopardising his quasi-judicial role, now Hunt left his door open to them, holding a series of formal meetings with James Murdoch and his executives. But much more important: where Cable's special adviser had refused to engage with Fred Michel, now Hunt's adviser – Adam Smith – started to act as a secret backchannel, providing a gushing source of information and support with no regard to the limits which Cable had observed. Michel phoned, emailed and texted Smith hundreds of times as the bid was being discussed. One forty-eight-hour period saw Michel send him thirty-five texts. And repeatedly Smith responded in helpful terms.

At the Leveson Inquiry the following year, Hunt was cornered by the evidence of this backchannel. He admitted that he knew Smith was in contact with News Corp but claimed he had not known the scale of the contact nor the tone and content of most of it. He also denied telling Smith to ignore the quasi-judicial boundaries, although he admitted that he had never told him to observe them. Smith, then aged twenty-nine, presented a rather different picture. It was clear that he was a key member of Hunt's team: they had worked closely together for four and a half years; their offices were on the same corridor; they met and spoke by phone regularly on a daily basis. Smith told the Leveson Inquiry that Hunt and others in the department 'were all generally aware of my activities' and that, in some cases, they had asked him to sort out particular problems with Michel. Michel also said he thought that Hunt was aware of the backchannel, that he understood that when he was told something by Smith or any of Hunt's other advisers, 'it was always on behalf of the minister and after having conferred with him'. This was very different to the separation which had been observed by Vince Cable and his officials, and very different to the 'strong legal advice' which had been given to Hunt by his own officials. In his defence, Hunt claimed that the permanent secretary in his department, Jonathan Stephens, had given his blessing to the back-channel. Stephens himself was asked about this by a House of Commons select committee and repeatedly refused to confirm it.

Lord Justice Leveson later concluded that the relationship between Adam Smith and Fred Michel had been 'a serious hidden problem' which gave rise to 'at least the appearance of bias in the process'. Smith had got 'far too close' to Michel; Michel had 'sought vigorously to exploit' the relationship; their communications had been 'highly unsat-isfactory'; and Hunt's decision to allow Smith to liaise with News Corp without giving him clear boundaries created a risk which 'should have been obvious from the outset'.

It should be said that the accuracy of some of Michel's messages to News Corp was seriously questioned at the Leveson Inquiry. Very often, Michel claimed to have been in touch directly with Hunt, when in truth it was Smith who had spoken to him. Nevertheless, the existence of the backchannel was clear, and the flow of information from Hunt's office was to become a powerful aid for News Corp.

On 10 January, four days after he had met James Murdoch, Hunt met the head of Ofcom, Ed Richards. An account of that private meeting then passed straight down the backchannel from Adam Smith to Fred Michel, who passed it all on to James Murdoch. This included Michel offering advice, which he claimed came direct from Adam

Smith, that they must attack the Ofcom report by finding technical legal errors in it. James then instructed his lawyers to do so, and they produced their own report which complained that Ofcom's process had been 'seriously flawed' and that Vince Cable had been 'biased against the interests of News Corp'. Knowing that this might fail, the lawyers also came up with a second tactic, similarly designed to bring the bid process to a rapid conclusion.

They devised an 'undertaking in lieu' – a scheme which would allow Hunt to accept the bid instead of referring it to the Competition Commission as Ofcom wanted. All of Ofcom's concerns focused on one part of BSkyB – the Sky News channel. James's lawyers suggested that if they took the channel out of BSkyB and spun it off as a separate and independent company, baptised internally as Newco, nobody could possibly complain that the takeover was having any effect on the number of organisations which owned news outlets. On 14 January, they sent Hunt their attack on Ofcom; on 18 January, they sent him their plan for Newco.

On 20 January, Hunt again met James and his team and told them that he was still minded to bring in the Competition Commission. But crucially he then added that he would consider the Newco plan as an alternative, although, to James's habitual fury, he also added that he would ask Ofcom to check it out for him. He would announce this to Parliament, he said, on Tuesday 25 January – the day that Rupert Murdoch was to take charge of events in London. That night, Michel sent Hunt a text: 'Great to see you today.'

It was on the next day, Friday 21 January, that Andy Coulson resigned, allegedly with encouragement from Rebekah Brooks in an attempt to release some political pressure over the hacking.

During the next few days, Hunt prepared his statement for Parliament. The opposing media alliance were locked out of the process, but Fred Michel was able to make regular contact through the secret backchannel to Adam Smith and occasionally directly to Jeremy Hunt. This allowed Michel to tip off James Murdoch that they were winning – that Hunt had already decided that he would green-light the BSkyB bid. Michel's messages to his bosses gave the clear impression that Hunt was now conniving with News Corp to conceal his decision from Parliament and public while he went through the motions of asking Ofcom what they thought of the crucial Newco plan. Hunt denied this at the Leveson Inquiry.

As a first move, Michel suggested, on 25 January Hunt would publish the existing report from Ofcom which had criticised the bid. That would expose News Corp to attack but Michel spoke to Adam Smith and reported that Hunt wanted them 'to take the heat . . . He very specifically said that he was keen to get to the same outcome and wanted JRM [James Murdoch] to understand he needs to build some political cover on the process.' After more contact with Smith, Michel then forecast a second move, that Hunt would steer the Newco plan through Ofcom: 'He said he would be able to send it to them with a specific question to limit their ability to challenge it . . . He said Ofcom would not be able to create major obstacles in that way.'

Michel relayed particularly comforting news about the timing of all this, providing a detailed summary of Hunt's plans. He claimed that: Ofcom would now look at the Newco plan, and two weeks later Hunt would tell Parliament that the Newco plan was a strong one, at which point, in Hunt's view, it would be 'almost game over for the opposition'. He assured James Murdoch that Hunt would ask the regulators for 'speedy feedback. He believes he can do it more quickly and understands the damages [*sic*] a long period can have.' The whole deal would be sealed by mid-February.

On the day before Hunt's statement to Parliament, Michel was given yet more inside information, reporting with some hyperbole to Matthew Anderson that his own access to this was 'absolutely illegal'. He then delivered a series of predictions about the content of Hunt's statement. On several occasions, Michel claimed that he not only knew the wording of the minister's statement but was attempting to negotiate particular phrasing to help News Corp.

On the morning of 25 January, Hunt duly made his statement to Parliament. It followed precisely the lines which Michel had predicted. The Ofcom report was published, provoking attacks on News Corp. The statement included three particular sets of wording which Michel had forecast, including those which he had claimed he was negotiating. And Hunt did indeed give Ofcom just two weeks to come up with a verdict on the Newco plan. It would all be over by mid-February.

That morning, Michel was still pushing Smith, complaining that Hunt was failing to say that their plans for Newco were strong. Smith replied by text: 'We can't say they're too brilliant, otherwise people will call for them to be published.' The appearance of collusion continued all day. That night, Michel texted Smith: 'I think we're in a good place tonight, no?' Smith replied: 'I agree. Coverage looks okay.'

News Corp had reason to be cheerful.

During the day, Rebekah Brooks had her office, home, phones and car swept for bugs. That evening, she might have shown Rupert Murdoch the incriminating emails which had been found in Ian Edmondson's computer and tried to persuade him that it was a good idea to hand them over to the police – that they might cause trouble for the *News of the World* but they could help the BSkyB bid by allowing News Corp to claim that it wanted to uphold the law. Two sources who were directly involved say they suspect Brooks never did show him the emails simply because she didn't want to upset him by giving him bad news.

The following day, 26 January, as Scotland Yard launched Operation Weeting, the bare wires moved closer together.

This was a new experience for those inside News International – a genuinely threatening police inquiry.

Rebekah Brooks seemed bewildered, according to some of those who worked alongside her. They say that, having clearly agreed that the three embarrassing emails be handed to police, she then saw press reports about the launch of Operation Weeting and claimed to know nothing about it. There were some who were now worrying out loud that she was in the wrong job. They complained that habitually she failed to read her emails, missed meetings and then made midnight calls to try to catch up, and that her social life involved too much white wine with the result that she was simply forgetting things. Worse, they feared she was still playing the denial game, keeping Rupert Murdoch sweet; failing to do enough for the police, who wanted a formal protocol to allow them access to evidence in News International's possession; and failing to stop the company policy to delete millions of emails as they migrated to new servers in the new TMS offices. That last omission had a potentially very destructive result.

As the Weeting detectives started their work on 26 January, the IT department finally followed the official policy to destroy more of the email archive. During the previous September, they had deleted all messages up to the end of 2004. Over the weekend following the launch of Weeting, they deleted everything they could find from 2005 and 2006. By 7 February, after several false starts, they had deleted all they could find from 2007. Will Lewis had already preserved the messages he believed were most important, and they were stored on a laptop. But, in amongst material which was of no importance, the archive had been stripped of a mass of evidence about all the years when Mulcaire was hacking as well as the footprints of the company's cover-up after he and Goodman were arrested. On 16 February, apparently alarmed, Jon Chapman called a halt to all deletions.

When Weeting finally got to grips with the company servers, they found that a total of some 300 million emails had been deleted over the years. They succeeded in recovering only 90 million. According to multiple sources, the laptop on which Will Lewis preserved the messages of 105 key users was not found by Weeting, although this has not finally been confirmed. The hard drive which had been removed from Rebekah Brooks's computer for safe keeping also was not found.

In the meantime, Weeting were struggling on a second front. Senior officers spent two months bogged down in negotiations with News International about privacy and journalistic privilege, trying to agree a protocol which would allow them access to the potentially revealing emails and paperwork which were being held by the company. When finally the two sides signed an agreement, on 25 March, Weeting detectives ran into new obstacles. It was then that they discovered that multiple millions of email messages were missing from the servers. And when they asked for the Harbottle & Lewis emails, they found that some unseen hand had deleted most of them from the servers – two of the seven folders which had originally been prepared for the law firm were completely empty; hundreds of messages were missing from the other five. But Jon Chapman contacted Harbottle & Lewis and asked if they had any records of their own. The law firm said they had no electronic copies at all – but, on 1 April, they disclosed that they had kept printouts of some of them. Chapman asked them to hand them over.

By the first half of April, alarm was changing to panic inside the Murdoch camp. Neville Thurlbeck reported that when he and Ian Edmondson were arrested on 5 April, detectives had asked him whether he had worked on stories about Milly Dowler. In London, James Murdoch was suggesting that they might close down the *News of the World* completely if that was the only way to stop the damage. Brooks was resisting. In New York, Lon Jacobs was arguing for a full internal inquiry, and James Murdoch, according to one source, was telling him he was ridiculous and had no business being involved. News Corp had announced, as apparently agreed in the Azores, that James was leaving London to work under his father's eye in New York.

And now there was yet another internal conflict in New York: Jacobs, the established in-house counsel, was finding his advice challenged by Rupert Murdoch's new vice president, Joel Klein, a controversial lawyer who had joined the company four months earlier and rapidly earned himself the unkind nickname of Gollum, partly because he looked a little like the character in *Lord of the Rings* and partly because some thought that, like Gollum, he wanted to get his hands on precious treasure – Lon Jacobs' job.

In London, Will Lewis and Simon Greenberg were pushing along parallel lines to Lon Jacobs, calling for a full inquiry. Lewis had contacted Clifford Chance, who had drawn up terms of reference and costed their work to act as an independent investigator. Brooks, however, still refused to give them a green light. Since January, in New York and London, they had been discussing the plan for News International to issue a 'mea culpa', admitting widespread crime and offering to settle with hacking victims. Amidst the internal conflict, this was still stuck in the pipeline at the end of March. As one of those involved put it: 'We were becoming increasingly embarrassed. We knew the rogue reporter line was not true, but we didn't know what was true. We had no internal inquiry, we never examined our emails, we hadn't got Mulcaire's notes.'

In their office on the tenth floor, Lewis and Greenberg sketched out on a whiteboard on the wall 'an escape map'. Down the left-hand side, they listed the things which needed to be done if the company were to have any chance of surviving: bring in Clifford Chance, hand over the Harbottle & Lewis emails, give clear evidence to select committees. In the middle, they recorded some worst-case outcomes: other News International titles being investigated by police, the whole company being investigated by police, the *News of the World* closing down. And on the right-hand side, at the top, they wrote two words and underlined them: Main Street. Underneath that, they wrote three more words: McCann, Soham and Dowler. Rebekah Brooks came into their office one day and asked what it meant. So Lewis explained – that just possibly they could contain the scandal if they followed their escape map. But if it turned out that it was not just celebrities who had been hacked, if it turned out that the *News of the World* had hacked really vulnerable victims – like the parents of three-year-old Madeleine McCann, who had been abducted in Portugal in 2007, or the two young schoolgirls who had been murdered in Soham in 2002, or Milly Dowler who had been abducted and murdered a few months later – then it would 'go Main Street'. That would change everything. 'It's manageable as long as it doesn't go Main Street.'

Meanwhile, James Murdoch found his foot still snared in Ofcom's regulations. The plan to complete the BSkyB deal by mid-February rapidly fell apart when Ofcom reported on 11 February that they were not convinced by the scheme to spin off Sky News into Newco. The new company might be independent, they argued, but they wanted more guarantees for its editorial independence and they objected, in particular, to James Murdoch's plan to chair it.

Worse, Jeremy Hunt refused to ignore Ofcom and, on 15 February, gave News Corp a twenty-four-hour deadline within which to concede all of the regulator's points, or else he would send the whole thing to the Competition Commission. An irritable and reluctant James Murdoch agreed and was then reduced once more to fury when, on 17 February, Hunt went back to Ofcom yet again to ask if they were now happy. Another two-week delay.

In the background, Fred Michel wheeled in the Scottish First Minister, Alex Salmond, who agreed to talk to Hunt about the importance of the bid for the Scottish economy and wondered if Sky News would like to organise a pre-election TV debate featuring himself. Michel and Adam Smith continued to swap information through their backchannel, co-operating on PR moves, occasionally sneering at Ofcom and the media coalition and MPs who opposed the bid. Michel urged Smith to tell his boss 'to show some backbone' by dismissing Ofcom's worries. He did, a little.

On 1 March, Ofcom – backed by a second regulator, the Office of Fair Trading – told Hunt that they feared Newco would not be financially independent: it would be entirely reliant for its income on BSkyB. This time, Hunt compromised: he told News Corp they would have to find some way to satisfy Ofcom but, in the meantime, agreed to announce on 3 March that he was 'minded to accept' the Newco plan yet wanted to run a short public consultation, which would end on 21 March. A week later, he would announce his final decision and, if all went well for News Corp, the deal would be waved through on 28 March.

But it didn't go well. With Mr Justice Vos in the background ordering more and more disclosure in the High Court while the *Guardian* and *Panorama* were breaking news stories, Hunt's public consultation produced multiple thousands of responses, almost all of them opposing the deal. The majority of them had been generated by two online campaigning organisations, Avaaz and 38 Degrees. Hunt was advised that the law would not allow his department to consider the responses in blocks. Each one must be dealt with individually. And Ofcom and News Corp were still at odds about the detail of Newco. The 28 March target slipped away. Rupert Murdoch's eightieth birthday had passed without victory. Michel agitated urgently for a quick conclusion. One of Hunt's officials emailed a colleague: 'Are we sure the process is going as fast as it can?' All through April, there was still no end in sight.

On 8 April, News International finally issued their 'mea culpa' admitting liability for hacking claims – a clear admission that they (and News

Corp) now knew that there had been widespread crime at the *News of the World*, and yet they took no disciplinary action against anybody, continued to make no serious effort to uncover the truth and continued to give minimum co-operation to the police. Two different sources say that, when Harbottle & Lewis in early April gave the company the hard copies of the emails which had survived in their office with their explicit references to paying royal police, Rebekah Brooks chose not to pass them immediately to Weeting but to delay, telling an increasingly impatient Scotland Yard that she did not want to hand over evidence piecemeal. Colleagues believed she wanted to stall for long enough to let the BSkyB bid be completed and for News Corp to hold its annual summer party in London. They say it was obvious that the emails 'went to the guts of the company'. Others argue that the delay was inevitable, that they had to check the emails for themselves, which involved interviewing a senior lawyer at Harbottle & Lewis, and that then they had to get the blessing of the News Corp board. They concede that both these moves were arguably unnecessary and that, whatever the intent, they had the effect of slowing down police progress.

Ian Burton called an internal meeting to discuss them and, according to one of those there, began by showing no great concern about the emails. When others at the meeting flicked through them and found emails apparently implicating Coulson and Goodman in bribery, Simon Greenberg is said to have exploded: 'What part of the *News of the World* paying police to steal the Queen's phone directory don't you think is serious?' He and Lewis insisted they be handed to police. But they were not. Following this meeting, James Murdoch heard about the embarrassing contents of the emails and, apparently recognising the potential damage to his precious Rubicon project, according to one source, he asked if they really had to hand them over now. To which the answer from Greenberg was 'fucking yes'.

It was days later, on 14 April, that Weeting detectives arrested Jimmy Weatherup and then threatened to arrest Ian Burton for attempting to hold the contents of Weatherup's desk in his office. This finally snapped the patience of Sue Akers, who called a summit meeting at Scotland Yard on 21 April. Flanked by her senior officers, she carpeted Lewis and Greenberg like a headteacher with disobedient students. 'She was quite threatening,' according to one who was there. 'Finger-wagging stuff, saying "if this is co-operation, you don't know the meaning of the word".' She also made it painfully clear that she was not happy to see Ian Burton in the room. Chastened, Lewis and Greenberg went back to the office and are said to have told Brooks: 'These are not nice people. Either you put us in charge, or we're gone.' Brooks agreed to put them in charge.

In New York, Lon Jacobs was pushing hard for an independent inquiry, hiring a law firm, Debevoise & Plimpton, to run it. However, Joel Klein switched the job to a different firm, Williams & Connolly, based in Washington DC. Jacobs' firm was left with a watching brief while Klein's firm handed the job to one of their most senior attorneys, Brendan Sullivan, who had become famous in the late 1980s for representing Colonel Oliver North in the Iran–Contra scandal.

In early May, Jacobs flew to Washington for a summit meeting in Brendan Sullivan's office. Rebekah Brooks and Will Lewis were coming in from London. They would all meet to hammer out a strategy. In the event, whether by accident or design, the London duo failed to arrive on time. After an empty afternoon, Jacobs was persuaded by Sullivan to go to his hotel for the evening. Later that night, Jacobs discovered that after he had left, Rebekah had arrived and that Sullivan had proceeded to discuss the case without him. He was so furious that he emailed Joel Klein and Rebekah Brooks to say he was sacking Sullivan with immediate effect.

But Sullivan was not sacked. Rebekah subsequently told friends in London that when she saw Jacobs' email, she had called Joel Klein to ask him what he thought and that Klein had expressed himself very simply: 'Fuck Lon.'

Sullivan duly declared that having spoken to Rebekah, he believed she was innocent. The real problem for Jacobs and some others in New York was that there was no sign of anybody conducting a serious investigation: not Rebekah or James in London; not Rupert and Joel Klein in New York. Those who feared there was far more dirt to be uncovered, including Jacobs and his chosen law firm, were sidelined.

Soon after the abortive meeting at Brendan Sullivan's office, Rupert

Murdoch announced that ten key players from the company must meet for dinner at his home in London on Thursday 19 May, to agree a strategy for the hacking. According to a detailed account which was later published by *Bloomberg Businessweek*, the players immediately split into two groups.

A group of six began the evening with cocktails in Murdoch's house round the corner from Buckingham Palace: Rupert and James Murdoch, the deputy chairman Chase Carey, Joel Klein, Brendan Sullivan and Rebekah Brooks. Sullivan and Brooks went into a huddle. The other group, of four, were sent to a nearby hotel to buy a drink: Lon Jacobs and his deputy, Jeff Palker; Will Lewis and his sidekick Simon Greenberg. Lewis, according to one of those there, said he had been saying for months that they must close the *News of the World*, speaking of 'greasy people producing rancid journalism – moral corruption dragging us into the mire'. When they merged for the meal, Rebekah Brooks took a seat directly opposite the chairman, according to the *Businessweek* report: 'Brooks expressed mild embarrassment at being in the prime position, even though she had arranged the seating personally. She turned to Carey and coyly insisted that he switch seats with her. Carey demurred.'

And then, without discussion, according to *Businessweek*, Rupert Murdoch announced his decision: 'This is going to be handled by Joel and Brendan. I will handle the board. Everyone else, stay out of it.' Brendan Sullivan then repeated his view that Rebekah was innocent. The message was clear. There would be no investigation; nobody from New York would challenge Rebekah or James; Lon Jacobs was out of the picture and, a fortnight later, he resigned.

By mid-May, Fred Michel was sending urgent signals to Jeremy Hunt's office pleading for a rapid decision: 'Otherwise we won't be done before mid-June, which will be catastrophic for many important reasons.'

And now the hacking scandal was banging on Hunt's door. The 'mea culpa' from News Corp on 8 April had worried him and he had asked his lawyers for advice. On 18 April, they had told him that the hacking revelations raised a question about trust 'to the extent that they suggested that you could not reasonably expect News Corp to abide by their undertakings, for example, if the wrongdoing was known of and endorsed or ordered at a senior level within News Corp'. Knowing nothing of Rupert Murdoch's decision to refuse to allow a real investigation, Hunt concluded that this was not a problem. But still the bid was stalled. News Corp had still not hammered out an agreement with Ofcom, and nearly 40,000 people had now sent objections to Hunt's department. Each of them had to be dealt with.

By 6 June, Michel was reporting that, in talking to Hunt's office, he had 'floated the threat that, if this were to go on for weeks, we could decide at any moment to withdraw' – an echo of James Murdoch's threat, in his speech in Barcelona seven months earlier, to pull BSkyB out of the UK altogether. It didn't work.

By this time, Scotland Yard were scoping Operation Tuleta, to investigate Jonathan Rees's involvement with the *News of the World*, and News International were running out of excuses for failing to give police the Harbottle & Lewis emails. During May, Brooks had agreed that a small sample of them should be shown to the former DPP, Lord Macdonald, who reported to the News Corp board, as he later recalled, that it was 'blindingly obvious' that they contained evidence of crime. Yet still Brooks had delayed.

There was more talk within the company of making the drastic tactical move of simply closing the *News of the World*. On 9 June, Simon Greenberg emailed Brooks: 'If we are the subject of further enquiries into computer hacking and possibly payments, this is why we should consider the shutdown option. Is the brand too toxic for itself and the company? I believe it is. Unparalleled moments need unparalleled action. Showing we get it is important for us and for Rubicon. You could be person to save the Rubicon deal.'

Weeting detectives had met her on 13 June to show her evidence of the scale on which her own phone had been hacked but she had said nothing about the emails. Finally, on 20 June, nearly three months after receiving them from Harbottle & Lewis, she agreed that Lord Macdonald should pass them to police together with the surviving records of Clive Goodman's allegations of crime, thus finally provoking the Operation Elveden inquiry into the bribing of police and other public officials.

However, Brooks was still fighting back. As the *New York Times* later reported, she was trying to create a diversion by asking former *News of the World* journalists to dig up evidence of hacking by other Fleet Street newspapers. On this account, Rupert Murdoch personally warned the editor of the *Daily Mail*, Paul Dacre, that 'we are not going to be the only bad dog on the street'. Dacre is said to have told senior managers at the *Mail* that he had heard several reports that Will Lewis and Simon Greenberg had encouraged business leaders, footballers and PR agencies to see whether they had been hacked by the *Mail*. Rebekah's efforts earned her nothing but friction, first from Dacre, who is said to have confronted her at breakfast in Brown's hotel with the complaint that 'you are trying to tear down the entire industry', and then from Lady Rothermere, wife of the *Mail*'s owner, who told her that the *Mail* had not broken the law, to which Brooks is said to have responded by asking her who she thought she was, 'Mother Teresa?'

On 22 June, Ofcom and the Office of Fair Trading finally agreed terms with News Corp. An adapted version of Newco would spin off Sky News. The bid could go ahead. On Thursday 30 June, Jeremy Hunt went to Parliament to announce the news, adding that the phone-hacking allegations were 'not material to my consideration'. He added just one final step – a brief final public consultation, with a deadline of noon on Friday 8 July. Victory was in sight.

On Sunday afternoon, 3 July, while Rebekah Brooks and James Murdoch partied with senior politicians in Elisabeth Murdoch's Oxfordshire garden, Fred Michel was at home, watching Rafael Nadal take on Novak Djokovic in the Wimbledon tennis final. He spotted Jeremy Hunt in the crowd and texted him: 'Come on Nadal!'

Nadal lost.

On the afternoon of Monday 4 July, the *Guardian* website posted a detailed story about the *News of the World*'s involvement in hacking the voicemail of Milly Dowler.

Part Three
Truth

If you shut up truth and bury it under the ground, it will grow and gather to itself such explosive power that the day it bursts through, it will blow up everything in its way.

Emile Zola in Dreyfus: His Life and Letters

No tyrant need fear till men begin to feel confident in each other.

Aristotle

14. 28 June 2011 to 19 July 2011

I spent six days following up the tip about Milly Dowler. The thirteen-year-old schoolgirl had become a household name when she disappeared while walking home from school in Walton-on-Thames, Surrey, on 21 March 2002. Six months later, her body was found in woodland twenty-five miles away.

At first, the source was so nervous that he insisted I must make no inquiries for fear of exposing him. As a safe routine move, I checked into the *Guardian*'s database of Fleet Street output to find some background. Suddenly, I realised I was reading a most revealing story, which had been published by the *News of the World* on 14 April 2002. It was not a big story – only 300 words long and buried away on page 30. It claimed that a mentally ill woman had tricked one of Milly's friends into giving her the missing girl's mobile number and had contacted an employment agency, pretending to be Milly looking for work. And then this: 'The agency used the number to contact Milly when a job vacancy arose and left a message on her voicemail . . . It was on 27 March, six days after Milly went missing, that the employment agency appears to have phoned her mobile.'

Two thoughts collided. First, that the *News of the World* had been either crazy or completely complacent to publish that without even attempting to pretend they had a lawful source for the information. Second, that this gave me a way forward. I contacted the nervous source and suggested that I could start asking questions without exposing him if I told people I was following up on the *News of the World*'s old story. He agreed.

I called Glenn Campbell from the BBC, who had worked on Milly's disappearance in 2002. He offered to try to track down sources in Surrey police who had been involved in the original inquiry. I went off in search of other leads. Rapidly, I found a big one in my own office. Steve Whittamore's records of his work for the *News of the World* clearly showed that the paper had commissioned him to blag British Telecom records for the home addresses and ex-directory phone numbers of three Surrey families called Dowler, including Milly's parents, Bob and Sally. That was illegal.

Within hours, Glenn Campbell reported back that his source on the 2002 Surrey police inquiry had told him that there had been 'a hell of a lot of dirty stuff going on'. The source had given him three precious nuggets. First: 'We knew they were into Milly's answerphone, but there was just so much going on that we didn't, rather couldn't tackle it.' Second: 'The press interest was just so intense that often we'd arrange landline calls between the SIO [Senior Investigating Officer] and the team and chief, as we didn't trust our mobiles. Paranoid or what, but looking back, it was most probably sensible.' Third, Operation Weeting were investigating the hacking of Milly's phone and had been taking statements from officers on the original inquiry.

I spoke to current sources in Surrey police and confirmed all three points. They were particularly worried about emerging evidence that their own officers had had their phones hacked, including one who had been having an affair at the time. Glenn Campbell's Surrey source then added that they had known about the hacking at the time because the *News of the World* quite shamelessly had quoted the voicemail to them when the paper was preparing its story. They had also suspected that the voicemail of Milly's parents might have been targeted. I contacted Scotland Yard, who refused to help: 'It's a "not prepared to discuss", I'm afraid.'

The original source had two other claims: that the *News of the World* had not only hacked Milly's messages but had also deleted some of them, apparently because her voicemail box had filled up and they wanted to make room for new messages; and that some of those deletions had given Milly's parents a false hope that their daughter must be alive and checking her voicemail.

I brought in Amelia Hill, who contacted Jingle and soon reported back that the *News of the World* had hacked Milly's phone, and deleted messages because the voicemail box was full. Months later, new evidence surfaced and cast serious doubt on this last point but at the time, it was supported by the evidence which was available. Amelia added that Weeting had visited the parents a few months ago and were pursuing the case with the Crown Prosecution Service.

That weekend, I drafted a story and sent it to Glenn Campbell and Amelia Hill to check that it was accurate and did not jeopardise their sources. I was worried about Milly's family being caught unawares by all this, so I sent Surrey police press office a summary of the story and asked them to warn the Dowlers and to try to put us in contact with somebody who could speak for them, possibly their solicitor. On Sunday evening, 3 July, I emailed the final version to Alan Rusbridger. With the mental image of ambitious tabloid reporters eavesdropping on Milly's distressed family and friends imploring her to get in touch, I added a message: 'I think this may be the most powerful hacking story so far.'

On the following day, I had a call from Mark Lewis, who had managed somehow to get himself hired as the Dowlers' solicitor and who agreed to prepare a statement. Rusbridger and his deputy, Ian Katz, went through the story with the *Guardian*'s in-house lawyer, confirmed with me that there were at least two sources for every key point and then, at 4.30 on Monday afternoon, 4 July, we published it on our website.

There was a white flash and a mighty explosion.

Newspapers who had spent so long ignoring the scandal finally reacted like newspapers. It helped that, when they contacted Scotland Yard, reporters were told off the record that the Yard 'would not argue with' the *Guardian*'s report. Surrey police came to my house in search of more information about the hacking of their detectives. Mark Lewis denounced the hacking as 'heinous' and 'despicable' and told me the Dowlers were happy with the story.

Glenn Mulcaire was not so happy. Max Mosley called to tell me that the investigator was anxious and remorseful and ready to talk. On the Tuesday morning, I met Mulcaire at the office near Trafalgar Square where Mosley was employing him. He was indeed miserable and made no attempt to deny anything. I persuaded him to issue a public state-ment through me, apologising for the hurt he had caused, describing the 'relentless pressure' for results at the *News of the World* and adding that he had not realised that he was breaking the law. 'I never had any intention of interfering with any police inquiry,' he said.

I came out of that meeting to find that David Cameron had told reporters that the hacking of Milly's phone was 'a dreadful act'; the Labour leader, Ed Miliband, had called for a public inquiry into news-paper malpractice; five major companies had suggested they would withdraw several million pounds' worth of advertising from the *News of the World*; and some readers were cancelling their subscriptions. Moral outrage was invading the power game.

Rebekah Brooks suddenly found herself up to her neck in news coverage.

She had been editing the *News of the World* when they had hacked Milly Dowler's phone, and that morning I had published a summary of our evidence about criminal activity on her watch. She issued a statement that it was 'inconceivable' that she had known about the incident. News International were soon briefing reporters that 'anyone except Rebekah' could lose their jobs over the hacking scandal.

That evening, Amelia Hill revealed that Operation Weeting were reviewing every high-profile case of the murder or abduction of a child since 2001 to look for evidence of hacking. Cambridgeshire police confirmed that the parents of Jessica Chapman and Holly Wells, who had been murdered in Soham five months after Milly, had also been warned by Weeting that they had been targeted by Glenn Mulcaire.

The outrage rolled out like storm clouds. That same evening, the first editions of Wednesday's papers revealed that the *Financial Times* were calling for Brooks to resign and – to our great surprise – that *The Times* were joining the criticism. A bold leader comment described the hacking of Milly's phone as 'beyond reprehensible' and added: 'It ought to go without saying that nothing of this nature can ever happen again. But then it ought to have gone without saying that nothing of this nature could ever have happened in the first place.'

And then we saw the first edition of the *Daily Telegraph* with a devastating front-page story: Operation Weeting had found evidence that some of the fifty-two families who had been bereaved by the terrorist bombings in London in July 2005 had had their phones hacked by the *News of the World*. They quoted Graham Foulkes, whose twenty-two-year-old son, David, had died in the attacks. 'How low can you get?' he asked.

The next forty-eight hours saw a stream of new revelations squirting out of the holes in the crumbling walls of News International's defences: the hacking of families of British military personnel who had died in Iraq and Afghanistan; the targeting by Mulcaire of George Osborne, the Chancellor of the Exchequer; and of Michael Mansfield, the barrister who had challenged the official version of events at the inquest into the death of Princess Diana. I ran a detailed account of Detective Chief Superintendent Dave Cook's meeting with Rebekah Brooks, when he had warned her that Alex Marunchak had used the *News of the World*'s resources to spy on him while he was investigating murder allegations against Jonathan Rees and Sid Fillery.

In Scotland, Strathclyde police revealed they were investigating allegations of hacking there by the *News of the World* and of perjury by Andy Coulson at the trial of the Scottish radical, Tommy Sheridan. Stories were running on the front page of Fleet Street papers and all around the world, although Murdoch's Fox News continued to ignore it. On Wednesday, in an emergency debate in the House of Commons, an increasingly confident Ed Miliband raised the stakes by urging that the BSkyB bid must now be blocked.

In the nine months since he had become Labour leader, Miliband had followed Blair and Brown in attempting to befriend the Murdoch papers. Early on, he had arranged a private meal with Rebekah Brooks, although reports hinted it had not gone well with Miliband inquiring twice about her children even though she had none; and suggesting she should read *Sun* editorials from the 1930s although the paper had not been launched until the 1960s. But now it was safe to end the pretence of alliance.

News International did their best to fight back, insisting that they would be 'absolutely appalled and horrified' if it were confirmed that the *News of the World* had hacked the phones of dead soldiers' families. They said that Rebekah Brooks had been on holiday when the paper published the story about Milly Dowler's voicemail and also when they ran stories about Holly Wells and Jessica Chapman. The clear implication was that we should blame her deputy, Andy Coulson.

They also tried some tactical leaking, laced with falsehood and hypocrisy. In the midst of the turmoil, Will Lewis's old friend, Robert Peston of the BBC, disclosed that News International had 'uncovered emails that indicate payments were made to the police by the *News of the World* during the editorship of Andy Coulson'. Peston reported that the company had handed them to Scotland Yard.

News International then followed up by claiming that this demonstrated their 'full co-operation with the Metropolitan Police'. Not only did they fail to mention that they had sat on this information for four years; that they had retrieved the emails only because the police had told them to do so; and that they had then delayed handing them over for nearly three months: they also failed to mention that they had promised the police that they would say nothing about them, for fear of tipping off suspects who might then destroy evidence. They were rewarded with the private fury of Sue Akers and her officers, and a helpful front-page story in *The Times*.

By noon on Thursday 7 July, the boycott by advertisers had gathered devastating force, with thirty-three companies withdrawing their business from the paper and a particularly vocal Mitsubishi describing the seventy-two hours of revelation as 'unbelievable, unspeakable and despicable'. Some newsagents were saying they would refuse to sell the paper on Sunday. Equally bad for News International, old allies were changing sides.

The Press Complaints Commission finally withdrew their 2009 report which had cleared the *News of the World* and criticised the *Guardian*'s coverage. The London mayor, Boris Johnson, who had been happy to describe the *Guardian*'s stories as 'codswallop' now called for allegations of corruption to be investigated 'ruthlessly and openly'. David Cameron denounced the *News of the World*'s behaviour as 'absolutely disgusting' and promised a public inquiry, though he refused to join the calls for the resignation of Rebekah Brooks. The *Guardian*, the *Daily Mirror* and a swelling group of MPs from all parties were now calling for an end to the BSkyB bid.

And then, that Thursday afternoon, the Murdochs made a move which was stunning in its desperation. They announced the death of the *News of the World*. Sunday's edition would be the last. It would carry no advertising, and the income from sales would be given to charities. 'Wrongdoers turned a good newsroom bad,' James Murdoch explained. Rusbridger and I were dumbstruck by the move. Nobody had called for this, nobody had expected it. The ruthlessness was amazing to see – to chuck not just one or two bodies but the entire newspaper over the battlements to save their grab for BSkyB.

But if they thought this would clear the air or even relieve the pressure, the Murdochs were wrong. They had done too little for too long and, in the flood of revelation, this looked less like a commitment to good conduct than a confession of guilt. Within minutes of the news breaking, Twitter was alive with bitter complaints that the Murdochs had sacrificed several hundred jobs to save their own and Rebekah Brooks's. Thirty journalists from the *Sun* walked out in protest. A throng of MPs now called loudly for Brooks to resign. Within an hour, Tweeters had discovered that, two days earlier, News International had registered the domain name sunonsunday.co.uk, clearly suggesting that the closure was a PR move and that the *News of the World* would reopen at some point as the *Sun on Sunday*. The leak to Robert Peston two days earlier now looked nastier than ever – an attempt to smear their own newspaper before they sentenced it to death.

By Friday, Murdoch's Fleet Street allies were running for cover. The right-wing *Daily Mail* attacked Murdoch by name: 'Never again must one man be allowed to hold such power.' Stephen Glover at the *Independent*, who had tied himself in such angry knots in his efforts to support the official line, now attacked the closure of the *News of the World* as 'a desperate ploy by a dysfunctional company' and called for Brooks to resign. Brooks herself addressed the *News of the World*'s surly staff, telling them that there was still more dirt to be revealed: 'I think in a year's time, every single one of you in this room might come up and say "OK, well, I see what you saw now."' True to the paper's form, one of the journalists secretly taped her and leaked her comments.

By the time she had finished speaking, Andy Coulson had been arrested on suspicion of conspiring to hack phones and pay bribes to police – exactly two years to the day since we had published the Gordon Taylor story. Clive Goodman, who could have been forgiven for thinking he had seen the end of his nightmare, also had been arrested, on suspicion of conspiring to pay bribes to police. It was clear that the arrests had been informed by the Harbottle & Lewis emails which had been suppressed for so long by Murdoch's executives.

That Friday afternoon, Amelia Hill and I posted a story on the *Guardian* website, challenging News International's claim to be co-operating with police, disclosing that Weeting were investigating evidence that a senior executive had deleted millions of emails from their servers; that the company had infuriated police by leaking the story about the Harbottle & Lewis emails; and that prosecutors were considering charging those who had removed material from Jimmy Weatherup's desk on the day of his arrest in April and initially refused to hand it over.

Parliament was in uproar. Those who had always resented Murdoch's power now spoke out, a sleeping army waking up from years of silent fear. Others who had been happy to support him now raced to abandon him. David Cameron, in particular, shrugged off his cosy friendship with Rebekah Brooks, saying that if it were his choice, he would accept her resignation. He formally announced two public inquiries, one into the press, another into the police. 'The truth is, we have all been in this together,' he said. 'The press, the politicians and the leaders of all the parties – and, yes, that includes me . . . Throughout all this, all the warnings, all the concern, the government at the time did nothing.'

But the really bad news for the Murdochs came from Jeremy Hunt. This was the day of the deadline for the final consultation on the BSkyB bid, the day they had planned to celebrate victory. Yet things had changed. Public revulsion had by now produced 156,000 responses, almost all of them hostile. Hunt announced that he had decided to delay his decision. The bid was not dead, but it was in deep trouble.

At the beginning of the week, BSkyB shares had been trading at 850p. By Friday evening, they had fallen to 748p, wiping an estimated £1.7 billion from the company's value.

★   ★   ★

Watching from my study as the masonry collapsed around the Murdochs' heads, I could only guess at what was going on behind the scenes that week. Much later, sources from News International and News Corp described their panic and confusion, all redoubled by the warring factions within the empire fighting like cats in a sack.

They say that as soon as they saw the Milly Dowler story on the *Guardian* website that Monday afternoon, they understood that the hacking scandal was finally a real threat to the BSkyB deal. As one of them put it, it 'broke the fallacy' that the two could be kept apart. Their immediate decision was that James Murdoch must take centre stage instead of Rebekah Brooks. But it was not as easy as that.

By Tuesday evening, some of James's team were saying that Brooks had to get out of the building: either she knew about the Dowler hacking and had to go; or she didn't know but was nevertheless responsible because she had been the editor, so she still had to go. They believed that her staff were briefing the press against James. Some of Brooks's camp believed James's people were briefing against them. James nevertheless continued to defend Brooks, aware perhaps that an argument with Brooks was effectively an argument with his father. Brooks herself was buoyed by an email from Tony Blair offering his help. 'I have been through things like this,' he wrote.

By Wednesday, Rupert Murdoch had joined the shouting match, according to one source, who says he was furious when *The Times* ran their leader condemning the Dowler hacking and, from the US, phoned the editor James Harding to complain, loudly and bitterly. Harding is said to have made it clear within the company that he thought Rebekah Brooks must go immediately and even to have threatened to write another leader, calling for her resignation. In the confusion, Brooks told friends that she had offered her resignation to James Murdoch, who had refused to take it; and this was soon leaked to the press by her camp. Against that, James's team say that she never offered to resign but simply had an inconclusive discussion with him about whether she should consider it. On the Wednesday afternoon, she met Ken Macdonald, the former DPP, for legal advice.

At the beginning of the week, as the Dowler story broke, the signals which Fred Michel was reporting from government were still encouraging. On the Tuesday night, the prime minister's press secretary, Gabby Bertin, sent supportive messages to Brooks. Jeremy Hunt was still saying that the hacking had nothing to do with the bid. On Wednesday morning, Craig Oliver, who had replaced Coulson as the prime minister's director of communications, texted Fred Michel to say he was looking forward to dining that evening with him and Will Lewis, and hoped the location would be discreet.

But the Labour opposition smelled blood in the water. After Ed Miliband stood up in the House of Commons on Wednesday and urged that the bid must be stopped, Will Lewis called Miliband's office and insisted that the hacking had nothing to do with the BSkyB deal. 'That gave away their fear,' according to one of Miliband's senior advisers. 'We decided to keep pushing on it.'

It was against this background that Rupert Murdoch not only approved the death of the *News of the World* but made a second bid for respectability by setting up a Management and Standards Committee, which, he said, would gather evidence about the hacking and liaise with police and report to Joel Klein in New York. However, still blinded by his enduring affection for Rebekah Brooks, he not only refused to sack her but appointed her to run the MSC's investigation.

At around this time, according to two sources, any hope of Murdoch family unity was broken by a heated conference call between the chairman and his four eldest children, during which Elisabeth said boldly that not only should Brooks resign but that James too should 'step back'. She was overruled. After this call, according to *Vanity Fair*, Elisabeth spoke privately to her father and persuaded him that James should take some leave. Rupert Murdoch told James that he should take a break from his job and possibly resign but then, after a sleepless night, changed his mind. Later, Elisabeth was quoted as having told James that he had 'fucked the company' – a line which, according to one source close to her, was inaccurate in its language but correct in its gist.

By Thursday morning, with the death of the *News of the World* to be announced that afternoon, the sources say that Brooks was effectively absent without leave. One says she had 'some sort of breakdown', hiding in her office, refusing to take meetings or phone calls and allowing contact from others in the building only via her husband, Charlie. She was due that evening to go to the *Sun's* annual Police Bravery Awards where, two years earlier, she had huddled comfortably with John Yates and Sir Paul Stephenson from Scotland Yard. But not tonight. She cancelled – at the suggestion of the police, according to one senior officer.

Fred Michel was anxiously working on Adam Smith in Jeremy Hunt's office, and on Thursday evening he was able to send James Murdoch an accurate account of Hunt's meeting with the prime minister at which they had agreed to hold public inquiries into the police and the press. But the government was clearly shifting. Hunt's department posted a new note on their website, saying that he would 'consider all factors' in making his decision about the bid, and then he announced the delay.

On Friday morning, Rebekah Brooks came up with a masterplan, emailing James Murdoch soon after seven to suggest they set up a full internal inquiry 'as an internal announcement from you that gets leaked', which would 'slam Les, Colin etc and it will vindicate my position (or not)'. The plan got lost in the chaos with Lewis and Greenberg now openly saying that she had to resign.

That afternoon, after bitter wrangling among the factions, it was agreed that James Murdoch should give an interview to ITN News to position News Corp as a law-abiding company which wanted to help the police. His advisers instructed him at all costs to avoid endorsing Rebekah Brooks; but he lost the script. Although he did claim (disingenuously) that 'the process of information-discovery that we went through, proactively and voluntarily' had led to the creation of Operation Weeting, he then proceeded to say that he was convinced that Brooks's leadership was right, she was doing the right thing and, in relation to the hacking, that 'I'm satisfied that she neither had knowledge of, nor directed those activities.'

That caused more shouting in the office.

I was still picking up warnings that there might be some kind of surveillance on me and the *Guardian* editor. On my advice, Rusbridger

345

commissioned an upmarket security consultancy to make sure there was no listening device in his home. Stupidly, the consultancy subcontracted the job to a specialist who was close friends with the group of corrupt investigators around Jonathan Rees, thus creating the risk which they were supposed to eliminate. The specialist, we heard, searched through paperwork in Rusbridger's study and possibly photographed pages from his private diary.

Sunday saw the *News of the World* pushed into its grave, with a final remorseful leader column which admitted 'appalling wrongdoing'. The Church of England's commissioners were threatening to sell £3.7 million of shares in News Corp. John Yates had given an interview describing his refusal to reopen the hacking investigation after our Gordon Taylor story as 'pretty crap' and privately had written to Rusbridger and me to apologise for his mistakes. And we saw the first signs of News International turning to attack as a form of defence.

The *Sunday Times* described the *Guardian* as a 'lefty newspaper' with a long history of fear and loathing of Rupert Murdoch and 'a visceral dislike for multinational business'. In the *Sun*, Trevor Kavanagh mourned the closure of the *News of the World* and suggested darkly that 'we should examine closely the motives of those who brought it to its knees'. The *Sun* tried to do a story accusing me of having held a meeting with a private detective in the Obsidian bar in Manchester, in order to hire him to spy on the *News of the World*. I'd never met the detective or been to the Obsidian bar, so that fell by the way, but the will to smear was easy to see.

None of this aggression amounted to any real problem – until I accidentally opened a chink in our defences. Glenn Campbell from the BBC and I had succeeded in collecting a pile of evidence about News International targeting Gordon Brown's confidential information: the *News of the World* had used Glenn Mulcaire to try to listen to his voicemail; the *Sunday Times* had used a blagger who on six occasions had obtained details from Brown's bank account; they had also, as I already knew, used another blagger, Barry Beardall, to trick a London law firm into providing details of a property he had bought; and the *Sun* had obtained confidential medical details about the cystic fibrosis which had been diagnosed in Brown's infant son, Fraser.

On Monday afternoon, 11 July, a week after the Dowler story, we posted on the *Guardian* website a strong account of the targeting of Brown, including the fact that the *Sun* had obtained confidential information about Fraser, which was accurate. But in the opening paragraph, I had tried to squeeze everything into a single sentence which accused News International of 'obtaining information from his bank account, his legal file and his family's medical records'. That was the chink in our defences: we knew they had obtained confidential information, but we didn't know that they had got this direct from his family's medical records.

Two days later, the *Sun* splashed its front page with the headline 'Brown wrong', telling its readers: 'The *Sun* today exposes the allegation that we hacked into Gordon Brown's family medical records as FALSE and a smear.' They had a point, but they had wildly overstated it: nobody had accused them of hacking the medical records. We didn't know how they had got the confidential information – by blagging, hacking or through a leak from the hospital. The *Sun* story claimed that they had been given the information by 'a shattered dad whose own son also has the crippling disease'. But how had he got it?

The *Sun*'s managing editor, Richard Caseby, insisted that we publish not only a correction, which was fair enough, but also an apology. In emails and phone calls, Caseby pressed his point by explaining that, if the *Guardian* didn't do as he said, the *Sunday Times* would 'work you over' at the end of the week and expose Rusbridger as 'the biggest fucking hypocrite on earth'. Digging deeper, I heard that the *Sun* had not quite told the truth about their source; that their 'shattered dad' was, in fact, married to a health worker, whose name I was given. One source claimed that the *Sun* had paid her £2,000, potentially a criminal offence if true. I relayed the information to the office of Gordon Brown, who passed it to his local health authority in Fife and persuaded them to investigate.

But that didn't stop Richard Caseby. In a high-volume expletive-scattered call to an executive at the *Guardian*, he continued to demand an apology before interrupting himself to say: 'Right, I have just heard that Fife has cleared our source.' He didn't seem to understand that he had just knocked the legs out from under the *Sun*'s version of events. It turned out that Fife had merely run a cursory check of their records and found no evidence at all. Months later, they conceded that it was 'highly likely' that one of their staff had been the original source.

I was hundreds of miles away, at my daughter's graduation ceremony, when, to my surprise, I heard that the *Guardian* had agreed to publish an apology. That was irritating. The *Guardian* had been unmoved by Caseby's aggression but had decided to apologise on the grounds that the sentence in the story had been inaccurate. I thought a simple correction would have been enough. I heard that Gordon Brown was furious about the *Guardian*'s decision.

The *Sunday Times* then followed up by attempting to run stories claiming that in the past, the *Guardian* had hired Jonathan Rees and another private investigator to gather information by illegal means. Rusbridger told them this was news to him and invited them to take their evidence to the police. It was clear that they had been talking to Rees: they also asked whether it was true that in the previous week, Rusbridger had had his home swept for bugs. Rusbridger told them that no organisation would comment on its security measures.

All this looked very much like a diversionary tactic from a company which still had its eyes on the big prize, BSkyB.

On Sunday 10 July, two days after Hunt had announced he would delay his decision, Rupert Murdoch once more had flown into London. He had suggested a PR move to improve his appearance: that he might travel on a commercial flight, like an ordinary man. In the event, he had used a private jet and soon delivered a PR gaffe when replying to a TV reporter who asked about his main priority, by pointing to Rebekah Brooks and saying: 'This one.'

His real priority was to deal with the tsunami of political disrespect which was flooding his company, much of it now channelled into a single event – a vote in the House of Commons on Wednesday, called by Ed Miliband, urging Murdoch to kill his bid for BSkyB. Fred Michel reported a call from an adviser in the prime minister's office: 'No. 10 are very worried about the vote on Wednesday. They think that it's highly possible that Miliband will win.'

Still acting as though the special relationship were undamaged, Fred Michel contacted one of the senior advisers in the office of the chancellor, George Osborne: 'Quick question for your advice. Do you think it would be possible/helpful to get a senior government person to come out condemning strongly phone-hacking, ask for a thorough police investigation but insisting on the need for the legal process to be followed with the bid? Incredible that a business decision on a massive takeover could be left to Parliament to oppose/influence, no?' It didn't work. The Murdochs had lost their influence in Westminster. The point was made bluntly at an internal meeting when James Murdoch and his team defended the bid, arguing as ever that there was no legal basis for blocking it, only to be told by one of Will Lewis's team: 'You don't get it: everybody hates you.'

Internal records from Jeremy Hunt's department reveal that he now recognised that the hacking scandal and the BSkyB bid were linked in the public mind. On Monday morning, stepping back fast from his previous sympathy for the bid, Hunt decided to write to Ofcom to ask them for advice on whether his decision should be affected by the closure of the *News of the World* or by the recent revelations. Of potentially even greater significance, he asked the regulator to consider whether News Corp was a 'fit and proper person' to hold a broadcasting licence in the UK. This was a line that had been pushed over the previous week by Tom Watson and other MPs. If Ofcom were to rule that News Corp were not fit and proper, they would not only lose the chance to buy the 61% of BSkyB which they wanted, they would also have to sell the 39% which they already owned. They would be turfed out of British broadcasting.

An hour later, with nowhere to go but backwards, the prime minister himself spoke out against the bid: 'If I was running that company right now, with all the problems and the difficulties and the mess frankly that there is, I think they should be focused on clearing those up rather than on the next corporate move.'

That Monday morning, Murdoch found his London colony in disarray, with a new back-stabbing leak as an outward sign of their internal friction. Robert Peston of the BBC had been given details about the Harbottle & Lewis emails, revealing that they appeared to show that the *News of the World* had agreed to pay a royal protection officer £1,000 to get phone contact details for the royal family. The leak was no help at all to James's efforts to push through the BSkyB deal, but it potentially took some pressure off Rebekah Brooks by adding the misleading spin that 'as soon as the newer management of the *News of the World* became aware of what was in the emails, they were told them [*sic*] that they had to give them immediately to the police'.

The move backfired within hours, first by provoking Sue Akers into going public with her anger, condemning the leak as 'part of a deliberate campaign to undermine the investigation', and second by causing yet more irritation on the tenth floor of the Murdoch building in east London.

James's team was feeling the pressure. One of his closest advisers, Alice Macandrew, had resigned. James wanted to plough on with the BSkyB bid and was frantically looking to Rebekah Brooks to quell the hacking storm. She emailed him to say she had just spent an hour on the phone with Tony Blair, who was suggesting that they set up an inquiry similar to the one which he had established under Lord Hutton to investigate his decision to invade Iraq in 2003. This would 'clear you', she told James, 'and accept shortcomings and new solutions'. She added that Blair was offering to give them more advice but – evidently recognising that this might not please his own party who were confronting News Corp in Parliament – he had suggested that this 'needs to be between us'. Most of James's advisers were struggling to rein him in, to persuade him to abandon the bid and take refuge in New York; but James would not hear of it, and the confusion generated an inadequate compromise. On Monday afternoon, James wrote to Jeremy Hunt to say that News Corp were withdrawing their Newco plan. That meant that Hunt would have to refer the bid to the Competition Commission, precisely the move which News Corp had once so feared. Now, with public opinion fervently against them, they told themselves that a six-month delay would help them and that they were better off dealing privately with a regulator than publicly with a politician. But the tide was too strong.

Monday evening added insult to ignominy. Murdoch's own Sky TV broadcast an episode of *The Simpsons* in which Lisa published a newspaper describing the miserly millionaire Monty Burns as 'a hateful man nobody likes' and Burns reacted by buying every news outlet in Springfield to silence all his critics. When the people of the town rebelled against him by producing their own news, Burns concluded: 'It's impossible to control all the media – well, unless you're Rupert Murdoch.'

Tuesday saw Gordon Brown – in an interview with me and Glenn Campbell from the BBC – condemning News International's 'most disgusting' tactics; the former deputy assistant commissioner Peter Clarke, who had commanded the original hacking inquiry, telling the home affairs select committee that the company had lied to police and damning them as 'a major global organisation deliberately trying to thwart a police investigation'; Sue Akers telling the same committee that Weeting were trying to contact as many as 4,000 potential hacking victims and that they were also looking at 'the criminal liability of directors' of the company; and, most alarming of all, David Cameron telling his MPs to back Ed Miliband's motion in the Commons debate the next day. That was very bad news for the Murdochs.

On Wednesday morning, Chase Carey flew in to London for an urgent meeting with James and Rupert. The two older men agreed they must make the ultimate sacrifice – they had to kill the BSkyB bid. James objected but lost the argument. Carey put out a statement: 'It has become clear that it is too difficult to progress in this climate.'

In two short weeks, imminent victory had turned to total defeat. That afternoon, the House of Commons passed by acclamation the motion from Miliband which condemned the Murdochs. It was backed by all six parties in the House. Miliband made a rousing speech: 'This is a victory for people – the good, decent people of Britain, outraged by the betrayal of trust by parts of our newspaper industry . . . The will of Parliament was clear, the will of the public was clear, and now Britain's most powerful media owner has had to bend to that will . . . The painful truth is that all of us, for far too long, have been in thrall to some sections of the media, including News International. For far too long, when these things happened, we just shrugged our shoulders and said "That's the way it is" – but no longer. The events of the past seven days have opened all our eyes and given us the chance to say "It doesn't have to be like this.""

Early on Sunday morning, 17 July, a chauffeur-driven black Audi set off from the peaceful farmland of west Oxfordshire and rolled down the M40 towards London. In the back, Rebekah Brooks sat alongside her husband, Charlie.

For days, she had known that Operation Weeting wanted to interview her. She had been told to present herself at noon at Lewisham police station in south London. In spite of the efforts of her lawyers, she had been unable to discover whether she was to be interviewed as a witness, or arrested on her arrival and treated as a suspect. Her lawyers feared the worst. And it was with this knowledge that two days earlier, on Friday morning, 15 July, she had finally announced her resignation.

The last move had come from Lewis and Greenberg who had met with the Murdoch family on the Thursday, told them that the police wanted to interview her, that it was crazy to leave her in charge of the MSC inquiry or anywhere near the company. They had no need to push: the Murdochs had agreed rapidly. Lewis and Greenberg had been dispatched to give her the news, to which she replied: 'You people are mad.' With the police on Friday morning instructing that she be out of the building by lunchtime, at noon she was marched down to the front door with a security guard.

She had released a statement saying that she left with 'the happiest of memories and an abundance of friends', describing News Corp as 'the finest media company in the world'. In reply, she had received sympathetic messages from Tony Blair and indirectly from David Cameron, even though publicly he welcomed her departure. Ever the power broker, she had negotiated a generous deal with Rupert Murdoch: a severance payout which was reported to be worth £10.8 million; an undertaking that News Corp would fund her lawyers for any criminal or civil action arising from her work; and a security team whose brief – rich in irony – included protecting her from news media.

This last task had been given an internal code name, Operation

Blackhawk. The man in charge of it was Mark Hanna, News International's director of security, who hired a group of former soldiers who were experts in surveillance to help him. They wanted £5,500 a day to keep Brooks safe. Murdoch had agreed to pay. Blackhawk did its job – its men texting each other outside her country home over the weekend to report the lurking presence of her former colleagues from Fleet Street, or, as they put it: 'Lots of rats at the bottom of the road.' In the wings, this created a small pantomime, which involved bin bags, pizzas and a great deal of confusion.

At noon, Rebekah arrived at Lewisham police station and was immediately arrested and held while her chauffeur waited outside. A quarter of an hour later, Charlie Brooks, who had gone to their luxury flat at Chelsea Harbour, went down to the underground car park, clutching a brown Jiffy bag and an old Sony laptop to his chest, walked round the corner to where there was a row of large green wheelie bins and dumped them. But he wasn't throwing them away. Two hours later, Mark Hanna drove into the car park, took a brown briefcase out of the car, chatted for a moment with Charlie and went over to the bins to retrieve the Jiffy bag and the laptop. He then left, with Jiffy bag, laptop and briefcase safely in hand. An hour later, at about 3 p.m., a small squad of Weeting officers arrived to search the Brooks flat. Clearly, Mr Brooks had something to hide, but if this was intended to be secret, things were going badly: all of it was caught on the CCTV cameras in the car park.

It took a little time for Fleet Street to hear about Rebekah Brooks's arrest. They were still chasing the flood of scandal, which was now lapping on the edges of the US. She had not been the only casualty on Friday. In New York, Les Hinton had resigned from his prestigious post as chief executive of Dow Jones and publisher of the *Wall Street Journal*. Hinton had started to attract heat as more questions were asked about his knowledge of crime at the *News of the World* and in particular about his knowledge of the Harbottle & Lewis emails whose content had been leaked so assiduously by some of Brooks's team. Politicians were asking whether he had deliberately misled the media select committee on the two occasions he had given evidence to them.

Still, his resignation was a surprise. Hinton had been Murdoch's friend for fifty-two years, his 'representative on earth'. But loyalty has its limits. According to one source from the senior ranks of News Corp, his departure was another part of Brooks's severance deal with Rupert Murdoch: 'She would not go alone. She said if she was going, Les had to go too.' By mid afternoon, news of Brooks's arrest had broken, and Hinton's problems were swept aside.

Soon the CCTV cameras in the underground car park were busy recording more of the pantomime. First, at about five o'clock, they caught the police search team leaving with armfuls of seized material. Then, at about 9.30 that evening – with Rebekah Brooks still being questioned – they recorded the arrival of one of Mark Hanna's security men, who drove in to the car park, made a quick phone call and, with a few furtive glances, lifted a well-stuffed black bin bag from his car and took it over to the green wheelie bins, where he hid it. Minutes later, a friend of Charlie Brooks came down to the car park and was rewarded by the security man with two boxes full of pepperoni and barbecued steak pizza (with piri piri stuffed crust).

The security man then texted his Operation Blackhawk controller a line famously used by Richard Burton to his commanding officer in *Where Eagles Dare*: 'Broadsword to Danny Boy. Pizzas delivered. The chicken is in the pot.' The controller replied 'Hah! Fucking amateurs' and went on to suggest they should have used a dead letter box or 'a brush contact by the riverside'.

Night fell. Soon after midnight, a small convoy of cars delivered Rebekah Brooks home. Her husband was there. Much later, he explained that by this time he and his friend had consumed not only the pizza but six bottles of wine. Perhaps it was for that reason that he failed to retrieve the bin bag that evidently had been left for him. And by the time he tried to do so, at about one o'clock the following afternoon, it was too late. A conscientious cleaner, Mr Nascimento, had got there first. Worse, Mr Nascimento had opened the bin bag and seen the old Sony computer and a stash of other interesting-looking material and taken it to his manager.

Brooks had gone in search of it, telling the manager: 'A friend left this bag for me last night, and there's been a bit of a mix-up.' The manager said he would look into it and, aware that the morning papers were full of the news of Rebekah Brooks's arrest, he then called the police, who soon swept onto the scene – or, as one of the Blackhawk security men put it in a text, 'Filth all over the underground car park ref Pizzagate.'

All this was to have painful ramifications for Charlie Brooks and his wife.

Scotland Yard, however, had problems of their own. John Yates's reputation was disintegrating rapidly: every step that Weeting took was a boot mark on his face, exposing his own failure to investigate properly. During the previous week, he had appeared before the home affairs select committee to defend himself and been told by the chairman, Keith Vaz, that his evidence was 'unconvincing'. Andy Hayman had been doing no better. His attempts at the same committee session to justify the weakness of the original hacking inquiry had ended in ridicule, with MPs describing him as 'a dodgy geezer' and 'more Clouseau than Columbo'. Now, it all got worse.

The day before Rebekah Brooks resigned, Operation Weeting had arrested Neil Wallis, the former deputy editor of the *News of the World*, on suspicion of involvement in the conspiracy to intercept voicemail. That might have passed as a simple news story, if the Metropolitan Police Commissioner, Sir Paul Stephenson, had not then released a very surprising statement – that in October 2009, four months after the *Guardian* published the Gordon Taylor story, as the *Guardian* and the media select committee continued to uncover the hacking scandal, Scotland Yard had hired Neil Wallis as their media consultant. Among other things, Wallis had been giving advice directly to Sir Paul and to John Yates. What kind of influence had Wallis had?

That evening, Alan Rusbridger wrote to Dick Fedorcio, who had personally been responsible for hiring Wallis, reminding him of the two occasions on which he had visited the *Guardian* – first with Sir Paul, then with John Yates – to insist that the *Guardian*'s coverage of the hacking was 'over-egged and incorrect'. Rusbridger asked him a series of questions: 'Why did you not think it appropriate to tell me at the time of these meetings that you, Paul and John were being advised by

Coulson's former deputy? What advice did he give you about the coverage of the phone-hacking? Was Wallis consulted in advance of these meetings or subsequently informed of the nature or contents of our discussions?'

By Sunday morning, as Rebekah Brooks's convoy was heading for London, the row about Neil Wallis had escalated. The *Sunday Times* reported that earlier in the year, Sir Paul and his wife had accepted twenty nights' free accommodation, worth £12,000, at a Champneys health farm – whose media consultant was Mr Neil Wallis. And one more twist: the farm had a 'kriotherapy' unit to treat ailments in sub-zero temperatures – which was run by Charlie Brooks. And Sir Paul had used it during his stay.

At 7.30 that Sunday evening, Sir Paul Stephenson resigned as commissioner of the Metropolitan Police.

Monday morning saw a new allegation, that John Yates had helped Neil Wallis's daughter, Amy, to get a job at Scotland Yard. It was by no means the worst complaint about Yates, but it was yet another boot mark. The Professional Standards committee of the Metropolitan Police Authority announced that they were meeting that morning to consider the conduct of Yates, Sir Paul, Peter Clarke and Andy Hayman.

At 2.00 that Monday afternoon, John Yates resigned as assistant commissioner.

It was the biggest show in town. At 2.00 on the afternoon of Tuesday 19 July, Rupert Murdoch and his son, James, would appear before the House of Commons culture, media and sport select committee to answer for their failings. The queue outside Parliament had been building since early morning. I joined it.

Sitting on the pavement, watching the TV crews and the demonstrators in the street, I remembered the day just over two years earlier when Alan Rusbridger and I had been called to give evidence to the same committee, with the clear warning that we were to be barbecued for our supposed errors. The email for Neville Thurlbeck had saved us. The question now, not only for me but for multiple millions who would watch live on television, was whether the Murdochs could save themselves.

They had done their best to avoid the occasion. When the committee chairman, John Whittingdale, first invited them, Rupert Murdoch had refused to attend, and his son had replied that 19 July was inconvenient but he would be willing to see them in August. Whittingdale, who had been a friend of Les Hinton and a vocal supporter of BSkyB, threatened to place empty chairs in front of the committee for the world to see and to report their absence as a contempt of Parliament, with the theoretical possibility that the serjeant-at-arms could invoke his ancient power to arrest them. In the event, a formal summons delivered to them by the serjeant's deputy brought them to heel.

There was a mood of rebellion in the air. Vince Cable, on radio, had put it well: 'It's a little bit like the end of a dictatorship, when everybody suddenly discovers they were against the dictator.' There was also some real sadness. The previous day, Sean Hoare had been found dead at his home in Watford. I had really liked Sean. He had done so much to expose the rotten core of his old paper, and he was good company while he did it, funny and warm with an endless supply of tales. The conspiracy theorists had all started tweeting that he must have been murdered. It wasn't true. His job, as he used to say, had been 'to take drugs with rock stars'. That was what killed him, aged only forty-seven.

After four hours on the pavement, we finally made it into the committee room. I sat with my back to the wall, looking down a row of seats where the Murdochs' supporters would gather: Rupert's wife, Wendi; Joel Klein; assorted lawyers and PR merchants. In front of them, a little to my left, were the two chairs waiting for Rupert and James. Further to the left was the committee, arranged around their horseshoe-shaped desk, with the familiar faces of Paul Farrelly and Tom Watson nodding a greeting from the far side. We were all very quiet, more nervous than excited, simply because this was such a reversal of power, as if schoolkids were about to discipline the head teacher and his deputy. How could this room possibly dominate the dominators? Yet when Rupert and James finally came in, they were just two men in dark suits, Rupert much smaller than I had expected, a corporate giant but still merely a man.

Within minutes, the first part of the Murdoch strategy became clear. They played the humility card. James Murdoch took the first question and interrupted his own answer to say how sorry he was, and then Rupert interrupted him: 'This is the most humble day of my life.' That was a good line, which sounded as if it owed something to Edelman, the world's largest PR firm, which had been hired by the Murdochs the previous week and had already encouraged Rupert to meet Bob and Sally Dowler to say he was sorry, and to place advertisements in every national newspaper on Saturday, headed in very large print: 'We are sorry.' James went on to say that the company was now trying to behave in a humble way, and Rupert repeated that it was the most humble day of his career. Twice.

That wasn't going to be enough. Humble was one thing. But were they also guilty?

Led by Tom Watson, the MPs confronted them with the history of clear and public evidence of crime in their newsroom. How could they not have noticed: the *Guardian* in September 2002 running 3,000 words on the *News of the World*'s involvement in Jonathan Rees's network of corruption; or Rebekah Brooks in March 2003 telling a select committee that her paper had paid police in the past; or the ICO in December 2006 reporting that twenty-three of the paper's reporters had taken part in Steve Whittamore's 'illegal trade'; or the claims at Glenn Mulcaire's sentencing in January 2007 that he had been working not just for Clive Goodman but for others at the paper?

The Murdochs soon turned to the second part of their strategy. From their lofty position in the crow's nest at the top of the company, they drew a line under themselves and said simply and repeatedly that they had failed to notice a thing that was going on beneath them. At this moment, their refusal to run an effective internal inquiry became their best line of defence, like a reverse version of the Nazi defence at the Nuremberg war trials: 'We didn't know they weren't obeying orders.'

Rupert Murdoch had an extra layer of help with this: his age. He frowned, shook his head in confusion and disappeared into unnaturally long pauses, tapping his fingers on the desk in front of him. One of his closest advisers claims he always does this when he is asked to say something important, that he is so worried about saying the wrong thing that he gets lost in a mental spin. Whether it was natural character or furtive design, it worked. Confronted repeatedly by awkward questions, he vanished into vagueness.

What had he talked to Tony Blair about, for example? A blank look and a shrug: 'We argued about the euro, I think.' What instructions had he given to the editor of the *News of the World*? 'I'm not really in touch. I have to tell you that.' Had he not wondered why News International had paid such large amounts of money to Gordon Taylor and Max Clifford? 'I never heard of them,' he said.

James was in more difficulty. His crow's nest had been in London, with direct responsibility for News International. He had agreed to settle with Gordon Taylor, because that was the advice from senior counsel, but that was all he had known. Which seemed a surprising way for a chief executive to spend £1 million. And Clifford? 'I was not involved in that piece.' Really?

A third strategy came into view. The Murdochs explained that they had 'rested' on the investigations of others: on Scotland Yard, even though its most senior officers were now accusing News International of lying to them; on the Press Complaints Commission, although its chair, Lady Buscombe, was now pleading that the *News of the World* had lied to them; and on Harbottle & Lewis, whose narrow remit to review a collection of emails was now presented as a full-scale investigation with the aim, as Rupert put it, 'to find out what the hell was going on'.

I didn't believe a word of it, but, in spite of all the efforts of the MPs, the Murdochs held their ground. Then they were presented with a surprising gift. From my right, a young man rose from his seat, walked in front of me and, instead of heading for the door, he turned to approach Rupert Murdoch. I thought he was going to hit him and – in spite of all my battles with the mogul – I tried to shout a warning. Too late. The man produced a paper plate full of whipped cream and shoved it into Murdoch's face. It was a deeply stupid thing to do. The MPs lost their line of questioning, all the press and public were excluded from the room, and an eighty-year-old man who had been attacked without warning found sympathy tilting towards him. Until that moment, neither side was winning. Now the Murdochs were ahead. When the hearing stuttered to its end soon afterwards, both of them were wounded, but neither had fallen.

Still, they were not in the clear. Scotland Yard were running three investigations into their journalists; Strathclyde police another; Ofcom were officially investigating whether they were fit and proper to hold a broadcasting licence in the UK. In the US, the FBI had started an inquiry into whether News Corp had broken the Foreign Corrupt Practices Act by allowing UK officials to be bribed. The Australian prime minister, Julia Gillard, had ordered a review of media laws, and News Corp's subsidiary there was checking for evidence of crime in their newsrooms. Biggest of all, the prime minister had announced that within months Lord Justice Leveson would chair a public inquiry, with powers to compel witnesses and order disclosure of records, to look at News International, the press, the police and government. The hearing was finished, but the show was not over.

15. Exposed!

It was like watching a headmaster addressing the morning assembly. He sat up on the stage at one end of the room, in his charcoal grey suit and his serious spectacles, and, speaking slowly and gravely, more in sorrow than in anger, he told the hundreds of silent faces lined up in neat rows before him of the bad behaviour and indiscipline which had come to his attention. Lord Justice Leveson was delivering his report.

It was the morning of Thursday 29 November 2012. Leveson spoke in the Queen Elizabeth II Conference Centre, a few minutes' walk from Parliament. Around the corner, Rebekah Brooks and Andy Coulson stood in the dock at Westminster Magistrates' Court for a preliminary hearing on charges that they had conspired to pay public officials for information. Seventeen months had passed since the *Guardian* published the Milly Dowler story.

The Leveson Inquiry, sitting in public, had taken evidence from 337 people. Some were ordinary members of the public, who had found their lives suddenly ransacked by the press. Others were from the peaks of power: the prime minister, three former prime ministers, numerous Cabinet ministers, government officials, chief constables, detectives, film stars, newspaper editors and a cohort of reporters. All of them were cross-examined. Some were compelled to disclose emails, text traffic, paperwork. More than 300 others submitted written statements. It was an unmatched exercise in exposing the concealed world of governance.

Some came in grandeur. Before Rupert Murdoch spent two days in the witness box, his staff visited the drab waiting room next to Leveson's court and distributed cushions and flowers and laid a white tablecloth and silver cutlery on the battered old table for the mogul's lobster lunch. Others took a simpler approach. Ed Miliband prepared his evidence in the same room without luxury additions, asking at the end for a few minutes on his own, during which the sound of Journey playing 'Don't Stop Believin'' could be heard through the door, fortifying the Labour leader's morale.

Some witnesses rebelled against the very idea that they could be called to account at all. During preliminary seminars in October 2011, the former editor of the *Sun*, Kelvin MacKenzie, stood in front of Leveson and referred to 'this ludicrous inquiry . . . this bloody inquiry'. The editor of the *Daily Mail*, Paul Dacre, declared he could detect 'the rank smell of hypocrisy and revenge in the political class's current moral indignation' at his profession. Without waiting for a word of formal evidence, the *Sun's* associate editor, Trevor Kavanagh, told Leveson that his inquiry was 'a cloud over freedom of speech'.

Once the inquiry started, in November 2011, some newspapers continued to behave as though Leveson were not watching them. When Hugh Grant's girlfriend gave birth to a child that month, tabloid reporters and photographers surrounded her home with such persistence and occasional aggression that Grant eventually went to court and got an injunction to stop them. When an eleven-year-old British boy, Sebastian Bowles, died with twenty-seven others in a coach crash in a Swiss tunnel in March 2012, while Leveson was still sitting, British newspapers ignored requests to respect the family's privacy. They published a picture of his grieving nine-year-old sister on private property preparing to carry flowers to the scene of the accident as well as photographs which had been taken from Sebastian's Facebook page in apparent breach of privacy settings. His family had to close down the dead boy's blog after quotes and a photograph from it were published without their consent, and they found so many reporters outside their home that they were forced to live behind shuttered windows for more than a week.

Some newspapers attacked Leveson directly. When the Education Secretary Michael Gove told the Commons press gallery that the inquiry was having a 'chilling effect' on press freedom, Leveson called Downing Street to find out if the government no longer supported its work. He was reassured by the Cabinet Secretary, Sir Jeremy Heywood. In the hands of the *Mail on Sunday*, this became a front-page story, headlined 'Leveson's "threat to quit" over meddling minister' with a claim that the judge had made an angry call to the Cabinet Secretary and 'demanded that the Education Secretary be gagged'.

Some papers adopted a threatening tone not only to the inquiry but to some of those who dared to step forward to speak to it. A former *Daily Star* reporter, Rich Peppiat, told Leveson in detail how he had been encouraged to fabricate stories. He was then confronted and denounced by one of his former bosses in the conference centre's canteen. The *Daily Mail* attacked some of Hugh Grant's evidence as 'mendacious smears'. The *Mail* also went to court to try to stop Leveson taking evidence from anonymous sources. They failed, but at least three former *Mail* reporters then backed out of helping the inquiry for fear of losing their careers if their assistance became known.

Nevertheless, by the time Leveson summarised his report to that assembly of journalists in November 2012, he had exposed Fleet Street to some of the humblest days of its life. Above all, he provided a platform for dozens of media victims who variously told him of the blackmail, bullying, malice, invasion of privacy and toxic falsehood which they had suffered. Some were celebrities whose phones had been hacked and who had been pursued by reporters and photographers to the point where their lives were no longer free. The most impressive were ordinary people.

Kate and Gerry McCann recalled the aftermath of the abduction of their three-year-old daughter, Madeleine, during a family holiday in Portugal in May 2007 – how newspapers recycled unchecked and baseless allegations from the Portuguese press which poured acid on their grief, and falsely accused them of selling or murdering their own child. In his report, Leveson concluded: 'They had become a news item, a commodity, almost a piece of public property where the public's right to know possessed few, if any, boundaries.'

Leveson went on to investigate what happened when the *News of the World* obtained a copy of Kate McCann's diary, in which she had recorded her agony, a document which was so private that she had not shown it even to her husband. Portuguese police had seized it, translated it and then allowed a copy to reach a local journalist. The *News of the World* had bought it for 'a substantial sum', translated it back into English and then confronted the significant legal problem that they had no right to publish it. The editor, Colin Myler, told Leveson that his news editor, Ian Edmondson, had spoken to the McCanns' representative, who had consented to publication. Edmondson, however, told a different tale, explaining that, in reality, Myler had told him to contact the McCanns' spokesman and to 'make it very woolly', specifically not to tell him that the paper had the complete diary for fear that the McCanns would take legal action to prevent publication. Leveson said this was 'devastating evidence'. Gerry McCann said his wife had felt 'distraught and morally raped'.

Margaret Watson, whose sixteen-year-old daughter had been stabbed to death by another schoolgirl, described how her girl was then portrayed by the *Glasgow Herald* as a snob and bully. Mrs Watson recalled the pain which this had caused not only herself and her husband but also their only surviving child: 'It was all too much to bear for our dear son, Alan, and he took his own life. He was found holding copies of the articles.'

Christopher Jefferies told Leveson how he had suddenly become a tabloid victim because he was the landlord of a young woman, Joanna Yeates, who was found murdered on Christmas Day 2010. He was arrested as a suspect but released without charge. The real killer was caught three weeks later. In the meantime, some newspapers had published what Jefferies described as 'a mixture of smear, innuendo and complete fiction' about him, effectively naming him as the killer. These stories were not only libellous – Jefferies sued eight newspapers over a total of forty of them – but also risked serious prejudice to any trial which he might have faced, and the *Sun* and the *Daily Mirror* were later fined for contempt of court with the judge describing Jefferies as 'the latest victim of the regular witch-hunts and character assassination conducted by the worst elements of the British tabloid media'.

It was the stories of these victims which built the platform on which Leveson constructed his report. Addressing his silent audience that day, he said that the object of his inquiry had been not simply to make recommendations, but also 'to expose precisely what has been happening'. He was not alone in attempting to do that. With Scotland Yard, two select committees and court actions still dragging detail out into the open, the power elite found its secret world uniquely threatened with exposure.

The threat to James Murdoch began with a discreet text message at 4.37 in the afternoon of 19 July 2011, as he and his father were navigating their way through the choppy waters of their appearance before the media select committee with MPs alleging that the pair had known about crime at the *News of the World* and engineered a cover-up.

Watching from the side of the room, I could see the MPs repeatedly rocking the Murdochs' boat but never quite upsetting them. Several had got close by challenging James Murdoch over his decision to pay huge damages to Gordon Taylor in 2008. Surely he must have known that Taylor's lawyer, Mark Lewis, had found evidence of illegality. But James was well prepared and claimed he had agreed to settle simply because that was the advice of counsel and without exploring the reasons. I could see that the MPs needed to push him further into the detail. I remembered sitting in front of this same committee two years earlier and distributing the document which saved my skin.

Quietly, I slipped my phone out of my pocket, found Tom Watson's number and sent him a message across the room: 'Did James know about email for Neville? If not, why settle Taylor case? If so, why not tell police?'

I caught Watson's eye and held an imaginary phone to my ear. He nodded. I waited. The idiot with the whipped cream broke up the hearing, but when the MPs resumed, Watson intervened to put one more question to James Murdoch: 'When you signed off the Taylor payment, did you see, or were you made aware of, the "for Neville email", the transcript of the hacked voicemail messages?'

James snapped back his answer: 'No, I was not aware of that at the time,' he said.

Now he had committed himself. Now he was vulnerable.

The next day, my colleague David Leigh called Tom Crone, who had handled the detail of the Taylor settlement, and urged him to say what he knew. Crone had no reason to like us and said only that he would think about it. The following evening, he and Colin Myler issued a joint statement: 'Just by way of clarification to Tuesday's select committee hearing, we would like to point out that James Murdoch's recollection of what he was told when agreeing to settle the Gordon Taylor litigation was mistaken. In fact, we did inform him of the "for Neville" email which had been produced to us by Gordon Taylor's lawyers.'

With that, James Murdoch was tipped out of his boat. If Crone and Myler were right, James had concealed his knowledge of crime for more than two years. As he struggled to keep his head above water, the media select committee over the following months extracted a sequence of disclosures, each of which threatened to push him under.

These revealed that in May 2008, Myler had met James to discuss Gordon Taylor's lawsuit, armed with Crone's written opinion that the email for Neville was 'fatal to our case'; and that, the following month Myler and Crone together had seen him a second time. According to Crone: 'Since the "for Neville" document was the sole reason for settling and, therefore, for the meeting, I have no doubt that I informed Mr Murdoch of its existence, of what it was and where it came from.' James had stalled, they said, wanting to see the legal opinion from Michael Silverleaf QC, who duly reported that the email for Neville 'has disclosed that at least three journalists appear to have been intimately involved in Mr Mulcaire's illegal researching into Mr Taylor's affairs' and that the *News of the World* had harboured 'a culture of illegal information access'.

Was James Murdoch really going to maintain that he settled the case with Gordon Taylor without knowing any of this evidence? Faced with the new disclosures, he changed his story. He was summoned back to the committee to give evidence for a second time, on 10 November 2011. The chairman, John Whittingdale, confronted him: 'Even if it was not described as the "for Neville email", were you made aware of the existence of an email that contained the transcripts of voice intercepts which, in Tom Crone's words, was "fatal" to your case?'

To which he answered: 'Yes.'

This directly contradicted the answer which he had given four months earlier to Tom Watson, who had asked him if he had known about 'the "for Neville email", the transcript of the hacked voicemail messages'. To which he had answered: 'No.'

He went on to agree that he understood that this email was very damaging to the company's defence that nobody other than Clive Goodman had been involved. To any reasonable onlooker, that was enough: as far back as June 2008, the executive chairman of News International had known that the 'rogue reporter' line was untrue, but he had not told anybody – not Parliament, which had been misled; not the police, who had clearly not captured anybody other than Goodman; and not his shareholders, in spite of his duty of candour to them.

James Murdoch wriggled with great energy. He had known about 'a transcript of voicemail interceptions that were made on behalf of the *News of the World*', he now agreed, but he had not known that this had been produced 'for Neville' and so had not been aware that it implicated anybody else or required further investigation. It was very hard to understand how Mulcaire could have been producing illegally obtained voicemail for the newspaper without some human being who worked there necessarily being involved.

Undaunted, he wriggled on. He understood that it now appeared that he had discussed the Taylor case with Colin Myler in May 2008, but he did not recall this and, therefore, did not recall Myler passing on any of the 'fatal' evidence which Tom Crone had given Myler. And, he agreed, he had decided to wait for Michael Silverleaf's opinion before deciding how to settle with Taylor, but, he claimed, he had then settled the case without reading the opinion for which he had asked.

Furthermore, he said, it was not just in 2008 that he had remained unaware of the evidence in the Taylor case. When it was splashed across the front page of the *Guardian* in July 2009, he still had not known about it, even when the *Guardian* the following week gave the email for Neville to the select committee. This had all been handled by Rebekah Brooks, he claimed, because she had become chief executive in June 2009. This happened to be provably inaccurate: Brooks's appointment had been announced in June 2009, but she had not taken over until September.

Beyond that, he claimed that in spite of the public storm which had broken around the Taylor settlement after the *Guardian* story, he had not stopped to ask why his company in February 2010 then agreed to pay £1 million to stop Max Clifford suing them. That, too, had been dealt with by Brooks. 'It was discussed with me in general terms but not from an authorisation perspective,' he told the committee.

James was alive but still struggling in the water when that hearing finished. The committee then obtained one final piece of evidence, which appeared to contradict him. News Corp disclosed that in the midst of his meetings with Crone and Myler, James had received an email chain which included Myler telling him that 'unfortunately, it is as bad as we feared' and Crone explaining that 'we knew of and made use of the voicemail information from Glenn Mulcaire'. James had sent a brief reply a few minutes later. Confronted with this, James wrote to the committee to claim that although he had replied, he had not actually read the message which he had received. He suggested that this was because he had received it on a Saturday 'when I was likely alone with my two children'. In spite of his pressing childcare arrangements, he had then invited Myler to call him at home that weekend.

Mark Lewis, who had been at the centre of the Taylor case, was called back to the committee and put the case against James in its clearest form: 'I think James Murdoch would like to give you the impression that he was mildly incompetent rather than thoroughly dishonest.' In their final report, published on 1 May 2012, the committee also used strong language, concluding that it was 'extraordinary' that James had authorised such an expensive settlement without knowing the evidence and 'simply astonishing' that he had not understood that the 'rogue reporter' defence had collapsed.

At the end of all this, James Murdoch could still insist that he had not been proved to be part of a cover-up, but the cumulative damage to his credibility and reputation was serious. In New York, he was marginalised. 'Because his surname is Murdoch, he can command meetings with people who fly in to report on what's going on,' according to a senior News Corp executive, 'but he's just treading water and has no function.' His close ally, Beryl Cook, stepped down as head of human resources. His right-hand man, Matthew Anderson, also resigned. In the run-up to the media select committee publishing its report, James himself resigned his two UK posts, as executive chairman of News International and chairman of BSkyB.

★　　★　　★

For Rupert Murdoch, the threat of exposure was never so tightly focused.

Like his son, he stumbled into trouble with the media select committee, for example by telling them that News International had hired the law firm Harbottle & Lewis 'to find out what the hell was going on'. That was emphatically denied by Daniel Cloke and Jon Chapman, the two News International executives who had hired the law firm. It was also denied by Harbottle & Lewis themselves, who told the committee: 'There was absolutely no question of the firm being asked to provide News International with a clean bill of health which it could deploy years later in wholly different contexts for wholly different purposes.'

He stumbled into more trouble when he was summoned to appear before the Leveson Inquiry, spending two days in the witness box, under attack over his relationships with senior UK politicians and his handling of the hacking scandal. He denied all wrongdoing. He had never asked a politician for a favour, he said. And he had simply not known the facts about the hacking. Indeed, he claimed, it was he who was the original victim of the cover-up at News International. His evidence was greeted with great scepticism. He emerged bruised and diminished. But at the end, his line of defence was not quite broken.

However, he faced a more powerful threat from a much bigger accusation: that he had been running a rogue corporation. The hacking scandal turned out to be one particularly well-defined part of a pervasive pattern.

One of Murdoch's most senior newspaper executives, Andrew Langhoff, resigned as European director of Dow Jones when the *Guardian* revealed that the *Wall Street Journal* had been channelling money through other companies in order to secretly buy thousands of copies of its own paper, misleading readers and advertisers about its true circulation and compromising its authority by giving one of the companies helpful editorial coverage.

The *New York Times* exposed the detail of how one of his US subsidiaries, News America, which sold advertising on supermarket shelves, had been accused of undermining a rival, Floorgraphics, by hacking into its computers to get information about its plans and customers. Court hearings which would have exposed the facts were halted when News Corp settled with Floorgraphics – and then settled again with two other companies, Valassis and Insignia, who complained that News America had been variously using threats, bribes and smears to try to steal their customers. It cost News Corp a total of $650 million to silence the three legal actions. In an uncomfortable echo of James Murdoch's problems with the Gordon Taylor case, News Corp refused to say whether Rupert Murdoch had been aware of the evidence of foul practice when he authorised these settlements.

BBC's *Panorama* investigated allegations about another News Corp subsidiary, NDS, who were crucial to the success of Murdoch's pay-TV business. NDS used an Israeli military scrambling system to encrypt the signal which was sent from the News Corp satellite to millions of homes. Without the encryption, potential customers could simply take the service without paying. Those who have worked with Murdoch say that he was particularly closely involved with NDS. *Panorama* reported that in the late 1990s NDS had not only encrypted Sky's signal but had sabotaged the business of its biggest rival, ITV Digital, by hiring a computer hacker who obtained and distributed codes which then allowed people to watch ITV Digital without paying. ITV Digital eventually folded. News Corp denied *Panorama*'s allegations. Similar claims against NDS had been made in 2002 by the French pay-TV company, Canal Plus, who sued the company. Those allegations also were denied. A court hearing which would have exposed the facts was cancelled when News Corp bought the part of the Canal Plus business which was at the heart of the affair.

A Murdoch subsidiary in Russia, News Outdoor, which sold advertising space on billboards, was accused of bribing local officials. The Chinese office of the *Wall Street Journal* was accused of paying bribes to get information. Whenever a rock was lifted in the News Corp business, it seemed to reveal another allegation of rule-bending or lawbreaking from a company which lived by only one rule: to win. Even in the world of sport, it had cheated to win, breaking the rules of Australian rugby league to pay nearly $4 million in secret salary top-ups to players in the team which Murdoch owned, Melbourne Storm. (It worked: the team won four Premiership titles.)

The picture which emerged was of a rogue corporation which thrived precisely because of its ruthlessness – the more money it made, the more power it accrued, the more money it could make. And if it was running on the fuel of amorality, that really didn't matter. All that counted was the bottom line.

While Murdoch escaped allegations that he had covered up crime at News International, he was damned for his oversight of his own business. Lord Justice Leveson concluded that there had been 'a serious failure of governance within the *News of the World*, News International and News Corporation'.

The media select committee went further. Rupert Murdoch, they said, had 'turned a blind eye and exhibited wilful blindness to what was going on in his companies and publications. This culture, we consider, permeated from the top throughout the organisations and speaks volumes about the lack of effective corporate governance at News Corporation and News International. We conclude, therefore, that Rupert Murdoch is not a fit person to exercise stewardship of a major international company.'

Murdoch's reputation was deeply damaged. Symbolically, the Church of England in August 2012 made good on its threat to wash its hands of News Corp, disposing of all its stock in the company. Murdoch's summer party in London, which had become an annual pilgrimage for the UK's power elite, was cancelled. A group of institutional share-holders, led by Amalgamated Bank, sued the company over its handling of the hacking and its purchase of Elisabeth Murdoch's TV company, Shine, and in April 2013 forced News Corp to accept more independent directors, a whistle-blower's hotline, scrutiny of its political activity and possibly an end to Rupert Murdoch being both chairman and chief executive. They also won damages of $139 million.

There was more financial pain from the scandal in London. In the year following the Dowler story, News Corp paid $224 million in damages, compensation and fees for lawyers and other consultants. There was damage too to Murdoch's family and to his dreams of handing the chairmanship to one of his children. *Vanity Fair* reported that three months after the scandal exploded, Murdoch and his children had met, on 8 September 2011, in their yachts off the coast of Ibiza. The family remained divided. Rupert Murdoch and James were barely on speaking terms, according to one of their senior executives. And the cold gap between Elisabeth and James became publicly visible a year later when she gave the MacTaggart lecture in Edinburgh, glancing back to her brother's bold claim in the same lecture three years earlier, that the only guarantor of independence is profit, by complaining of the absence of moral language in the worlds of government and business. 'Profit without purpose is a recipe for disaster,' she said.

Elisabeth said she would not serve on the board of News Corp nor seek to succeed her father. James's older brother, Lachlan, had already fled the snake pit in New York. James himself remained, discredited, unfavoured, powerless.

Exposure is one thing, victory another. Even as the truth emerged about the secret life of the power elite, there were signs that they were not yet ready to change their ways.

All those involved in uncovering the hacking scandal had lived with the fear that the Murdoch papers might turn on them. In the months after the Dowler story, hard evidence emerged that they had indeed tried to punish some of them, using their favourite weapon: prying into their sex lives.

Tom Watson had a history of animosity with the *Sun*, going back to 2006 when he had pushed for Gordon Brown to replace Tony Blair as prime minister. Watson told Leveson that during the Labour Party conference in Manchester later that year, he had been approached by the *Sun*'s political editor, George Pascoe-Watson, who had told him that 'Rebekah will never forgive you for what you did to her Tony' and that 'Rupert Murdoch never forgets'. Three years later, under Brooks's editorship, the *Sun* ran a series of stories calling him 'Two Dinners Tom' and a mad dog, falsely accusing him of being part of a plot to publish smear stories about Conservative MPs. Watson sued for libel and won substantial damages.

Now it was revealed that in the autumn of 2009, as Watson and colleagues on the media select committee dug into crime at the *News of the World*, both the *Sun* and the *News of the World* had targeted him again. Watson says he was warned by several people that Brooks was complaining about him. One source at the *Sun* says that she called in reporters to ask if they had 'any dirt' on him. They had none, but the *News of the World* picked up on a rumour that he was having an affair. This appears to have come from the paper's notorious undercover specialist, Mazher Mahmood, who emailed the news desk with the heading 'Labour sex scandal', claiming that 'Tom Watson as we speak is shagging' an Asian woman who belonged to the Labour Party. The paper then tasked their surveillance expert, Derek Webb, to shadow Watson for five days at the Labour Party conference in September 2009 in search of confirmation. They found none. The story was untrue. Colin Myler had to content himself with walking through the conference and describing the troublesome MP as 'a fat bastard' within his hearing.

It was also disclosed that the *News of the World* had used Derek Webb to run at least two surveillance operations on solicitors working for the victims of hacking. The first, in March 2010, was aimed at Mark Lewis as he gathered new clients to sue News International in the wake of their successfully stopping Max Clifford's case. The *News of the World* turned to Webb, who located Lewis's former wife and daughter and secretly videoed them as they visited local shops. It is not clear why they did this. The second surveillance, in January 2011, targeted Charlotte Harris as her case with Sky Andrew threatened to destroy News International's remaining defences. Again, Webb was commissioned to follow her, apparently searching for evidence that she was having an affair with a solicitor in Manchester. She had never met the solicitor in question. Questioned by the media select committee, Tom Crone admitted that he had seen information which had been gathered about Lewis and Harris. 'It involves their private lives,' he said.

These efforts were fruitless, but News International successfully wreaked havoc in the life of the only front-bench politician who spoke out about the hacking scandal before the Dowler story: Chris Huhne, who was the Lib Dem home affairs spokesman when the *Guardian* published the Gordon Taylor story. Huhne consistently badgered the company to come clean. In June 2010, when he had become Secretary of State for energy in the new coalition government, the *News of the World* exposed the fact that he was having an affair. He left his wife, Vicky Pryce, who then took revenge on him by disclosing to the *Sunday Times* that in 2003, he had persuaded her to accept penalty points on her licence for a speeding ticket which he had incurred. The *Sunday Times* controversially handed police their email exchanges with Pryce, exposing her as their source and compounding the damage to Huhne. It is not clear whether the company's hostility to Huhne contributed to this decision. In March 2013, both Huhne and Pryce were jailed for eight months for perverting the course of justice. Huhne's political career was destroyed.

Separately Gordon Brown, who had denounced News International after the Dowler story, then found himself the object of a sequence of hostile stories in *The Times*, *Sunday Times* and *Sun*. The stories were false, and the three Murdoch titles were forced to print a total of eight apologies to him in one six-month period. James Harding, who had reportedly infuriated Rupert Murdoch by publishing a leader comment which denounced the hacking of Milly Dowler, was suddenly ousted as editor of *The Times*. David Cameron, who had been News International's darling, was vilified by the *Sun* after he called for Rebekah Brooks's resignation and set up the Leveson Inquiry.

In the months after the Dowler story, Amelia Hill was warned that the *Sun* were trying to trace her former partners to do a story about her sex life; and I was warned that the *Sun* had put a 'hit squad' on me who were contacting former students from my masterclass in reporting technique, in search of evidence that I had advised them to use illegal techniques or attempted to seduce them. As it happened, I had done neither.

The *Sun* declared war on the *Guardian*. In November 2011 the *Guardian* columnist Marina Hyde claimed that the *Sun* had sent a reporter to doorstep one of Leveson's counsel, Carine Patry Hoskins, and suggested that this was like 'defecating on his lordship's desk while doing a thumbs-up'. Hyde's claim was incorrect. The *Guardian* published a correction, but the *Sun*'s managing editor, Richard Caseby, followed up by sending Alan Rusbridger a toilet roll with the message: 'I hear Marina Hyde's turd landed on your desk. Well, you can use this to wipe her arse.'

Early the following month, December 2011, I had a private conversation with a senior police officer who had some important news: Operation Weeting had found new evidence about the hacking of Milly Dowler, and it now looked as though the *News of the World* might not have deleted the messages which had given her parents false hope she was still alive. That was not good news. The Dowler story had set off the chain reaction which finally brought the scandal to a head. It had gone all around the world. And if an important piece of the story was now falling apart, it was clear that Caseby, the Murdoch titles and other enemies we had made in Fleet Street would move in for a monstering.

I spent the following week trying to work out what had happened. There was some good news. Police had confirmed everything else in our story: that the *News of the World* had hacked the missing girl's phone; that Surrey police had known about it at the time and taken no action (because, as one officer later put it, the press were 'untouchable and all-powerful'); and that it was very likely that the paper had also hacked the phones of detectives who were trying to find her. It was also confirmed that the paper had hired Steve Whittamore to blag confidential information about her family. Finally, they confirmed that Mrs Dowler had been given false hope when messages were suddenly deleted from Milly's phone. But how had those messages come to be deleted?

Digging deep into Surrey police's dust-covered archive, I learned, Weeting detectives had found new evidence which suggested that the deletions had happened before Glenn Mulcaire was instructed to hack Milly's phone and that it was far more likely that the voicemail had been wiped by a crude automatic system on Milly's voicemail which removed any messages which were more than seventy-two hours old, even if she had not listened to them.

The picture was blurred. There was evidence that Neville Thurlbeck had told Surrey police at the time that he had personally got hold of Milly's PIN number and that somebody may have listened to one of her messages long before Mulcaire was instructed. Other evidence revealed that Surrey police had switched off the automatic deletion system on the fourth day after her disappearance and yet some voicemail appeared to have been manually deleted after that, during the period when the *News of the World* certainly were eavesdropping. Surrey police at the time suspected that the paper were deleting messages. Indeed, three weeks after we published our story, Surrey officers had visited the Dowlers to tell them that, although they had no direct evidence on the point, they thought Mrs Dowler's belief that the paper had caused her moment of false hope was 'completely reasonable and absolutely possible'. But the bottom line was simple: the new evidence cast serious doubt on part of our story. The fact that the evidence had not been found until months after our story was published made no difference.

On 12 December 2011, counsel for the Metropolitan Police at the Leveson Inquiry made a short statement concluding that it was unlikely that the *News of the World* had been responsible for Mrs Dowler's moment of false hope.

There duly followed several days of high-energy monstering, which was described by the Dowlers' counsel, David Sherborne, as 'a storm of misreporting'. The serious doubt was converted into a certainty that we had got it wrong and even that we had done so deliberately. Richard Caseby told a House of Lords committee that Alan Rusbridger had 'effectively sexed up his investigation into phone-hacking'. A *Sunday Times* columnist said baldly that the *Guardian* had 'made it up'. The problem with one part of the story became, in the mouth of Kelvin MacKenzie, the claim that the whole Dowler story had been wrong. The impact of that one angle was held to have been responsible for the creation of the Leveson Inquiry; and for the closure of the *News of the World*, with Caseby declaring that 'the *Guardian's* false allegation directly resulted in 200 people being thrown out of work'.

By contrast, Weeting sent a detailed report to the Leveson Inquiry advising that 'reaching a definitive conclusion is not, and may never be possible' and, months later, Lord Justice Leveson wrote: 'The fact remains that the *News of the World* hacked the phone of a dead schoolgirl. The revelation of that story rightly shocked the public conscience in a way that other stories of phone-hacking may not have, but it also gave momentum to growing calls for light to be shed on an unethical and unlawful practice of which there were literally thousands of victims.

In that context, whether or not *News of the World* journalists had caused the "false hope" moment is almost irrelevant.'

But at the time, it was frustrating and frightening to be at the centre of such a storm of aggression, particularly as they had a point. Beneath the exaggeration and hostility, the fact was that I had stated as a fact something which now appeared likely to be wrong. That was bad enough. Worse, I had exposed the *Guardian* to precisely the kind of attack which until then we had generally avoided with such success.

Walking through my home town at the end of that week, I noticed an elderly woman in a long brown coat beckoning me from the other side of the street. I'd never seen her before but I crossed over and said hallo. To my surprise, she gently reached her hands up on to my shoulders and said something very warm about my work on the hacking. I thanked her and said we'd made a few nasty enemies, who were queuing up to give us a serious kicking right now, and, with her hands still resting on my shoulders, she looked up into my eyes, smiled and said quietly: 'Well, fuck 'em.' Which seemed like good advice.

The full story of the *News of the World*'s activity in the Dowler case emerged later. It turned out that they had not only used Mulcaire and Whittamore to gather information illegally but that twice they had interfered in the police investigation.

The first occasion came after they picked up the message from a recruitment agency, apparently offering Milly a job interview. In fact, the agency was trying to contact a Ghanaian woman called Nana, whose phone number differed from Milly's by only one digit. Instead of alerting police to what they believed was very important evidence, the paper decided to find the missing girl themselves. Neville Thurlbeck led a squad of seven reporters and photographers who staked out the factory where they thought she would go for her interview. When she failed to show up, a woman reporter called the agency, posing as Milly's mother, to get more information; another journalist called them, claiming to be working with the police; and Stuart Kuttner threatened to destroy the agency if they did not co-operate. It was only when all their efforts to land the story on their own had failed that they chose to tell Surrey police that they believed they knew where the missing girl was. A reporter contacted Surrey police and played the intercepted voicemail down the phone to them, insisting that they confirm the story. Kuttner followed up with a similar email, quoting voicemail messages and insisting that he was '110% certain' that Milly had applied for the job.

Second, both the *News of the World* and the *Sun* told Surrey police they wanted to offer a substantial reward for information about Milly. The police told them this was a bad idea, since they would need to divert manpower to deal with the calls and they feared some of them would come from hoaxers. After weeks of stalemate, senior officers were told that the *News of the World* planned to go ahead 'with or without our blessing'. Both papers then offered the reward, generating some 600 calls to Surrey police, none of which led to any significant new line of inquiry.

Richard Caseby continued his campaign. As the row over the Dowler deletions subsided, Operation Elveden arrested a detective on suspicion of passing information to a newspaper. This turned out to be Detective Chief Inspector April Casburn, who was subsequently jailed for trying to sell the *News of the World* inside information about Scotland Yard's work on the phone-hacking, but Caseby wrongly assumed that this was somebody who had been helping the *Guardian*. He sent an email to Rusbridger: 'Hi Alan. I hear Amelia Hill's source in Operation Weeting just got busted today. She must be terribly upset – they were ever so close. Some people at the *Guardian* say much too close.' He was wrong about that, too.

In the background, Scotland Yard were dealing with the Management and Standards Committee (MSC) which had been set up by Rupert Murdoch in July 2011 to 'co-operate fully with all authorities' in investigating his papers. It was not always easy.

Voluntarily, early in 2012, the MSC started to review the *Sun*, and handed over material which led to two group arrests involving ten people who held or had held very senior positions at the paper. There was a backlash led by Trevor Kavanagh who used his *Sun* column to declare this a witch-hunt against legitimate journalism, adding that 'there is nothing disreputable and, as far as we know at this point, nothing illegal'. He was wrong. But the subsequent Fleet Street attack on the police was strong enough to persuade Scotland Yard to abandon plans to run another group arrest of *Sun* journalists and instead to arrest them more discreetly one at a time.

At the same time, the MSC handed over evidence which led to the arrest of police officers, prison officers and other public officials who were accused of taking bribes from the *Sun*. Curiously this included Detective Chief Superintendent Dave Cook. He had been a source for the newspaper but he had never been paid for his help. However, he had become a thorn in News International's side, complaining about the *News of the World* surveillance on him when he first became involved in the inquiry into the murder of Daniel Morgan; suing them for hacking his phone; and offering to testify to the Leveson Inquiry about their links to Jonathan Rees's network of corruption. Cook was arrested by the Independent Police Complaints Commission after the MSC handed over emails which showed he had supplied information to a reporter from the *Sun*. At the time of this book's publication – more than two years after his arrest – prosecutors still had not decided whether he should be charged with any offence.

Meanwhile, for months, according to minutes of meetings between the two sides, News International executives had been asking police nervously whether the company itself might end up in court. In May 2012, after receiving legal advice from prosecutors, the Weeting detectives formally told the MSC that they were investigating the company – and the full co-operation with authorities stopped dead. Police concluded that the Murdoch camp had been handing over material on junior reporters in the hope that this would persuade them not to prosecute the company.

For several weeks, the MSC refused to provide any more material while a tense series of meetings took place. Minutes suggest that News Corp's new in-house counsel, Gershon Zweifach, turned on the political pressure to resist a corporate charge, citing the 46,000 people employed by the Murdochs and warning that 'the downstream effects of a prosecution would be "devastating and apocalyptic". The US authorities' reaction would put the whole business at risk.'

Police began to see some of their requests for information refused or delayed. Material which was handed over now was sometimes heavily redacted, leaving detectives to guess whether it was important. When they asked to see the final report of the MSC review of the *Sun*, they were told that it did not exist. Some senior officers found this hard to believe and concluded that, if this were true, it might be because News Corp had realised that such a report would be so damning that it would be better not to write it. Scotland Yard also believed that News Corp had changed the MSC's terms of reference so that their work no longer required them to follow clues into the higher reaches of the company. They were suspicious too that no material was ever handed over about suspect activity at the *Sunday Times* – the paper which had been so involved in the dark arts that they had hired a specialist, David Connett, to handle them and put him on a freelance contract so that they could disown him if he got caught. Senior police speculated that the MSC had been given a particularly narrow brief for the title. One News Corp source says that, having checked *Sun* records for the previous ten years, they searched *Sunday Times* records for only three years, i.e. back to 2008, thus neatly avoiding the Connett phase, which was from July 2003 to July 2005.

A year later, in May 2013, the tension was continuing, with one very senior officer, Detective Chief Superintendent Gordon Briggs, telling the MSC 'the higher up the organisation our investigation goes, the more you appear to withdraw co-operation', while the chair of the MSC, Lord Grabiner, threatened to go to the Cameron government's Attorney General to protest that any charge brought against the company would be an abuse of legal process.

It was not only the Murdochs and their companies which were exposed. Leveson and the select committees also took the lid off Scotland Yard's reaction to the *Guardian*'s stories, revealing the internal machinations of their prolonged failure to tell the truth to press, public and Parliament.

When John Yates stepped out in front of Scotland Yard on Thursday 9 July 2009, he made a point of saying that he came to the case with an independent mind. He did not say that, like so many of his colleagues, he had a history of dining and drinking with key people from News International including Rebekah Brooks and Andy

Coulson; nor that he was a particularly close friend of Neil Wallis, that they had known each other for ten years, went to football matches together and, just the previous month, had enjoyed one of their regular dinners, at Scalini's in Chelsea. This mattered, because the *Guardian* story had suggested explicitly that the police might now have to investigate 'reporters and the senior executives responsible for them'.

Yates's statement that day was riddled with significant omission and falsehood. He said that 'this case has been the subject of the most careful investigation' without saying that it had been cut short for want of resources and had failed to pursue the mass of evidence it had collected. He did not mention that the original inquiry had found numerous indicators of the involvement of others at the *News of the World*; that they had failed to give this to prosecutors; or that a cursory study of the material seized from Mulcaire had identified 418 potential victims.

When finally he was called to account, Yates's defence was that he had not known the facts. But to a significant degree, this was his own fault. Before he made his statement, Yates had agreed that Phil Williams, who led the original inquiry, should prepare a detailed memo about the operation. That took Williams three days to prepare. Yet, without waiting to have sight of it, Yates stepped out and suggested that he had 'established the facts'. Would he have done that if the suspect organisation had been a crime family or a paedophile network, not a media company with a close relationship with the police?

Beyond that, evidence uncovered by the Leveson Inquiry suggests that Yates knew more than he said. At 11.00 in the morning that day, we now know, he had chaired a meeting of a Gold Group (police jargon for an operational command meeting) to discuss the *Guardian* story. Under the heading 'Potential Vulnerabilities', the minutes of that meeting recorded: 'Could be criticism that MPS [Metropolitan Police Service] has not looked after wider private individuals.' This reflected the fact that the original inquiry had contacted only twenty-eight of the 418 potential victims they had found. That day, Yates had instructed officers to check back and identify those who now needed to be warned. And yet he told the press that afternoon: 'Where there was clear evidence that people had potentially been the subject of tapping, they were all contacted by police.'

The following morning, Friday 10 July, Yates chaired another Gold meeting about the *Guardian* story. The minutes record that he was told that the original inquiry had not analysed the call data which might have identified other perpetrators at the *News of the World*; and that the paper had reacted to the attempt to search Clive Goodman's desk with 'resistance and threats to use force', followed by 'a general lack of co-operation'. Yates duly agreed to hold a second press conference that afternoon and to ask the *Guardian* to hand over any evidence it might hold. However, his officers then reported back on their search for unwarned victims with the news that they included Andy Coulson, who was now sitting at the right hand of the man who looked set to become the next prime minister. Yates now made a series of striking decisions.

He cancelled the plan for a second press conference; decided not to ask the *Guardian* for evidence; and agreed that they would warn Coulson but also that they would speak to senior officials in the Home Office and the London mayor's office – the two organisations who were responsible for Scotland Yard – and ask them not to mention this to the Home Secretary or the mayor because of 'political sensitivities'.

That evening, News International released its statement accusing the *Guardian* of misleading the British people, repeatedly citing Scotland Yard's actions in support of the claim; and the first edition of *The Times* carried the column by Andy Hayman claiming that the original investigation 'left no stone unturned' and had found only a handful of victims. The Metropolitan Police said not one word to challenge any of this.

More light is possibly thrown on the state of Yates's knowledge by a statement submitted to Leveson by Keith Surtees, Phil Williams's deputy on the original inquiry. Surtees said: 'On more than one occasion in meetings I attended in 2009 with Assistant Commissioner Yates, I voiced my concern that the original investigation could and should be reopened or re-examined and suggested either Her Majesty's Inspectorate of Constabulary or another force undertake such a task.'

Surtees said his immediate boss, Phil Williams, could confirm this and added crucially that he had also 'set out my view that the criminality extended beyond Mulcaire and Goodman. It was a view held jointly by DCS Williams and myself that the phone interception and other criminal conduct of Mulcaire and Goodman was not limited to them and that the criminality extended further.'

Surtees went on to say that he had recorded his view of the need for a second investigation in the logbook which he had kept in 2006 – and that Yates had had access to that log in 2009: 'In short, whatever information I obtained and documented in 2006 was relayed and/or available to AC Yates in 2009.'

Yates not only dismissed the need for a new investigation in his first press statement but continued to do so for the following two years, without ever hinting to Parliament or public that Surtees had expressed his concern or given him this information. Yates's claim to ignorance was further undermined by his own evidence to the Leveson Inquiry, that his 'establishing the facts' on 9 July was not the end of his research: 'It was a continuing exercise of reviewing, considering, reflecting about whether we were on the right track and whether we needed to do something different.'

The week after Yates's statement in July 2009, the Director of Public Prosecutions, Keir Starmer, got involved, and there was a new round of bad judgement. As with Scotland Yard – as typically with the power elite – events were screened by the easy assumptions of official secrecy.

Keir Starmer said publicly that his officials had studied all the material they had been given by the original police inquiry. In fact, they had studied none of it: all they had done was to look at their correspondence with Scotland Yard. Nevertheless, Starmer declared that his office had been given no evidence of other victims or perpetrators. However, the *Guardian* then challenged him to explain the email for Neville. Starmer was worried, as he later admitted to Leveson: 'It seemed to me to suggest that both the author and the recipient were possible suspects.'

Starmer decided to consult lead counsel from the original inquiry, David Perry QC, who worried him even more by telling him, first, that the police in 2006 had said clearly that they had no evidence of the involvement of other journalists, and, second, that he did not think the police had shown him the email. Clearly alarmed, Starmer sent a message to Yates to 'invite him to consider' opening a new investigation. He even drafted a press release to announce this. But Yates then spoke to him on the phone twice in an hour, persuaded him to stall, then had a meeting with him and argued that the email for Neville 'will go nowhere'. Phil Williams followed up with a long memo to Starmer urging that the email had no evidential value. Starmer sent it to David Perry who – without access to any of the original case papers – agreed with Williams. So Starmer backed down. There would be no new investigation. Nothing of this was revealed at the time. It was on that evening, Thursday 16 July, that Yates and other senior officers dined with Rebekah Brooks at the *Sun*'s Police Bravery Awards.

Yates faced a new difficulty when he and Phil Williams were called to give evidence to the media select committee three months later, in September 2009. Preparing for this, Williams wrote a draft statement, which included the following very revealing passage: 'The size of the potential pool of people that Mulcaire had an interest in could be in the region of 600 individuals . . . Out of this pool of 600-plus persons of interest, there were in the region of seventy to eighty who the phone companies could indicate may have had their voicemails called . . . At the time, the strategy recognised that there was still extensive research to be done with the phone companies to identify what the full extent of victims might be . . . This could be a vastly bigger group of people, and in reality we would probably never know the true scale.'

That clashed directly with several of Yates's public comments. That whole passage was cut from the final version of the statement given to the committee. Yates sat in front of them and told them baldly: 'There was nothing to take us any further forward from an investigation point of view.'

Four months later, Yates was confronted with another problem, the Freedom of Information application from the *Guardian* to which Scotland Yard had responded with many weeks of stalling in breach of their legal duty before finally conceding that they would have to disclose that Mulcaire's records included ninety-one PIN codes. In January

2010, on the eve of that disclosure, Phil Williams wrote another internal memo, headed 'Options for dealing with the potential victims issue'. Williams noted that at the end of his press statement about the Gordon Taylor story, Yates had said he would ensure that potential victims would now be warned if 'there is any suspicion that they might have been' hacked. The Freedom of Information request, Williams observed, was 'a good question', and he saw the immediate problem: 'The key part of that statement is for us to decide what constitutes "any suspicion that they might have been". From the moment the reply to the Nick Davies letter is sent out, with the answer ninety-one, we need to be ready to stand by our interpretation.'

Ignoring the obvious inference that if a professional phone-hacker had obtained somebody's PIN code, that in itself raised the suspicion that they might have been hacked, Williams suggested they narrow the definition to include only those of the ninety-one where the available evidence showed that Mulcaire had also dialled into their voicemail and stayed on the line long enough to listen to a message. The difficulty, he explained, was that thirteen of the ninety-one who met even that restrictive definition, still had not been warned.

He suggested they might immediately warn those thirteen before sending the information to the *Guardian*. Or they could get the phone companies to do so, which would have the advantage of spreading responsibility to them but the disadvantage that 'this would take an unknown time, and it is important to send out the Nick Davies FoIA this week'. Both options would have had the effect of concealing the police failure to fulfil Yates's undertaking. In the event, they said nothing about the unwarned thirteen, nothing about the failure to warn others among the ninety-one and, when the *Guardian* ran a story about the significance of the ninety-one PIN codes, they complained, and Yates and Dick Fedorcio visited Rusbridger. Quietly, they also warned seventeen more victims.

In the background, Scotland Yard wrote a memo for government ministers which included the claim that 'Where there was evidence or mere suspicion that an individual had been subject to unlawful interception by use of a PIN, all reasonable steps were taken to ensure that individuals were informed.'

Even when, a year later, in January 2011, he finally agreed that the DPP should review all the evidence in the case, Yates tried to take the credit. It emerged at the Leveson Inquiry that, following the Sienna Miller revelations, Keir Starmer had told Scotland Yard that this was his plan. Yates had come to his office. Starmer recalled: 'By then, I had reached the stage where I really was not in a mood for being dissuaded.' But in agreeing to the review, Yates urged that he should be allowed to pretend that the review was his own idea. With the DPP's consent, he then wrote Starmer a fundamentally misleading letter in which he said: 'I consider it would be wise to invite you to further re-examine all the material collected in this matter.'

We discovered only later that during the months following the *Guardian's* first story, senior Yard personnel – including Sir Paul Stephenson, Dick Fedorcio and John Yates – continued to meet, drink or, more often, dine with senior figures from the *News of the World* on a total of at least ten occasions. In November 2009 – while his decision to refuse to reopen the inquiry was being challenged by the *Guardian* and MPs – Yates was happy to dine at the Ivy with the paper's editor, Colin Myler, and its crime editor, Lucy Panton. He continued to meet socially with Neil Wallis. The then deputy commissioner, Tim Godwin, warned Yates about these meetings at the time, but Yates ignored his request to cut back on his contact with journalists.

It was in this context that Yates and Dick Fedorcio gave their blessing to Wallis becoming a media consultant for the Yard and that Yates helped Wallis's daughter to find a temporary job. The Independent Police Complaints Commission found that, while these events involved 'blurred boundaries, imprudent decisions and poor judgement', neither Yates nor Fedorcio had been guilty of corruption. (Fedorcio faced disciplinary charges for gross misconduct but quit before they could take place.) The IPCC found that Sir Paul was guilty of no misconduct over his free stay at Wallis's other PR client, Champneys. The real question is whether or how this social contact influenced police thinking. Yates and his colleagues continued to insist that it had made no difference. There is no objective way of finding an answer.

Lord Justice Leveson concluded that there was no evidence that the social contact had influenced Yates or any other officer and that the real problem was that from the outset Yates had adopted an 'inappropriately dismissive and close-minded attitude' which was aggravated by genuine misunderstanding about the meaning of RIPA and some inaccurate briefings. Yates and Phil Williams had been dogmatic and defensive, Leveson said, in part because the allegations were being made by a newspaper and appeared to be attacking the police.

Certainly, there was some hostility to the *Guardian*. One of the paper's crime correspondents recalls that at a police social event during the hacking saga, the then commissioner Sir Paul Stephenson, a little red in the face and apparently enjoying the refreshments, informed him that the whole story was 'a load of middle-class wank'.

Having reviewed all of the evidence, Leveson made numerous criticisms of Yates and some of Williams but concluded emphatically that neither man had acted in bad faith at any stage.

One footnote. When Keith Surtees submitted his statement to Leveson, he complained about the minutes of one of the Gold meetings on Friday 10 July, the day after Yates's controversial statement about the *Guardian*. Surtees said they were 'not a wholly complete or accurate reflection of what was discussed'.

Separately, researching this book, I noticed that two of the Gold minutes were obviously inaccurate, including those for one of the meetings on 10 July. In both cases, the header which listed the time, date and those attending was for one meeting, while the text below recorded the proceedings of a different meeting. I asked Scotland Yard to explain. They never did.

On the sidelines, the Press Complaints Commission too was exposed. In amongst hundreds of pages of internal paperwork which they disclosed to the Leveson Inquiry was one particularly revealing memo from Tim Toulmin, who had been the PCC director when they produced their report which not only exonerated the *News of the World* but also attacked the *Guardian*. Their report's most damning line was that we had suggested in our Gordon Taylor story that the hacking had continued after the jailing of Goodman and Mulcaire but had been unable to produce any evidence to support this. This happened to be untrue: there was nothing in the *Guardian* story to suggest that. And the memo revealed that the PCC knew that. Preparing their report,

Toulmin had written to the commission: 'There is no suggestion in the latest *Guardian* allegations that such activities are ongoing at the *NoW* or anywhere else.'

Toulmin left the PCC before the scandal broke. The chair, Lady Buscombe, resigned in the wake of the Dowler story.

All of this exposure and the brief humbling of Rupert Murdoch easily seduced us into thinking that we had won a great victory, that truth had caught up with power. Very soon, however, as attention faded and the scandal slipped into the past, the elite simply took back their power, as if we had never challenged it – as if the tide had stayed out just long enough to allow us to build our castles in the sand, and now we watched as waves of irrestistible force returned to wash them all away.

Scotland Yard hit back by arresting a serving detective from Operation Weeting on suspicion that he had been helping Amelia Hill and me to write stories about the hacking. They then attempted to use the Official Secrets Act to force the *Guardian* to disclose internal records of our work on a selection of stories, including the hacking of Milly Dowler. This provoked a wave of angry protest, and the Yard backed down. The Crown Prosecution Service then ruled that the arrested detective should not be prosecuted, and he retired from the force.

However, the Yard followed up with a far more effective – albeit hypocritical – move. Ignoring the fact that the senior ranks of the Metropolitan Police had spent years obscuring the truth about the hacking while whistle-blowers in their lower ranks helped us to expose it, they now lobbied successfully for a crackdown on whistle-blowing, insisting that in future all officers must record all contacts with all journalists – even though that was highly likely to silence any officer who wanted to defend the public interest by speaking out against wrongdoing or abuse of power. Other police forces around the country followed the same authoritarian line.

In the same way, using the unacceptable behaviour of the *News of the World* as a springboard, senior police exploited the scandal to lobby the Home Office to make it easier for them to seize all journalists' notebooks and computer records, and to make it more difficult for all journalists to conceal the identity of confidential sources.

But it was Lord Justice Leveson's report which finally confirmed that the rules of the power game had not changed. In the weeks before he published, right-wing newspapers came out to fight, vicious as ever. When forty-two Conservative politicians wrote to the *Guardian* arguing that there should be 'sensible changes in the law' to create genuinely independent press regulation, the *Daily Telegraph* dragged out past occasions when fourteen of them had been criticised by the press and suggested they were hypocrites who were 'tainted by scandal'.

The *Mail* published an extraordinary twelve-page attack on one of the six assessors who had been advising Leveson, Sir David Bell, a former chairman of the *Financial Times*. Headlined on the front page 'Leveson: Disturbing Questions About A Key Adviser', the *Mail* used the fact that he had formerly been the chairman of the trustees of Common Purpose, which runs leadership courses for senior managers, to suggest that he was involved in 'a quasi-masonic nexus' which was devoted to secretly injecting liberal ideas into 'every cranny of the inner sanctums of Westminster, Whitehall and academia'. The *Sun* recycled the story with the headline 'The leftie plotters with a common purpose' and told its readers: 'The shadowy enemies of a free press are circling newspapers like the *Sun*. They want the Leveson Inquiry into press standards to result in state regulation. The *Sun* would only be allowed to print what officials permitted you to know.'

A group of newspaper publishers and editors then formed 'the Free Speech Network' and paid for a series of advertisements which pictured notoriously undemocratic leaders from Cuba, North Korea, the Soviet Union, Iran, Syria and Zimbabwe over the advice to 'Say NO to state regulation of the press'.

In the event, when he finally published his report in November 2012, Leveson proposed neither statutory regulation nor state regulation. Instead, he invited news organisations to set up their own regulator which would have to function without interference from them or from government. It would handle complaints, investigate persistent offending and run a new arbitration system to deal with libel and breach of privacy with the power to impose fines. As an incentive, those who joined would be exempt from the worst of the costs and damages if anybody still chose to sue them in court. To ensure that it really was independent of press and politicians, the new regulator would be inspected periodically by a 'recognition body'. All this would be underpinned by a law which would require government to uphold and protect the freedom of the press; require the courts to protect member organisations from some costs and damages; and give the recognition body authority to do its work.

In advance of the report, David Cameron had said that he would implement it in full unless it was 'bonkers'. And yet within hours of its publication, in a painful echo of the bad old days of government fear of Fleet Street, the prime minister kicked away its cornerstone, rejecting the underpinning law which was essential to Leveson's plan. There were some who genuinely feared that any kind of legislation was a threat to press freedom, if not immediately then potentially in the hands of some oppressive future government. There was also more of the same naked aggression and distortion.

Publishing the report, Leveson had said: 'This is not and cannot reasonably be characterised as statutory regulation of the press.' While some commentators honestly debated genuine concerns about his plans, hostile newspapers continued to tell their readers that he had called for regulation by statute and even by the state. In something close to parody, the Press Complaints Commission attempted to lead the debate by appointing a 'foundation group' of six experts to oversee the transition to a new regulator – and appointed Trevor Kavanagh as one of its members.

In a lecture in London at the end of January 2013, the respected former editor of *The Times* and *Sunday Times*, Sir Harry Evans, looked back at the past two months and condemned 'the cynicism and arrogance of much of the reaction to Leveson coming from figures whose inertia assisted the cover-up conducted into oblivion by News International'. The distortion of Leveson's ideas was, he said, 'staggering'. To portray his careful construct for statutory underpinning as state control was 'an amazingly gross distortion'.

When he published, Leveson had also said that the handling of his report should itself be the first test of his advice that contacts between government and the senior ranks of media companies should be transparent. The government nevertheless proceeded to hold a series of meetings with the senior ranks of media companies behind closed doors, refusing to confirm that they had even taken place. While opinion polls showed public support for Leveson running at over 70%, government stalled. By March 2013, the report was mired in confusion and compromise, with its supporters and opponents equally frustrated. The *Daily Mail* then exposed the sex life of a barrister who had subjected its editor to particularly fierce questioning at a Leveson hearing.

And in the wings of this pantomime, News Corp was reviving. In February 2012, they launched the *Sun on Sunday* to replace the *News of the World*. The following September, Ofcom published the results of their inquiry into whether the company was 'fit and proper' to hold a broadcasting licence. The regulator laid into James Murdoch, concluding that his handling of the hacking had been 'both difficult to comprehend and ill-judged . . . [and] repeatedly fell short of the exercise of responsibility to be expected of him as chief executive and chairman'. Nevertheless, they found that the company was entitled to broadcast in the UK: the Murdochs could keep their 39% stake in BSkyB.

Their annual report in May 2012 showed that the company's global profit had soared by 47% from $639 million to $937 million, primarily from its film and TV interests. In the twelve months following the Dowler story, News Corp shares rose by 23%, valuing the company at $73 billion and the Murdoch family trust's stake alone at $9.5 billion. During that year, Rupert Murdoch was paid just over $30 million; and James Murdoch received $16.8 million.

News Corp's political influence also revived. Rupert Murdoch's visits to London saw him dining with senior Conservative politicians, while senior Labour figures agreed to write guest columns in the *Sun on Sunday*. Soon, the mogul was throwing his political weight around in the old familiar way, voicing his support for Republican electoral candidates in the US while the *Sun*, still punishing David Cameron, flirted with the right-wing UK Independence Party in the UK.

There were some who did not revive. As with the collapse of any big structure, the masonry fell downwards, inflicting most damage on those below the Murdochs. Having lost his job, Les Hinton was denounced by the media select committee, who accused him of misleading them and of being 'complicit in the cover-up at News International'. Hinton strongly denied this though the complete absence of the 'full rigorous internal inquiry' which he had told them about in 2007 was particularly striking. Tom Crone and Colin Myler also lost their jobs, though Myler was then hired to edit the New York *Daily News*. Both men also were damned for giving misleading evidence to the select committee which found that they 'deliberately avoided disclosing crucial information and, when asked to do so, answered questions falsely'.

However, the most severe damage was reserved for journalists who had worked for Rupert Murdoch and for some of the public officials with whom they had dealt. As the months unfolded, more and more of them fell victim to Operation Weeting. Their trials were to provide the final chapter of the scandal at the same place where the whole saga had begun seven years earlier with the trial of Clive Goodman and Glenn Mulcaire: the Central Criminal Court at the Old Bailey in central London.

16. Final reckoning

Friday 4 July 2014. Court 12 at the Old Bailey. At one end of the room, on a raised podium, the judge sits in his red robe and horsehair wig. In front of him, the well of the court is crammed with barristers and journalists. And opposite him, standing in the glass-fronted dock, neatly lined up almost like pets on display in a shop window, tamed and passive, there are five men. All guilty.

Andy Coulson has been convicted of conspiring to intercept communications. Now, he must be sentenced. The judge confronts him with 'the very great deal of phone-hacking' which he allowed and which he used to boost his reputation and his career. He talks about 'the intensely personal messages' which were intercepted from the famous and also from the ordinary people who happened to stray into the path of Coulson's journalists; and about Milly Dowler. He tells the court it was 'unforgivable' that Coulson not only ordered the eaves-dropping on her phone but decided not to tell the police that he and his colleagues thought they had found evidence that the missing girl was still alive. 'Their true motivation was not to act in the best interests of the child, but to get credit for finding her and thereby sell the maximum number of newspapers.'

Coulson stands quietly while the last fragments of his reputation are swept away by the judge. For a moment, I feel sorry for him, for the sheer depth of his fall. This is the man who, according to one of his former colleagues in Downing Street, enjoyed the small but special privilege of being allowed to walk into the prime minister's office without knocking. Ruined. But then I remember the day during the trial when the jury was played a tape-recording which David Blunkett made one day in August 2004, when Coulson came to tell the Home Secretary he was going to expose his relationship with Kimberly Quinn.

I remember Blunkett's voice, full of panic and fear as he pleaded for his privacy; and the sheer mechanical coldness of Coulson as he insisted on his right to convert this man into a headline. And I remember all the others who suffered the same fate, left behind like roadkill as Coulson roared off into his gilded future.

The judge tells him the maximum sentence he can give is two years, but he will reduce it, in part because of the delay since the offences were committed. Coulson is jailed for eighteen months.

Greg Miskiw, Neville Thurlbeck and James Weatherup stand beside Coulson in the dock, the willing lieutenants who ran the news desk for years. Before the trial began, the three of them took one long look at the mountain of evidence which Operation Weeting had gathered against them and pleaded guilty to conspiring to intercept communications. Now, the lawyers for Thurlbeck and Weatherup have pleaded to the judge that they were only obeying orders. Thurlbeck's barrister says the hacking was 'known and approved by more senior figures' at the paper, naming Stuart Kuttner as one of those who was responsible. Weatherup's says it was 'endemic', adding that 'the suggestion that phone-hacking was the work of a small clique is wrong and misleading'.

The judge notes that none of them had the courage to step forward and give evidence at the trial and is unimpressed by their professions of apology: 'I am afraid that that has the appearance of regret for the consequences of getting caught rather than true remorse.' Miskiw and Thurlbeck are jailed for six months, the sentence again reduced because of the delay since the offences. Weatherup, a lesser player, is given four months, suspended for a year.

Finally, it is the turn of Glenn Mulcaire, who also pleaded guilty before the trial began, not only to conspiracy to intercept communications but specifically to hacking Milly Dowler. His lawyer has claimed that Mulcaire thought he was targeting the missing girl to help the police. The judge swipes aside the claim. 'It is incapable of belief,' he says. But he tells the man who committed crime for a living: 'You are the lucky one.' Since he has already been sent to prison, in 2007, albeit for only a fraction of his offences, Mulcaire will not have to go back to jail. 'The sentence will be six months' imprisonment, suspended for twelve months.'

Somewhere offstage there is a sixth guilty man, Dan Evans, the features writer who became the *News of the World*'s second specialist phone-hacker. He not only pleaded guilty before the trial began but also agreed to help the police, stepping into the witness box to tell the jury that Coulson hired him specifically because of his skill at intercepting voicemail. He will be sentenced separately.

There are three important people who will not be sentenced. Rebekah Brooks and Stuart Kuttner have been acquitted on all charges by the jury. And Ian Edmondson, who started the trial alongside his former colleagues, has been sent for a separate hearing after becoming too ill to continue.

It is three years to the day since we published the Milly Dowler story; nearly eight months since this trial began. Court 12 has been like a laboratory for the study of excess, examining in microscopic detail the crime that was committed in Rupert Murdoch's newsroom and studying, too, the sordid inner world of tabloid journalism. It has also been a minor exhibition of passive power.

By the time the jury returned their verdicts, the version of events which had been promoted for so long by News International and Scotland Yard had been smashed into tiny shameful fragments. Not just one rogue reporter, but also a rogue editor, three rogue news editors and two specialist hackers. Not just eight victims, but 5,500 for Glenn Mulcaire and an estimated 1,600 for Dan Evans. As the prosecuting counsel Andrew Edis QC put it, the *News of the World* had been 'at the highest level, a criminal enterprise'.

An email from a junior editor, which was disclosed during the trial, caught the reality of what had been happening behind the closed doors of Murdoch's paper: 'Sometimes I think we're just dazzled by traces and checks and shady stuff and don't try obvious journalistic techniques.'

The shady stuff turned out to include not only the casual commission of crime but also the tabloid assumption that normal human boundaries existed only to be breached: one of Jude Law's own family being paid to sell the actor's private life behind his back; a model who acted as a honeytrap for celebrity sex stories and ending up selling the paper a picture of her own foetus; the truth about Sally Anderson, who had been one of Mulcaire's victims but who had also invented and sold a completely false story that David Blunkett had made her pregnant; plus a routine campaign of industrial espionage which had seen the *News of the World* using Mulcaire's hacking to steal stories from rival papers. I had known that they had hacked the *Mail on Sunday*'s then investigations editor, Dennis Rice, but Weeting found that they had also hacked the paper's news editor, deputy news editor and chief feature writer, as well as journalists on the *Sunday Mirror* and the *Sunday People.*

Inevitably, the court's microscope returned often to the Murdoch papers' endless hunger for the sex lives of public figures, and then revealed a startling hypocrisy: that between 1998 and 2006, while they were busily humiliating other people by exposing their affairs, Rebekah Brooks and Andy Coulson were themselves secretly doing exactly the same thing in spite of their marriages. Weeting detectives had discovered this when they seized a laptop computer on which Brooks had written to Coulson in 2004, urging him not to end their relationship. She had written this while she was editing the *Sun*, in which, for example, she had lambasted the leader of the firemen's union during a strike: 'It's bad enough that Andy Gilchrist is a Marxist rabble-rouser. But now we expose him as a lying, cheating, low-life fornicator. In a strike that puts lives at risk, we need men we can trust. Not a hypocrite who lies about his family so he can drop his trousers.' So it goes.

In the same vein, during the trial, the man who had sold Fleet Street so many of those sex stories – Max Clifford – was himself prosecuted and convicted for a series of indecent assaults on girls and young women. He was jailed for eight years. The newspapers who had been happy to feed off him had then monstered him as though they bore no responsibility for giving him the power and the wealth and the prestige that he had used to intimidate his victims.

The *News of the World*'s own arrogance and aggression were themselves the source of some of the most damning evidence against them. They were faced with the surviving copies of the Harbottle & Lewis emails with their brazen references to the apparent payment of bribes, but the police had found out about them only because News International had tried to fool the media select committee by quoting the law firm's dubious judgement on them as evidence of their innocence. Coulson was faced with the collection of compromising emails which Clive Goodman had downloaded as an insurance policy after he was arrested in 2006: the prosecution had them only because Coulson had bullied and betrayed his royal editor to the point where he not only handed over the emails but acted as a hostile witness, telling the jury that Coulson personally had authorised his hacking of the royal household.

But the trial was never a foregone conclusion. The threads of evidence which linked that bundle of crime to the defendants in the dock were sometimes thin. It was at this point that the passive power played its part. Rupert Murdoch had no need to do anything to intervene in the trial, but his money gave the defence the kind of muscle which is rarely seen in a courtroom, delivering squads of senior solicitors, junior solicitors and paralegals who sifted every fragment of evidence, testing and probing, wrong-footing witnesses with a misremembered date, a forgotten detail; providing the jurors with neatly organised bundles of laminated paperwork, all backed up by daily transcripts of the evidence and by IT support which would make Google jealous.

By comparison, the Crown Prosecution Service struggled – as any section of the underfunded state now struggles – desperately short of muscle to deal with the weight of evidence which fell on the court from more than three years of endeavour by Operation Weeting. They could afford just one full-time solicitor and one admin assistant to deal with it. The prosecution worked tirelessly but delivered witnesses whose testimony sometimes collapsed under scrutiny, simply because nobody had checked it. They gave the jurors bundles of paper, some of which proved to be misleading or incomplete. Towards the end of the trial, Andrew Edis decided that the jury must have a computer with an electronic index to help them find their way through the mass of paperwork in front of them. He had to offer to pay for it out of his own pocket. He was earning less than a tenth of the fees of the lead barristers for the defence. When it came to calling character witnesses, the defendants picked from the power elite: Stuart Kuttner was able to produce the former Archbishop of Canterbury to vouch for his honesty.

But even a well-funded prosecution would have struggled with a more fundamental problem. There was a shortage of important evidence. It was more than a decade since Rebekah Brooks had left the *News of the World* and so naturally paperwork had been lost, memories had faded, people had died (Sean Hoare, for example). Weeting never did recover the editorial computers that had been thrown away when the *News of the World* moved office, nor 210 million of the 300 million emails which had been deleted from the company's servers over the years, nor the hard drive from Brooks's computer. There was no way of knowing which way that missing material might have tilted the trial. Fear, too, played its part: Weeting interviewed dozens of journalists who declined to come forward as witnesses and scores of hacking victims who wanted no part in the trial. And often, over the years, the *News of the World* had been devious in covering its tracks. Dan Evans told the court how he had taped one particularly important voicemail, which had then been put into a Jiffy bag and delivered to the office so that it appeared to have been hacked and delivered to them by some unknown outsider.

While the prosecution urged the jury to stand back and look at the big picture and to accept that the editors must have known about the crime in the ranks below them, the defence urged them to move closer, to look at the detail, to see the gaps, the problems, the doubts. After the five guilty pleas before the trial began, only Brooks, Coulson and Kuttner faced the phone-hacking charge. All three said they had never heard Mulcaire's name until he was arrested. Brooks said she had not even been aware of his contract; Coulson and Kuttner that they knew of the contract with Mulcaire's company but had had no idea what he was doing for his money.

The hacking case against Brooks was pure inference – that the sheer volume of interception meant she must have known – and Murdoch's money allowed her to land a particularly powerful blow. Her lawyers were handed all 11,000 pages of the scribbled and scrawled notes which Caryatid had seized from Glenn Mulcaire. The Caryatid detectives had taken one look at them and decided they didn't have the resources to check them. Weeting did the job, but it took them the best part of a year. Brooks's team did it in three months and then had the manpower to deliver a very helpful analysis. Since Brooks had been editor for more than a third of the time that Mulcaire was working on contract for the paper, it was possible that his notes would record well over 1,000 taskings on her watch. However, Brooks's lawyers set aside all those notes where it was not 100% certain that they had been written during her editorship, and all those where it was not 100% certain that Mulcaire had been tasked to intercept voicemail as opposed to blagging confidential data. Since a considerable mass of his notes were incomplete and/or ambiguous on either date or task, this allowed them to tell the jury that there were only twelve occasions when it was 100% certain that Glenn Mulcaire had hacked a phone while she was editor. In her case, the big picture became much smaller.

Strangely, the most powerful evidence of hacking – what the judge described as 'the high point of the prosecution case' – came from the same source as the most powerful emotion, a murdered schoolgirl. It was not just that Weeting had found fourteen pages of Mulcaire's notes about the hacking of Milly Dowler, with the names of Greg Miskiw and Neville Thurlbeck in the top left-hand corners; but Surrey police had found, in their archive, records of the phone calls and emails with which the *News of the World* had tried to bully them into confirming the paper's false story that the girl was alive and applying for work. These included emails from Stuart Kuttner, who told the court that he had known that the newspaper had obtained Milly's messages but that he could not remember asking where they had come from and certainly had not known they were hacked. Both Brooks and Coulson insisted that they had known nothing of this, Brooks emphasising that she had been on holiday in Dubai at the time.

Coulson alone faced more difficult evidence, including the recording which Blunkett made openly when Coulson visited him to confront him with the story about his affair. Now, the prosecution had the tape, on which the jury could hear Coulson saying: 'I am certainly very confident of the information . . . It is based on an extremely reliable source.' Faced with that, Coulson went into the witness box and admitted that – contrary to years of denial to Parliament and the prime minister – he had known that the story was hacked, that Neville Thurlbeck had even played him the tapes. He claimed he had been shocked and had told Thurlbeck never to do it again. That put him in the position of knowing that one of his staff had broken the law, but not actually of doing so himself. It also put him very close to the edge of conviction. The rest of the evidence pushed him over. Weeting found an email in which he had dealt with the possibility that one of his journalists was leaking stories by ordering in writing: 'Do his phone.' Dan Evans and Clive Goodman both told the jury that he had been deeply involved.

Brooks was also charged with conspiring to commit misconduct in public office by authorising payments totalling £38,000 to a civil servant in the Ministry of Defence. The cash had been paid. The civil servant admitted selling information. But the trail of emails which tied Brooks to the payments was ambiguous, well short of proof that she understood that it was a public official on the receiving end. The jury found her not guilty. Coulson faced two similar charges together with Clive Goodman, who could have been forgiven for thinking he had seen the last of the inside of a courtroom back in 2007.

This involved the emails from the Harbottle & Lewis collection in which the two of them apparently discussed paying cash to Palace police officers. Weeting had followed the payments through News International's accounts and found they were made to false names with false addresses. Coulson said he had never believed that Goodman really was paying police. It was suggested that Goodman might have been pocketing the money himself, though Goodman told the jury that the real recipients were other journalists whom he would not name and that he had pretended they were police officers to encourage his editor to make the payments. The jury could not reach a verdict, and Coulson and Goodman were told they would face a new trial. Separately, Coulson was facing trial for perjury over evidence he had given at the trial of Tommy Sheridan in Glasgow in December 2010.

The other charges – of hiding evidence from Weeting – crumbled into a mess of confusion and doubt. Charlie Brooks appeared at first to be in trouble over the CCTV images of him using the bins of the underground car park as a hiding place while police searched their flat.

When Weeting retrieved his mysterious bin bag, they assumed that the laptops he had hidden must belong to Rebekah. They were wrong, and the bag proved to contain no evidence of crime, only Charlie's porn, his unpublished novel, some paperwork and a conker. When the prosecution tried to tie both Brookses and the security head, Mark Hanna, to the disappearance on the same day of various electronic devices, the evidence stretched and snapped, and all three were acquitted. Rebekah Brooks and her PA, Cheryl Carter, were found not guilty on a similar charge of hiding Brooks's old notebooks from police.

For Weeting, the trial was a fair result. On phone-hacking: six guilty; two not guilty. On paying public officials: one not guilty; two for retrial. But Fleet Street focused on the acquittal of Brooks and the collapse of the charges on destroying evidence, complaining loudly that the whole prosecution had been a waste of public money and claiming that the trial had cost £100 million. In reality, the total cost of Weeting had been £18.7 million, for this case but also for others in the pipeline; and the cost of the prosecution in court had been £1.7 million. Murdoch had spent at least thirty times as much on the defendants. So it goes on and on.

By the time the big trial was over, the police had run riot through the world of tabloid journalism, arresting or interviewing 210 people including 101 journalists from six different national newspapers; thirteen private investigators; and thirty-seven public officials who were suspected of taking cash bribes. Eleven public officials had already been jailed. Eleven more trials were scheduled on charges of hacking phones, paying cash to public officials and breaking into allegedly stolen mobile phones, while the CPS was still reviewing other cases which could generate still more trials on similar charges including email-hacking. Among those waiting to hear whether they would be prosecuted were Coulson's deputy editor, Neil Wallis, who had been arrested for a second time; his features editor, Jules Stenson; his in-house lawyer, Tom Crone; and four senior journalists from the Mirror Group. Police had also interviewed as a suspect Murdoch's former UK chief executive, Les Hinton, and were planning to do the same with Rupert Murdoch himself. In the wings, Murdoch's UK company – now rebranded as News UK – had paid compensation or damages to 718 of Mulcaire's victims, while many more of Dan Evans's alleged victims queued to sue.

There were some interesting loose ends. I established that the Mail newspaper group was one of the favoured few who had been approached as victims by Caryatid in the autumn of 2006, when they had been told about all four of the *Mail on Sunday* journalists who had been on the wrong end of the *News of the World*'s espionage. Oddly, neither the *Mail on Sunday* nor the *Daily Mail* had published a word about their own role as victims of the scandal. Even stranger, the Press Complaints Commission had published two reports (in 2007 and 2009) which supported the *News of the World*'s lies about itself without ever mentioning that there were at least four other victims to add to the official list of only eight. This was particularly weird since the editor of the *Daily Mail*, Paul Dacre, was one of the commissioners who produced the 2006 report; and the editor of the *Mail on Sunday*, Peter Wright, was part of the commission which was responsible for the 2009 one, which also rubbished the *Guardian*. Did they not know?

And there was an intriguing piece of evidence about the police which surfaced during the trial: the minutes of a meeting at the *News of the World* on 20 January 2010, as Rebekah Brooks was trying to persuade Max Clifford not to take them to court for hacking his phone. The minutes noted that when Scotland Yard first disclosed Mulcaire's notes about Clifford, 'there was nothing there'. That had sent Clifford's lawyer, Charlotte Harris, back to the High Court for an order to disclose an unredacted version of the notes. And, according to the minutes, it had also provoked a comment from the then editor, Colin Myler: 'CM said that Andy Hayman and John Yates had indicated to him previously that this was probably going to be the case.' Was that accurate? Did one of those men really tip off Myler about the material they would be disclosing? I contacted all three. None would comment.

Back in Court 12, the judge has finished reading his comments. The guilty men stand silent and contrite, perhaps aware that the door at the end of the dock opens on to a dark staircase which leads to the grim old cells in the basement below. The machinery of justice which so badly failed to deal with them for years has finally trapped them. The oldest form of democracy in the land – not voters but jurors – has finally found a voice. The judge sighs and looks to the dock where Coulson, Miskiw and Thurlbeck now know they have lost their freedom. 'Go down please,' he says. The door to the cells is open.

Epilogue

This was never simply a story about a journalist who broke the law. The rogue reporter turned out to be working for a rogue newspaper which, in turn, proved to be part of a rogue corporation. Beyond that, the rogue corporation had been allowed to flourish – and to break the rules and to make comrades of the police and the government – because it had grown up in a wider system which positively encouraged it and other corporations to do all of these things.

All this is relatively new. This 'neoliberalism', this revival of laissez-faire capitalism, has reversed several hundred years of struggle by labour movements, political campaigns and radical thinkers across the world who saw the effects of a free-market economy, red in tooth and claw, and who determined that they must create democratic governments with power to take hold of the commercial wealth of their societies and to enforce rules which would protect working people and to create institutions which would provide for their health and education and welfare. This neoliberalism was conceived by conservative economists and then put into effect in the early 1970s by the military dictatorship of Augusto Pinochet, who tortured and murdered his political opponents in Chile and was celebrated by conservatives for the freedom of his economy. It was promoted most powerfully from the early 1980s by the right-wing governments of Ronald Reagan and Margaret Thatcher, and then reproduced and reinforced by the Australian governments of Bob Hawke and Paul Keating; in New Zealand by Robert Muldoon; in Canada by Brian Mulroney; and so on around the world, penetrating by the 1990s even the dark empires of China and the former Soviet Union.

Neoliberalism worked, for some. It generated economic growth which in turn delivered short-term political benefits for the governments who sponsored it and enormous wealth for those who owned and ran the corporations which were its flagships. But . . .

When you allow global corporations to roam global markets, you make them more powerful than nation states; when you 'roll back the state', you reduce the power of the people in each nation; when you 'cut back regulation', you allow the biggest corporations to dominate and exploit their territories; when you break trade unions and tear up employment laws, you allow those corporations to ride roughshod over those who work for them. The simple, beautiful idea that people should run their own societies disintegrates, allowing the few to rule and the many to follow.

Over and again, you allow the hard logic of the market to usurp human choice and so you create a society with the morality of an anthill, where all human life is reduced to labour, all freedom flattened by the demand for efficient production, all weakness punished, all violence justified, where schools and hospitals are cut while crime and alienation flourish and millions are thrown into the deep pit of unemployment.

You privatise your industries, so you lose control of the essential raw materials of life; you cut taxes for the rich and cut welfare for the poor, so you manufacture deep layers of inequality, great pools of poverty. Listen to the words of Joseph Stiglitz who, from his vantage point as chief economist at the World Bank in the late 1990s, watched as neoliberalism infected the whole planet: 'Those at the top have learned how to suck money from the rest in ways that the rest are hardly aware of. That is their true innovation.'

And all of this is cloaked in the twisted language of the power elite in which the ways of the wealthy have always been disguised as a service for the needs of the poor. The predecessors of those who promoted this neoliberal backlash sat on the boards of Victorian coal mines, explaining gently that they must preserve the right of children to work down the pit and that they must resist the do-gooders who would take away the free choice of those children and deprive their families of their income. They were the shipmasters who argued that it was nothing less than their duty to provide good strong cheap labour from Africa for the king's dominions in the West Indies and beyond, whose growth was essential to England's own well-being, and that good people must understand that the conditions endured by a savage on the verge of starvation in darkest Africa were far inferior to those of a bonded labourer in the care of an employer who had every reason to ensure that he was well kept.

War is peace, freedom is slavery, ignorance is strength.

So it was that a whole generation of English men and women were told that they should lose the welfare state and the trade unions and the protective laws for which their ancestors had fought and that the balance of power should be tipped backwards by a century and more, because this would make them free; and, in case they hesitated for a moment and questioned the idea that the wealthy elite would know and care more about their welfare than their own parents and grand-parents, they were also offered a little cash. 'Vote to return to laissez-faire capitalism, and we will cut your taxes. You may lose your society but you will gain a bigger TV.' A very great theft was organised on the simple basis that its victims had nothing to lose but a decent life.

Like all corporations, News Corp has taken advantage of this reversal to increase its wealth and to increase its power – over governments and their regulators, over competitors and their own workforce. However, far more than most corporations, News Corp also was instru-mental in engineering this reversal. Like some ideological vanguard, Rupert Murdoch and his lieutenants have used their news outlets to shift the centre of power – the centre of thinking – far over to the right; and they have used their political muscle to press these ideas on governments who sought their support. They have done this not only in the UK but also in the US and Australia, wherever their business has flourished. They have left us with a world that demonstrably is a worse place to live, unless you happen to belong to the power elite.

And the importance of this in the aftermath of the hacking scandal is to shake ourselves free of the illusion that because we won a really important battle, we won the war; that by exposing some secret machi-nations, we stopped the machinations occurring. In truth, very little has changed.

Some people resigned – from the PCC, the police, Murdoch's company. Others soon replaced them. One paper closed. Another replaced it. The BSkyB bid was blocked, but there is nothing to stop Rupert Murdoch coming back to try again, to use his reservoir of cash to buy the rest of that marvellously lucrative business, so that he has an even bigger reservoir of cash to buy still more, to become still bigger, to become the biggest.

And when Rupert Murdoch dies, another chairman will replace him. It might not be a man or woman from his bloodline, but that chairman's power will be the same. Or if Rupert Murdoch sells every newspaper he owns in the UK – or if he sells every newspaper he owns in the world – there will always be another ambitious businessman waiting to fill his place, some Russian oligarch or Middle Eastern oil magnate or Chinese billionaire.

For a while, we snatched a handful of power away from one man. We did nothing to change the power of the elite.

Appendix

Private investigators who worked for Fleet Street

Many of those listed here have been convicted of crime, but it should not be assumed that any others have broken the law. Some are tracers and tracing is not illegal. A tracer may lawfully blag confidential data if there is a public interest in doing so. It should also not be assumed from inclusion in this list that any newspaper was aware of any criminal act that may have been committed.

Barry, Rachel. Blagger, phone and medical records. *Mail on Sunday, News of the World, Sunday People, Sunday Express*. Convicted, October 1997.

Beardall, Barry. Blagger, political targets. *Sunday Times*. Convicted of unrelated fraud, April 2001.

'Blue'. Blagger, all records. *Mail on Sunday, Sunday Times*. Founder member of Narcotics Anonymous (NA) group.

Boddy, Micky. Blagger, phone companies. Most Fleet Street papers. Worked with Gary Lowe and NA group.

Boyall, John. Middleman. *News of the World, Sunday Mirror*. Member of Whittamore network. Trained Glenn Mulcaire and Andy Gadd. Previously worked with former South African intelligence officer John Ferrer Smith at Argen Investigations. Convicted, April 2005.

Bullen, Shaun. Blagger, phone companies. Unidentified papers. Employed by Code Ten agency. Member of Southern Investigations network.

Burrows, Gavin. Middleman. *News of the World, Sunday People*. Ran Rhodes Associates.

Campbell Smith, Philip. Covert surveillance and email-hacking. *News of the World*. Former British intelligence officer in Northern Ireland. Convicted, February 2012.

Clarke, Steve. Phone-tapper. *News of the World*. Former police officer. Ran Metshield.

Coghlan, David. Phone-tapper. Worked with Phil Winton. Former army intelligence officer. Convicted, February 1987 and January 1995.

Coulson, Dean. Middleman for phone-tapping. Worked with Active Investigation Services (AIS). Convicted, February 2008.

Creasey, Steven 'Sid'. Covert surveillance, email-hacking, phone-bugging. *News of the World* and TV. Former London detective. Convicted of unrelated crimes.

Dewse, Chris. Tracer, driver records. Member of Whittamore network. Charged but not prosecuted.

Dowling, Stuart. Manufactured bugs for phone lines. Worked with AIS. Convicted, January 2007.

Edwards, David. Phone-tapper. Used by NA group and Phil Winton. Former British Telecom engineer.

Fillery, Sid. Police corruption, blagging, suspected burglary. *Daily Mirror*, *News of the World*, *Sunday Mirror*, *Sunday Times*. Ran Southern Investigations. Convicted of child pornography offences, October 2003.

Ford, John. Blagger, all records. *Sunday Times*. Former actor, trained by Al Green.

Gadd, Andy. Tracer, all records. *News of the World*. Ran Trackers agency.

Gelsthorpe, Scott. Middleman. As London police officer with Jimmy Young, ran AIS which worked for the *News of the World* and allegedly other titles. Convicted, January 2007.

'Green, Al'. Blagger, all records. *Sunday Times*, *Today*. Trainer for NA group.

Gunning, John. Blagger, phone companies. Numerous papers. Worked for Southern Investigations and with Whittamore network. Convicted, March 2006.

Hackett, Chris. Blagger, all records. *Sunday People*. Ran Code Ten agency with Darren Whalley. Convicted, June 2008.

Hall, Mickey. Phone-tapper. Worked with AIS. Former soldier. Convicted, January 2007.

Hart, Christine. Known as 'Queen of the blaggers'. Targeted human sources rather than records. *News of the World, Sunday People, Sunday Mirror* and *Daily Mail.*

Hart, Lloyd. Tracer, all records. *Daily Mirror, Sun, Sunday Mirror* and Express Group. Worked for Code Ten agency. Ran TDI agency, later ELI.

Jones, Taff. Blagger, phone companies. Member of Whittamore network. Worked for Severnside Investigations. Former soldier and Hell's Angel. Charged but not prosecuted.

Lawson, Glenn. Tracer. Unidentified press client. Worked for Abbey Investigations.

Lowe, Gary. Middleman. Most Fleet Street papers including Mirror Group and *Sunday Times*. Former soldier. Worked with Southern Investigations, NA group and Phil Winton. Ran Chimera agency and later Premier.

MacDonald Murray, Michael. Blagger, all records. Worked with Southern Investigations. Former London detective. Convicted of smuggling drugs, February 1975.

McInerney, Alan. Blagger, all records. *News of the World.* Ran Pearmac with Ray Pearson. Worked for AIS. Convicted, August 2005.

McLoughlin, Steve. Surveillance. *News of the World.* Ran Burgess PDQ agency in Manchester.

Palmer, Rob. Tracer. *News of the World.*

Pearson, Ray. Blagger, all records. *News of the World.* Ran Pearmac with Alan McInerney. Worked for AIS. Convicted, October 2005.

Rees, Jonathan. Police corruption, blagging, suspected burglary. *Daily Mirror, News of the World, Sunday Mirror, Sunday Times.* Ran Southern Investigations. Convicted of perverting the course of justice, December 2000.

Ross, John. Middleman to corrupt police. *Daily Mail* and others. Former detective, sacked after being cleared on corruption charges.

Scott, Jacqui and Malcolm. Tracers, all records. Most Fleet Street papers.

Stafford, Jonathan. Blagger, all records. *Sunday Mirror* and *News of the World.* Former actor, specialised in imitating celebrity voices. Ran Newsreel.

Whalley, Darren. Blagger, all records. *Sunday People.* Ran Code Ten agency with Chris Hackett. Convicted, June 2008.

Whittamore, Steve. Blagger, all records. Most Fleet Street papers. Tracer since late 1960s. Trained John Boyall. Ran JJ Services. Convicted, April 2005.

Winton, Phil, aka Phil Catt. Phone-tapper. Unidentified tabloid clients. Worked with Gary Lowe and NA group. Ran No Hiding Place. Convicted, January 1995.

Young, Jimmy. Middleman. As London police officer with Scott Gelsthorpe, ran AIS which worked for the *News of the World* and allegedly other titles. Convicted, January 2007.

List of Illustrations

Index

Index